Forged in Battle

Forged in Battle

The Civil War Alliance
OF
Black Soldiers
AND
White Officers

Joseph T. Glatthaar

THE FREE PRESS
A Division of Macmillan, Inc.
NEW YORK

Collier Macmillan Publishers
LONDON

The Free Press
A Division of Macmillan, Inc.
866 Third Avenue, New York, N.Y. 10022

Collier Macmillan Canada, Inc.

Printed in the United States of America

Library of Congress Cataloging-in-Publication Data

Glatthaar, Joseph T.
    Forged in battle: the Civil War alliance of Black soldiers and
white officers / Joseph T. Glatthaar.
        p.   cm.
    Bibliography: p.
    Includes index.
    ISBN 0–02–911815–8
    1. United States—History—Civil War, 1861–1865—Participation,
Afro-American.   2. United States. Army—Afro-American troops—
History—19th century.   3. United States. Army—History—Civil
War, 1861–1865.   4. United States—Race relations.
E540.N3G53   1990
973.7′415—dc20   89–11620
                                                                          CIP

BOMC offers recordings and compact discs, cassettes
and records. For information and catalog write to
BOMR, Camp Hill, PA 17012.

For My
Parents and Brothers

Contents

Preface and
Acknowledgments

One summer morning in 1985, while researching at the State Historical Society of Wisconsin, I came across an interesting collection of letters from a white officer of black troops during the Civil War. He was a man utterly committed to the concept of the United States Colored Troops and to a vigorous prosecution of the war. "I do not think that I would exchange my position in this Regiment for one of equal rank in any white Regiment," he confessed to his brother, and on another occasion he urged, "When your time is up, just enlist, or go in for the war *if it lasts forty years*, as I intend to do if I can." The force of his words intrigued me.[1]

Later that day, at lunch with my friend and graduate adviser, Dr. Edward M. Coffman, I mentioned the letters, and we began to discuss some of the problems that confronted whites who crossed the color barrier to command black soldiers. Over the next few days my thoughts kept drifting back to that officer and all those like him, until finally I decided to drop all other research and pursue this new project.

Since then it has carved a course for itself. As I studied these men, their conduct as officers, and their racial attitudes, I also had to look at their black soldiers, to see what they thought of their officers. This soon snowballed into an examination of the entire black experience in military service—for both enlisted men and officers—and not long afterward it became clear that my primary interest was the interaction between the racial groups within the United States Colored Troops. Here were almost 180,000 Afro-Americans, enslaved in the South and discriminated against in the North, who had responded to the call to arms in the hope of creating a better world for themselves and their children. Alongside them were 7,000 whites, who volunteered to officer these black soldiers in the face of overwhelming discrimination and abuse. Although both groups carried with them mental and emotional baggage about the other race, whether from personal experience or preconceptions, within the structure of their military units—where they ate, slept, fought, and often died together—they had to reconcile themselves to one another.

This task would have been formidable enough under almost any circumstances, but it was particularly difficult during the Civil War. Both Northern and Southern whites scrutinized the performance of the United States Colored Troops through tinted glasses, more to reaffirm their convictions about black inferiority than to see if the black race had the character to merit freedom and equality. In addition, the United States Colored Troops became the great symbol of hope for blacks in both the North and the South. Through valor on the field of battle, black soldiers could serve as the army of freedom and also prove themselves an invaluable asset to the Union in its moment of crisis. And all this was predicated on the ability of blacks and whites in the United States Colored Troops to forge bonds and labor effectively together.

My object is to explore the inner working of these black commands, to investigate conduct, attitudes, and experiences among the participants. Within the context of military service, I examine the interaction of the two racial groups to understand better not only these black commands and their contributions to Union victory but also the aspirations, prejudices, and behavior of their officers and men and the society from which they came.

In an effort to determine the impact of the war on its participants and the long-term implications of extensive use of blacks in the military service of their country, this study extends into the postwar years. In the case of the white officers and black soldiers, the war affected them in some ways uniquely, yet as soldiers they endured hardships and suffered catastrophes just as did other troops, and their readjustment problems may shed some light on the experiences of all participants in the Civil War. The experiences of the United States Colored Troops established precedents for blacks in military service that lasted nearly ninety years, and in some respects this country still has not fully overcome them.

During the course of this endeavor, I accumulated many debts.

The University of Houston provided me with a Research Initiation Grant and a Limited Grant-in-Aid. The United States Military History Institute also helped to defray my expenses there with a United States Army Military History Fellowship. During my travels, friends were extremely gracious: in Leavenworth, Celia, Bob, Ruthie, Bobby, and Rex Baumann; in Madison, Mike and Ceil McManus; in New York, my brothers Tom and Mike, my parents, and close friends Tom and Marie Goodman, Bob McFarland, and Steve and Debbie Meinsen; in North Reading, Massachusetts, Mr. and Mrs. John McFarland—Mr. McFarland did not live to read the final version, but his wonderful stories about his service in World War II, his keen wit, and his generous hospitality have left a lasting mark on me, as well as on hundreds of others; in the Washington, D.C. area, dear friends Keith, Erin, and Caitlyn Cotton; Tom, Colleen, and Holly David; Steve and Marlin Perkins; Rob Richards; and, especially, Niels C. Holch; and in North Carolina, Tom and Yvonne Hoban.

I received royal treatment at dozens of archives, but I would like to single out a few people in particular. Carl Anderson of the Houston Veterans Administration assisted in obtaining pension records. David Keough took great care of me in the absence of Richard Sommers at MHI. Ira Berlin, Leslie Rowland, and others from the Freedmen and Southern Society Project not only turned out invaluable research volumes but shared their resources with me one spring day. At the National Archives, where I spent more weeks than the staff cares to recall, Maida Loescher, Tim Nenninger, Peyton Howard, Mike Pilgrim, and William Lind did me numerous favors. Michael Musick, their excellent archivist, who specializes in the Old Army, drew on his extraordinary resourcefulness again and again. Frankly, Mike's knowledge and skills are irreplaceable. Last but not least is Sara Dunlap Jackson, who more than anyone else is at the heart of Afro-American history. She is a dear friend who supplies me with research material, and with her good humor, personal and professional advice, and warmth and enthusiasm for people.

Back in Houston, Steven Mintz advised me with my sampling, James Kirby Martin shared some insights, and James Jones plowed through the last chapter and provided his keen criticism. Great friends at the Jefferson Davis Papers—Lynda Crist, Mary Dix, and my former professor Sanford W. Higginbotham—kept me in mind whenever they saw something of interest. Clara and Danielle endured, or maybe relished, my prolonged absences. They should be commended in either case.

Stan Schultz of the University of Wisconsin-Madison, a friend and former professor, took time to guide me in my sampling. Robert F. Durden of Duke University reviewed the manuscript and provided some excellent recommendations. William Frassanito advised me on a photograph, and Richard Tracy shared his wonderful collection of Charles Augustus Hill Papers with me. My undergraduate adviser and dear friend Dr. Richard Smith lent me a wonderful photograph of black troops in his hometown of Delaware, Ohio, and Yvonne Hoban expertly prepared the maps. I also want to thank Dr. Elizabeth Yew of the Jewish Home and Hospital for the Aged in New York and Dr. William D. Sharpe, editor of the *Bulletin of the New York Academy of Medicine*, for providing thoughtful criticism of medical care in the USCT. Gerry McCauley and Joyce Seltzer of Free Press helped to make it all possible.

Finally, Edward M. ("Mac") Coffman has been and always will be my great friend and adviser. Since the project's inception, he has been there every step of the way, providing comments, criticisms, suggestions, and good cheer. He waded through two very different drafts, as if he had nothing else to do. And, unknowingly, he served as a model both personally and professionally. A day does not pass that I do not think how fortunate I am to have been his pupil.

I have three final notes. Originally, many of these black commands had state titles, followed by the parenthetical abbreviation A.D., for "African Descent," or the word *Colored* to designate the race. In 1863 and 1864, the War Department changed the names of these units to United States Colored Troops, with numbers and arms of service to distinguish them. Thus, the 1st Mississippi Cavalry (A.D.) became the 3rd U.S. Colored Cavalry, the 1st North Carolina Heavy Artillery (A.D.) changed to the 14th U.S. Colored Heavy Artillery, and the 1st Kansas (Colored) Infantry transformed into the 79th U.S. Colored Infantry (New), to distinguish it from the 79th U.S. Colored Infantry (Old), which the War Department merged with other troops to form the 75th U.S. Colored Infantry. To avoid massive confusion, I have relied on the later designations, a sensible solution for both the reader and author. Only four Northern black regiments— the 5th Massachusetts (Colored) Cavalry, the 54th Massachusetts (Colored) Infantry, the 55th Massachusetts (Colored) Infantry, and the 29th Connecticut (Colored) Infantry—officially retained their state designations. The War Department called all its black units United States Colored Troops, and most people abbreviated this to USCT. I have elected to follow that course of action.

Throughout the text, I regularly refer to officers as white and enlisted men as black within the USCT. In fact, a small number of white enlisted men held the highest positions in noncommissioned officers' ranks, but their mission was to help organize and train Southern black soldiers; whenever vacancies occurred, regimental commanders promptly commissioned them. There were also at least

110 black officers, most of whom served briefly either very early in the recruitment of black units or at the end of the war. Whenever I discuss either of these small groups in the text, I refer specifically to black officers or white noncommissioned officers.

Finally, I have quoted heavily from the sources, and whenever possible I have kept their spelling and punctuation.

In late September 1865, Garland H. White, the black chaplain of the 28th U.S. Colored Infantry, wrote, "The historian pen cannot fail to locate us somewhere among the good and the great, who have fought and bled upon the alter of their country." I have come to a similar conclusion, and if there are any errors in this project, I take sole responsibility.[2]

1

Breaking Down
the Resistance

Famed Civil War historian Bruce Catton once wrote, "Of all the incalculables which men introduce into their history, modern warfare is the greatest. If it says nothing else it says this, to all men involved in it, at the moment of its beginning: Nothing is ever going to be the same." Seldom have words more aptly described the experience of American blacks and whites in the 1860s. Racial prejudice was so powerful that most whites regarded the notion of arming blacks and encouraging them to fight for their freedom as lunacy. Yet, after sixteen months of war, the Federal government established as its official policy the recruitment and use of blacks as soldiers in its army, and from its white population came volunteers to serve alongside them as officers. Even in the Confederacy, which went to war to protect its peculiar institution of slavery, officials and private citizens openly debated the idea of using blacks for its army in the last year of the war, and in its waning weeks actually authorized their enlistment as privates. Whites had, in effect, become slaves to the demands of war.[1]

When President Abraham Lincoln spoke those immortal lines at the dedication of the Gettysburg battlefield cemetery—"Four score and seven years ago, our fathers brought forth, upon this continent, a new nation, conceived in Liberty and dedicated to the proposition that all men are created equal"—nothing could have been farther from the truth for black Americans. From the arrival in 1619 of twenty Africans on a Dutch trading vessel at Jamestown, Virginia, blacks had suffered abuse and indignities at the hands of both Northern and Southern whites as a result of deep-seated convictions about the inferiority of the black race. In the South, nearly four million blacks lived in bondage at the time of the Civil War, along with another quarter million whose rights were so circumscribed that, for them, the expression "free black" was truly a contradiction in terms. In the North there were fewer than a quarter million blacks, and like their Southern counterparts, they too were "free" but unequal.

Whether blacks were slave or free, prejudice had stifled their opportunities for self-fulfillment and personal development and made them feel shortchanged as human beings. They yearned for freedom to learn and improve, to attain a better life for themselves and a much better one for their children. Yet blacks knew that to achieve genuine freedom they must somehow emasculate the power of racial prejudice, first by striking a blow at the institution of slavery and then by demonstrating to whites the folly of racism. A chance to prove themselves was all they demanded.

As the rising tensions between North and South were transformed into war, blacks began to wonder if this was the cataclysmic event that would provide them with an opportunity to win freedom and respect. In the South, especially among slaves, the question evolved at a staggered pace. Bondsmen from the Border States or in areas where fighting took place learned rather quickly that the war offered them the possibility of freedom. Those in more distant parts of the Confederacy, deprived of access to much information and misled by rumors, had to "read" their owners to determine the seriousness of the war. Like nearly all others, they had been deceived by the magnitude of the struggle initially, and it was only when weeks became months and then a year and more, and the young white men ushered into uniform and disappeared, some returning in coffins, that most slaves began to realize that this might be the "War for Freedom." [2]

Nevertheless, they had to act cautiously. Insurrection, despite all its temptations, would most likely have resulted in a bloodbath, with few tangible results. Nearly all the power and weapons were in the hands of whites, and a massive revolt would have left countless slaves dead and injured in brutal reprisals. Instead, slaves in the Border States had to pick their chances to flee for Union lines very carefully, while others had to await the arrival of the Federal ranks. [3]

Free blacks in the South, who had better means of learning about the world around them, realized that the war placed them in a precarious position, yet one that also offered a chance to improve their status. In the eyes of Southern whites, free blacks were the least trustworthy and most unessential segment of Southern society, and as the sectional controversy became more critical, whites began to restrict their limited freedom. Once the war was upon them, their loyalty to the Confederacy was clearly at issue. Some quickly aligned with the Confederates, because they "had dared not refuse" or hoped their cooperation would lead to an improved status in the postwar South. Others sought an opportunity to band with the North but were fully conscious of the consequences of openly adopting the Union cause prematurely. Still, some accepted the risks and supported the Federals as their only possible hope of gaining civil rights. Such was the case of future soldier Hamilton Robison, who was "driven out by the Rebels" from his home in Loudoun County, Virginia. Robison's family made it to Ohio safely, but they had to abandon all their property in a hasty escape. No matter how they responded initially to the war, though, all hoped that the struggle would strike a fatal blow at prejudice and result in an uplifted status for all blacks. As a wealthy "Man of Color" from New Orleans explained to a Union general in 1862, "No matter where I fight; I only wish to spend what I have, and fight as long as I can, if only my boy may stand in the street equal to a white boy when the war is over." [4]

For Northern blacks, however, things were different. From the moment Fort Sumter fell in 1861, Northern blacks flooded the War Department and Lincoln with offers to serve in the Union Army. A Boston black man argued that if the government removed the disability that prevented blacks from entering the army, "there was not a man who would not leap for his knapsack and musket and they would make it intolerable hot for old Virginia." In a shrewd plea for the enlistment of blacks, two men wrote the secretary of war, stating that they had voted for the administration and adding, "the question now is will you allow us the poor priverlige of fighting— and (if need be dieing) to support those in office who are our own choise." Clearly, Northern blacks perceived this as their great opportunity to strike a blow at prejudice and prove their worth and loyalty to the Union. [5]

To make the proposal of black enlistment more palatable to the Northern white public, a number of blacks proposed the use of "efficient and accomplished" or "competent" white officers, predating the solution eventually adopted by the Lincoln administration. But for the time being, the Federal government refused to accept black soldiers. Few predicted a long war, and the government had problems accepting all the white volunteers who wanted to serve in this moment of crisis. [6]

Nevertheless, in the early stages of the war the Federal government took the first step toward emancipation and the organization of black units in the Union Army when it adopted the policy of confiscation of slaves as contraband of war. As a result of two centuries of slaveholding, Southerners had an excellent understanding of the value of black labor, and when the war broke out they immediately employed slaves in all sorts of military construction projects, as well as in the raising of foodstuffs and other items useful to the Confederate Army. In fact, their contributions were so significant that the Confederate provisional governor of Kentucky, George W. Johnson, announced that "the presence of the negro race adds greatly to the military spirit and strength of the Confederate States." Normal Federal policy was for the military authorities to return into bondage any slaves who ran away from their Southern masters, in accordance with the Fugitive Slave Law, and in spite of the work their masters had them performing.[7]

Yet Brig. Gen. Benjamin Butler, a leading Massachusetts Republican and Federal officer in Virginia, viewed the matter differently. One night three slaves who were working on the erection of an artillery battery slipped away from Confederate lines in a canoe and arrived safely at Butler's headquarters at Fortress Monroe on the Yorktown Peninsula. When a Confederate officer under a flag of truce came to retrieve the runaways the next day, Butler refused to return them. Possessing a shrewd, manipulative sort of mind that won him renown as a trial attorney before the war, Butler declared that slaves as used by the Confederacy were no different from cotton or machinery that contributed to the Confederate war effort and were therefore subject to confiscation. Then, in an act nearly as important as the confiscation itself but undertaken with very little thought as to its consequences, Butler directed the men to go to work for the Union Army for pay building a bakery.[8]

In one swoop Butler had established a precedent for the confiscation of runaway blacks who worked on Confederate military projects and their employment by the Union Army. Secretary of War Simon Cameron promptly endorsed Butler's decisions, and two months later Congress passed "An Act to confiscate Property used for Insurrectionary Purposes," which established it as the law of the land. Kansas senator James H. Lane, a great supporter of the use of blacks in military service, recognized the tremendous value of this policy when he advised a general officer, "Confiscation of slaves and other property which can be made useful to the Army should follow treason as the thunder peal follows the lightning flash." A decision based exclusively on military grounds had, in effect, emancipated slaves.[9]

At first this policy pertained only to slaves who worked on Confederate military projects, but as Federal armies penetrated well into the Confederacy, the Union government could not enforce such a restrictive rule. Huge numbers of slaves, who had regarded the Union Army as a sanctuary or who received encouragement from Federal soldiers, escaped bondage by fleeing to Yankee lines. Much to the chagrin of these runaways, Federal authorities attempted to return all slaves who had not worked on Confederate military projects, and slaveholders actually used Union troops to assist in the process. This, however, proved to be a substantial burden on the army and a highly controversial policy inside and outside military circles, particularly when dealing with Southerners in Confederate states, and by early 1862 the War Department prohibited the use of Federal troops in the return of runaway slaves.[10]

Once the government terminated this practice, troops who were sympathetic to the plight of slaves or who recognized the military value of bondsmen fleeing from their Southern masters began to help fugitives and to shield them from their owners. An Illinois soldier observed a slaveholder riding into camp seeking one of his slaves. The master quickly spotted the black man and seized him by the neck, but the fugitive bondsman broke loose and ran. When the slave owner went to ride after the man, he found his horse missing. Some disapproving soldiers had stolen it. In other regiments the same sort of conduct occurred. According to an 18th Michigan infantryman, a future officer in the USCT, his regiment assisted so many fugitive slaves that the locals cursed them as the "nigger thievery regiment," an appellation the troops regarded with pride.[11]

As more and more slaves poured into Union lines, an increasing number found employment with the army. Henry W. Halleck, commanding general of the Union Army, stated the justification rather concisely when he wrote, "In the hands of the enemy they are used with much effect against us. In our hands we must try to use them with the best possible effect against the rebels." Some worked as cooks and servants for officers while others labored for the Quartermaster's Department, which in turn freed soldiers for other military duties. Whites clamored for the use of blacks as pioneers, teamsters, and laborers in military construction projects—in a sense to take over the peripheral military duties—which would enable the government to utilize more of its soldiers for field duty. This type of policy, some hoped, would also spur enlistments, because one drawback to military service was the fatigue duty that in many instances blacks could now do.[12]

Eventually, however, the number of blacks who came into Federal lines was more than the army could handle. The army was able to employ many of the males; though there was little work for the women and children, the military had to feed and care for them. Authorities gave some brief consideration to the idea of sending many blacks, particularly families, to the free states, but as Adjutant General Lorenzo Thomas noted, "the prejudice of the people of those states are against such a measure." It was more practical, the government concluded, to keep them in the vicinity and have them cultivate land on abandoned plantations. Unfortunately, Confederate volunteers and guerrillas regarded them as an important target, and the Federals had to allocate manpower to protect these plantation workers.[13]

Like the heavy casualties and hardships that white troops endured, this policy of accepting fugitive slaves and employing them for government purposes helped bring the war to a critical juncture. When the Federals stripped Southerners of their laborers, it became increasingly difficult to appease and entice them into a pro-Union position. In addition, more and more Northerners were calling for emancipation and the enlistment of black troops. Early in the war only blacks and some abolitionists had urged the Lincoln administration to draw on the black race for troops. But as the length of the war extended with no termination in sight, and as blacks took up more nonmilitary roles with the army and Northern whites were reluctant to enlist, emancipation and the adoption of blacks in the military won more and more supporters. Slowly but steadily, it became clearer to troops in the field that a war to preserve the union and protect slavery was "nonsense," as a Pennsylvanian termed it.[14]

In the first fifteen months of the war, there had been opportunities and attempts to arm blacks. Before Brig. Gen. Thomas W. Sherman embarked on an expedition to the coastal islands of South Carolina, Acting Secretary of War Thomas A. Scott authorized him to use the services of anyone, "fugitives from labor or not, who offered it," and he could employ them any way he saw fit, including arming them. Sherman elected the conservative course and did not use blacks for military purposes. His successor, however, did.[15]

In late March 1862, Maj. Gen. David Hunter, a West Point graduate and a committed abolitionist, took over for Sherman in South Carolina. Presuming his authority from the orders given his predecessor, Hunter declared martial law and promptly emancipated all slaves in Georgia, South Carolina, and Florida. He then called in, at gunpoint, all escaped male slaves and announced to them that he was organizing military units with fugitive blacks and was now taking volunteers. This harsh tactic alienated a sizable portion of the black population and hurt recruitment in the islands for some time to come. To complicate matters, Hunter never communicated these steps to the War Department. The Lincoln administration learned of Hunter's activities through newspaper reports and Treasury Department correspondence.[16]

Technically, Lincoln had the authority to uphold Hunter's actions. That summer Congress passed the Militia Act of July 17, 1862, which empowered the president to organize blacks and use them "for any military or naval service for which they may be found competent." Nevertheless, the president elected not to endorse Hunter's decisions. Lincoln had an extraordinary sense of public opinion, and at the time he believed the Northern populace was not quite ready for such a step. As a New York private and future officer in the USCT commented, "It is the wrong idea that this is the time to urge abolition measures." It took heavy casualties and unforeseen sacrifices throughout the rest of the summer and early fall before the public was willing to tolerate more drastic action.[17]

Nor did Hunter help his own cause with the Congress. When he finally submitted a report of his actions to the War Department, which the secretary of war passed along to the legislative body, it was a flippant, almost disrespectful lecture on civil rights. Radicals loved it, but his tone and language alienated many moderates as well as opponents of emancipation and black enlistment. In the end Hunter was his own worst enemy, and Lincoln was unwilling to associate himself with these tainted efforts.[18]

Kansas was another scene of black recruitment in 1862. Big Jim Lane, the U.S. senator from that state who resigned to accept a commission as a brigadier general and recruit military units back home, organized a regiment of black soldiers without authorization from the War Department. Lane, not one to be bothered by such trifles as rules, had apparently hoped that the existence of such a military unit would result in governmental approval. When the War Department notified him twice that he had no authorization to raise a black unit, Lane simply ignored it in the best frontier fashion. By January 1863 the federal government accepted the services of the black regiment, but by then many of its troops had already seen combat.[19]

Finally, there was a bizarre episode of black recruitment in Louisiana. After the fall of New Orleans in April 1862, Benjamin Butler stepped in to command the occupation forces. Butler, who had acted so boldly in Virginia on the contraband issue, now voiced his doubts about the efficacy of using black troops to the War Department. One of his subordinates, however, did not hesitate to endorse the concept.[20]

Brig. Gen. John W. Phelps, a West Pointer and an abolitionist, viewed the enlistment of blacks as both a military and a social necessity. Phelps believed blacks could offset the Federal manpower shortage in the area, and the military structure would be a useful tool to facilitate the transition of blacks from slavery to freedom when the inevitable collapse of Southern society occurred. First Phelps openly welcomed and even encouraged fugitive slaves to come into his lines. Then he organized them into five companies and requested arms and accoutrements for their use.

Meanwhile, Butler—who had not yet learned of Phelps's activities—ordered his subordinate to use the fugitives to cut down trees and build fortifications. To this an outraged Phelps replied that he would order black soldiers to perform such labors but he would not act as a "slave driver." He promptly tendered his resignation and requested an immediate leave of absence.

In what was for him a rare instance, Butler responded to Phelps with considerable tact. He mentioned that only the president had the authority to raise black military units and that at present Lincoln declined to exercise that authority. The construction of fortifications, he continued, was essential for defense, and the use of fugitives was nothing new. The government had already drawn on black labor in other theaters. As for the resignation, he gently scolded his wayward subordinate for such a request when the national crisis required the aid of all its countrymen, particularly someone with the vast military skills that Phelps possessed. Nevertheless, he agreed to forward all correspondence on the matter to the War Department.

Unsoothed, Phelps replied that his conscience would not permit him to work under such conditions and again requested that Butler endorse his resignation and grant his leave of absence.

What made this entire event so peculiar was that within a few weeks, Butler made a 100 percent turnaround on the issue of blacks in the military. Encouragement from Secretary of the Treasury Salmon P. Chase and military necessity convinced Butler to accept free black militiamen for federal service a scant three weeks later, and the War Department supported the decision.[21]

In fact, federalization of black militiamen was monumental, but not in the way it appeared. These were free blacks whose ancestors had fought alongside Andrew Jackson in the Battle of New Orleans in 1815 and had organized, albeit halfheartedly, for the Confederate government. With Federal occupation of New Orleans, they had immediately tendered their services to Butler. They were men of considerable means—either skilled workers, professionals, or entrepreneurs—and some, such as Francis E. Dumas, had accumulated vast holdings and even owned slaves themselves.[22]

What was so striking about Butler's decision was that he accepted them for service with their black officers. At one time the 1st, 2nd, and 3rd Louisiana Native Guards (later 73rd, 74th, and 75th U.S.

Colored Infantry) all had black captains and lieutenants; and one regiment, the 2nd Louisiana Native Guards, even had a black major, slaveholder Francis Dumas. Much to the dismay of these officers and men, Butler's tenure as commander of the region was brief, and his replacement, Maj. Gen. Nathaniel P. Banks, disapproved of black officers and methodically drove them all from the service. Not until the end of the war, when the War Department appointed Martin Delaney as major of the 104th U.S. Colored Infantry, did a black obtain such high rank, and the authorities had no intention of placing Delaney in command in the field. Thus Butler again played a central role in the adoption of both black enlisted men and officers by the Union Army.

Back in Washington, Lincoln had been mulling over the idea of emancipation and black enlistment for some time. Personally an abolitionist, Lincoln subordinated his views for the good of the war effort, mainly for fear of alienating the loyal slaveholding states. But by midsummer 1862, he decided it was time to act. After McClellan's Peninsula Campaign in Virginia failed and springtime gains in the West halted in northern Mississippi, it became apparent that an amicable solution to the war was impossible. Both sides had suffered tens of thousands of casualties, and the Confederates obviously were not going to back down. Lincoln decided that hostilities had reached such a scale—and that the Federal armies had lost so many men—that a return to the way the nation was before the rebellion was simply unacceptable. Slavery had been the major divisive issue between the North and South, and if the Union won the war, he was going to resolve the matter permanently. Thus, on September 24, 1862, Lincoln declared that all slaves in areas still in rebellion against the Federal government on January 1, 1863, would be free.[23]

Lincoln also made it clear that the Union planned to enlist blacks for military service. Northern recruitment had slowed to a trickle as a result of the high casualties and limited progress in the war, and this enlistment would be a means of tapping into both the free black and slave populations. In addition, by enlisting slaves, he would be placing arms in the hands of the people who had the greatest incentive to fight—and against their former masters. If Southerners had a psychological edge over Northerners because they were fighting for their own independence, they lost it to blacks, who were seeking basic human rights.

Though Lincoln most probably decided on emancipation and the use of blacks as soldiers at the same time, in fact he authorized the use of black troops *before* emancipation. On July 22, he presented a proposal to the cabinet that called for the emancipation of slaves in Confederate-held territory. Secretary of State William Seward, a veteran politician, supported the move but recommended that Lincoln wait until the Union won a major battle. Otherwise it would look like the desperate grasp of a losing government. Unfortunately, the next significant Federal victory was at Antietam, two months later. By then Lincoln had directed Brig. Gen. Rufus Saxton to raise a black regiment in South Carolina—Thomas Wentworth Higginson's famed 1st South Carolina Infantry—and agreed to permit Butler to muster black militiamen in New Orleans into federal service.[24]

Reactions to the Emancipation Proclamation were mixed. Many Northern blacks and abolitionists lauded the decision, while others criticized it for not going far enough. According to the proclamation, slavery would continue to exist in loyal areas, and Lincoln only freed slaves over whom he and his armies had no control. On the other hand, criticism of the Emancipation Proclamation for having gone too far was considerable. An exaggerated report reached the Illinois governor that two companies in one of his volunteer infantry regiments "have laid down their arms and gone home, swearing they will not fight to free the negroes." Opposition to the proclamation in the Army of the Potomac was open, mainly because its popular commander, Maj. Gen. George B. McClellan, was a noted critic of abolitionism. From Virginia a Wisconsin officer warned Lincoln that "a decided majority of our Officers of all grades have no sympathy with your policy; nor with anything human. They hate the Negro more than they love the Union."[25]

Despite the resistance of many whites, the recruitment of blacks into military service proceeded at an almost breathless pace, which in turn produced a new administrative weight that quickly overwhelmed the Adjutant General's Office. Queries for information, requests for appointments to recruit and serve in these new units, mountains of paperwork for enlistees, and orders to organize and equip these commands became so burdensome that the War Department decided to create a single entity under the umbrella of the Adjutant General's Office, called the Bureau of Colored Troops, to manage its affairs. Headed by Maj. Charles W. Foster, the bureau's purpose was to systematize the process of raising black units and securing officers for them, and also to serve as a clearinghouse of information on these United States Colored Troops. With Foster at the helm, the Bureau of Colored Troops administered more than 186,000 black and white officers and men, and at one time had over 123,000 soldiers in uniform—a force larger than the field armies that either Lt. Gen. Ulysses S. Grant or Maj. Gen. William T. Sherman directly oversaw at the height of their campaigns in 1864 and 1865.[26]

2

The White Man's War

For the white men who eventually commanded black soldiers, the experience of fighting in state volunteer units during the first few years of bloodshed compelled them to make some subtle yet critical adjustments in their attitudes toward blacks. Prior to the war, virtually all of them held powerful racial prejudices, but prolonged military service and the tragedies of combat forced them, as it did all soldiers, to reconsider their commitment to the war effort and to redetermine how they and the Northern public must contribute for the Union to earn a decisive victory. The early years of the war shook the very foundations of Northern society and demanded that it sacrifice some cherished values and practices to preserve more essential ones. In this atmosphere, at first tentatively and then with increasing strength, the Union latched onto the concept of employing blacks as Federal soldiers, and these white veterans concluded that they must have a hand in the creation and development of this new resource.

Before the war, most Northerners regarded race relations as a Southern concern. Comparatively few blacks lived in the North, 1 percent of the population in 1860, and they either gathered in urban pockets or sprinkled themselves throughout the countryside, where few whites had regular contact with them. Yet like Southerners, Northern whites had powerful prejudices against blacks. One man who commanded black soldiers in the war sized up the sectional attitudes toward the African race rather well when he wrote that Southerners regarded blacks as little higher in the scale of animated nature than apes and gorillas, and their value was reckoned as one would estimate that of his horse or ox, by the money they would bring on the auction block, or by the utility of the work they could be expected to perform without compensation from their masters; while north of the Mason and Dixon's line they were regarded by many with aversion and often with loathing.[1]

It was one thing, most Northerners reasoned, to regard the enslavement of the black race as cruel and inhumane; it was another to ask Northerners to regard blacks as their equals or welcome them as neighbors and friends.

Even those men who elected to fight alongside black soldiers in the war had held prejudices in the prewar years. Like the rest of Northern society, most of them had little or no contact with blacks before the war, and they preferred to keep it that way. When they did encounter blacks on anything resembling an equal standing, the whites generally squawked. Three years before Jeff Hoge volunteered to serve with black troops, he regarded a black in his college class as intolerable: "There is a Nigar in the Grammar class that I am in," he mentioned to his aunt. "I feel higly honored, wouldent you to be in a class with a Nigar." In fact, nearly all of those men who were outspoken critics of slavery and later served in the USCT never dreamed that a black man was their equal. Despite frequent contact and all their efforts on behalf of the black race, they too felt no remorse over using such demeaning expressions as "niggers," "nigs," or "darkies," or regarding their intelligence as inferior and behavior as childlike. Rare indeed was the individual who believed in full political and social equality.[2]

Nevertheless, the mere fact that most of the whites considered blacks inferior did not mean that these men who later commanded blacks in the war viewed enslavement as proper or justifiable. To the contrary, the common bond between nearly all of them was their distaste of the slave system. In the prewar years their motivations and commitments to antislavery groups varied considerably, from radical activism to nonparticipation, but virtually all of them regarded the institution of slavery as wrong.

The most visible, albeit smallest, group who later commanded black soldiers in the war consisted of prominent abolitionists and scions of antislavery leaders. For decades a cluster of abolitionists had fought the institution of slavery almost single-handedly, gradually increasing in strength over the years. Unfortunately, with few exceptions, abolitionism was a reform movement that had essentially the same leadership for thirty years. By the time of the war, its leaders wisely recognized that they were unsuited for the rigors of combat.

Fortunately, abolitionism was a family-oriented movement. The Welds, Beechers, Birneys, Garrisons, Tappans, and Adamses were just a few families that had several members in the abolitionist movement. While the family heads could not oversee the continuation of their labors on the battlefield, several of these families sent relatives to help the movement. William Birney, son of James Gillespie Birney, the abolitionist Liberty Party candidate for president in 1840 and 1844, was a lawyer and intellectual of distinction. After outstanding performance on several battlefields, he eventually rose to the rank of major general. Before that, though, he helped raise seven black regiments and had a hand in the abolition of slavery in Maryland. Charles Francis Adams, Jr., was the son of Free Soil vice presidential candidate Charles Francis Adams and grandson of President John Quincy Adams. He served successfully in a Massachusetts cavalry regiment before entering the 5th Massachusetts (Colored) Cavalry in 1864. Despite the pacifistic predilections of abolitionist William Lloyd Garrison, he made no effort to stop his son George Thompson Garrison from picking up the sword on behalf of blacks in the 55th Massachusetts (Colored) Infantry. Nor were the Beechers without a representative. James Chaplin Beecher, son of the famous minister Lyman Beecher and half brother of renowned author Harriet Beecher Stowe and minister Henry Ward Beecher, commanded the 35th U.S. Colored Infantry after service in two New York regiments.

One of the most interesting and promising young men to serve in the USCT was Lewis Ledyard Weld, nephew of antislavery activist Theodore Dwight Weld. Under his uncle's influence, Lewis adopted abolitionism at an early age. His Yankee education led him to Yale, where he passed an entrance examination by reading Cicero "with a 'perfect rush,' " conjugating some Latin verbs, and reading Xenophon, all before several faculty members. Weld graduated in 1854, and after teaching school he drifted to the Kansas imbroglio where he hung out a law shingle and worked to combat the extension of slavery. A committed Republican, he eventually became secretary of state for the Colorado Territory and for a time was acting governor, all before the age of thirty. When the war broke out, Weld and his two brothers made a pact that one would sit out to support their widowed mother, and Lewis drew the lot. The death of one brother and his other brother's discharge for disability paved the way for his entrance into the USCT.[3]

Probably the most famous offspring of a prominent abolitionist who served with black troops was Robert Gould Shaw. Young Shaw's father, Francis George Shaw, was an extremely wealthy merchant whose philanthropy included all sorts of reforms, abolitionism among them. Robert Gould Shaw attended Harvard but left before graduation for a career as a merchant. All who knew him praised his integrity, forthrightness, and quiet compassion. His sympathy for the downtrodden and the commitment to reform that he inherited from his father drew him to abolitionism. On the outbreak of hostilities, the twenty-three-year old Shaw volunteered his services and quickly entered the officers' ranks in a Massachusetts regiment. His death and burial beside his black troops during the war led to his depiction as a martyr by his abolitionist friends.

Only one prominent white abolitionist, Thomas Wentworth Higginson, graced the officers' ranks of the USCT. Born in the shadows of Harvard College, Higginson graduated from that school in 1841 and later took his postgraduate degree in divinity studies there. According to his leading biographer, intimate contact with the reform-minded Channing family, which he joined through marriage, and the writings of abolitionist Lydia Maria Child converted him to the antislavery cause. A man of immense learning and exceptional literary skills, he accepted a position as pastor of a Unitarian church in Massachusetts, but his fervent antislavery preachings did not sit well with his conservative congregation and he resigned. Higginson ran unsuccessfully for Congress on the Free Soil ticket and was a strong supporter of the Kansas free state movement. He won national fame, however, for his efforts to rescue runaway slaves who fell into the hands of U.S. marshals and for his support of John Brown and the raid on Harper's Ferry. During the war he commanded a company of infantrymen and organized and served as colonel in the first official black unit organized by the Federal government.[4]

Other men who eventually commanded black troops during the war also had connections to abolitionism, yet they either lacked the notoriety or family connections to the abolitionist leadership. Penrose Hallowell, who served in the 54th and 55th Massachusetts (Colored) Infantry and had relatives among the antislavery ranks, was a Philadelphia Quaker and "naturally an Abolitionist," but not active in the movement. As a young scholar at Harvard, though, the oratory of abolitionist Wendell Phillips spellbound both him and his brother, and the two of them volunteered to serve as bodyguards for Phillips. Henry C. Corbin, later an officer in the 14th U.S. Colored Infantry, had the good fortune of attending an integrated school run by an ardent abolitionist. There he learned that abolitionism was God's work and that the laws of God superseded the laws of man. Adolphus W. Greely, on the other hand, adopted abolitionism because his father, a man of modest means, had concluded after extensive readings on the subject that slavery was wrong and taught his son so.[5]

In several instances, abuses committed by slaveholders convinced Northerners that they must work to terminate slavery at all costs. Benjamin Thompson had just moved to Florida and opened a store when the secession crisis hit. Suspected of being a spy by the locals, he had his mail opened illegally, his store ransacked by the Vigilance Committee, and the bulk of his goods confiscated for the benefit of the state, with reimbursement to come in good time. Thompson blamed Southern whites and their paranoia over slavery for these abuses and sought retribution through military service. Some fifteen hundred miles away in Missouri, Warren Olney discovered that when it came to the issue of slavery, there was no such thing as freedom of speech. Although mildly sympathetic to slaves, he felt no sense of commitment to their cause and actually cared little about the institution. It was the inhibition of free speech that led to his conversion to abolitionism: "The fact that I dared not freely speak my sentiments was most exasperating, and hardened every conviction on the slavery question." When war broke out, Olney headed immediately for Iowa, and as he crossed the border he turned and waved a clenched fist at Missouri for its intolerance.[6]

Just as evangelical religion had been a driving force with abolitionists, because it branded slavery a sin and demanded that its converts work actively to terminate the evil wherever it existed, so it was with whites who elected to command black soldiers. Spearheading this religious influence in the ranks of the white officers was the clergy itself. Along with those who served as chaplains, a considerable number of men cast aside their prewar frocks to pick up a sword in the USCT. Thomas Wentworth Higginson, twice a pastor, was the most famous clergyman who served in a combat role, but there were numbers of others. Presbyterian minister James M. Alexander was one of several who vacated a comfortable position as chaplain in a white unit for a colonelcy in the USCT. He thought he could transform his charitable work with the freedmen into something very valuable to the war effort by raising and training a black regiment. Some even accepted lower rank to serve in combat roles in black units. Edwin M. Wheelock, chaplain in the 15th New Hampshire Infantry, accepted a first lieutenancy in the USCT, as did Methodist minister Hiram Roberts. Whenever Roberts's command was without a preacher on Sundays, he gladly filled the void. For these clergymen and for many others, service in the USCT offered them an opportunity to take an active role in fulfilling their dreams of abolitionism and uplifting the black race.[7]

Yet evangelicalism had touched the hearts of many of the future

officers in the USCT without ever recruiting them to abolition soci-
eties. The bulk of the whites who later served in the USCT originally
came from the region most strongly affected by the various revivals.
From the mid-1820s into the 1850s, revivals roared through a belt
that stretched from northern New England across to northern Ohio,
with central New York, the famous "Burnt-Over District" (for its
role in revivalism and reform), as the focal point. Over the years
many of these families left this hotbed and scattered throughout
the North, but their children, who reached majority age around
the time war broke out, grew up in households where abolitionism
was encouraged or at least received a fair hearing.[8]

Along with evangelicalism, education was another common thread
among whites who eventually commanded black troops in the war.
In part, service in black units favored well-educated whites, who
were able to pass the required examination to become an officer in
the USCT. Thus an unusually large number of teachers and students
before the war, as well as many others who were college graduates,
later commanded black troops. But there was more to it than that.
The purpose of education, particularly at the college level, was to
promote learning in the broadest sense, to encourage students to
recognize varying points of view. Most colleges sought to provide
an atmosphere for free and open discussions on all sorts of subjects,
including abolitionism. When a future lieutenant in the USCT, then,
participated in a debate on which race—the white, black, or Indian—
was the most mistreated, his classmates may not have won him
over to the plight of blacks, but they certainly exposed him to their
arguments. In such a climate, students were likely to become not
only more sensitive to abolitionism but even converts to the antislavery banner.[9]

With superior educations, these men held much better jobs than
did most Americans. Nearly all of them had skilled or professional
positions that required either extensive training or an exceptional
education. Carpenters, blacksmiths, coopers, and printers made
up a sizable proportion of prewar occupations, as did lawyers, doctors, engineers, and clergymen. Indeed, very few of them had the
unskilled jobs that were so prevalent in mid-nineteenth-century
America.[10]

Although most of the whites who fought in black commands hailed
originally from the Northeast, at the time of the war many of them
had now settled on the Midwestern frontier. There they had little
exposure to race relations, but they were close to the violence over
slavery in Missouri and Kansas, which gave them a personal interest
in the speedy resolution of the war. In addition, those who moved
to the frontier had that adventuresome, pioneering spirit. They had

demonstrated a desire to step forward and tackle the challenge of the unknown in hopes of great returns. As recent settlers, their intercommunity bonds were not long standing, and powerful attachments to local institutions had not formed as they had in older, more established areas. This played a major role in the willingness of white soldiers to move over to positions in the USCT, because when the war broke out, the government recruited white volunteer units on the local level. In older areas, longtime relationships served to weld individuals to their comrades and military organizations in an unusually strong manner. Those bonds simply did not exist to the same degree in units assembled in newly settled areas, which made it easier for a soldier to leave his comrades for promotion in a strange unit.[11]

Of course, most of the whites who joined the USCT were ardent Republicans. Back in 1854, Delavan Mussey was distressed by the public's unwillingness to elect many abolitionists to public office. He found "consolation" in the victories of Seward, Sumner, and others, but pined, "Would God there were more of them." Needless to say, his transition from Whig to Republican was smooth. Another stalwart, James Brisbin, was such an outspoken abolitionist and Republican that in the election of 1860, he campaigned for Lincoln in Virginia, a dangerous undertaking. Others moved more cautiously to Republicanism, switching just in time for the election of 1860, but when war broke out, they were fully committed to the party of Lincoln.[12]

Among the white officers, however, there was also a substantial cluster of Democrats who held to their party in 1860. John A. Bross was a "Stephen A. Douglas" Democrat who "had been taught to regard everything which savored of what men were accustomed to call 'abolitionism,' with distrust." Jeff Hoge heard Congregationalist minister Lyman Beecher preach in Galesburg, Illinois, and felt, "He preached too much Abolitionism for me," and refused to hear him again. He complained to his aunt that Beecher had predicted, "The Republican triumph [of 1860] would be a glorious triumph. It would be the first step toward reforming the nation." He was so annoyed that he "had a notion to tell him I dident believe it." A few weeks later Hoge jokingly reconsidered his political affiliation, because as a Douglas Democrat he was in the extreme minority at college, especially with women. "I have a notion to turn Publican myself, be a Publican while I am among Publicans."[13]

When the secession crisis began, these men, Republicans and Democrats, banded together in support of the federal government. They viewed Southerners as the cause of the crisis to the union not only by their secession but by their infringements of civil liberties under the claim of protecting their chattel property. Several years earlier John Wilder had noted in his commencement address at Union College in New York that the Southern laws protecting slavery and "the arbitrary and offensive manner which has been adopted for their enforcement, is repugnant to the cherished principles of Northern Freedom, & is calculated to awaken the most determined hostility & resentment." Since then, things seemed to have gotten worse. Nevertheless, few of them had any insights into Southern fears and suspicions, and many thought Southerners used secession as a trump card to win their way, as one skeptic noted on New Year's Day in 1861:

> The Southern, or Slaveholding states, seem determined to try and better themselves out of the Union. The professed cause is the interference by the North, with the institution of slavery, which they say has now culminated in the election of an abolition President, as they style Lincoln; but the real causes are their lossing control of the government, and with it, executive patronage, and the emoluments of office, the humiliation, proud aristocrats that they are, to be governed by a "Mudsill." [14]

Those men who later commanded black soldiers solidified behind their president and government, but most of them were a long way from committing themselves to service in the USCT. Support for the Federal government was one thing, as was sympathy for the plight of blacks in the South, but it was a huge leap from there to employing blacks as soldiers, let alone commanding them. It would take several years of hardship, wounds, fatalities, and sacrifices before they were willing to join hands with blacks to win the war.

Nearly all the whites who commanded black men had prior military service, and like other Federal soldiers, they sought the same goals. A small minority entered the Union Army to free the slaves, as did Charles Francis Adams, Jr., who discussed enlistment in terms of family honor to win his father's blessing: "For years our family has talked of slavery and of the South, and been most prominent in the contest of words, and now that it has come to blows, does it become us to stand aloof from the contest?" Yet most of them, despite personal disapproval for slavery, sought foremost to restore the union. A Massachusetts captain, later an officer in the USCT, who supported the antislavery movement, wrote his mother that he had seen no blacks at Harper's Ferry, "nor do I desire to. The Constitution & the Union are enough for me to fight for." For most of them, regardless of their views on the institution of slavery, this was a time of crisis and their country needed their service.[15]

Of course, a number of men enlisted for purely personal motives.

Probably the most striking example was James Horrocks, a university student in England who got a neighborhood girl pregnant. He promptly fled to the United States and enlisted in a New Jersey artillery battery to "get money quick." Horrocks eased the minds of his parents by telling them, "I fully intend to desert if I don't get good treatment," and enlisted under a false name to shield him from punishment if he did desert. Horrocks also vowed "not to risk getting a scratch in this war," although he admitted "it would be different if I was fighting for my own country." Strangely enough, Horrocks later became a fairly good soldier in both the New Jersey unit and the USCT. Fortunately for the Federal government, his motive for enlistment was not representative of future officers in black units.[16]

Competing with Horrocks was William F. Spurgin, a West Pointer of the class of 1862 who left before graduating to serve in the war. Although he received his appointment to the United States Military Academy from Indiana, Spurgin offered his services to the Confederacy because he had been born in Kentucky. He wrote Jefferson Davis a letter stating that he had resigned his commission with the United States, "not wishing to do violence to my principles and feelings by remaining longer in the Northern Army. If my services are acceptable I would be pleased to serve in the Southern Army." He never received a reply from Davis, but his principles were apparently never too rigid. During the war he served in an Indiana regiment and later commanded black troops.[17]

Early in the war, the greatest fear of the enlistees was not to die or suffer wounds; rather, it was to miss the great experience of their generation, an opportunity to defeat the Confederates in battle. The failure to win the battle and the war at First Bull Run, many of these men felt, was fortuitous because it gave them a chance to prove their prowess. "It is the general opinion that this war matter will be settled within the next six months," wrote a sergeant and future officer in the USCT in November 1861, "and if we don't pitch in soon we will not have a hand in it." They proudly accepted the cheers of roaring crowds as they played the role of national saviors, with no concept of what they were getting into and how much they would have to sacrifice to win.[18]

The novelty of army life at first suited them well, as a Minnesota private and future captain in a black regiment indicated: "Well they say that soldiers are nothing but Machines, and I think there is some truth in that but if Uncle Sam will keep us oiled with Pork and beef he can run *us* for some time without much repairing." In those early days of the war, the only issue that aroused the ire of the men was the selection of commissioned and noncommissioned

officers. Some, naturally, found theirs satisfactory, but many others complained that "No matter what a man's qualifications are, or what his character may be, if he only have *influence* there is no trouble about his getting an appointment." At the time, the selection of officers seemed significant to the men, but it was nothing compared to the problems they soon encountered.[19]

At first the marching and drilling seemed fun, but week upon week, month upon month of training sapped their initial enthusiasm. The rigid and hierarchical military structure stripped away the freedom to which these men were accustomed and forced them to live the same as their comrades. Only officers and non-commissioned officers made decisions, and the privates merely carried them out. Such a life-style prompted one man to comment, "Soldiering is a lazy life & I think it is the next thing to slavery   a man becomes dependent & looks for his officers to provide for him & bid him to do this & that."[20]

Boredom set in as they waited while senior officers stockpiled supplies, accumulated more manpower, and ruminated over the military situation. Instead of whipping Confederates, they were lying around in camps throughout the North. One man wrote home of the heavy casualties the " *'Bloody 6th* [Ohio Cavalry]' " inflicted. "It was a very *hard fought-battle;* of the Enemy *One-hundred were killed,* and several taken *prisoners of war. . . .* the boys killed 100 old and young *rats* 75 very large ones and run some more into holes in the ground." Losses were not from Confederate lead but accidental wounds and diseases that raced through camp and took fearful tolls. As one soldier accurately concluded, "There is more reality than poetry in a life on the Tented field."[21]

When they finally did campaign, it proved to be far less enjoyable than many of the men had imagined. Most had envisioned themselves marching through the Southern countryside or along the streets of Richmond, beautifully accoutered and in perfect step, to the delight of poor Southern whites and slaves, whipping the Confederates decisively at every turn. Few had considered sore, blistered feet; exposure to all the elements; and moldy or worm-infested rations and worn-out clothing. Without previous experience, they could not conceive that campaigning would teach them the hard way to throw away all excess baggage, as one soldier wrote home: "I shall have to come down to nothing but a rubber blanket before a great while. I haven't thrown away that Bible yet but I'm afraid it will have to go, when you are on the march continually day & night every ounce tells like thunder." None of them had thought that they would do so much marching with no idea what the plan was and where they were going. As Sam Evans wrote home, "If you want to find a *'Know*

Nothingism' in its purity, just come into the army and you can find it, Col. down to private." And as the weeks transformed into months and even years, familiar sounds and experiences of military life replaced those from the civilian world. One New Yorker who later became a lieutenant in the USCT described it well when he penned:

> Our experience during the past year has dispelled all the novelty, mystery & glory of a soldier's life. The rattle of the drum is more familiar to our ears than ever was the school bell & the booming of cannon accompanied by the howling of the shell, as it approaches us commands rather less emotion than we were want to bestow to the firing of blanks at a fourth of July celebration in Chatauqua.[22]

Nor was their baptism by fire quite the experience they had predicted. To a Massachusetts captain, his first fight, against Stonewall Jackson's command in the Shenandoah Valley, was terrible: "It was hell—there's no doubt of that—or at least about as good an imitation as is often produced in the upper world and I doubt if Satan himself could have improved upon it much." A private in a New Jersey battery admitted, "The first time that bullets whistled past my ears I confess that my heart fluttered, but 10 minutes afterward I did not seem to care anything about them nor for shot and shell that buzzed past us." He also learned in his first fight that "a *miss* is as good as if it were a mile off." Eventually, many accustomed themselves to battle, kept their wits, and simply performed their duty. Others, however, constantly battled fright, particularly before entering an engagement. A Connecticut sergeant, later a lieutenant colonel in the 29th Connecticut (Colored) Infantry, recalled, "I never could rid myself of a sneaking desire to turn and run for all I was worth, but I wouldn't have run for a good deal more than I was worth." [23]

Before these white men entered the USCT, nearly four of every five of them had been in battle or "seen the elephant," as the soldiers liked to call it. Well over 40 percent had been in more than two major battles, and over 20 percent had seen action in five or more major battles prior to service in black units. By the time they took command of black soldiers, they had no false notions about the battlefield.[24]

Combat, they discovered, was a paradox. While it heightened the senses of some soldiers, it dulled the senses of others. It was grand, thrilling, and awesome and at the same time horrible, destructive, and demonstrative of the great weaknesses of mankind.

Combat both made and broke men. It was a place where youths could prove their manhood, where individuals could pass the test of courage in front of their peers. Under the enormous stress of battle, soldiers learned whether they and their friends could be counted on in moments of crisis or whether they were untrustworthy and unreliable. It dictated its own set of standards, which were very different from those in the peacetime world. For some, combat reaffirmed a belief they already had in themselves and their comrades. But performance in battle also elevated nobodies to greatness and demoted prominent individuals to insignificance. According to one future USCT officer, "Many were mere boys, many men of scant education; many were thought to be men of small soul and to fill places in civil life with little credit. Yet one could not fail to note the wondrous changes wrought in the lives and characters of some of these patriots." In civilian pursuits the lives of some soldiers were mundane and their accomplishments minor, but with a uniform on their back and a weapon in hand they blossomed. Like Ulysses S. Grant, they somehow managed to excel in combat. For some it was the structure of military life, while others drew strength from the unique opportunity the war offered to measure themselves against their peers. Regardless, the military experience provided these men with confidence in themselves that they never had before.[25]

But these future officers also knew that one taste of combat expunged any romantic notions they may have had about it. "I never knew a man who really seemed to enjoy battle," wrote a sergeant and future USCT officer, "and I suspect such men are few in number." An Illinois soldier who suffered a wound at the Battle of Perryville conceded, "I would be very glad if the war would be closed by the time I am able to go back to the Regt." They viewed the bloodshed as a necessary evil and simply resigned themselves to it. In a fatalistic way, these men realized they must do their duty, take the risks, and hope for the best. The ultimate goal of restoration of the union demanded they endure combat, as one future lieutenant in the USCT explained to his sister: "We have the men now & if we have to fight why lets be at it & get home & if we fall in the battle why I feel that all is well." [26]

Whites who later commanded black units fought on every major battlefield in the early years of the war, and their experiences range from humorous to nearly tragic for themselves. They represent both the bizarre and brutal aspects of war.

Illinois Sgt. William Parkinson, future USCT captain, for example, had one of the most humorous but at the same time dangerous occurrences at the Battle of Fort Donelson in February 1862. In that fight Parkinson was at the head of his company in the front rank and lay down on his stomach to load and fire. A comrade named Sim Copple managed to lay about five feet behind the line and directly to Parkinson's rear. When the sergeant lifted his head to fire at the enemy, "Sim blazed away, & I thought in my sole my head was bursted wide open, I jumped up on my knees & said God Almighty dam you, come into the ranks & fight. I then called McKee & told him if he did not keep them damd boys in the ranks, I would get out of their way, for I would not stand two fires." [27]

Nor were these men without their close calls from the enemy. At Shiloh in April 1862 one man had a ball strike his cartridge box, a buckshot pass through his hat, and a grapeshot strike his neck, but he somehow came out of the battle all right. In the Seven Days' battles in the summer of 1862 the Confederates absolutely riddled one future commander of black troops: "Three guns, one after another, were shot to pieces in my hands, and one of these was struck twice before I threw it away. My canteen was shot through, and I was struck in three places by balls, one over the left eye, one in the left shoulder, and one in the left leg, and the deepest wound was not over half an inch, and I came off the field unhurt." [28]

In the Battle of Fredericksburg in late 1862 one future officer in the USCT, along with some comrades, advanced too far forward. When the Confederates counterattacked, they nearly captured him. "You are scared," he later described. "Your only desire is to get under cover, to increase your distance between you and the foe." To escape, he ran so fast that he became sick and vomited, but he nonetheless made it to safety. [29]

Without doubt, wounds were one of the most terrible aspects of combat and a problem that occurred with unusual frequency among future officers of the USCT. (Since most of the white officers entered the USCT before the staggering casualties of the campaigns of 1864— in which black commands frequently took a back seat—they suffered a disproportionate number of injuries in combat during service with white volunteers.) As many as one in five of them suffered wounds, one man as many as nine, before entering the USCT. At the Battle of Fair Oaks in early June 1862, while a corporal in a New York regiment was removing a cartridge from his box, a ball struck his hand, severing his second finger and damaging his third, and ricocheted into his stomach, leaving a severe bruise on his abdomen. Had the ball not hit his belt buckle, the soldier probably would have died. It was well over one year before he returned to a field unit, this time the 7th U.S. Colored Infantry. Jeff Hoge lasted only a short while before a Confederate ball struck him at the Battle of Perryville, his first fight. After his regiment stood in the rear and observed the battle for about an hour, an officer ordered them forward to support a battery on the top of a hill. There they hugged the ground for several minutes until a brigadier general ordered them forward. Hoge's company was in the reserve and had advanced some fifty yards when a ball "cut through my Blouse on my right breast, then went into my arm near the Shoulder. it passed down along and under the bone to the point of my elbow. Just came near breaking through to the skin." When Hoge realized that he could not use his arm, he headed for the rear, and once he reached safety, he became so weak that he could barely walk and staggered to an ambulance. Later that day a surgeon removed the ball "in a short time," but Hoge was recovering and out of action for two and a half years.[30]

From the battlefield, wounded soldiers went to a field hospital, where they received medical attention. According to most Civil War soldiers, the mere mention of army hospitals instilled terror in their hearts, and the sentiments about field hospitals were even stronger. There surgeons, grossly overworked and possessing rudimentary equipment and widely varying degrees of medical knowledge, struggled to save the lives of hundreds, sometimes thousands of soldiers who arrived with ghastly wounds from the huge balls of soft lead that Civil War armies fired at one another. For wounded soldiers, it was the ultimate nightmare. One future officer in the USCT who suffered a wound at Gettysburg and lay on the battlefield for several days described a battlefield hospital vividly when he wrote to his girlfriend, "Of all places that a human mind is capable of thinking of, a battlefield hospital is the worst   dead men and men mangled in all shapes legs and arms in heaps and then the groans and cries is awful for one that is wounded to face." [31]

Death played a more visible role for mid-nineteenth-century Americans than it did in the world of their descendants, yet the rate of death in the war caught even these people unprepared. The staggering numbers who died from injuries on the battlefield were just a part of it. Because of inadequate medical care and the life-style of soldiers, substantially more men died of disease in the Civil War than fell in the combat arena. As an assistant surgeon in an Illinois unit and later surgeon in a black regiment informed his wife in early 1863, "I have seen but little of the desolation of war and yet I have seen enough to prevent me falling in love with the profession of a soldier. The waste of health and of life is immense here, where no battle has been fought." [32]

The death these men faced was not the deep, dark death that children feared at night. It was an ever-present force that demanded reconciliation. Most of them acknowledged the randomness of their form of death and merely resigned themselves to the possibility of its coming. "I am a man, Mary, and a *soldier* and if my country needs my life she is welcome," wrote a Rhode Island private who later served as a lieutenant in the USCT. Others found comfort in religion, as did a Hoosier who was so ill he nearly lost his will to survive, yet somehow did: "I never was made to view death so closely before   All my plans and schemes for future life dwindled into nothingness. *A Savior was all I needed.*" The saddest death, conceded a future captain in the USCT, occurred when soldiers did not reconcile themselves to it. As he cared for a dying friend from home who was "unprepared for death," he regretted that the man "clings to life as his all." [33]

At times death was so commonplace that soldiers felt almost unfazed by another fatality. A New York regiment stationed in the sickly Port Hudson, Louisiana, area, decreased in size by two-thirds in its first year in the service. According to one of its sergeants, a future officer in the USCT, the loss of more and more comrades eventually dulled the senses of the survivors: "What hardened wretches we have become. The word came, 'Eph. Hammond is dead, hurry up and make a box for him.' He was one of the best-liked men in the regiment. Yet not a tear was shed, and before his body was cold he was buried in the ground. We will talk about him more or less for a day or two and then forget all about him. That is what less than a year has done to us." He then concluded, "At that rate two years more and we will be murdering in cold blood." [34]

Eventually, though, the totality of these losses came back to haunt them, as did the death of a friend or family member, and Federals assessed blame for these needless deaths on their foe, the Confederates. Had the Southern states not seceded, their reasoning went, the Union government never would have asked them to fight battles and expose themselves to the elements for such a prolonged period of time. "I attribute his death," wrote an Ohioan whose brother had just died in the service of his country, "to this Unjust and Unholy Rebellion on the part of the enemies of Our country." He then admitted, "It is wrong to harbor revenge in our bosom, but it Sticks in me. Some Secesh shall suffer for that if I am lost in the attempt." Since all soldiers knew at least someone who had died in the war, this hostility touched nearly everyone. [35]

This grim world contrasted starkly with civil life. As one soldier noted, "there are stern realities in war which cannot be portrayed by words or letters." Every day was a struggle, he felt, because at night he would "dream of home and home associations, to dream of everything pertaining to beauty civilization & intelligence [and] to wake up & find death & desolation all around you to start up & go into the ranks & prove yourself a man then & there. I say to depict this scene & the feelings of the actors requires a language which no man was ever known to possess." [36]

After extended service, few of these men found military service more than barely tolerable. A Michigan captain, later a lieutenant colonel in the USCT, wrote his wife, "The fancy Part of Soldiering is played out this is the Reality." Another future commander of black troops quipped to his brother, "For a man to enjoy the service, he must not be averse to much strong drink, must not be encumbered with morals & must possess an unsatiable appetite for confusion." Six months or more in the military stripped away the myth, and the reality was harsh. "There is not much glory in soldiering to one who has his mind set on a life of higher usefulness—striving to elevate his fellow creatures to a higher intellectual & moral standard," wrote a New York private. "He looks on war as a direful necessity,—a stern duty which calls him away from the more peaceful & pleasant duties of life." [37]

To compound the problem, the war had not gone well for the Union in 1861 and 1862. The Federal government had called into service hundreds of thousands of men, and the country had lost tens of thousands of soldiers, yet by all appearances it was no closer to victory. The war that Union troops had worried about missing was now a war they believed might never end. As a Wisconsin cavalryman, later a lieutenant in the USCT, moaned in mid-1863, "I little thought when I went in to this thing that it would take three Years to get out of it. but I am affraid that it will be so." [38]

No doubt, the harsh realities of the war were disillusioning. A considerable portion of the Federal troops had enlisted in a fit of patriotism and learned the unfortunate lesson that war was for the most part an awful experience. Their object was to get out of the service as soon as possible, whether by desertion, feigned or legitimate illness, resigning their commissions, or the expiration of their enlistment term.

For the men who later accepted commissions in black units, as well as for many other Union soldiers, the unanticipated hardships of the war jolted them, but they remained committed to the fight. "I shall deem it a duty to serve the good nay holy cause of Liberty and obedience to the Laws to the last, i.e. so long as *any one* need Serve it," a New Yorker and future lieutenant in the USCT told his sister. They had families at home that needed them, and most had careers that they would have preferred to pursue; nonetheless, they remained in uniform and did all they could for the war effort. "I would like to be at home with my friends," an Iowan and future officer of black troops maintained, "but as long as things is as they are I think it is my duty to stay where I am." A Connecticut sergeant and future officer in the 29th Connecticut (Colored) Infantry expressed the sentiment best when he wrote, "I don't like the Service

& the war & shall be glad enough when peace shall be proclaimed & I can return again to my books & peaceful pursuits, for all that I am in it to the end." And in the end, it was their sense of being obligated to aid their government in the preservation of the democratic republic that sustained these men.[39]

Along with this renewed commitment came a new approach to the war. Though it evolved gradually, taking hold in some early on while others were latecomers, it transformed the entire war effort in the North. As the hardships of military service stripped away any notions of glamour the troops had held previously, these Yankees also cast aside any illusions they had about their Southern foe and what it would take for the Union to win. At the beginning of the war, few Federal troops believed deep down that most Southerners were truly committed to secession or that it would be so difficult to defeat them. In battle after battle, though, the Federals had suffered staggering losses and endured tremendous hardships, with the war apparently no closer to termination. This forced many Northerners to reconsider their war aims and recommit themselves to a Union victory at any cost. The result was a gradual escalation of the war. The Union, these troops concluded, must prosecute the war more vigorously than it had.

They began to see the Confederate nation, its soldiers and civilians, as the enemy. This was difficult to accept initially, especially since just a few years before they had been brothers under the same government. But as the losses piled up and the personal sacrifices extended from weeks to months and even years, Federal troops began to recognize that individuals were able to make substantial contributions to the war effort without wearing a uniform. As one future officer stated in rather blunt and extreme terms, "Every man in the South is either for or against us and if he is not for us he must be treated as an enemy in armes and his property confiscated and he taken prisner or Shot on the Spot as they will cut our throtes if they get a chance at a Single man." What Northerners had originally perceived as a class conflict against Southern elites gradually became a war that pitted one section against another.[40]

As the fighting dragged on, troops respected the needs and possessions of Southern civilians less and less. The sanctity of property, held inviolate by the United States Constitution and protected by most Union forces at the outset of the war, gradually declined in importance. More and more, Federal troops considered it outrageous that their government allocated manpower and occasionally risked lives to protect the property of people who were in rebellion against that government. One future officer in the USCT complained to his mother, "I would sooner be an apron string guard than guard

Rebble property." By late 1864, many Federals had made the leap
from a debate on the protection of private property to a belief in
its destruction as a legitimate and effective means of waging war.
Anything that Southerners could use to aid their war effort became
a target of Union troops.[41]

Many Northerners, both in and out of uniform, had also concluded
that to augment their military force the government was going to
have to challenge some cherished values and practices. Rather than
rely exclusively on volunteering, the government had to compel men
into serving through conscription. In addition, a considerable number of Northerners realized that the course of the war demanded
that they subordinate their racial prejudices, albeit stubbornly in
many cases, to the needs of the nation in its time of crisis. They
converted a liability into an asset by confiscating black laborers
whose efforts supported the Confederacy and then admitting them
into the armed forces to fight against their former owners, all as a
result of the Emancipation Proclamation.

Of course, not everyone arrived at these conclusions simultaneously, even among the whites who eventually sought commissions
in the USCT. When Lincoln announced his decisions to emancipate
the slaves of Rebels and draw on the black population in the North
and South for military service, there was considerable public outcry,
and some future officers of black troops joined the chorus. One
soldier wrote a friend, "I am as much in favor for the Union as
any one but I am not in favor of shedding my blood for the sake of
the black tribe although I think Slavery is a ruination to our government." Another man, an Illinois sergeant, wrote, "I am not opposed
to it, but I call it a very poor thing, and it has done more harm
than good." He complained that the morale of the army had fallen
considerably since the proclamation. Family and friends were now
writing soldiers and telling them to desert because their generals
were secessionists and they were now fighting to free blacks. Such
arguments, he insisted, were having great effect on the more ignorant troops who were "raised to believe that Slavery is one of the
Sacred things instituted *by God.*" Many of them had been slowly
coming around to the abolitionist viewpoint until "that *Rebel Back
Bone Braker* of Old Abe's, one of the harmlessest things Ever written
on paper, only the dissatisfaction it creates in the North and Army,
it does the negro neither harm nor good." [42]

Because of their stance on abolitionism even before the war, a
large portion of the men who later commanded black units rejoiced
over the Emancipation Proclamation. "The President's Proclamation
freeing the Slaves of all Rebels is in the papers this morning," an
Ohioan noted on the second of January. "Thank the Lord for this!

I hope that this will open a way whereby the Lord can lay his blessing on our arms & give us victory. May the Good Lord bring this unholy rebellion to as speedy a close as is consistent with his holy will." In concurrence, a Minnesotan who had always opposed slavery wrote home, "I now feel that we are upon the right road at last." [43]

Lincoln's cautious handling of the emancipation decision had caused abolitionists considerable consternation. Since the outbreak of the war they had endured the contradiction of opposing the institution of slavery yet fighting a war to preserve a union with slaveholders and to defend a constitution that protected slavery in the states. Lincoln's decision for emancipation helped harmonize the issues. They now fought the war to restore the union and the sanctity of the Constitution, and out of wartime necessity the government had to liberate the slaves. [44]

Others, who had no significant ties with abolitionism, had also come to the conclusion that freeing the slaves and placing arms in their hands was the best means of prosecuting the war. Since the days of Thucydides, man had witnessed the uncanny ability of war to carve its own path. Some twenty-four centuries later, a Michigan officer and future lieutenant colonel in the USCT insisted, "The raped [rapid] occurance of important events that this war carries with it and brings on changes turn mens minds on Some of the questions that agitate Sensitive people at home." The war, he argued, had made emancipation and the enlistment of blacks possible, not Lincoln's decree. "The Rebelion will soon come and Slavery with it as a natural result of the war not as one of the war measures," he explained to his daughter six months later. "The Army will use all the negroes it can to advantage notwithstanding owner Protests against the abolition war." [45]

Just as the war had changed this man's views on slavery, so it had those of many others. With more flair, the commanding general, Henry W. Halleck, reiterated the theme in March 1863 to Grant: "The character of the war has very much changed within the last year. There is now no possible hope of a reconciliation with the rebels. The union party in the South is virtually destroyed. There can be no peace but that which is enforced by the sword. We must conquer the rebels or be conquered by them. The north must either destroy the slave oligarchy, or become slaves themselves." The first eighteen months of the war brought substantial numbers into the antislavery camp, primarily for military reasons. Like their president, many of the men who had served extensively in the army now recognized the value of slavery to the Confederate cause and also foresaw the contribution blacks could make to the Union war effort. An Ohioan, avid Democrat and future officer in the USCT explained his support for emancipation by saying, "My doctrine has been any thing to weaken the enemy." He then headed a committee for the 70th Ohio Infantry that endorsed the proclamation and called on the government to employ blacks "in whatever manner they can be made most serviceable to the United States army, whether it be to handle the spade or shoulder the musket." He approved the destruction of slavery not as a moral issue, but because it was a valuable auxiliary to the Confederate cause.[46]

For the first time many of these men came into contact with the institution of slavery and the black race, and this exposure helped convince them of the justice of the Emancipation Proclamation and the concept of black military service. "I thought I hated slavery as much as possible before I came here," a Pennsylvanian and future officer in the USCT wrote from Virginia in early 1862, "but here, where I can see some of its workings, I am more than ever convinced of the cruelty and inhumanity of the system." After six months in the South, a New Yorker also regarded the institution as disgraceful: "This cursed slavery that gives one man power over another to whip or do as he pleases with him   I would just like to see a man whipping a negro   I would try the virtue of my sword if he did not stop it." They saw firsthand the whipping posts, slave pens, and the racially mixed offspring and heard stories from former slaves of other cruelties, and they were absolutely infuriated. When a fifteen-year-old slave made his way to the 70th Indiana Infantry and safety, he told of his escape, recapture, and his escape again, this time while under gunfire from his master. The boy became cook for some of the troops, and his stories of slavery convinced at least one soldier to do more about the plight of blacks, including service in the USCT later in the war. "To hear this child tell about the thrashing he has received from a brutal master and the chains and weights he has carried in the field," wrote the soldier, "is enough to make a man feel like it would be God's service to shoot them down like buzzards."[47]

In addition, personal experiences with blacks elevated the race in the eyes of their future commanders. Through special assignments such as supervising freedmen on abandoned plantations, through everyday military work, or through working with hired servants, these soldiers came into contact with blacks and took away an enhanced regard for them. Henry Crydenwise attended a religious meeting of freedmen and found it to be an enlightening experience: "I was very much surprised at the intelligence which they displayed in their remarks and exhortations. They show great knowledge of the Scriptures and in relating their experience use some beautiful illustrations." An Illinois surgeon misjudged his black servant as a "very stupid" person until he asked the fugitive why he had left a relatively kind master. The freedman argued that " 'We are all human' " and " 'It wasnt right for one half of the men to live off the other half,' " which impressed the physician. For some, these early experiences boldly challenged their prewar prejudices and left a lasting mark.[48]

In this atmosphere a considerable number of men who later commanded in the USCT endorsed the proposal for black enlistment. Those who were longtime abolitionists viewed this policy as a fulfillment of their grandest wishes. Many others, because of their experiences in the war and with the black race, also applauded the administration program. "I don't know but what I am getting to be a little *abolition afied* myself," wrote future USCT officer Jeff Hoge. "I think from the looks of things now that this war will either free all the Negros or be the destruction of our national independence. I am in favor of letting them do anything they can to aid in putting down the rebellion." Prejudice aside, they had seen these people laboring on public works or for the military and regarded them as diligent employees; there was no reason to believe they would not also serve as diligent soldiers. "We Regard the Positions in Col[ored] Troops as honorable as any," wrote a Michigan officer, who had been no fan of abolitionism before the war, to his wife. This man "heard many a good Officer Say that he wished he had of Sent in his name," as he eventually did himself.[49]

Unfortunately, some based their approval on harshly prejudicial grounds. One rationale for the use of black troops was that they could perform better than whites in the Southern climate, which may of course have been the case for freedmen who lived there but not for Northern blacks. Strangely enough, these men unwittingly relied on the same argument that slaveholders used to justify the enslavement of blacks in the United States. Another popular reason for black enlistment, even among their future commanders, was that they could serve as Confederate targets as well as whites could, and that each black casualty spared a white one. After an Ohioan listened to a speech by Adjutant General Lorenzo Thomas on the administration's plans to recruit black units under white officers, he wrote his father, "My doctrine is that a Negro is no better than a white man and will do as well to receive Reble bullets and would be likely to save the life of some white men." A Michigan enlisted man indicated that such sentiment was widespread when he recorded: "After the emancipation proclamation, the idea that a black man could stop a bullet as well as a white one grew into the organization of Colored Troops." One future officer in the USCT went so far as to state to his aunt that he hoped "when Uncle Abraham gets his Niggers armed and in the field he can get along without us."[50]

Once black units organized and fought, whites were soon sold on them. Many of the men who later commanded black troops had no intention of doing so until they read about the exploits of black soldiers and personally observed them. After reading favorable newspaper accounts of black troops in Louisiana and watching them in South Carolina, a Connecticut soldier wrote home, "The more I see & hear of them the more I want a hand in the matter & wish more that I had 'jumped at the chance.'" While recuperating in a hospital, a New York sergeant, later a lieutenant in the USCT, decided to perform an unofficial inspection of a black unit and found it clean and stylish, with a tidy camp. He vowed, "When I get out of the hospital I mean to try and get the boys to be more like them." One future officer enjoyed strolling through the camp of a black command, and that enticed him; while combat performance impressed another man: "The Niggers whipped the Southron Chivelry at Millikens bend the other day. Banks is using the blacks at Fort Hudson and they fight well." Understandably, these whites were also the first to recognize the propaganda value of exposing as many white soldiers to black units as possible, to gain more officers but, more important, to win general acceptance of the concept of blacks in the military.[51]

Nevertheless, acceptance of the notion of black soldiers, even by some of their future commanders, was going to take time. A surprisingly large number of future officers of black troops took no notice, at least in their diaries and letters home, of the Emancipation Proclamation or the directive to enlist blacks, and only some time afterward did they endorse those decisions. Some of them had bad experiences with blacks early in the war or felt that blacks, indirectly at least, were responsible for all the hardships and losses the Federals had had to endure in the war. Moreover, prejudice was a very difficult concept to eradicate. The number of white Northerners who threatened to shoot any black soldier who served near them or who wished they could gather all blacks in this country and explode "one Bomb shell that would Disperse the whole of *them*" was considerable. One of the great recruiters and organizers of black units, George L. Stearns, conceded in April 1863, "The Republicans want them to go to the war and the rest of the people because they want to get rid of them." He predicted that if Lincoln conscripted all blacks—men, women, and children—and sent them into the South, he would insure his reelection.[52]

An Indiana soldier and future officer in the USCT pointed out the revolutionary nature of arming blacks and calling on them to fight whites to his mentor, the prominent abolitionist Caleb Mills, when he wrote: "Would not even *you* have shrunk from the thought of the negro taking up arms against the white man for his freedom?" Just a few years before, John Brown had sought to do that very thing at Harper's Ferry, Virginia, much to the shock and condemnation of both the Northern and Southern populations. Thus it was asking a great deal of them not only to endorse the use of black troops but also to abandon their old organizations and friends, in the face of such overwhelming prejudice, to command black troops. Many of them required more exposure to the war and the black population before they willingly accepted the concept of the USCT. And many of them needed more than that—specifically the dissolution of their bonds to their original military organizations.[53]

3

Recruiting the Officers

From the very beginning it was evident that white men would officer these new black units. Lincoln and the War Department believed they must make this program as palatable as possible to the Northern public and soldiery, to diminish the controversy in an already controversial proposal. One of the best means to do that was to reassure Northern citizens that white men would always be in charge. Moreover, since the creation of armies and navies, officers' commissions had been a good way of securing support or rewarding followers, and black units in the Civil War were no exceptions. By establishing a policy that only white men could command black soldiers, the government offered recompense to those who were willing to endorse the plan and assist in its execution. Yet the process of becoming an officer in the USCT was quite selective, and conflicting interests made the decision difficult.

Because most Americans had doubts about the innate ability of blacks to fight effectively, they hoped that highly competent white officers would significantly upgrade black units. Here again, blacks felt the severe constraints of prejudicial contradictions. On the one hand, casting aside the numerous examples in American history in which blacks had fought well, substantial numbers of both soldiers and civilians believed that blacks were inferior humans, more akin to savages, and therefore would be extremely difficult to control once in a killing frenzy. When blacks fought their former masters, some feared there would be no means whatsoever of restraining them. On the other hand, many viewed blacks as lazy, irresponsible, and childlike—all qualities unsuited to effective military service and to a considerable degree in contrast with the image of the savage. Nevertheless, the conclusion was that the best white men could handle the immense responsibility of commanding black soldiers.

Even vigorous friends of blacks and advocates of black military service had reason to support this government policy. In the eyes of some of its greatest white supporters, it was an equitable trade-off. Of course, barring blacks from command positions stifled their opportunities for advancement, but ideally the selection process would secure quality officers, who in turn would help build outstanding black units. The hope was that the benefits derived from excellent performance on the battlefield would offset the losses to the black race caused by the limitations on the growth and development of black leadership in the military. Equally important, in late 1862 and throughout most of 1863, the employment of black soldiers was still in the experimental stage. To ensure its continuation and success, for the benefit of all blacks, many believed it was best to give them the finest officers available—who happened to be white veterans. Once the public began to accept black soldiers and acknowledge their wartime contributions, then they could resurrect the idea of black officers.

As a result of this policy decision, the Federal government avoided the elevation of blacks to officers' rank. With hesitation, the War Department assented to the commissioning of some black chaplains and surgeons, but in the early stages of black units the federal government made it clear that only white men would serve as combat officers. Those free black militia officers in New Orleans whom Maj. Gen. Benjamin Butler had accepted into federal service in September 1862 were rapidly weeded out for purposes of racial purity by his successor, Maj. Gen. N. P. Banks. Banks removed the black officers under the guise of incompetency, even though many of them had performed well in combat, and the government extended the policy by rejecting any proposals for promotion of blacks until late in the war.[1]

From the very first attempts to raise black units, the military established a pattern for the selection of white officers. Maj. Gen. David Hunter, in his abortive efforts to organize black military units in South Carolina, looked to "the most intelligent and energetic of our non-commissioned officers: men who will go into it with all their hearts" for his company-grade officers and convinced the son of Senator William Pitt Fessenden, James, to head the outfit. Hunter wanted bright men of high moral character, committed to the black race, and with military experience.[2]

His successor, Brig. Gen. Rufus Saxton, called on Massachusetts

Capt. Thomas Wentworth Higginson, prominent abolitionist, intellectual, and minister, to raise the first black regiment. Higginson then selected as his field officers men who were sympathetic to the plight of blacks, and for his company officers he chose "the finest, sharpest men I could find," as he testified before the American Freedmen's Inquiry Commission, a committee designed to advise the president on policies dealing with freedmen.[3]

Interestingly, Higginson's field officers had no previous military experience. His belief was that a bright individual could learn how to command troops fairly rapidly, while good character was essential for effective command. Brig. Gen. Daniel Ullmann, who organized the famous black Corps d'Afrique in Louisiana, adopted the same policy and helped open the door to individuals outside the military.[4]

When abolitionist Governor John A. Andrew of Massachusetts cast around for someone to command a Northern black regiment, the 54th Massachusetts (Colored) Infantry, prior military service was mandatory. "I am desirous to have for its officers—" he wrote, "particularly its field officers—young men of military experience, of firm anti-slavery principles, ambitious, superior to a vulgar contempt for color, and having faith in the capacity of colored men for military service. Such officers must necessarily be gentlemen of the highest tone and honor." To locate these men, Andrew merely searched the educated antislavery society circles from the prewar years, "which next to the colored race itself have the greatest interest in the success of this experiment." There he found Capt. Robert Gould Shaw, Capt. Penrose Hallowell, and others.[5]

Adjutant General Lorenzo Thomas, however, concentrated his efforts to obtain officers for black units exclusively in existing volunteer units. Thomas was an old Regular Army man, an 1823 West Point graduate who had devoted nearly his entire adult life to staff duty. There was some speculation that Secretary of War Stanton considered Thomas as corrupt, although Thomas's continued service seems to indicate he met Stanton's standards of honesty. More likely, Stanton believed Thomas's drinking problem was interfering with his ability to manage the tremendous volume of paperwork generated by the war. Regardless, in March 1863 the Lincoln administration sent Thomas to the Mississippi River area to announce to the troops the new government policy of enlisting black troops. Thomas was to explain what the government position was and why the government adopted it. Then he was to encourage individuals to volunteer to raise and command these organizations composed of freedmen.[6]

In fact, many of Thomas's talks were carefully orchestrated. In the Seventeenth Corps, for example, with all the popular senior officers at his side, the beloved corps commander James B. McPherson told the men in his introductory remarks about the government policy of creating black military organizations and how it would free white soldiers for active campaigning. He would gladly muster out any officer who disagreed with the policy, McPherson declared to the troops, if the officers would just step forward. Skillfully, the revered McPherson had put opponents of black enlistment on the spot. They would either have to announce before McPherson; division commanders such as John A. Logan; the adjutant general of the United States Army; and the entire division their opposition to black enlistment or meekly endure it. Those soldiers who later grumbled about the policy, wrote a future officer in the USCT, looked like cowards while others, because of McPherson's handling of the affair, were won over even before the adjutant general spoke. On one occasion Thomas joked that McPherson had stolen his thunder by stating the government's case better than he ever could have done.[7]

The result of all these efforts was a substantial increase in the number of both government-organized black units and white men who sought officers' commissions. To deal with the expansion, the adjutant general authorized the creation of division boards to certify qualifications of candidates for officer's rank in the new black units. Each division commander was to organize a panel of officers, one from each brigade, to question candidates on their military knowledge. This device proved unwieldy, though, and in May 1863 the War Department created the Bureau of Colored Troops, headed by Maj. Charles W. Foster. The purpose of the bureau was to systematize the process of raising black units and securing officers for them, and also to serve as a clearinghouse of information on the USCT. Prospective candidates were to write to the bureau to receive permission to appear before a board of examiners. The boards—which met regularly in such cities as Washington; New Orleans; St. Louis; Davenport, Iowa; Nashville; Cincinnati; and, at the end of the war, Richmond—determined who qualified for an officer's commission and for what rank the individual had demonstrated competence. The boards passed weekly results on to the bureau, which in turn assigned successful candidates to various black commands.[8]

Following the lead set by Higginson, Ullmann, and Andrew, the Bureau of Colored Troops made it clear from the outset that it wanted only intelligent white men with high morals who were willing to make a commitment to uplifting the black race. The main problem was that they could test for intelligence and have others attest to morals, but they had no viable means of ascertaining the true desire of candidates to labor for the benefit of the black race. Thus, everyone involved in the organization of black units tried to stress the criticality of obtaining men who genuinely wanted to work with black soldiers. Thomas told Maj. Gen. William Rosecrans that he wanted "only those for Officers whose hearts were in the work and who would exert themselves to the uttermost and treat the Negro kindly," a message which "Old Rosy" conveyed to his men. Capt. R. D. Mussey, who organized black units in Tennessee, announced: "No person is wanted as an officer in a Colored Regiment who 'feels that he is making a sacrifice in accepting a position in a Colored Regiment,' or who desires the place simply for higher rank and pay." Mussey wanted officers who would strive to make the black units "equal, if not superior to" white organizations. And Brig. Gen. August Chetlain, also involved in the recruitment of black troops, stated publicly that he did not want any man who considered service with blacks a "sacrifice" or who "desires appointment simply for higher rank and salary." [9]

This publicity campaign, in conjunction with the examination, helped elevate the position of officer in the USCT, at least in the eyes of those who eventually received commissions. Occasionally people perceived the process as elementary, as did a Massachusetts soldier and future lieutenant of black troops who wrote home, "Any one with a good education no matter what his other qualifications are is sure to get a commission." Most men, however, agreed with a future officer in the USCT who argued that because of the high standards, "It seems to be the determination to make this one of the most effective branches of the service." Upon receipt of their commissions, they had met or surpassed levels of knowledge and skill that few volunteer officers had demonstrated, and this gave them a sense of satisfaction. "Any one if he has money can get a position in a white reg't but not so here," insisted Henry Crydenwise, with a USCT commission in hand. Officers in black units were "a better class of men, more moral, more religious, better educated and understand their business better than those in white reg'ts." He concluded by guessing that over one-half of the officers in white units could not pass the examination. [10]

Although the concept of selectivity was appealing, it was not a major attraction to the black units. Soldiers and civilians sought commissions in the USCT for a variety of other reasons. Many of them felt sympathy for the black race and wanted to help elevate them through military service, while others saw this as an opportunity to aid the cause of the union more than they could through service in white volunteer units. Serving in the USCT provided many soldiers with an opportunity to increase their salary and obtain a command position that simply was unattainable in their volunteer unit. Still some people had their own personal reasons for seeking a commission in the USCT.

A sense that service in black units was tantamount to missionary work was a strong attraction to many individuals. For them defeating the Confederates was only part of the problem. The Federals must uplift the black race as well, to insure that in the postwar years blacks were able to look after themselves. A New York soldier regarded this as a chance to get the black man into the war in a bold way, "to elevate and enlighten him that he may be prepared for the future which shall open before him." "Here then," he concluded, "is a great field for christian & philanthropic labor." [11]

Others saw this work as the culmination of all their abolitionist activities in the prewar world. "Now is the time to prove that I am what I have always professed to be—an Abolitionist," insisted one future officer in the USCT. Another one considered command of a black unit the culmination of his fondest dreams: "Perhaps I shall be permitted to carry out the day dreams and night dreams of my youth, when I was devising ways and means for marching at the head of an army of blacks, proclaiming liberty, and rallying the slaves to my standard." Four months later, he remarked, "I look upon this as a life work for all of us." [12]

A sizable portion put forth their names for service in the new black units because of their strong commitment to the war. These men believed that it was their duty not just to perform military service but to do it in whatever way they could best contribute to victory. After extensive service in volunteer units, they concluded that the USCT needed their expertise. An Ohioan recorded in his diary, "The Administration has determined to make use of the colored population as soldiers, placing white officers in command. It is not a popular branch of the service now, but what is the difference, when I am conscious of doing right, and serving my country." Along the same lines, Sam Evans wrote to his brother, "Some body must direct thes[e] men. Shall I require as a necessity some one to do what I would not myself condescend to do. no I could not do that It would be very unjust." By commanding black troops, he was able to turn a government expense into a tremendous government asset. [13]

Of course, desire to become an officer was an extremely powerful motivator. An officer's life, most soldiers agreed, was better than that of an enlisted man. It had greater responsibilities, but pay was much better, as were various minor benefits, and there was a certain amount of prestige associated with rank. Officers, after all, had their privileges. [14]

Some men had sought promotions in their old outfits, without success, and the USCT offered an assured elevation in rank. A Massachusetts private, stifled in his attempts to gain promotion in his regiment, nevertheless insisted, "I have no aspirations for a Co.

obtained in any manner but through my own exertions." The new black units gave him that chance. Another soldier, a Pennsylvanian, was much more direct to his sister: "You know that, with my restless disposition, I could not be contented as a brigade bugler while there was a possibility of doing better." [15]

Money certainly was a strong attraction. "I would drill a company of aligators for a hundred and twenty a month," an Illinois soldier told a friend. That amount was substantially better than his monthly pay of thirteen dollars. [16]

Others had more unusual reasons for vying for a commission in a black unit. Some wanted to become officers so that they could resign whenever they wanted, a luxury that did not exist in the enlisted ranks. Much to their chagrin, the War Department began refusing to accept letters of resignation in 1864 except under unusual circumstances. Also, men who were entering the service from civilian life in 1864 and 1865 found it extremely difficult to obtain officers' rank except in the USCT. By then the War Department authorized the organization of very few volunteer units, and most of their officers came from experienced commands. [17]

Still, some had personal reasons for attempting to win a commission in a black unit. Stephen P. Jocelyn had wanted an appointment to West Point when the country erupted in war. For him, the USCT provided a chance for experience as an officer that would enable him to obtain a Regular Army commission after the war. When the size of a New York captain's regiment fell to 130 men, he decided to go at it with black soldiers rather than risk his good reputation with the type of replacements New York was sending. In a very different case, Sgt. Henry Crydenwise had to investigate the murder of a black man by a white soldier. When he uncovered evidence to convict the man, the provost marshal took no notice, to Crydenwise's dismay. As he noted, "a negroes life is little more regarded than that of a dog" and vowed, "Tis time something was done to teach people that a negroes life cannot be taken with impunity for every slight offence." This cruel lesson encouraged him to seek a commission. [18]

Regardless of their motives, many of the soldiers who sought commissions in the USCT required an added impetus. They needed the dissolution, or at least a weakening, of the bonds to their original unit before they seriously considered leaving their comrades. This usually took the form of an extended separation, but some sort of internal problem in their volunteer organization also prompted soldiers to leave. Detached service, time in Confederate prisoner of war camps, and wounds or illnesses that required extensive medical care were the most common causes of the dissolution of the bonds, but there were others as well. Company commander Marshall Harvey Twitchell suffered a head wound in the Battle of the Wilderness and was out of action for one hundred days. With only twenty-two men left in his company, and because his commander had passed him over for promotion twice, he decided to to try his luck in the USCT. A Connecticut sergeant informed the folks at home that he was considering the opportunities available in black units: "As I become more & more disgusted with our commanding officer I begin to think more & more of taking my chance." Because not enough men in the 72nd New York Infantry reenlisted, the handful who did volunteer for a second tour of duty got transferred to the 120th New York Infantry, a unit to which they had no ties. Around that time Pvt. George Tate of the 72nd became ill. Seven months later, when Tate recovered, he elected to join the USCT instead of going to the new white regiment.[19]

Soldiers and civilians initiated the process by applying to the Bureau of Colored Troops for a commission in the USCT. This usually took the form of a letter simply stating that the individual wanted to be a candidate for a commission in a black unit, that he was an upstanding citizen or had served meritoriously in his volunteer unit, and that he had participated in various engagements. The soldier's commanding officer frequently prepared the letter and circulated it throughout the organization for the signatures of other officers to endorse or comment on the candidate's qualities. Typical was the letter for Gardiner A. A. Deane, a bugler in the 3rd Iowa Cavalry. One officer mentioned that Deane had been a soldier since August 1861 and had fought at Pea Ridge and in various skirmishes. "He is a young man possessing very fair abilities, with a moral character untarnished. He is well versed up in company duties especially those of an administrative or executive character." Another officer mentioned how Deane "conducted himself with coolness and courage" in battle, and the regimental surgeon stressed Deane's "rare business qualifications" and his "sober" habits. Iowan Charles R. Riggs had nineteen officers attest that he was "a man of good moral character and possessing the necessary qualifications for an efficient officer," and twenty-seven officers endorsed the candidacy of Benjamin Densmore. All three men were successful candidates.[20]

Although many did not deem it necessary, some men felt compelled to reassure the government in their letter of application that they were friends of the black race. A Connecticut soldier requested a commission because he believed "Slavery is a curse to the Country & aught to be put down that Slavry is a national Sin & hoping that the Almighty will rule this rebellion to the overthrow of the Same & restore our country to peice & posterity again." A New York cavalryman indicated two reasons why he wanted a commission.

First was "the love that I feel for my country & to the Black man who for ages has been ground under the iron heal of despotism & with such a position I could searve my Country as well or better than I can now." Second, he wanted better pay to care for his widowed mother and two sisters.[21]

Unfortunately, some officers in volunteer units abused the process for their own advantage by refusing to aid good soldiers and supporting the candidacy of those they wanted to dump from their commands. A Connecticut sergeant doubted his colonel would write the letter because "he does not wish to lose his best men from the Reg."; instead, he received help from his captain. On the other hand, to check corrupt practices, Maj. Gen. William Rosecrans had to establish guidelines for applications and endorsements. He complained that "applicants have been recommended for no other apparent purpose than to get rid of worthless or obnoxious men, or to obtain in this way a furlough to visit St. Louis. Officers are informed that in future they will be held to strict accountability for their recommendations" and subject to examinations of fitness and possible dismissal themselves for falsely endorsing a candidate. Rare indeed was the officer who was truly candid, such as Robert Scott, who considered candidate Sgt. George W. Allen "competent but in my opinion *not trustworthy.*" As first sergeant in the 4th U.S. Infantry, Allen had tried to desert. Because of such abuses to the system, a handful of good candidates never made it before the board of examiners, but, more important, a number of incompetent or immoral ones passed the examination and became officers in the USCT.[22]

The USCT also offered an opportunity for foreigners to obtain military commissions in the Union Army. Because volunteer units selected their own officers or governors appointed them, foreigners had little chance of receiving commissions. Until the War Department established competitive rules for attaining officers' rank in black units, their only recourse was to get commissions by being on a general's staff. Edelmiro Mayer, born in Argentina and a member of its army for more than ten years, had fought in thirty-two battles and had risen from cadet to major. He earned a commission as a captain in the 4th U.S. Colored Infantry and two years later, when he resigned, Mayer held the rank of lieutenant colonel. Ex-British regular officer Frank J. Dobie unsuccessfully requested a commission, as did Baron Engelbert de Brackel, who produced "testimonials of meritorious service in the Armies of Prussia and the Pontifical States," with ten years of experience. He wanted to organize and command a "Corps of Negroes . . . , having not at this reguard any one of the opinions which prevail among some american officers," more specifically race prejudice.[23]

Candidates also had to provide letters of endorsement that vouched for their moral fitness. For men already in the service, these usually accompanied or were part of the application. An officer's word sufficed. Civilians who sought commissions in the USCT needed letters of reference from prominent citizens or community leaders, a common practice at the time. Unsuccessful candidate Webster H. Abbott, a private in the 4th Minnesota Infantry, had a letter from a Treasury Department official who mentioned that Abbott's father "is an earnest working Republican a faithful supporter of the administration," as was the son. Lewis Ledyard Weld received a letter of endorsement from a man who had considerable clout with abolitionists and the administration—his uncle Theodore. The elder Weld forcefully wrote of his nephew, "Having known him from his birth, he has always been an abolitionist without an *if.*" Uncle Theodore Dwight Weld also said that Lewis "has great power over an audience; is one of the most facile speakers off hand, that I have heard. I doubt if there be an officer in the Army, who could stir up a regiment by a speech to a greater enthusiasm." These were strong words of praise from a man whom many regarded as the greatest public speaker of his time until he was afflicted with chronic hoarseness.[24]

Again, some officers failed to mention any bad habits the candidate may have possessed. One lieutenant wrote that a private was "capable of performing any Company business which might delve upon him," but failed to mention the private's drinking problem, which led to his being reduced in rank twice and eventually caused him to resign his commission in the USCT. Nor was this man the only officer in the USCT who brought with him such a problem.[25]

Strangely enough, the boards did not consider the contraction of venereal disease during enlisted service as evidence of immoral conduct. Nevertheless, if a man contracted it after accepting a commission in the USCT, authorities immediately brought charges against him for conduct unbecoming an officer. This was stricter than the Regular Army and white volunteers, which generally let such mishaps slide.[26]

Once the candidate provided satisfactory letters of recommendation, the Bureau of Colored Troops ordered him to report to a board of examiners. On receipt of the order, candidates usually had a little time to prepare for the examination, which consisted of an oral grilling by a panel of four examiners on such topics as tactics, army regulations, general military knowledge, arithmetic, history, and geography. Most of them, however, needed more than a scant few weeks of part-time study, and if they had not used some forethought and begun preparations earlier, they were in considerable trouble.

Soldiers certainly had an advantage on the examination, but it was a much smaller one than most people thought. Civilians were at a disadvantage when it came to military questions, but soldiers, particularly enlisted men, had suffered from the deterioration of many of their fundamental skills while in the army. During wartime few of them found use for arithmetic, history, and geography, and their knowledge in those areas thus declined considerably. In addition, many enlisted men knew military jargon and thought they knew tactics, but they knew little of army tactics from the command perspective and less of army paperwork and regulations.

Adequate preparation, then, was critical. Benjamin Densmore read important military works such as Baron de Jomini's *The Art of War*, Dennis Hart Mahan's *Outposts*, and Henry W. Halleck's *Elements of Military Art and Science*, although that approach was unusual. Most troops studied a tactics manual and army regulations and simply hoped for the best when it came to the nonmilitary sections, as did the civilians.[27]

Occasionally, men hooked up with others to help prepare for the examination. Daniel Densmore, Benjamin's brother, had the good fortune to meet someone else who was preparing for the test, "so we go in and catechise each other, making a fine school for us both." Troops in the Second Brigade, First Division, First Corps in the Army of the Potomac agreed that teamwork and structure were more effective means of preparing for the examination before the board and set up their own school of instruction for anyone who wanted to attend.[28]

The most famous effort at preparing candidates for the examination before a board was the Free Military School for Applicants for Commands of Colored Troops. The brainchild of Philadelphian Thomas Webster, the purpose of the school was to provide the essential remedial work to enable candidates to pass the examination. Webster, who had raised black units in Pennsylvania and had encountered the problem of the shortage of qualified whites to command these troops, learned in September 1863 from Maj. Gen. Silas Casey, head of the examining board in Washington, that nearly 50 percent of those who took the examination failed it. Most of them had considerable military experience and merely needed a few weeks of close study of army regulations, tactics, and general knowledge to receive satisfactory scores. Not one to spurn a challenge, Webster concocted the idea of a school to prepare men specifically for the examination for command of black troops. He accumulated a faculty, which included a former colonel of a Pennsylvania infantry regiment and a West Pointer, published a brochure to advertise its existence, and opened its doors to civilians and soldiers in late December 1863. Within four months, the school was so successful that it was receiving nearly 170 applications per week, graduated between 24 and 30 students per week, and had won approval from the War Department for its services. Its 96 percent pass rate during its first ninety days in existence was nothing short of phenomenal.[29]

Col. John H. Taggart, the chief preceptor, kept a tight reign on his students. They attended three hours of classes a day, six days per week, plus drill, dress parade, and nighttime study. Rules were strict and discipline tight. As one graduate commented, "A man who cannot put up with a rigid military discipline, would make a poor officer to enforce it on others when necessary." Infractions led to dismissal from school, as did evidence of incompetency or unwillingness to work hard. Students were only to stay for thirty days, but testimony from graduates of the Free Military School indicates that a number of them spent considerably longer there.[30]

Under Taggart's leadership, the school assigned candidates to one of four levels, depending on the student's military knowledge. The bottom class studied the school of the soldier, the next level learned the school of the company, then school of the battalion, and finally the school of the brigade. The Free Military School also offered remedial work in arithmetic, algebra, geography, and ancient history.[31]

In addition to classroom labors, the students devoted considerable time to actual fieldwork. Each man started in the ranks as private and worked his way up to brigadier general or brigade commander. They also took time drilling recruits at nearby Camp William Penn, a rendezvous for black organizations. According to a graduate, regardless of the weather, they drilled themselves and blacks and learned the different formations and maneuvers, and "If a man attempted to dodge he was at once informed that they had no time to spend on him he was not the right material to make an officer and he had better fall out and go back to his regiment at the front." [32]

When a student felt competent in his studies, the school examined him over the course of two days. On the first day, a professor tested him in the academic subjects, and the following day Col. Taggart grilled him on his military knowledge. Success on these tests meant the candidate was ready for the real examination. Graduates then went to Camp William Penn, where they awaited the call from the Casey board for their examination.[33]

Admission to the school required that candidates write a letter of application accompanied by letters of support. For civilians, getting time to attend the school was seldom a problem, but those men already in the service had considerable difficulty obtaining leave for schooling. In a Union Army pressed for manpower, commanders and the War Department were loath to grant leaves, especially during campaign season, but pressures from Webster and also the needs of the USCT forced a change in policy. In late March 1864 the War Department authorized army and department commanders to grant thirty-day furloughs to enlisted men to attend the Free Military School. Even then, though, there was discretionary authority, and an applicant had no assurance of receiving a leave.[34]

Some men, such as Pvt. William Baird, had no time constraints. At the conclusion of the Gettysburg Campaign in July 1863, Baird contracted dysentery and ended up in a Philadelphia hospital. There someone loaned him the pamphlet on the Free Military School, and he decided to give it a try. He struck a deal with a doctor that he would attend the school and return to the hospital every evening. After Baird promised not to abuse the privilege and swore that he did not drink liquor, the doctor consented.

For individuals like Baird, who questioned the quality of their prior education and doubted their ability, the Free Military School was both toil and a great learning experience. Baird worried constantly that if he did not show evidence of hard work, the faculty would dismiss him from the school. During his time as a student, he came down with smallpox and missed ten days of classes. When he returned to school, Baird learned that he was sixty pages behind in tactics. That afternoon he returned to the hospital and studied most of the night. The next morning he arose early and reported to his instructor that he had mastered all the tactics material. His professor drilled him on the spot, and Baird used wooden miniatures to demonstrate the different formations successfully, no mean accomplishment. More than military knowledge, the Free Military School gave Baird self-confidence, and that was essential if he was to be a good officer.[35]

Financial problems and bickering within its Supervisory Committee and with both the commander of nearby Camp William Penn and the War Department led the Free Military School to close its doors on September 15, 1864. According to Taggart, 484 Free Military School graduates had passed the examination before Casey's board, a very respectable number. If the school had a drawback, it was the localized nature of its students. Nearly all came from Eastern armies, and a preponderance of the student body had resided before the war in Pennsylvania or nearby states. Due to lack of publicity and to expense involved, the Free Military School was never able to tap into candidates from distant military departments. Nevertheless, the school performed a vital function during the war, helping to train officers for the USCT. It was, as the eminent historian Dudley Cornish has written, the "grandfather of the Officer Candidate School."[36]

According to War Department specifications, the boards of examination were to subject each candidate to a "fair but rigorous examination as to physical, mental, and moral fitness to command." They accepted letters of testimony to vouch for moral qualifications and had a physician on hand to ensure the candidates' physical fitness. Thus the boards were able to concentrate on the candidates' mental qualifications.[37]

Yet the War Department did not provide the specifics of the test, and for that the various boards looked to Maj. Charles W. Foster, head of the Bureau of Colored Troops. Foster thought that a lieutenant should know how to read and write, understand the rules of grammar, and have a thorough command of the school of the soldier and company movements. A captain should master all that and be "perfectly familiar" with the school of the battalion. "Great care," Foster urged, "should be exercised in recommending persons for appointment as field officers." Above and beyond what a captain should know, they should be "conversant with brigade evolutions, and be possessed of general acquirements, sufficient to enable them to discharge the duties of their positions in such a manner as to do credit to the Service." He also insisted, "A fair knowledge of U.S. Army Regulations should be required for all grades."[38]

Col. R. D. Mussey, who had the War Department establish an ad hoc board at Nashville, provided slightly different advice to his board members: "My idea is that a few questions on important subjects will determine a man's character as a military student, and show his fitness or unfitness for the position he seeks." Mussey called for a candidate to demonstrate both theoretical and practical knowledge. He then urged board members, "Do not ask leading questions; do not seek to refresh the candidate's memory; do not inform him whether his answer is correct; you are to examine, not to teach him." He also wanted them to observe the candidate and listen to the conciseness and accuracy of his answer. It was, after all, a test to see if the candidate had the knowledge and character to command others in combat.[39]

With authorization in hand, candidates appeared before a specifically designated board. There was almost always a backlog of examinees, and they often had to wait up to one week. Candidates reported promptly each morning and learned whether or not they would be tested that day. If they were too far down the list, the officer merely dismissed them for the day, and the process repeated the next day, Monday through Friday. Because of the expense, particularly in Washington, Major General Casey, as general supervisor of the entire examination process, made arrangements for enlisted men to board at the Old Soldier's Home, at no cost. Thus candidates had an opportunity to meet one another, either at the boardinghouse or the examination site, go sightseeing, or study together, as most elected to do. There were "a dozen of us all in the same business," a Connecticut enlisted man wrote home as he awaited the test before the Casey board. "We ask and answer questions and post one another up." [40]

Young Freeman Bowley came directly from a private military academy and sought a commission in the USCT. As he waited in the outer room, a candidate who had just undergone the grilling grumbled that he knew nothing about muster rolls and company papers. Bowley panicked. He knew nothing of that either, yet he had enough good sense to run out to a bookstore and there he purchased a copy of *The Company Clerk; What to Do, and How to Do It.* Fortunately, he did not get the call that day, and through much of the night he studied the book thoroughly, in time for the exam the next day. [41]

The length of the actual examination varied from board to board and candidate to candidate. Some thought their grilling lasted four or five hours, which may be an accurate estimate or how long it seemed to them. One soldier stated flatly that his examination before the Casey board lasted only twenty-five minutes, and another man wrote his brother immediately afterwards that his was three-quarters of an hour. Although evidence on the examinations is limited, it appears that the higher the rank sought, the longer the examination. Maj. J. Smith Brown, for example, sought a colonelcy before the St. Louis board and had to answer 293 questions. At 30 seconds per question, his examination would have lasted two and one-half hours. One successful candidate recalled, "Each one of these officers took me in turn, and when one was tired or exhausted his fund of questions another would be ready with a quiver full of arrows to fire at me." [42]

Essentially, the various boards asked the same questions. Although there were some minor structural differences in the examinations, all boards quizzed candidates on tactics, army regulations, general military knowledge, history, geography, and mathematics. Candidates for cavalry or artillery, understandably, had different tactics questions than did infantrymen. In addition, candidates for positions of quartermaster were exempt from tactics but had categories such as regulations and orders of the War Department and method and system of the quartermaster. Scoring for the examinations was based on a scale of one to nine, one to seven, or one to five, depending on the board, with one as the lowest in most cases but occasionally the highest. [43]

The examination of Horace Bumstead before the Casey board indicates an emphasis on tactics and regulations. Bumstead, who successfully passed for the rank of major, had to answer forty-nine rather specific tactics questions, plus dozens of others that flushed out the details of his answers. For example, they asked: "How many ranks form a company? Distance between the ranks? Where is the 3d sergeant posted? . . . Where are the lieut-col. and major when in column? . . . What is the distance between the battalions in column at half distance? What does the general do before closing the column of a subdivision in rear of the battery?" Familiarity with the tactics volumes, written by Casey himself, was the key to mastery of the examination.

According to Bumstead, who recorded the questions immediately after the test, he received only eleven queries on army regulations. They included: "How are non-commissioned officers reduced to the ranks? . . . Is an officer justified in striking a soldier? May he not strike or even shoot a soldier in case of mutiny or desertion? How often does a capt. account for clothing he received for his men?"

The final segment of Bumstead's test before the Casey board, and in some respects the most interesting part of the examination, was a hodgepodge of geography, history, and mathematics questions, twenty-one in all. The purpose, clearly, was to ensure that successful candidates had reasonably good, liberal educations, which in turn indicated intellectual development and broad-mindedness. Some of the board's queries were: "What is the largest city in the United States? Who were some of the distinguished men of ancient times? Who have been the greatest generals of modern times [clearly a loaded question]? Have you studied Greek and Latin? Can you repeat the first verse of John in Greek? What is the equation of a line?" [44]

By contrast, the examination before the St. Louis board of civilian George P. Tinker, a former second lieutenant in the 117th Indiana Infantry, was somewhat different. Tinker began by reading aloud a passage and then writing it out from dictation. His tactics questions dealt primarily with the various formations and orders that a company commander would issue to execute the movement. They also quizzed him on the positions of various officers and noncommissioned officers in different formations.

In the field of army regulations, the board asked him mainly about the paperwork of a company—the clothing book, morning reports, and muster rolls. He answered questions on the roll call well, but he thought ten companies made up a battalion, when in fact they made up a regiment.

In general military knowledge, Tinker stumbled. He was asked a number of questions on such things as investment of the enemy, sieges, and bivouacs, which he struggled to answer. Tinker also defined strategy as " 'The means whereby we suprise the enemy' " and tactics as, " 'It means the drill and disipline.' "

Tinker's history test provided some unusual results. He knew quite a bit about the Revolution and the War of 1812. " 'High taxation and refusal of representation' " was the cause of the revolution. He also knew who Aaron Burr was, a popular question with the St. Louis board. When it came to civics and non-American history, however, Tinker made repeated mistakes. He thought each state had one U.S. senator for every five members of the House of Representatives and that senators served four-year terms. He knew nothing of Peter the Great, believed Cromwell defeated Napoleon at the battle of Waterloo, and thought the Crusades were a "sect of people."

On the geography section, Tinker performed miserably. He did not know where Cuba was, considered Virginia and the Carolinas as Gulf States, and named the Atlantic, Pacific, and Mediterranean as the five great oceans of the world. He insisted that he had never heard of the Indian Ocean. Despite living in Indiana, he could name only two Great Lakes, thought the Connecticut River flowed through New York, and maintained that London rested on the banks of the Nile River.

Finally, Tinker had mixed results on his arithmetic test. He was able to perform some fairly difficult division problems, which included weights, but he could not add ½ and ⅓, divide ¾ by ¼, or, in a trick question, determine whether ¹⁵⁄₁₈ or ⅚ was greater.

In the end, Tinker failed the examination. He received somewhat "inferior" scores for a second lieutenancy in tactics, army regulations, and history, but in general military knowledge, geography, and arithmetic he scored poorly. On a nine-point scale, he received ⁵⁄₁₂ in general military knowledge, 1 in geography, and 1 and ⅙ in arithmetic.[45]

No doubt, scores on tests were quite subjective. Isaac Gannett, first lieutenant of the 7th Kansas Cavalry, did not perform significantly better on the history portion than did Tinker, yet Gannett received a score of 4 and ⅚ to Tinker's 3 and ⅙. In geography, Gannett answered eight questions correctly and nine wrong, for a score of 3 and ⅓. Tinker, for his score of 1, answered eleven of twenty-four questions right. Evidently, other factors, such as directness of answers and performance on previous portions of the test, affected final scores.[46]

In an examination of this type, with the flexibility granted to each board and the subjectiveness of the grading process, complaints were inevitable. On passing his examination before the St. Louis board, Daniel Densmore criticized the process to his brother, even though he did well:

The object of the examining board seems to be to ascertain whether the applicant is a live man, quick at catching ideas, disposed to inform himself and ready in his address—and to that end a glimpse at the cut of a man's job would go as far as a correct examination in tactics, boots properly blacked would rate as high as a problem well solved, and a certain thoughtful air which says man and not parrot tells more than labored precision of dates or happy recitation of events.[47]

One man, D. O. Van Trump, wrote a protest letter filled with charges of West Point elitism and prejudicial questions to the *Missouri Democrat* on the St. Louis board after he failed the examination. He complained, "If an incorrect answer be given, or none at all, then comes a scowl and look of contempt as much as to say, you contemptible ignoramus, what business have you before this enlightened board of 'West Pointers;' and then that sarcastic reply, 'that will do, sir, that will do.' " He concluded that "boys, just from school, or those who understand figuring, stand the best show, while modest men of mind and merit, are rejected." [48]

Another soldier, this one a major of engineers in the USCT who sought a promotion to lieutenant colonel, argued that his examination lasted barely two hours and failed to delve into the subject of engineering deeply. "The questions asked were oral, no problems given to solve, no propositions to demonstrate, no written examples required." "The examination," he insisted, "was a farce." He had eight years of engineering experience, over six in the Army Corps of Engineers, and had served on the staffs of four different army commanders. None of the officers who examined him was very knowledgeable. To this charge, Col. I. Hale Sypher, head of the Gulf board in New Orleans, responded by calling the major a "*young Hercules*" and claimed that the major was unable to answer such elementary questions as, "What are the three angles of a triangle equal to[?]" Sypher maintained that he was a civil engineer by profession and another board member was a practical engineer, and that they grilled the major on applied mathematics, railroading, fieldworks, permanent fortifications, and architecture, along with the standard topics. He promptly brought the major up on charges of conduct unbecoming an officer for his criticism of the board.[49]

In fact, some military officials asserted that there were considerably different standards between the various boards. The Bureau of Colored Troops restricted successful candidates from the New Orleans board to the Department of the Gulf, because that board was notoriously lenient. When Colonel Sypher tried to raise the standards to the level of the Casey board, Maj. Gen. E. R. S. Canby agreed that the Casey board standards were not too high, but he felt it "would be inexpedient to raise the standards now that a considerable number had passed under more lax standards." Col. R. D. Mussey had a running battle with the Bureau of Colored Troops to eliminate such divisional boards as the one at Stevenson, Alabama, and Chattanooga, Tennessee. He learned that a man passed the Stevenson board as a major and afterwards a board member commented that he would have passed as a colonel had he been taller. One successful candidate, highly recommended by the Chattanooga board, wrote a twenty-three-line letter to Mussey and in it he spelled " 'Cyrus' S-y-r-u-s, and makes six other Orthographic blunders." He regarded the board as a "farce," and called for its abolishment and "uniform and systematic" standards in the Nashville board, similar to those of the Casey board.[50]

Many at the time believed that the Casey board maintained the most rigorous standards. The evidence, however, is biased. The most vocal proponents of the Casey board were its head and its own examinees, who had no experience before other boards. Nor was the Casey board always very demanding. While Stephen P. Jocelyn, who rose to a general officer's rank in the Regular Army after the war, took his examination, Casey read a newspaper and paid little attention. The two questions he asked concerned chemicals, when he learned that Jocelyn had been an assistant druggist before entering the service. On the other hand, the St. Louis board performed so well that the department commander sent inefficient officers before it as a means of ridding the service of them. Most likely, those two boards levied the strictest requirements on their candidates.[51]

According to the Bureau of Colored Troops—and its records appear incomplete because they do not include the division boards—it received over nine thousand applications for commands in the USCT, and nearly four thousand took examinations for original commissions or promotions. Some 60 percent passed. More important, only one in every four applicants received a commission in the USCT, because of the effective screening process of both the bureau and the boards.[52]

Nevertheless, some unqualified officers inevitably slipped past even the more rigorous boards of examination. One officer in the USCT thought "in a number of instances the said Examining Boards have been composed of a set of ignorant men," and on other occasions candidates " 'pulled the wool' over the eyes of Examining Boards." Mussey was a great complainer about the occasional laxity of boards, but he also had the good sense to blame poor preformance of officers on "getting their heads turned by promotion," rather than the examination process.[53]

In addition, performance on the examination was no guarantee of performance in the field, as the War Department and the boards

of examiners certainly knew. Col. George W. Baird, a former private
in the Invalid Corps who supposedly passed the Casey board with
the highest score it ever awarded, struggled as a regimental commander, yet this was not the fault of the Casey board. Despite all
the attempts to question, screen, and even pressure candidates,
such efforts could not examine the intangible qualities that frequently determined success or failure, such as the ability to make
critical decisions under the enormous stress of battle or the knack
to recognize the exact moment to implement them. One officer in
the USCT termed it "pluck & quick decision of character enough
to fill any emergency which may arise," along with knowledge in
the ways of the military. And in fairness to everyone who served
on the boards of examiners, the same system that provided the
USCT with Baird and officers inferior to him recognized the talents
of William R. Shafter, Stephen Jocelyn, and many others.[54]

Forty hours after his examination before the Casey board, a courier
handed John McMurray a sealed letter that contained his results.
With butterflies in his stomach and weakened knees, "I opened the
envelope with trembling fingers, while my pulse moved with quick-
ened beat, caused by desire and expectancy." McMurray passed as
a captain. One candidate could not wait for the results through
proper channels and attempted to bribe a clerk to learn his results.
The clerk promptly reported the man to the members of the board,
and they in turn voted the candidate unfit for any commission in
the USCT.[55]

For those who failed, the decision was final. They returned to
their volunteer units to fulfill their enlistment agreements, or back
to civilian life. Officers who had mustered out of their white units
and into the USCT and then failed the examination received a discharge from the War Department.[56]

Each board determined what rank successful candidates had
passed and then categorized them into first and second class. They
then arranged them within each class from one to seven and sent
weekly reports to the Bureau of Colored Troops. This procedure
enabled the Bureau to place successful candidates properly in regiments and companies with seniority dictated by performance on
the examination.[57]

Yet within this system, as with most, irregularities occurred. Capt.
Edward Martindale failed the examination for colonel in the USCT,
but the New Orleans board recommended that Martindale receive
the position anyway, and he did, "on account of his excellent record
in military life, bravery, general intelligence and aptitude for military
service." This, however, was a rarity. Much more common was the
use of commissions in the USCT as a means of favoring friends of

politicians. When Senator Henry Wilson, head of the Senate Military Affairs Committee, wrote Col. James Brisbin requesting that Albert Austin receive a second lieutenancy without an examination, the colonel complied. Maj. Gen. Oliver Otis Howard wanted an acting staff member, Pvt. Joseph Sladen, promoted and assigned to him for permanent duty, but there were no slots in the soldier's volunteer unit. As a department commander, Howard simply convened a board, briefly questioned Sladen, and then awarded him a lieutenancy in the USCT. The War Department accepted Howard's actions and assigned Sladen to the 14th U.S. Colored Infantry, although he never served a day with it. After the Savannah Campaign, Howard's brother Charles and William Beebe, both staff members, decided they wanted commands. When plans fell through, Brig. Gen. Rufus Saxton, commander of the Department of the South, talked them into taking a black unit, the 128th U.S. Colored Infantry, with full powers to select their own officers. Even such stalwarts as Col. R. D. Mussey, who worked continuously in the USCT yet never served as commander of the 101st U.S. Colored Infantry, to which he was assigned, agreed to the appointment of several individuals and waived the examination.[58]

The most obvious example of using commissions as patronage was the decision of the War Department to permit Governor Andrew Johnson to control all commissions in the USCT for units raised in Tennessee and to exempt all Johnson appointees from having to appear before the board of examiners. Johnson was trying to walk a tightrope in Tennessee by retaining the support of unionists, many of whom did not want black soldiers, attracting disunionists, and supporting government policies to crush the rebellion, such as the enlistment of blacks. He wanted to move cautiously, while George Stearns, the commissioner of recruiting and Mussey's predecessor, preferred a more vigorous policy. Moreover, control of commissions was a viable tool to help make black units more appealing to Tennesseans. As military governor, Johnson wanted the same privileges that other governors had received—the right to appoint officers over troops enlisted in his state. The War Department came down fully behind Johnson, and this forced Johnson and Stearns to work out their difficulties. Mussey, who took over for Stearns in February 1864, was more nonconfrontational but also more committed to the elimination from the service of the incompetents that Johnson appointed. He argued: "It is a shame to set such men over these Troops. They need the very best of men," and suggested that the Bureau of Colored Troops cashier Johnson appointees whenever it became necessary.[59]

Most candidates, once they received news of success on the examination or notice of an appointment in the USCT, thought the hard part was over. In actuality, it had just begun. Soldiers and civilians found it difficult to leave old friends and enter an organization with few or no friends, serving alongside a different race, about which they had heard all sorts of prejudicial stories, in the face of opposition by many in their own army and the threat of death if captured by the enemy.

To help make the decision easier, they sought support from the folks at home. For some, all their family and friends had to do was set the proper atmosphere by advocating total victory. A New Yorker's father revealed, "Bad as I want the war to stop I don't want them to compromise. may as well fite it out now as ever," and his girlfriend told him, "I think any man who feels an interest in his country's welfare will volunteer to do all in his power to crush out this Rebellion which has nearly ruined our country." Shortly after receiving such words, he sought a commission in the USCT. For others, it was support when they made their decision. A Minnesotan received encouragement from his father, who wrote that the USCT "is perhaps a thankless service but nevertheless important and if successful may aid in the cultivation of the blacks to a capacity they might not have attained in civil life among the 'chivalry' even were they emancipated by them and the utmost favor allowed possible in such society." New Yorker Henry Crydenwise had the choice of a lieutenancy in his regiment or a captaincy in the USCT and decided in favor of the black unit: "I am well aware that many are strongly prejudiced against colored soldiers and that with some I should loose caste by becoming an officer in a colored regiment but I cannot think that the petty prejudices or even the frown of others should deter us from persuing what we conceive to be a line of duty." When his family and fiancé had no objections, he was thrilled.[60]

Unfortunately, support from the folks at home was not always forthcoming. When a New York artilleryman learned that his brother-in-law intended to join a black unit, he made clear his thoughts on the matter: "I sincerely hope you will take my advice and persuade James to come out from beneath it flee from its presences and no more allow such ideas to remain in his mind   'A chaplain of a *nigger* regiment!' My God! deliver him in due time from falling into that error." The clergyman shrewdly disregarded the urgings of his relative by marriage and found service in a black unit to be extremely rewarding.[61]

Because many of them had endured so much, they were very sensitive to negative reactions from folks back home. When Sam Evans decided to join the USCT and notified his family, his brother supported him but his father reacted severely to the news: "I had much rath[er] you had not asked my opinion, or even informed me, that you were making yourself so willing, to accept a degraded position, (I wouth rather clean out S__t houses at ten cents pr day, then to take you[r] position with its pay.) you have made an enviable reputation, as a '*good & worthy soldier. . . . Alas what a step!*" Jolted by his father's reaction, Sam angrily retorted, "The fact is, you have never marched so far with a heavy load and Sore feet as I and have never noticed so plainly the priveleges of a commissioned officer. I beg leave to differ from you as to it being a 'degraded position'   I would much rather have *my position* than the '*one*' you say you would rather have." His father, unwilling to let the matter rest, insisted he would prefer to have the race extinguished than lose a single company of white troops, and that friends of blacks should lead them in combat, not his son. His father then warned him that a few officers could do nothing in the face of one hundred armed and mutinous blacks. Evidently, the father failed to recognize the transformation his son had undergone after a year of war. Sam continued to try to soothe his father's racist anxieties, but time alone overcame his father's dissatisfaction.[62]

In a similar incident, when Lycurgus Grim notified his aunt that he was entering the USCT, she attacked abolitionism and accused him of endorsing miscegenation. Grim exploded in rage at her statements. "What do you mean by, '*This miserable crusade,*'" he penned indignantly. "Are you so unjust to philanthropy, to human nature[,] to the honor of our country as to still be a friend and an advocate of slavery?" As to the charges of supporting miscegenation, the outraged soldier wrote: "If you are candid in what you say, you certainly have a very *low* opinion of my natural manliness, and hence it would probably be better if our correspondence should cease. If I regarded my own feelings I could not correspond with a lady who believed that I entertained opinions so inconsistent with the dignity and honor of the white race, much less could I correspond with a lady who herself entertained such opinions." His aunt, apparently stunned by Grim's outburst, insisted that she was only joking and that she did not believe those things. Grim accepted her explanation and apologized for his remarks, which settled the affair.[63]

Just as support from home was important for those who considered accepting commissions in the USCT, so it was from comrades in their volunteer unit. After prolonged service together, soldiers in the white volunteer organizations understood one another better than did the folks at home, who had not endured the hardships and undertaken quite the same reevaluation of the war. It was imperative that comrades at least respect the decision of successful candidates, and nothing eased the pressure like warm support from friends in the old unit. A Pennsylvania private, more self-confident than most, described the response of his comrades to his appointment in the USCT: "You ask me how my friends received me, most of them with open arms notwithstanding my present calling was not approved of by some of them, but I was mighty independent & in fact could afford to be & so could anybody with a pair of shoulder straps on & a few hundred dollars in ones pocket." Most, however, needed friends to stand by them. When David Cornwell's commission as first lieutenant arrived, his buddies flocked about to congratulate him, and he felt much better about his decision. An Illinois corporal, after receiving an offer of a commission in a black unit, consulted his friends and they recommended that he take it because the extra money would enable him to obtain the education he missed due to the war.[64]

Soldiers quickly learned that the best way to avoid the sense of guilt over leaving the boys and to insulate themselves from negative reactions on racist grounds was to convince several or more men to seek commissions in the USCT simultaneously. While in winter camp, one of three tentmates in the 13th New Hampshire Infantry proposed that they all apply for commissions in a black unit. At first the other two men rejected the scheme, but gradually one and then the other relented. The three studied together for the examination, scored well, and then received assignments to the 30th U.S. Colored Infantry. In fact, numerous black units had an unusual number of officers who came from the same volunteer unit. Many of the officers in the 1st U.S. Colored Cavalry came from the 3rd New York Cavalry, and eighteen officers in the 90th U.S. Colored Infantry served previously in the 128th New York Infantry. Perhaps the most striking example was the 3rd U.S. Colored Cavalry, in which forty-four officers came from the 4th Illinois Cavalry and twelve from the same company.[65]

For Edwin Hobart, the decision to leave his volunteer unit was easy. He had mulled over an offer for some time, without making a firm decision. Then, the day before he eventually left, he and some comrades had raided a watermelon cart in Natchez and an officer got Hobart's name and command. The next day, when the lieutenant came to have Hobart arrested, he had already fled to the sanctuary of his new black unit, so that his old officers could honestly say there was no such soldier as Corporal Hobart in the regiment. His choice was service in the USCT or a stay in jail. For others, however, the decision was not that simple. "The more I think of it," wrote a Connecticut enlisted man, "the more I am loth to leave the co[mpany], & the Reg[iment]." Nevertheless, many of them could not resist the calling.[66]

"We are getting a very fine class of officers indeed," Maj. George Stearns testified before the American Freedmen's Inquiry Commission. "I think they will average better than the officers of white regiments." For the first time, the federal government screened candidates for officers' rank in volunteer units during wartime. It was, no doubt, an outgrowth of racism, of a belief in the innate inferiority of blacks and the need of exceptional white individuals to mold them into competent military organizations, yet it was also a positive development for both blacks who served under these officers and the American military establishment in general. While the system did not weed out all incompetent or immoral candidates, the quality of the officers was definitely superior to those in white volunteer units. As retired Maj. Gen. Silas Casey, forty years a soldier, wrote ten years after the war, "I have no hesitation in saying that the officers of the colored troops, *who passed the Board*, as a body were superior to them [volunteer officers in white units], physically, mentally and morally." In forceful language Casey went on to argue that the government had an obligation to obtain such officers for its men: "Let it be impressed deeply on the conscience of every man of influence and authority that when he places in command an incompetent officer he is guilty of manslaughter. The country has lost millions of treasure and thousands of lives by the incompetency of officers." Even though the system stifled efforts by blacks to gain commands of their own, this was a genuine attempt to prevent such careless abuses in black units and to secure for them qualified white officers.[67]

4

Filling the Ranks

Without doubt, one of the most difficult and disagreeable duties for these aspiring white officers was the recruitment of blacks to serve in the USCT. Both their superiors and the government exerted tremendous pressure on them to recruit organizations rapidly. To complicate matters, the government frequently did not provide them with the proper tools to recruit effectively, nor was it able to create an environment conducive to the recruitment of black soldiers. Finally, it was not always propitious for blacks, particularly freedmen, to join the army when their families, caught in the transitional trauma from slavery to freedom, required security and assistance in obtaining such essentials as food, clothing, and shelter.

In the case of many black soldiers, however, recruitment was unnecessary. The Union Army offered freedom to all blacks who enlisted, as well as an opportunity to fight for the termination of slavery, and this was enough incentive to entice thousands to risk the hazards of running away to Federal lines for sanctuary. Thus, when Kentucky slave Elijah Marrs told several friends he was going to Louisville to join the Union ranks, some other slaves expressed interest in enlisting too. During the day, all who planned to slip off to the Federal recruiters in Louisville rolled up their sleeves as a signal of participation. That night, after religious service, a timid crew of twenty-seven left on foot, fearful of the whippings and other punishments for being caught, yet hopeful of the rewards for success. On a few occasions the entire scheme almost collapsed because of the inherent risks, and at one point, they had to hide off the road while a party passed, which they assumed was a slave patrol in search of them. Nevertheless, they pushed on, and around sunrise they had arrived in Louisville. By 8 A.M. they were standing in line at the recruiting office and soon were recruits in the USCT. Later that day their former masters appeared in town, searching for their chattels, but all had enlisted except one, who was rejected as a minor.[1]

Other times, slaves shunned companionship for secrecy and made the journey alone. Charlie Reed, a Kentucky bondsman whose master had bought him five years earlier for $1,000, left the plantation to work on a railroad early in the war and was eventually apprehended and returned. Shortly afterward, he ran off again, this time for the Union Army, and enlisted promptly. In full uniform, he proudly returned to the old farm, but his former mistress refused to let him in the house. Farther south, in Alabama, a slave concluded that, rather than stick around and get beaten by the overseer, "I's gwine run off the first chance I gits. I didn't know how to git there," he continued, "but I's gwine North where there ain't no slaveowners." While out on a hunting party, he took the gamble and fled for Union lines. "I travels all that day and night up the river and follows the North Star," he recalled. Moving by night and hiding during the day, living on rabbits, fish, nuts, and anything he could find, the slave nearly starved to death in search of the Federals. One day, he heard guns firing in the distance, but he could not tell whether Union or Confederate troops were in front of him. Tired, hungry, and scared, he did not know what to do, when suddenly some soldiers sneaked up on him and ordered him to raise his hands. Fortunately, they were Federals, and he was soon within Union lines, clad in a blue uniform.[2]

Those who had run away to Union forces and were too young to enlist or who reached the safe haven before the government recruited black soldiers often found employment with officers in white volunteer units as cooks and servants. Once opportunity availed itself or they reached majority age, they swore the oath and put on a blue uniform, too. Shortly after the fall of New Orleans, young George Ellis ran off to the Federals and became a servant of Lt. Edward Caufy of the 26th Massachusetts Infantry. When the unit mustered out of service, Ellis went to Massachusetts to live with Caufy, where the young black learned to read and write and, in January 1865, having reached the proper age, Ellis enlisted in the 55th Massachusetts (Colored) Infantry. In the case of William J. Haynes, a slave in Henry County, Tennessee, he ran off to Kentucky, where he received a job as a cook for men in the 13th Wisconsin Infantry. By the time Haynes enlisted, at the first opportunity in May 1863, he had already been through two battles.[3]

While the desire and resourcefulness of slaves provided the Federal government with thousands of black soldiers, the supply was neither large nor consistent enough to sustain the formation of a substantial force of black troops. The War Department had to adopt an aggressive program to bring blacks into military service, and it rested the responsibility for this primarily upon the shoulders of the officers who were going to command them.

Filling the ranks was one of the most critical aspects of military service, and the conduct of recruiters affected every other officer and man in the USCT. Aside from gathering essential manpower for military service, those dealings also set the tone for initial relations between the whites and blacks who constituted these military organizations. For many blacks, this was their first encounter with Northern white men, and for others it was their introduction to federal government officials. Blacks who suffered abuse at the hands of Northern recruiters challenged their white officers to win their confidence even more than usual, while those who received honest and considerate treatment in the recruitment process sensed a genuine commitment on the part of Northern whites toward abolitionism and reunion, and they were much more likely to grant their white officers the benefit of the doubt when problems arose in the early going. Thus, either directly or indirectly, the handling of recruitment affected everyone in the USCT.

Pressure to recruit black soldiers came from the highest circles of government and industry. Despite considerable opposition in the military and the public at large, the government quickly grasped the tremendous value of recruiting blacks in lieu of Northern whites. White volunteers simply were not coming forward as they had once done, and conscription was very unpopular. By placing weapons in the hands of blacks, the government was sparing the white population. Moreover, extensive recruiting of whites in the Northern states began to cut deeply into the industrial work force. From the standpoint of Northern manufacturing leaders, it was much more practical to enlist "unemployed" blacks, particularly in the South, than to gobble up white men who were making considerable contributions to the war effort through their jobs. These industrialists pressured the House of Representatives to pass a resolution by nearly a 2 to 1 vote to encourage black enlistment to relieve whites "unacclimated and unused to manual labor, and lessen the number to be taken from their homes and from the industrial pursuits in the Union States." Such exertions filtered down through the War Department to the officers who were responsible for black enlistment, who in turn applied pressure on the recruiters.[4]

In addition, the officers who supervised the recruitment of blacks developed a system that generated its own pressure to stimulate recruitment. Standard War Department policy was that the actual strength of each command dictated how many officers it could muster into service and what rank those officers could hold. Not until nearly one hundred men had enlisted in the same company could all its authorized officers be commissioned. When Adjutant General Lorenzo Thomas traveled west to announce the president's policy on the use of black soldiers and to help organize units, he frequently authorized one individual to recruit a regiment, who then offered officers' ranks to other soldiers on condition that they raise specified numbers of blacks for military service and pass the examination. Any prospective officer who did not raise his command within a "reasonable length of time or be slothful or negligent in the discharge of his duties," had the offer of his commission revoked.[5]

Supposedly aiding the white officers in the recruitment process, but in many instances competing with them, were the civilian recruiters. Originally the federal government intended to hire a cluster of prominent free blacks who would do the work for a reasonable fee and guarantee the proper treatment of enlistees and their families. The policy came off track in mid-1864, though, when Congress granted Northern states authority to recruit throughout most of the Confederacy and credited recruits to those Northern states. Such incentives were irresistible for Northern governors, who in their lobbying efforts had depicted the policy as one of great benefit to the federal and state governments and the black race. As agents of the various Northern states, the civilian recruiters came south seeking freedmen who would offset state manpower quotas established by the federal government. The more freedmen they enlisted, the more money they made and the fewer citizens from their state had to volunteer or be drafted.[6]

In truth, these civilian recruiters contributed only marginally to the war effort while exasperating both senior military commanders and officers in charge of the organization of black units. After four months of work, more than one thousand state agents had registered with the Provost Marshal General's Office, and they had enlisted less than three thousand freedmen. By the end of the war these agents had brought only five thousand blacks into the service. According to Maj. Gen. William T. Sherman, who was no friend of blacks, the state agents merely consumed his rations, occupied critical transportation space, and generally interfered with his ability to wage war. At one point these state agents so frustrated Sherman that he barred them from using government transportation and rations, which he could better use for troops. Sherman was not alone in these opinions.[7]

Worse yet, many state agents were corrupt or interested solely in making a profit from the work. Col. R. D. Mussey complained that barely any of the thirty-six agents operating in his department "care a snap of their finger for the negro or are interested in Colored Troops." One agent sounded out an officer of Mussey's to see if he was susceptible to bribery, and another openly proposed a scheme to defraud the government. Eight days later Mussey complained that these agents received a large part of the bounty for enlistment that was supposed to go to the freedmen, as well as a premium for obtaining recruits, and that dishonesty was rampant. By then he had 107 agents in his department, 100 of whom he considered worthless.[8]

Federal and state authorities provided prospective officers in the USCT and state agents with very few tools to spark enlistments. For one thing, the government offered limited financial incentives. Pay was low and unequal for blacks throughout much of the war, and it was certainly no better than what a black laborer received from the federal government or in the private sector. All black enlisted men, regardless of rank, received seven dollars per month plus three dollars for clothing, while white privates earned thirteen dollars along with the three for clothing; remuneration for corporals and sergeants was higher. Yet federal and state governments attempted to compensate enlistees by granting them a sizable sum of money called a bounty. These bounties varied from state to state, even locality to locality, throughout the course of the war. Usually the federal government provided some money, as did the state and the local community, and in the end, the bounty could be substantial. Unfortunately, many of the freedmen who enlisted never saw the money. During the course of the war federal and state governments discriminated against blacks in the size of the bounty, and a number of recruiters, both white officers and state agents, defrauded unwitting freedmen of the proper sum. Other blacks enlisted with the consent of their former owners, who received all or part of the bounty, while in return the enlistees were "granted" freedom—which was something all slaves won, regardless of whether they had endured the hardships of military service. Thus, the Federal government had adopted the peculiar policy of calling on the black race to defend a government that had discriminated against it or permitted its enslavement, with exceedingly limited financial incentives to enable enlistees to provide for their families, while it had to use substantial monetary allurements to attract Northern whites whose government and democratic republic was at risk. Under these conditions, a considerable number of blacks entered the service only under false pretenses or through the use of force.[9]

The ability to offer bounties, however, failed to address the most serious problems white officers had to face in their recruitment duties. A lack of cooperation on the part of military officials, the illegal and unethical activities of a handful of recruiters that spawned distrust in the black community, and Southern resistance to black enlistment all hampered efforts to recruit black units.

Opposition to the enlistment of black soldiers by a number of prominent Federal officers—something that plagued the USCT throughout the war—was one significant impediment. These military officials felt that the black race, because of its alleged inferiority, could best serve the war effort as laborers in the quartermaster, commissary, and engineer departments, rather than in military garb with weapons in their hands. Since 1861, when Butler employed the runaway slaves in the construction of a bakery, the government had begun to hire more and more black laborers, so that by 1863 it had become critically dependent on their services. As the government began to press for the creation of more and more black units, particularly in 1864, recruiters eyed these laborers as an excellent source of manpower. Sherman, inspired at least in part by his racial views, argued from a military standpoint that efforts to strip him of his laborers would significantly hamper his campaign for Atlanta, and he threatened to imprison anyone who interfered with them. Lincoln, with his deft touch, assuaged the brilliant but irascible general while insisting that he must aid recruiters. Nevertheless, Sherman was not the only complainant. Officers in South Carolina, Florida, and Louisiana had to deal with the same problem—recruiters raiding their work force. In the end, although military commanders could not prevent the execution of the recruitment policy, they could hinder the efforts of recruiters or, as Sherman did, simply provide them with no assistance whatsoever.[10]

Another major stumbling block to black recruitment was the treatment blacks had received at the hands of the Union government and its sworn representatives, Federal troops. Once the government endorsed Butler's decision to declare freedmen contraband of war, huge numbers of blacks poured into Federal lines. Those whom military authorities returned to slavery had a particularly keen reason for distrusting anything to do with the Union Army. Others whom authorities put to work lived under poor conditions, sometimes exposed to the open air all night, were seldom paid for their labors, and failed to receive full rations and clothing allowances because of fraud in the quartermaster and commissary departments. Mistreatment reached such heights that a handful of officers in the Virginia theater accused the government of "degrading" the freedmen to a "lower level than before." In Kentucky, conditions for the families of black troops were so poor that they seriously undermined the morale of the troops and prevented enlistment of other freedmen, "fearing that their wives and children will not be cared for during the winter." One private's son died, most likely from exposure, after callous disregard for the welfare of his family by military officials.[11]

Federal officers compounded the problem by trying to meet manpower quotas through mass conscription of blacks. Such attempts in Virginia drove freedmen who did not want to serve in the Union Army to hide in nearby woods, and beneath beds and even inside chimneys in South Carolina. According to one black man in Nashville, while he was en route home from Sunday church, a guard stopped him and demanded his pass. When he showed it, the guard confiscated it and impressed him, along with nearly two hundred others. The guards later burned all the passes to conceal their illegal acts. Word of such actions spread rapidly throughout black communities and served as a powerful deterrent to future enlistments.[12]

Still another obstacle to enlistment in the USCT was the fraud committed against a substantial number of blacks. Because many blacks making the transition from slavery to freedom had few insights into the workings of the federal government and could neither read nor write, and because bounties were so high, some whites schemed to profit from their lack of knowledge and experience. Working in collusion with state agents, a number of white soldiers received kickbacks for providing black refugees for enlistment. In one instance, two officers in the 15th U.S. Colored Infantry, one a colonel and the other a lieutenant colonel, defrauded the government by falsifying records to claim that enlistees came from Alabama, which enabled them to sell the recruits to New York agents. Had they reported the enlistees' true place of residence (Tennessee), the Northern state agents could not have enlisted them.[13]

On other occasions state agents worked directly to rob unwitting blacks of their just deserts. Adjutant General Lorenzo Thomas complained that some agents were encouraging blacks to act as bounty jumpers, who enlisted, collected part of the bounty, deserted, and then enlisted again, and each time the agent received a commission for his efforts. In Virginia, Benjamin Butler notified the secretary of war that "I found a most disgraceful trade being carried on here in comparison to which the slave trade was commendable." Northerners paid freedmen in Virginia fifty to one hundred dollars to go north, where agents charged from five hundred to one thousand dollars for each black man to serve as a substitute for a drafted white.[14]

Accurate estimates of the amount of money that various individuals took from needy black enlistees are unavailable, but it appears that fraud was a widespread practice. A chaplain in the USCT claimed that enlistment officials had defrauded some recent substitutes in his regiment of four thousand dollars, and a lieutenant in a different regiment commented with disgust that most of the new recruits in his unit "entered the service as substitutes for four to six hundred dollars, yet recruiters cheated them out of every cent." When black troops learned that recruiters had fleeced them, and then the army had great difficulty retrieving their money, their confidence in Northerners and the government plummeted. And once black civilians learned of the corruption, their response was identical.[15]

Finally, Southerners, particularly slaveholders, resisted attempts to recruit blacks and made the work of prospective USCT officers difficult and at times even hazardous. Certainly prejudice was a major reason for Southerners' opposition to black enlistment, but there were other factors as well. Southerners suffered considerable financial loss when slaves entered the Federal ranks. The government provided loyal slaveholders with three hundred dollars in compensation, less than one-half the prewar price of male bondsmen, and those who supported the Confederacy received nothing. They also lost valuable labor to the Union Army, both in slaves and free blacks, which they could not replace until after the war.[16]

In addition, the deeds of a few dishonest officers, such as Capt. Thomas Bunch of the 5th U.S. Colored Cavalry, alienated many moderate Southerners. Bunch went on an unauthorized recruiting jaunt purely for personal profit. He confiscated slaves for the army and then told slaveholders he would release them and destroy the papers for a fee of one hundred dollars. When the owners paid the money, he surrendered the enlistment papers but kept the men. Bunch also bullied and threatened the lives of those slave owners who refused to participate in his scheme. Federal authorities eventually put a halt to Bunch's recruiting expeditions, but they could not reverse the damage he caused to Southerners who supported the Union.[17]

Most Southerners reacted to recruitment efforts with general harassment and even with outright violence. When Col. J. P. Creager unknowingly recruited several slaves along with free blacks in Maryland, local authorities threw him in jail. His commanding officer, Col. William Birney, pressed the War Department to secure Creager's freedom, but it refused on the grounds that the military had no authority in cases involving civilians—not much reassurance to an already shaky crew of recruiters.[18]

Other encounters with Southern opponents of black military units, however, were not so peaceful. During a manpower sweep in Maryland, Lt. Eben White learned that a man named Sothoron had two blacks tied up in his home to keep them from enlisting in the army. When White approached the house, Sothoron and his son came out with shotguns and pistols to prevent the enlistment. After a verbal confrontation, White walked to a neighboring field, where several blacks were working, to see if any of them had an interest in enlisting. Before he could ask them, though, Sothoron and his son ran up and confronted White again, and this time in the course of an argument blasted him in the chest from close range with their shotguns, killing him. The Sothorons, who later shot White twice more and smashed his head with the butts of their shotguns, then fled to the Confederate capital of Richmond for sanctuary.[19]

In Norfolk, Virginia, a prominent physician and vigorous secessionist murdered another lieutenant in the USCT, Anson L. Sanborn. Sanborn was marching his newly organized company through the streets when the physician stepped out of a crowd with a pistol in hand and called him a "son of a bitch." Sanborn calmly halted the command and ordered the physician to fall in line under arrest behind the troops. As the lieutenant turned to resume his duties, the physician raised his pistol and shot Sanborn in the neck. Three months later the Federals executed the physician after a trial, but Sanborn's public assassination injured recruiting efforts severely for months afterward in eastern Virginia.[20]

Southerners also attempted to discourage blacks from enlisting in the Union Army by harassing them in all sorts of ways. Some told stories of how the Union Army mistreated its black soldiers and insisted that the Federals did not pay their black troops and placed them in the front line of every battle. One white officer felt it was imperative to speak directly with the slaves to disabuse their minds of "needless fear" originating in these stories, yet most bondsmen, jaundiced by years and years of slavery, regarded such tales with skepticism.[21]

Much more effective were the bands of Southern guerrillas who brutally checked any attempts by blacks to enlist. In Kentucky two white inhabitants cut the left ears off two black men who sought to join the Union ranks, and in another instance guerrillas whipped fifteen blacks to deter them. Some locals in Missouri caught a party of black men trying to enlist, whipped each of them, and returned them to their owners. One of the slaveholders was so furious with her bondsman for running off that she offered five dollars to anyone in the group who would shoot the slave on the spot; a partisan promptly obliged her.[22]

Problems with Southern guerrillas were bad everywhere slavery existed, but they was especially severe in Missouri and Tennessee. In both of those states, to make the recruitment of blacks a bit more tolerable for the white residents, federal authorities prohibited roving recruiting parties. Blacks who wanted to enlist had to travel to fixed recruiting stations, frequently over fairly long distances and through areas dominated by guerrillas. The results were murder and violence, as an officer in Missouri stated: "The guerrillas have shown a singular and inhuman ferocity towards them."[23]

Worse than the abuse and violence Southerners directed at the prospective white officers and black troops was the punishment they inflicted on the families of recruits. Many Southerners took out their frustrations over a slave's enlistment by abusing his wife and children or attempting to sell the family to slave traders in other states. Pvt. Richard Glover received a letter from his pregnant wife back in Missouri begging him to come home to protect her. The overseer whipped her with a leather strap from a buggy harness "most cruelly": "They abuse me because you went & say they will not take care of our children & do nothing but quarrel with me all the time and beat me scandalously the day before yesterday." Another woman claimed that her master beat her because her husband had enlisted, and when they had learned the soldier died in Federal service, he beat her even more brutally.[24]

Nearly as bad were the threats of or actual sale of the family to slave dealers in other states. According to law, slaves and their families automatically became free when they enlisted. Slaveholders, therefore, lost numerous hands and considerable money when a married slave joined the Union ranks. To soften the financial loss and gain some psychological revenge, a number began to market families immediately on learning that the male had run off to enlist. Maj. Gen. Rosecrans, head of the Department of the Missouri, tried to cope with the problem by forbidding the sale of any slaves outside the state, which at least simplified the process of soldiers locating their families. Much more effective in dealing with the problem was the tack adopted by a captain, who wrote a slaveholder when a new enlistee voiced fear that his family "might be sold or ill used":

Now all I have to Say is this man is now a Soldier, and is entitled to his family, and *I have promised him that he Shall have them and he Shall*, and you will greatly oblige me, to furnish them with clothing and transportation to the Mo river at Kansas City immediately.

You may Consider this beyond my authority. I Confess it is as an officer, but not as a man, having 100 men with me to execute political Justice where it is necessary.

The delivery of that Negro Woman Martha & her children will insure you the protection and respect of all under my Control, the failure to do so will place the whole matter with me, and I will tell you in the Spirit of Calmness that your *life* or property is but a small Consideration when opposed to the march of freedom.[25]

With all these obstacles in the path of white officers on recruiting duty, it is a wonder they were able to accumulate such sizable commands. A great deal of the credit, of course, must go to the blacks. Many of them, whether slaves or freedmen, were seeking any opportunity to flee their current conditions, yet they also exhibited a tremendous commitment to the Union war effort. As one of their future commanders noted, "The negros feel quite patriotic. they would nearly all enlist about here if they could get the chance." Nevertheless, to recruit effectively, prospective white officers had to adapt to meet the peculiar circumstances of Northern and Southern society and their diversity of racial attitudes, and eventually they fell upon techniques that were unusually successful.[26]

In the North, recruiting blacks was not a difficult chore. Northern black leaders supported the war vigorously and urged black men to join the Federal ranks to aid their downtrodden brothers and preserve the union, despite the unequal pay the government was offering them. According to a black chaplain, "Many like the Roman Cincinnatus quit the plow and the field and flew to their country's rescue. These, generally, moral and religious and somewhat intelligent men have left their pleasant country homes and came to the war from principle, beleiving that it will result in a great [benefit] to their race and the nation." In a similar vein, a black soldier fired off a letter to one of his prized customers to keep her informed of his whereabouts. "My object in writing is to inform you that I have enlisted in the army of the United States for one year; but having faith and confidence in my Father above, I live in hopes to get back home once more, when I expect to find my work and old customers waiting for their old whitewasher and house-cleaner to resume his old station." Like Northern whites, they were citizen soldiers who stepped forward in time of national crisis, and when the war was over and victory won, they fully intended to pick up their lives where they had left off. Overall the commitment of Northern blacks to military service was most impressive. More than 34,000 Northern blacks served in the Union Army, or over 15 percent of the entire free black population in 1860, an extremely high rate.[27]

In fact, the major obstacle was convincing whites that the enlistment of black soldiers was to their benefit. Frequently black recruitment brochures had two sections, one part for the whites and another for the "Men of Color." The section for Northern blacks was a recruitment notice, calling on them to prove their manhood through military service; the section for Northern whites explained why it was so important to recruit blacks. Such lines as, "Since volunteering can no longer fill the ranks of our armies, and recourse to conscription becomes necessary, unreasoning prejudice can only be blind to the fact that every colored recruit acts as an unpurchased substitute for a white man," were clearcut attempts to garner support for the recruitment policy. In addition, once the government adopted the use of black troops, Northern blacks were subject to the draft and could serve as substitutes for Northern whites, frequently for less money than white substitutes, which many found very appealing.[28]

The biggest problem with Northern blacks was convincing some of them to leave their comrades and serve as noncommissioned officers in units raised in the South. Military organizations desperately needed literate noncommissioned officers, and among the masses of freedmen the military found very few. The obvious solution was to draw on Northern blacks, but they found objections to the idea. Most Northern blacks, like Northern whites, preferred to serve with their friends and neighbors. They also regarded the pay differential as insulting. Until, in mid-1864, the federal government put black soldiers on the same pay scale as whites, black noncommissioned officers received the same pay as black privates, which was considerably below that of white privates. To rectify this shortage Maj. Charles W. Foster, head of the Bureau of Colored Troops, tried to secure at Camp William Penn in Pennsylvania "one hundred of the most active and intelligent, (men who can read and write) with a view to their assignment in the South West and appoint as noncommissioned officers, and for detail as clerks." This, however, was grossly discriminatory. The government would never have dreamed of doing such a thing with white volunteers, and the bureau had no right to force a promotion on anyone. A much more sensible approach was the one adopted by Colonel Higginson. His 33rd U.S. Colored Infantry, composed mainly of South Carolina, Georgia, and Florida freedmen, had few literate blacks. To obtain them Higginson called on his friends in the free black population in the North. With great candor he warned William Brown of Worcester, Massachusetts, "*If taken prisoner by the Rebels at any time, you would probably be sold as a slave.* This being the case, I do not think it your absolute *duty* to leave your family to come." Nevertheless, Higginson insisted, "You can be very useful to us, as there are but few in our regiment who can read & write with ease."[29]

In the face of all the obstacles, recruiting in the slave states was a much more difficult proposition. There individual recruiters established a headquarters in a community and combed the countryside in search of prospective enlistees. Once they had scoured the area, recruiters "borrowed" animals to convey the party to another community and repeated the process until they had enough men. With only oral authorization, recruiters had no means to prove they had permission to confiscate slaves or property for military service, which led to clashes with locals. The government frequently refused to provide funds to defray expenses, so that recruiters lived miserably on scanty rations and slept either without shelter or in barns. Ostracized by most Southerners, they received few acts of kindness in their labors.[30]

The great advantage to these individual recruiting missions was that the recruiter almost always commanded the men he enlisted. Thus, the likelihood that he would mistreat or defraud his own recruits diminished considerably. The disadvantage was that it was a very inefficient process, which often resulted in conflicts with the locals. Most masters owned only one or two slaves, which meant that recruiters had to visit dozens and dozens of scattered farms, and slaveholders were unlikely to yield gracefully to a Union officer who was absconding with his labor. Some of these problems recruiters could offset, as did a shrewd lieutenant seeking to fill his ranks in Virginia. After toiling for several weeks in search of men, he discovered that Sunday, the day of rest, was the ideal time to recruit blacks: "We have found that Sunday is the best time to recruit as the darkeys have a dance or 'shin dig' as it is called and to visit with each other on that day and gather from the distance of five or six miles and when they are together it is easier to get them to enlist besides saveing the time of looking them up singly." Additionally, such practices bypassed slaveholders and dodged a touchy situation between the slaves, their masters, and the recruiters. Yet despite the lieutenant's success, individual recruitment as a rule was an impractical method of raising black commands. In an army of nearly one million men, depending on individuals to raise tens of thousands of Southern blacks among a generally hostile populace was a ridiculous approach.[31]

Another technique the military adopted was the use of black troops to enlist others. Nothing impressed fellow blacks like the sight of handsomely uniformed and fully armed black soldiers. Equally important, former slaves did not always open their arms to Northern whites. Their experiences made them leery of the white race in general, and many blacks preferred to deal with them cautiously. By utilizing enlisted men in the USCT, recruiting officers immediately established a rapport with prospective enlistees and were able to gain the confidence of freedmen by giving them opportunities to observe and interact with black soldiers.[32]

Just as prominent Northern blacks were an effective device to

spur recruitment, so were new enlistees influential with other freedmen. At an enlistment meeting at Nashville in 1863, one black encouraged his comrades to seize the moment and join in the fight:
"Let us make a name for ourselves and race, bright as the noonday
sun." Then a black corporal named Jerry Sullivan took to the stage
to urge the crowd to enlist because "God is in this war. He will
lead us on to victory." Sullivan called on them to grab rifles and
shoot "those grey back coons that go poking about the country
now a days." He insisted, "Don't ask your wife, for if she is a wife
worth having she will call you a coward for asking her. I've got a
wife and she says to me, the other day, 'Jerry, if you don't go to
the war mighty soon, I'll go off and leave you, as some of the Northern
gentlemen want me to go home to cook for them.' " [33]

Although the use of black troops was effective, this recruiting
technique also had its drawbacks. It was, after all, one thing to
have black soldiers address an enlistment rally and quite another
to have armed black troops roaming throughout the South in search
of recruits—as many were authorized to do—which absolutely terrified the white population and alienated many loyalists. For another
thing, it delegated authority to too many people, which in turn
paved the way for additional abuses. Still another reason was the
intolerance many black soldiers showed toward freedmen who did
not want to enlist. The lyrics of a song popular with black soldiers,
religiously inspired yet with military connotations, included the
verse,

> One more valiant soldier here,
> To help us bear de cross.

For them this was the ultimate moment, an opportunity to fight
for their own freedom, and in their zeal many black soldiers simply
could not understand why some fellow black men refused to respond
to the call. They bitterly accused those who were not in the USCT
of being "rebels," and a number of them suggested to officers that
they force them into service. "That man don't know what is good
for him," two black enlisted men told an officer in the USCT. "*You*
know that freedom is better than slavery for him, and you ought
to force him to go away with us." Others urged the policy of conscription of freedmen on the same grounds, that it would give them a
"chance to get sense." [34]

A most effective technique for acquiring black enlistees was the
recruitment campaign. Substantial Union forces penetrated deep
into the Confederacy to secure large numbers of recruits, as well
as any other contraband of war, such as cotton and horses, located
by Federal troops. By including units from the USCT on these expedi-

tions, they gained the advantage of black soldiers recruiting fellow blacks, under the supervision of officers. And because they had such a large armed force, the Federals had the luxury of bringing the families of recruits to safety too.

For some time, it had become increasingly clear that effective recruiting demanded that Union troops secure the freedom of recruits' families and convey them to areas of safety. White USCT officers complained that the conditions of enlisted men's families were undermining discipline in their units and leading to desertion and a number of other offenses. In addition, more-committed black soldiers appealed to the humanitarian sentiments of officers and government officials and begged them to launch campaigns to free loved ones. Even Sherman lectured Adjutant General Lorenzo Thomas, "If negroes are taken as soldiers by undue influence or force and compelled to leave their women in the uncertainty of their new condition they cannot be relied on." Sherman believed that if the government enabled them to "put their families in some safe place and then earn money as soldiers or laborers, the transition will be more easy and the effect more permanent." [35]

In point of fact, Sherman was correct. The ideal situation was for black men to relocate their families in secure areas before enlisting. Unfortunately, the exigencies of the war demanded an immediate increase in manpower, and these recruitment campaigns appeared to be the best solution.

In practice the recruitment campaigns proved very effective. Higginson and his comrade, Col. James Montgomery, enjoyed great success in the Department of the South, as did Maj. Gen. Benjamin Butler in Virginia. In the Department of the Gulf, the greatest advocate of the recruitment campaign was Maj. Joseph W. Paine of the 4th U.S. Colored Cavalry, who personally supervised the enlistment of some five hundred soldiers for the USCT. Once he penetrated into a region, Paine first gathered all the horses and mules. Then he began to collect black men and their families, and he always brought the entire lot back to New Orleans, regardless of orders. During the Red River Campaign of early 1864, which nearly resulted in a Union catastrophe, Paine, "in defiance of 'red tape,'" foraged for hundreds of indigent black women and children whose men had entered the service. "By dint of great personal exertions," according to a comrade, he provided transportation for the black men, women, and children "at a time when everybody declared the idea impossible, and that they would have to be left." Such monumental efforts left a tremendous mark on those black soldiers whose families arrived in safety. Regrettably, Paine did not enjoy the laurels for long. His extraordinary exertions led to his death shortly thereafter, but his work convinced superior officers of the benefits of the recruitment campaign.[36]

Despite the efforts of such officers as Higginson and Paine to devise effective recruitment practices, illegal and unethical recruitment activities continued. Too many officers cared too little how they raised black units. Even within the USCT unsavory methods of recruitment were far too common, as conscription, or forced enlistment, was a frequent occurrence. It became clear to one USCT officer, while he was trying to enlist a group of freedmen, "that not one of these coons had the slightest intention of enlisting, I felt quite certain." To convince them, he had a huge black recruit force them to come along. None of these men ever deserted, and all of them served well, which prompted the officer to conclude, "They were grateful that I had taken the responsibility of settling the question of their enlistment for them." A second white officer admitted that he threw a black man in the guardhouse for three days to "persuade him to enlist." Still another officer explained to his wife that he had enlisted his company without any resort to force. He merely neglected to tell them that a term of enlistment "is for three years, But we are gradually letting them Know it." He then confided, "I believe though if we had told them it was for three years, Every one of them would a been forced in." Authorities frequently rebuked officers for such practices, but they rarely court-martialed anyone unless they had swindled money from the enlistees.[37]

Nor were recruiters very selective about the physical condition of the men they obtained. According to army regulations, before a man enlisted he had to undergo a physical examination to determine his fitness for service. Based on the physical condition of many of the recruits who reached the black units, the examinations were a farce. The 119th U.S. Colored Infantry reported one enlistee as fourteen years of age and another one even younger. An officer in the 59th U.S. Colored Infantry wrote home that through conscription the regiment had received some men who were deaf, blind, and lame. When substitutes arrived for the 67th U.S. Colored Infantry, an officer noted that a number of them had already seen service. One soldier still had three balls in him, another had been shot in the head and was nearly deaf, and a third one had a broken back. The worst instance, though, was in the 63rd U.S. Colored Infantry. An assistant inspector general reported in that unit, "More than half of the men are old and cripples both physically and mentally disqualified for being soldiers."[38]

For the initial examining physicians, as well as for the regimental surgeons who had to devote considerable time to the new black recruits, these physical examinations produced some rather shocking results. Never before had these physicians observed so many cases of severe bodily abuse. Physicians' comments alongside the names of Southern-born blacks in Illinois late in the war included "left ear cropped," "Scared heavily on back from whipping," and "scar on Back from Whipping." In books of medical examinations of recruits and substitutes in the 12th and 13th Districts in Illinois, nearly all the cases of serious burn scars were for Southern-born blacks, although they composed only a small percentage of the men listed.[39]

In black units constituted wholly with freedmen, evidence of abuse was even more apparent. A lieutenant who observed the physical examinations of his troops recorded in his diary,

> Some of them were scarred from head to foot where they had been whipped. One man's back was nearly all one scar, as if the skin had been chopped up and left to heal in ridges. Another had scars on the back of his neck, and from that all the way to his heels every little ways; but that was not such a sight as the one with the great solid mass of ridges, from his shoulders to his hips. That beat all the antislavery sermons ever yet preached.

When Surg. Humphrey H. Hood examined recruits for the 3rd U.S. Colored Heavy Artillery, the condition of some of these men appalled him. In early May 1863 he informed his wife that "I have occasion to see the backs of these men and anyone inspired to read might there read corroborative evidence of all that Mrs. Stowe ever wrote of the cruelty of slavery." He estimated that "At least one half these backs were scared with the lash," and the beatings were so frequent that recruits "talk about whipping as a thing of course and, like a tooth ache, an accident to existence unpleasant enough—but to be endured as best they may." Two months later he wrote of a black who had lived in Charleston "till a big boy—that then he was brought to 'dis couter country where dey abused me mightily.'" His back, so stated Hood, "was terribly scarred" by a whip. The previous day he examined a young man, not quite twenty years old, who "must have been tortured. On his back there were whelts some fifteen or twenty in number, as large as my little finger. They were great cords of calloused flesh," which the soldier blamed on a "'tight master.'" Fifteen days later, he again told his wife of two more horrible cases. One was an eighteen-year-old man whose back was in a mangled condition: "One side of his back had been literally cut to pieces by a *raw* hide. There were scars as wide as my two fingers, where the skin must have been torn off. It was done eighteen months ago." According to the soldier, he received two hundred lashes for "*sleeping late* in the morning and so failing to make a *fire*" and was unable to move for one week. The other was about the same age, who "was scarred all over,—on his *arms, legs, breasts, back.*" When he asked the young fellow what caused the injuries, he replied, *"Nigger dogs."*[40]

Military officials also learned, much to their surprise, that a small number of recruits had been born in Africa. One of the abused recruits that Surgeon Hood had inspected originally came from Africa: "Today in the discharge of this duty I inspected a *native* African. He said he was brought to this country when a child and lived in South Carolina" until his owners moved west. An officer in the 73rd U.S. Colored Infantry reported a soldier in his company was "a pure African." The soldier "was stolen from his home six or eight years ago and brought with others in a slaver & sold in Charleston." The recruit, called Congo, had language problems but was "one of the most intelligent and one of the best soldiers I have," reported his commander. Strangely enough, recruiters may have found Congo as a slave on the plantation of William Epps, the brutal owner of Solomon Northup, a New York free black who was kidnapped and sold into slavery—a story that shocked many Northerners. The 39th U.S. Colored Infantry had an African by birth named David Briggs who enlisted in New York. Unfortunately, he died of malaria during the war, and little is known about him. The 55th Massachusetts (Colored) Infantry had an African-born soldier as well, but he came over as a free man and enlisted voluntarily. Nicholas Said, a native of eastern Sudan and a member of the ruling class in his tribe, spoke nine languages fluently, including five used in the Western world.[41]

With physical examinations completed, there was still much to do. Officers had to prepare five muster rolls for each batch of enlistees, plus two enlistment papers per man. As one white soldier who was awaiting his muster into the USCT noted, "It takes lots of writing to make one Negro Soldier." A Minnesotan on his first day with the USCT had to take a squad of newly enlisted men and find them quarters, secure them rations, obtain clothing (because most of the men were in tatters), and locate blankets to keep them warm during those cold January nights. All this he did without an officer's rank, because the government would not muster him into service until his command had a certain number of troops. At one point, he had to go directly to a general to receive authorization to obtain the blankets, as the bureaucratic quartermaster's department refused to issue them to anyone who did not have an officer's insignia.[42]

With all the chaos surrounding the recruitment process, it was not that unusual for enlistees to "get lost" in the system. At times recruits, and occasionally their families, went days without rations, shelter, or the issuance of new clothing. Under those circumstances, it should have come as no surprise that some of them deserted before the government could swear them into service or shammed illness during the physical, particularly when they enlisted during the winter months. But for the most part, these men were extraordinarily committed to military service, and they endured these hardships as they learned to accept many others—as a natural component of military service.[43]

According to the commander of the 59th U.S. Colored Infantry, they stripped the freedmen and unceremoniously burned their old clothes, bathed them, and finally suited them in army blue and "Lo! he was completely metamorphosed, not only in appearance and dress, but in character and relations also." The change was dramatic: "Yesterday a filthy, repulsive 'nigger,' to-day a neatly-attired man; yesterday a slave, to-day a freeman; yesterday a civilian, to-day a soldier." Another observer, a soldier in a white regiment, noticed the same transformation: "Put a United States uniform on his back and the *chattel* is a *man*." [44]

For black soldiers, donning the United States Army uniform was even more exciting than it was for white volunteers early in the war. To them, it signified their elevated status, their treatment as near equals. "This was the biggest thing that ever happened in my life," commented a former slave. "I felt like a man with a uniform on and a gun in my hand." While standing there during his first roll call, recalled Elijah Marrs, "I felt freedom in my bones." The uniform was a tacit recognition of their importance to the country and the war effort, as well as a chance to demonstrate to the white race that they could stand on their own and contribute significantly to the United States in its time of need. An officer in the USCT explained it well when he wrote, "One of the greatest incentives in fitting him for a soldier was the inspiration of his being an American citizen, and of being recognized as a soldier in the same uniform that white soldiers wear, with the menial service of serfdom forever buried. He felt himself lifted to a higher plane, worthy to be the Country's defender." [45]

Yet wearing the Union blue meant more than that. It also represented an opportunity to take an active role in freeing their families, friends, and strangers whose only link was that their distant ancestors came from the same continent. "We are fighting for liberty and right," exulted a black sergeant, "and we intend to follow the old flag while there is a man left to hold it up to the breeze of heaven. Slavery must and shall pass away." Black soldiers were the embodiment of the hopes and dreams of millions and millions of blacks in both North and South, and they vowed their willingness to endure any hardship, including the loss of their lives, to terminate slavery. *"If roasting on a bed of coals of fire, would do away with the curse of slavery, I would be willing to be the sacrifice,"* insisted Sgt. Alexander Atwood, who had been a grocer in Ohio before the war. Symbolic of this passion to fight for the Union and to end bondage was the regimental flag a North Carolina freedwoman gave the 35th U.S. Colored Infantry during the summer of 1863. It was made of blue satin with gold trim, and on one side it had the Goddess of Liberty trampling a serpent, and across the other in bold letters was the word *liberty.*[46]

One of their officers summed up nicely the entire experience of organizing black military units when he confided in his diary, "Now the man who declares that a man possessing devotion to his cause, fidelity, and soldierly pride, cant make a soldier, is simply, a hopeless ass." Not one of the two thousand black recruits he was in charge of at Riker's Island in New York City tried to desert. Yet plenty of questions still had to be answered. Although these blacks looked like soldiers, their white officers and the Northern public wanted to know if they would act and fight like soldiers. And by the same token, these black men, who now felt like soldiers, wondered whether their government and white officers would treat them like soldiers.[47]

5

Coping with Racism

*I*n a society with such widespread and deep-seated prejudice as the North, rare indeed was the individual untainted by racism. Even the white USCT officers—as a group far more enlightened in their racial views than their contemporaries—nonetheless bore the marks of their era and background. Despite their limited contact with blacks before they undertook their wartime positions, they had powerful preconceptions about blacks, founded, strangely enough, primarily on the words and writings of their enemy.

To be sure, some of the white officers certainly had no interest in the black race. They accepted commissions in the USCT to escape bad experiences in volunteer units or, more frequently, simply to become officers for pay and prestige, not because they cared for the men. Yet the vast majority of the white officers fully supported the war effort and service with blacks. For them, the war had always been or had become one of reunion and abolitionism. A sizable portion had adopted the antislavery plank reluctantly, as did one officer who lectured his sister, "I think the War *is* for the Union and nothing else—and it can be sooner restored without Slavery than with and when restored it will stay so," and concluded with a question, "Would'nt you sooner see the Union restored *without* Slavery than with it?" Others snatched at the opportunity for change and called for more than just emancipation. One officer thought this was "the best cause that man ever fought for in the preservation of the Union of the US of America and the equal freedom of all men in this country *regardless of color!*" Along similar lines, a surgeon in the USCT wrote in September 1864, "I am tired of war but I dont want an inglorious peace. The peace I want is one based upon equality, freedom, to all white black or copper colour." [1]

Nevertheless, virtually all of these men had some sort of prejudice against the black race. Thinking back nearly fifty years to his service in the USCT, a former officer pinpointed the problem when he wrote, "The colored man commenced his military life under the misapprehension and prejudice of an innate character. As the negroes had been dominated over for centuries by the white man, they were looked upon with suspicion, as though no good could come out of Nazareth, and all stories detrimental to their character, were accepted with unnecessary eagerness." These white men had learned about the black race from a wide range of sources, primarily such novels as *Uncle Tom's Cabin* and stories they either read or heard from supporters and opponents of slavery, but seldom through personal experiences. In their own minds they had formulated stereotyped images of the black race and drew on their early dealings to reinforce those suspicions. Hence, what developed among the white officers was a peculiarly contradictory portrait of blacks as a whole, varying in composition from one officer to the next, and at times overlapping, but in almost every case rooted in prejudice. Racist sentiments in the white officer corps, then, took diverse forms as individuals twisted events and experiences to meet their preconceptions while diminishing or overlooking everything that discredited them. In fact, their writings indicate that they adopted the same stereotypes espoused by white Southerners.[2]

At the core of the stereotypes lay qualities that white officers attributed as innate to the black race. Frequently these were characteristics associated with primitive civilization, which the officers believed existed throughout Africa. They also believed that blacks had progressed more slowly than whites in the areas of intellect, society, and culture; and the language these officers used to describe their black troops in the early days of service often reflected their assumptions that blacks were more akin to animals than to whites and that the development of the black race was somehow retarded. Thus, when whites discussed the natural qualities of blacks, they regularly alluded to them as children or animals, either subtly or overtly. Representative of these officers was one who boasted of the "animal spirits" of his men, and another who wrote his ailing brother, also in the USCT, that he should "yield to the demands of health. Turn the 'nagurs' out to grass and come away." [3]

Because their European ancestors had been able to force Africans into slavery, these white officers assumed that blacks had to possess particular characteristics that made them susceptible to this abuse.

To justify their original enslavement, one officer questioned their mental toughness and discipline. Had the black race possessed these qualities to begin with, whites could never have forced them into slavery. As evidence of this, he argued that black troops despaired easily and "did not stand the strain of daily duty and discipline with its attendant privations and hardships as well as the white soldiers" and "in long marches and severe labor the same lack of endurance was manifest." On the other hand, a justification for their enslavement, and also one for the utilization of blacks for fatigue duty among high-ranking Union officers, was their "nimbleness and power of endurance in a warm climate." Clearly this argument ascribed to blacks a diligence and consistency of labor in hot weather exceeding that of whites. Advocating these characteristics, one white officer went so far as to declare, "In cold weather the negro gets into a certain state or torpidity, from which 'tis very hard to rouse him"—qualities similar to those of hibernating animals—and several members of the medical community endorsed this sort of comment.[4]

In the eyes of their white officers, black soldiers were more akin to children than to adults. They were excessively trusting, irresponsible, and lacked initiative, "caring not for the morrow they look out only for the present." Another officer described them as "simple, docile, and affectionate almost to the point of absurdity." The black man, they insisted, "is a great child." Because of the inability of many black soldiers to manage their own affairs, some agreed with a lieutenant who believed "They will have to have some one to look after them like that many children or else they will starve to death." Yet at the same time black soldiers perplexed their white officers by squawking over being treated like children. A captain wrote to his brother in dismay, "One thing I observe a large portion of this race of negroes don't appreciate efforts for their future elevation." Actually, it was not that black soldiers were unappreciative; rather, life in the military, even with its rigid structure, offered freedmen ample opportunities to do things for themselves, to improve their own lot, and the troops were intent on taking advantage of it. Moreover, white officers were quick to categorize the conduct of their black soldiers as childish without fully understanding its complex nature. One of the most enlightened officers in the USCT, Colonel Higginson, could not understand how black soldiers who stood in an open field with "perfect coolness" under fire could come "blubbering in the most irresistibly ludicrous manner on being transferred from one company to another." He simply regarded it as another example of childish behavior, when in fact those soldiers had formed bonds with their old comrades and had found strength and courage within the group. These men had learned through actual combat experience that they could rely upon one another, but in a company of strangers they lost that assurance.[5]

Another innate characteristic that most white officers assumed their black soldiers possessed was a latent savagery. As descendants of primitive peoples, these black soldiers—so their white officers felt—naturally lacked essential self-control, which subjected them to emotional highs and lows and extreme behavior. "The negro is very fanciful and instable in disposition," stated an officer, voicing a widespread opinion. And in that sense, they thought of the black race as a ticking time bomb. Just as the fear of brutal violence in slave revolts loomed large in the minds of Southerners, so it made their Northern white officers uneasy. Many of them wondered how their black soldiers were going to react once they sighted blood. One claimed, "Owing to their excitability, they will throw themselves forward to the cannon's mouth; and in their rage, will even tear their opponents with their teeth, should they have lost their rifle or the arm bearing it," although his view was extreme. The bulk of them were more in line with a captain in the 80th U.S. Colored Infantry who wrote his wife, "I do not believe we can Keep the negroes from murdering every thing they come to." Nor were they too certain that they could maintain control of their troops in camp at all times once the government armed them, and in the back of their minds there was always a nagging fear of mutiny.[6]

The institution of slavery and its impact on the black man's personality also played a major role in the stereotyped image created by white officers. Again, as with the innate qualities that white officers imputed to their black soldiers, so they were selective in their opinions of the characteristics that slavery imparted to their men. Similarly, the officers' conclusions often conflicted.

Along with racism, a central element in the slave system was its overwhelming discipline. How the white officers believed that affected blacks as soldiers, however, was debatable. Butler, who somehow managed to entangle himself in the issue of black soldiers throughout his lackluster military career, testified before the American Freedmen's Inquiry Commission that the discipline blacks learned in slavery was an "advantage in favor of the negro as soldiers." They learned from an early age "to do as they are told." Adjutant General Lorenzo Thomas concurred. As slaves these blacks had accustomed themselves to strict obedience, something their white officers could utilize effectively.[7]

Yet, strangely enough, the extreme discipline that many advocates of black enlistment insisted would elevate the black race once its members entered military service was precisely what many white officers thought had stifled the intellectual and psychological growth of slaves and had made them less suited to soldiering. Slave life and discipline had engendered black soldiers with habits of "indolence and carelessness," or "stupidity and slow motion, natural or assumed." Self-reliance, according to some white officers, was at a premium among former bondsmen. Others insisted that slavery had stripped these blacks of their manhood. It had divested them of all elements of self-respect and denied them of their role as family leader. Slavery had made blacks "timorous," and one former commander asserted, "They have so long been under the rule of the white men that they have become completely cowed." Military discipline as opposed to slavery discipline, they argued, would be advantageous to blacks because it would increase self-confidence and provide the proper atmosphere for educating the black soldier in the ways of free society.[8]

Few white officers contested the benefits to the black race of military service, or gainsaid this notion that military discipline would be anything but a boon to black troops, yet some challenged assertions that the oppression of slavery had had such a devastating effect on blacks. A lieutenant found his black troops, nearly all just freed from the bonds of slavery, to be "civil[,] obedient and much more intelligent than I had supposed," and an inspector general who examined dozens of white and black units felt that, although the Southern black recruit might not possess reading and writing skills, he learned "rapidly" because "the habits of obedience which he has acquired from infancy facilitates his instruction." The hardships of slavery, some found, were a positive force. They had inured blacks better to the brutality of warfare and served as an extraordinary motivator in fighting their old masters. As a colonel in the USCT contended, the black soldier "is used to suffering and to seeing his own blood flow, he will not now be so easily shocked and dismayed by carnage, as those of the more delicate sensibilities." [9]

Naturally, white officers could not help comparing black troops from the North with those who had come from slavery. Nearly everyone seemed to notice differences between them, which was understandable, especially when Northerners contended that a free-labor society was vastly superior to one predicated on slavery, although there was no agreement among them on the specific distinctions. A captain of engineers in the Department of the South who supervised black troops in fatigue duty thought those from the free states were better: "They have more of the self-reliance, and approximate nearer to the qualities of the white man, in respect to dash and energy, than those from the slave States." A colonel in the USCT, after querying fellow officers, saw no difference between them. "The efficiency of each depends upon the officers placed over them," he explained to Senator Henry Wilson. Penrose Hallowell, some years after the war, thought his Northern black soldiers needed more discipline, along the same lines as Northern white troops, than did units recruited from slave populations, which required kindness to win over the freedmen. In direct contrast, a lieutenant in the USCT also wrote (considerably after the war), "I noticed that the men who were freemen, or had for a time enjoyed the rights of a man, are much more apt in learning military tactics, than those who came directly from the plantation." When a regiment of former slaves joined his brigade, he thought "they were more dense, and slower to catch on to the military duties of a soldier." [10]

In fact, Northern and Southern blacks themselves believed that there was a difference between them. Those who had been free before the war thought their broader range of experiences in the civilian world had prepared them better for military service than had slavery. As a Northern black soldier insisted, "There is men who has Been in Bondage   we cant expect them to Do as well as a man that has Been free." One prominent black chaplain, Garland H. White, himself a runaway slave, went so far as to argue that slavery had kept these people in such ignorance that they needed the government to force them into military service to harness their military potential and also to care for them: "I am sorry to say that while white & colored men from the north are breathing out their last breath upon the Battle field in freeing these stupit creatures, they are left Idle to rove over the country like ox that feed the army." [11]

As inevitable as the debate over the qualities of free blacks and freedmen was the one about the merits of blacks and mulattoes. The basis for the entire affair was the belief that whites were at the top of the chain of being and blacks were at the bottom, and varying shades were somewhere in between. Most whites merely assumed blacks were the most inferior because they had no white ancestry, as did an officer in a black unit who wrote his mother, "The pure African is a lower type—physically & mentally, he can't stand suffering like the white man & he dies easier—i.e., he wants tenacity of life." Much to the surprise of one surgeon in the USCT who polled the officers in his command, they were "decidedly in favor of the blacks, both for the physical and intellectual points. I was prepared for the former [mulattoes] but was surprised to find that the ruling spirits among the soldiers are found mainly among the black ones." A captain in a black unit mentioned that mulattoes in his command learned faster because of their experiences and duties as slaves, frequently working as house servants or skilled workers, while blacks tended to be manual laborers, particularly field hands. Nevertheless, he went on to state that mulattoes were "rather sullen and grow despondent easily," compared to blacks, who were "more even tempered." By the 1860s a handful of individuals were beginning to question the entire supposition that skin color predetermined ability, yet these white officers were all men of their times and had great difficulty seeing clearly beyond the blinders of prejudice, no matter how hard they squinted.[12]

In this atmosphere, racial slurs that depicted aspects of the stereotypes were commonplace. In the privacy of letters or officers' tents, beyond the ears of their troops, whites frequently conveyed vulgar tales, primarily as racial wisecracks or jokes, with the physical differences between blacks and whites as the main thrust. When an Illinois sergeant decided to accept a commission in the USCT, he explained his decision to his wife and then added a brief note to his young daughter, "Zetty   What do you say to it. Aint you afraid your pa will get black[?]" A lieutenant colonel lectured his daughter through his wife, "Tell her She must not *Paut* [pout] about it or She will get the *Swell* lip and be an out right Darky to all intents and purposes Except collor." He also claimed she had "Caught the *Negro heel*" when she visited his command the previous summer. Even bright and sympathetic individuals could not refrain from taking a poke at the black race. "I am tanned up as black as a mullatto," an officer wrote home. "It may be that I have been with a colored Regt so long that I am undergoing a metamorphosis. I expect every day when my hair will curl & heels elongate."[13]

In spite of all this prejudice, most white officers were optimistic about the prospects of blacks as soldiers. A surgeon who claimed not to go into "enthusiastics" on the subject insisted that "to talk of them as being equal to white troops is, it seems to me, to talk in the veinest nonsense," but he was an anomaly. After just a few days nearly all the officers were excited over the progress and promise of their troops. "I would rather have command of negro troops, with the same opportunities of improving themselves in drill, and discipline, than of the ordinary white recruits one gets," a captain stated for the record. An inspector noted that "the white officers are enthusiasts and think they would rather drill & discipline black men than white," and a year later a lieutenant in the USCT told his brother that his men would "make splendid machines." The reason for such zeal among the officer corps, as Maj. George Stearns explained to the American Freedmen's Inquiry Commission, was the general attitude of the black troops: "The negro gives his whole attention to the work, and takes pride in it." Moreover, blacks realized that nearly all their officers knew about soldiering from personal experience, and they accepted their officers' instructions much more readily than did white soldiers. As one officer noted, white troops regarded their officers more as "accidental Superiors" and challenged them frequently, whereas black troops were much more willing to admit they knew very little and that their officers were there for a purpose—to impart knowledge and lead the black men. While officers in white volunteer units had to supervise friends and neighbors, some of whom they may have known all their lives, "Officers of the colored troops will not have to contend against this disadvantage of a previous social equality with their men," no mean advantage, argued a colonel in a manual for officers in the USCT.[14]

In return, black soldiers demonstrated considerable affection for their officers. According to Colonel Higginson, "They attach themselves to every officer who deserved love, and to some who did not." Despite hostility to whites on the part of many black soldiers as a result of enslavement in the South and discrimination in the North, they proved surprisingly capable of putting that behind them and working with these whites for a greater goal—freedom and equality for all, regardless of race. Troops in the USCT, particularly freedmen, needed the guidance of their officers in both military and nonmilitary affairs, and in response they expressed genuine fondness for all officers who willingly helped and treated them with dignity and respect.[15]

Unfortunately, in a world filled with prejudice, and with black soldiers so dependent on their officers to perform various services and assist them in the transition from slavery to freedom, the temptation for white officers to violate that trust and take advantage of black soldiers was powerful. Living from one day to the next beyond the bounds of normal society, with death and destruction everywhere, and enduring hardship and making sacrifices on a daily basis, many soldiers, including some officers in the USCT, committed acts during their military careers that under normal circumstances would have been unfathomable. Yet in the case of the white officers there was more to it than that. Those officers who commanded freedmen worked with individuals who, to a considerable extent, were naïve about the ways of both the military world and free society. Many of the black soldiers had no alternative but to trust their officers in a wide range of matters. Unscrupulous whites, who either had criminal minds or foolishly confused inexperience with stupidity, utilized that trust for personal gain, usually to misappropriate funds from black troops in all sorts of ways, in hopes that the same naïveté that granted them access to the money would also enable them to get away with their crimes undetected.[16]

Without doubt, the most common offenses were defrauding the troops or embezzling their funds. Payday in the army was unreliable, so that when it arrived, troops frequently received anywhere from three to twelve months' pay, a fairly sizable lump sum even on a private's salary. Northern blacks, like their white counterparts, sent most of their money home to family members for support or to save for postwar life. Freedmen, however, had difficulty sending money by reliable means to family members, and banks in the Southern states were seldom trustworthy. Rather than hold it themselves, the men's common practice was to give it to their officers for safekeeping. Honest officers, who constituted the bulk of those in the USCT, provided their men with receipts and held the money or sent it to Northern banks, where the money drew interest. Dishonest officers invested the money for personal profit, borrowed from the fund without permission, or simply stole it outright. Others purchased items such as watches at a discount and tried to give them to the soldiers in lieu of money. To the good fortune of the black soldiers, most of them were shrewd enough to recognize the deceit and protect their earnings. A captain in the 9th U.S. Colored Infantry held money for twenty-five troops and attempted to resign by bypassing regimental authorities and fleeing with the money. Fortunately for the troops, he got caught. In the 2nd U.S. Colored Infantry, the troops gave a lieutenant two thousand dollars before a battle to hold for them. Instead, he attempted to leave the service with the money, and the regimental commander had the War Department withhold his discharge until the lieutenant returned the money.[17]

Eventually, to prevent such crimes, most units forbade all officers except one specifically designated for that purpose—usually the chaplain—from holding the money of the men, or they had headquarters supervise the process. These efforts were only partially successful, and in another case the head of the Bureau of Colored Troops, Major Foster, had to mark the amount of money officers owed their troops on muster and pay rolls. Foster then refused to pay the officers until they cleared their debts with the men.[18]

Regardless of the steps taken to prevent fraud and embezzlement, a few officers slipped away with substantial amounts of money. A lieutenant in a black artillery battery deserted after the war with $1,600, a tidy sum. In the 54th U.S. Colored Infantry a captain collected over $2,000 from his men and refused to return it. When the regimental commander had him arrested, the captain deserted with the funds. Attempts to apprehend both of these officers were unsuccessful, and those least able to endure the loss, the black troops, were out of the money.[19]

In other instances white officers did not rob or steal from their men; they merely abused their authority, solely because in their eyes black soldiers did not merit proper respect. A drunken lieutenant from a black artillery battery disturbed the peace, and a black corporal on guard duty arrested him. During the hubbub another lieutenant came to his comrade's rescue, drew his saber, and threatened to murder the corporal. Both officers received dishonorable dismissals. In a comparable incident, a captain in the USCT tried to sneak out of camp without proper authorization. When the guard refused to let him pass, the captain threatened to "shoot you, you damned nigger, you." The corporal forcefully responded that he was not a "nigger" but "a Federal soldier and wear the Federal uniform. I have taken the same oath that you have," he insisted. Again, a general court-martial dismissed the captain from the service. In both cases courts vindicated the conduct of black troops and penalized officers for failure to regard their men as soldiers in the U.S. Army, but these punishments failed to address the underlying cause—race prejudice.[20]

As a result, similar abuses frequently went unchecked. After seeing his colonel mistreat black soldiers for some time, an officer in the USCT concluded he was "a genuine pro slavery cotton hearted negro hater," and four months later he heard the colonel say, "the negro has no rights that white men are bound to respect." Such attitudes inevitably led to abuses by subordinate officers as well. And when officers did not commit such overt transgressions of military law or their soldiers never brought them up on charges, the end result was that some despicable characters remained in the service, harassing and abusing their troops at every turn. Such was an officer in the 29th Connecticut (Colored) Infantry, whose misbehavior toward his black troops prompted a black sergeant to write that the captain "ought to have been with the Greys instead of the Blues, he had so little use for the Colored troops."[21]

Disrespect for the authority and status of blacks as soldiers of the United States spilled over into personal lives, as numerous officers made outrageous charges against the wives and girlfriends of troops. A handful of officers treated black women with a modicum of dignity, and several even sent the wives and children of trusted troops to their own families in the North for safety and employment, but most officers viewed black women with the same prejudiced eye they cast on their black soldiers. Many white officers believed that because blacks were an inferior species between white men and animals, their moral conduct was substandard. Blacks lacked the self-discipline to control their sexual appetites, and their inadequate social development resulted in more loosely structured sexual relationships, or as one officer termed it, "peculiarly elastic notions of matrimony." On the Red River Campaign in 1864, black soldiers illegally concealed as many slaves, primarily women and children,

as possible on wagons to smuggle them back to freedom, and twice
their white officers searched the wagons and cleared them of the
stowaways. In fact, although white officers assumed the motives
were purely sexual, many of the slaves were family members of these
black troops. Had the wagon drivers been white, and the refugees
white women and children, no one would have made similar
assumptions.[22]

Naturally, these white males attributed virtually all this sexual
vivacity to black women, in part because of their role in Southern
society, and also because—by assigning qualities of passion and
lasciviousness to these women—they absolved themselves psychologically of their own occasional indiscretions. A surgeon expressed
his doubts about the fidelity of black women when a soldier who
worked for him was arrested for robbing the sutler. "In the mean
time," he wrote his own wife, "his young wife weeps for him—and
before his release will, probably, seek consolation with another husband." The assumption was that black women lacked even the rudi-
ments of morality, and males were little better. The commander of
Camp William Penn charged that many of the black women who
were working for officers as cooks and laundresses were of "immoral
character" and required them to furnish headquarters with "satisfactory certificates of respectability before they can be so employed."
Such a regulation concerning white women would have caused a
scandal. Even more enlightening, the order failed to address the
conduct of the officers, as if they were not culpable for their sexual
encounters.[23]

Because white officers were dealing with black women, they felt
free to take liberties that neither society nor their consciences would
have permitted had the women been white. At Fort Jackson, Louisiana, a number of officers committed repeated offenses against black
laundresses. During the trial of one of the lieutenants, whom authorities charged for his indiscreet acts, a laundress testified that he
had only felt her breasts once; otherwise, he "is a very nice young
man, he would not carry on like the rest of the officers, only laugh
sometimes." While the other officers taunted the women in vulgar
language, she "never heard him talk blackguard talk." Another laundress, however, claimed she overheard the lieutenant boast that
he had slept with every woman in the laundresses' houses. The
ringleader of the band of white officers was a captain who on one
occasion made obscene gestures to a laundress. Whenever any of
the whites served as officer of the day, all four of them forced their
way into the laundresses' houses under the ruse of searching for
enlisted men. They knew that in the hot months in Louisiana these
women slept naked and would have to get out of bed to open the

door, exposing themselves. Fed up with these intrusions, one night several women refused to open the door and the captain broke it down. A laundress then cursed at the captain, who in turn hit her with his sword scabbard and called her a bitch for having the whole regiment in her house. The laundress retorted that if she was a bitch, he was "a damned son of a bitch." A search of the premises uncovered no one. At the trials of these officers, they testified for one another, and the court decided the word of officers in the U.S. Army was superior to that of several black laundresses.[24]

In an even more bizarre episode, a captain entered the quarters of a married black enlisted man and had sex with a young black woman who boarded with the family. When military authorities caught him in the act and ordered him out, the captain yelled back, "You God damned sons of bitches, You God-damned whore house pimps." In his own defense, the captain argued that he could not resist the natural sexual enticements of the young black woman: "I have only obeyed naturs first law; and I hold, and do aske every member of the event if naturs law does not hold precedence to any law which man may promulgate." He then went on, "I do further hold gentlemen, that intercourse with the opposite sex is absolutely necessary to the preservation of perfect health." The judge advocate refuted his arguments and concluded by saying, "If it was absolutely necessary, as the accused asserts, for the preservation of his health, that he should be allowed promiscuous co-habitation, I present to the Court as my opinion, that outside the limits of the Camp is the best place for it to take place."[25]

Such callous treatment of black women did not pass unnoticed by the troops. One soldier in the 3rd U.S. Colored Infantry found these practices so appalling that he filed his complaint in print. "We have a set of officers here," he announced, "who apparently think that their commissions are licenses to debauch and mingle with deluded freedwomen, under cover of darkness." The conduct of these officers was so reprehensible that he insisted "their very presence amongst us is loathsome in the extreme."[26]

Amid all the prejudice, a number of black soldiers did not help matters by fulfilling the racist expectations of some of their white officers. Foolish displays of anger or misconduct—such as a private who erupted at his sergeant and threatened, in front of the regiment, to kill him over a trivial affair, or a black soldier who chopped off three fingers of another black infantryman in a dispute over a stick while collecting firewood—confirmed or augmented the racial stereotypes. Worse yet were three gang rapes that black soldiers committed against white Southern women, one of whom was only thirteen years old. In each case the victims and military personnel provided irrefutable evidence of the guilt of the men. Even though black troops had no monopoly on such misbehavior or brutality, in the eyes of many white officers, when whites committed such acts they were the acts of criminals, and when black soldiers did so, they were characteristic of the race. Moreover, the way blacks dealt with one another had an influence on their white officers. It was difficult, for example, to prevent whites from using the scurrilous expression *nigger* when blacks used it among themselves. To check the annoying practice, Colonel Higginson insisted that officers and noncommissioned officers refer to everyone by rank, but he was one of the few senior officers who was sensitive to such matters.[27]

Nor did black soldiers stand by unfeelingly in the face of such prejudice against them. They bitterly resented racial mistreatment and in fact had their own grounds for prejudice against whites. Northern whites did not have a good track record in dealing with either Northern or Southern blacks. They had discriminated against free blacks in the North, and it took a few years of violence and the deaths of hundreds of thousands of Americans for them to accept the policy of abolitionism. Whereas black soldiers enlisted for honorable reasons, they correctly argued that many white troops served purely for the money. In "Hangman Johnny," a song that black troops frequently sang, one verse began, "De buckra 'list for money," which referred to the mercenary motivations of white Union troops. In addition, whites discriminated against black troops in pay, equipment, work duties, and promotions, as well as in countless unofficial capacities, all of which blacks keenly noticed. There was a great deal of truth in Higginson's statement that "the negroes have acquired such constitutional distrust of white people, that it is perhaps as much as they can do to trust more than one person at a time." Their officers, blacks learned, were more white than Northern.[28]

Yet both the black soldiers and their white officers realized that they must set aside their differences and work together for the good of the Union and the black race. Despite their prejudiced beliefs, white officers were risking their lives and sacrificing much to command black soldiers, something the troops were fully aware of. From another standpoint, most white officers knew well that Northern and Southern society had mistreated blacks, that blacks were rightly skeptical of whites, and that they must earn the trust and respect of their black soldiers if the USCT was to accomplish anything in the war.

One of the quickest ways to gain the affection of the troops was to help them in personal matters. Invariably freedmen worried about the plight of their families, whose situations were tenuous at best. As a chaplain reported, "Our soldiers suffer considerable in mind on account of the unsettled condition of their families, many of whom are without homes or shelter and no one to care for them, scattered here and there and it does seem without any rights a white man is bound to respect." Family members complained that Southern whites destroyed the mail from soldiers and forced them to live elsewhere because the husband had enlisted. In one instance an officer learned that a soldier's former owner turned his wife and baby out of the home and took their twelve- and fourteen-year-olds to another state. At the time the soldier was in Virginia, his wife and baby were in Kentucky, and the owner and their two children were somewhere in Missouri. In most cases there was little officers could do directly, except complain within military channels, but their black troops appreciated any sort of help, and occasionally officers were able to remedy the situation. In Virginia a regimental adjutant wrote to the superintendent of Negroes to see that Pvt. Decatur King's wife received rations, even though she insisted on living in her own home rather than on the farm that the Treasury Department had seized and was operating. Another time, regimental officers got Brig. Gen. James Brisbin to intervene on behalf of two of their soldiers, whose master would let the wives leave to be with their husbands, but not with any clothing. To oversee the families of soldiers and to ensure proper treatment, several regiments formed registries of families that included addresses, regular reports on their condition, and where the men could send money to provide for them on paydays.[29]

Nearly all the white officers had had ample military experience before they entered the USCT, and they recognized the significant role played by family matters in soldiers' performance. They had seen the effects of personal hardships on friends or themselves, and they knew that no one could expect men to concentrate effectively when they were worrying about the welfare of their loved ones. No one was immune from such difficulties. Thus, while a black soldier endured the distress of his wife leaving him for another man, an officer shouldered the burden of his command and at the same time tried to scold his own father into abandoning his mistress and returning to his wife. By transcending the bounds of race and military structure, such misfortunes brought officers and men to-gether in ways they had never known before and helped to humanize the relationship between them.[30]

Moreover, specific deeds for the benefit of blacks earned officers lasting respect from their soldiers. A captain who rescued two run-away slaves in the face of nearly two dozen Confederates won the admiration of everyone in his regiment. Other officers, though, learned that less-heroic acts proved equally effective. After a young black woman fed a lieutenant and some of his men, she confided her desire to escape slavery. The lieutenant and men dressed her in a Union uniform and had her march, rifle in hand, alongside the troops aboard the transport ship to freedom. A lieutenant in the 115th U.S. Colored Infantry hired a young runaway black as his servant. Over the months they became fond of one another, and when the owner reclaimed the lad, the lieutenant successfully arranged for friends to smuggle his servant across the Ohio River and meet him in Virginia, where the War Department was transferring his regiment. On still another occasion, en route back from a recruiting campaign, a chaplain on horseback helped a black woman by carrying her child in his arms. The troops responded ecstatically. "I suppose it was the first time some of them ever saw a similar act of kindness performed by a white man for a colored child," the chaplain reasoned.[31]

Usually these were acts of little consequence that merely demonstrated to the troops that their officers cared about their well-being. When a trusted sergeant wrote a major that "I have bin so unfornate to luse the Site of one of my eyes and the other is a failing very fast indeed" and the surgeon "serve me no satisfaction whatever," the major got him sick leave. During a march on the second day with his company, a young lieutenant made a tremendous impression on the men when he carried the rifle of an exhausted private. "The looks of approval amply repaid me," he wrote later.[32]

One of the best ways to win over the troops was to provide them with little necessities that black soldiers had trouble obtaining for themselves. Each company had a fund derived from fines and a tax on the sutler to acquire many of these minor items that made a soldier's life easier, such as small sewing kits called housewives, or two-fingered mittens to keep hands warm yet enable them to fire their rifles, but they were not always available to troops in the South. White soldiers and Northern blacks usually had families on which they could depend to supply them with these things, but freedmen, whose families had neither the money nor access to such items, had no means of obtaining them. Into the void stepped numerous officers, who put friends and family members to work securing these little conveniences. Sometimes they paid for the items, and other times the officers looked for charity, as did a lieutenant who asked his brother, "Do you think that any sewing society in Newburyport would be abolitionists enough to make 50 to 100 pairs for colored soldiers[?]" He explained that his troops had received no pay for five months and even if they had the money, the mittens were not for sale on post. He then concluded with flawless logic, tinged with a bit of sarcasm: "I think that the colored soldiers deserve them as much as white soldiers as they are fighting for the same cause and as Newburyport raised so much money to buy colored recruits to prevent a draft they ought to do as much for the colored soldiers as they have done for the white ones and send them 'house-wives' and mittens." [33]

Because few white soldiers had to endure the day-to-day anxieties borne by black troops, particularly freedmen with families, the interdependence between black soldiers and white officers was unusually strong, and white officers had to cope with problems that officers in white volunteer units never even contemplated. With virtually no experience in dealing with the sundry problems that arose in the transition from slavery to freedom, black soldiers had no alternative but to turn to one another or their officers for help. Under those circumstances, and in the face of various other obstacles such as prejudice against the USCT, some white officers found the burden of command too taxing. A small number whose desire to be an officer outweighed the responsibilities of such commands, retained their commissions yet did little for the men. An officer in the 49th U.S. Colored Infantry, for example, did not know the names of half his company after twelve months with the men, and according to an old friend, "He has never showed any interest in the wellfare of the men in his Company." Another officer, a lieutenant in the 39th U.S. Colored Infantry, admitted his lack of interest in his men when he wrote, "I never had any faculty to distinguish one of those colored fellows from another." [34]

For most of these whites, however, the sense of dissatisfaction with service in the USCT eventually became intolerable. A captain resigned because "I am dissatisfied with the (Col'd) service, and while I feel it my duty to serve my Country, I feel it is my right to choose in what branch I serve," and an assistant surgeon sought a transfer because the other officers "out do me Entirely in 'Negro Worship.'" In the midst of such difficult command duties, the work frequently compelled officers to examine themselves and their motivations for service with black troops and to make difficult decisions. As an endorsement to the letter of resignation of a lieutenant, his commander wrote, "He has indeed gained that difficult knowledge, the knowledge of himself; and being of his opinion and believing also that his heart is not with the service, I would consider his discharge as a removal of a bad example to my command." [35]

For others, the early experiences of command in the USCT served to solidify their commitment to black units. A captain entered his assignment with the vow, "I do not intend to be and do not think I am prejudiced. I intend to study and judge them fairly." One month later, he told his wife, "A great many have the idea that the entire

negro race are vastly their inferiors—a few weeks of calm unpreju-
diced life here would disabuse them I think—I have a more elevated
opinion of their abilities than I ever had before. I *know* that many
of them are vastly the *superiors* of those (many of those) who would
condemn them all to a life of brutal degradation." After a scant
few weeks, a surgeon wrote, "I am steadily becoming acquainted
with very remarkable men whose lives in slavery and whose heroism
in getting out of it, deepens my faith in negro character and intellect."
Although a bit crudely, a captain contended, "As one is with them
he gets to liking them more & more & he begins to think as they
say some times round here, a white man is most as good as a nigger."
These whites immediately began to take pride in their commands
and defended their choice and work vociferously.[36]

Over time, strong relationships developed between black soldiers
and white officers. When Capt. Lewis Weld returned to his company
after four months of provost duty, the men responded with calls,
"We'll stand by you Cap'en," "You Know your old boys, Cap'en,"
and "We'se glad to get you back again Cap'en," and gave him three
hearty cheers. Such a warm welcome instilled Weld with a tremendous sense of satisfaction in his labors. In other instances, officers
and men established deep personal friendships. A Northern black,
who left his 55th Massachusetts (Colored) Infantry to help raise
and serve as a noncommissioned officer in a regiment of freedmen,
regretted leaving his former commander, Col. Alfred S. Hartwell.
In a letter to a white friend, the sergeant wrote, "he is the best
friend i hav this side of home but i was a fool and a big fool but
this will giv me sense." Even more revealing was the letter of condo-
lence a black private penned to the wife of his deceased commander:

> Allow me to say, that although a Colored man, a private in the
> 29th, I found in Colonel Bross a friend, one in whom every member
> of the regiment placed the utmost confidence, for, and with whom,
> each one would help defend the country to the end. . . . He was
> loved by every one, because he was a friend to every one. . . .
> Weep not for him who was one of God's chosen ones, who tried
> to deliver his people out of Egypt.[37]

One of the great lessons Colonel Higginson learned from his experience with the 33rd U.S. Colored Infantry was that "We abolitionists
had underrated the suffering produced by slavery among the negroes,
but had overrated the demoralization." Both Northern and Southern
blacks had very powerful images of the rights, privileges, and responsibilities of freedom, and they entered military service firmly committed to achieving them. They had great hopes that their white officers
would prove different from the bulk of the Northerners, that their

superiors in rank would fight alongside them to gain freedom and equality for all. The prejudice they encountered within the USCT was disillusioning, but by no means did it cause irreparable damage. Most of the white officers demonstrated enough compassion and commitment to the needs of the troops to win their confidence and support.[38]

From the standpoint of the white officers, they entered positions of command with a wide array of preconceptions about blacks, based predominantly on readings and gossip and strikingly similar to those held by Southerners, but through actual service alongside black troops many of them were able to shed much of their prejudice. Concomitantly, their optimism about the ability of blacks to become good soldiers increased. As one chaplain in the USCT predicted to the father of two officers of black troops, "The blacks will prove to be the best of soldiers—They very naturally feel elevated in their position—Know that the fight is largely on their account—and have naturally an irrepressible enmity to the 'Secesh.'" Providing they were able to maintain control of their black troops at all times, most white officers learned to feel very comfortable about service in the USCT. And as long as these white officers maintained their commitment to the eradication of slavery and the uplifting of the black race, they retained the respect and cooperation of their men.[39]

6

Training and Discipline

*I*n Civil War armies, training and discipline worked hand in hand. Nearly all fighting took place within viewing range, and in the face of such harrowing scenes it required the utmost discipline and control to keep troops at their positions. They fought in compact formations, in part a throwback to the days of inaccurate muskets when bayonet assaults were highly effective, but also because communication within units was difficult and closely packed men improved commanders' ability to maneuver their troops. Amid the clouds of smoke, deafening noise, and ghastly injuries of battle, soldiers had to be able to perform tactical maneuvers on order with speed and precision, and only through constant training did they learn to execute them properly. Such regimentation through both drill and discipline also fostered the concept of teamwork and bonded soldiers to one another, which in turn improved their battlefield performance by reassuring individual soldiers that they could depend on their comrades.

If USCT officers had one great asset, it was that most of them had previous military experience. Nearly all of it, however, was on the enlisted level. For the bulk of them, service as officers was an entirely new endeavor. In the enlisted ranks they had had an opportunity to observe good and bad officers and had determined certain qualities that were essential for effective command; nevertheless, their perspective was always from the soldier's point of view. Once they sewed officers' insignia on their shoulders, they began to see things differently. A lieutenant described the transition by writing,

"I threw off the dare-devil boy and took on the man." Another officer, who had suffered three wounds in a white regiment and seldom saw action in the USCT, also considered the change dramatic: "Scouting and fighting in the ranks had given place, under a commission, to solving problems of organization, care, drill, discipline and education of ignorant men, to be followed later by control and government of hostile communities." Promotion to the officer corps brought with it responsibilities that few of them had ever known before the war. As a lieutenant wrote to his sister, "One little knows the real work to be done in a company until he has tried the Organization of one." Duty as officers was a strange new world where performance was the only standard of evaluation, so a young man who had just earned a promotion to regimental commander commented: "I sometimes have my misgivings when I think that in military affairs success is the only criterion of worth, & mistakes, or failure in any degree is irretrievable condemnation. However, I ask no allowances, the damnation of failure shall be as completely my own, as might be the approbation for any success." [1]

Unlike their counterparts in most units raised early in the war, these officers did not have the luxury of months and months to teach all the duties and tactical formations. It was imperative that they concentrate on essential skills—those that could make the difference between death and survival—and fill in the others at a later date. Even with this approach, they invariably barraged troops with vast quantities of information and duties, and only through repetition and the vigilance of officers were the soldiers able to master everything that was critical for wartime.

With success or failure resting on their shoulders, the white officers tackled the problem of preparing their men for combat. Both officers and enlisted men in the USCT believed that only on the battlefield could they win the respect of white volunteers, and the best means to prepare for that moment was to drill the troops. This enabled the black units to learn the various tactical maneuvers and formations that were essential for combat, and it also imbued soldiers with a sense of confidence in themselves and their comrades that helped them cope with the ordeal of battle. According to the colonel of an excellent black regiment, "I knew that nothing but drill, discipline, and more drill, would fit the regiment for the field in such condition as to give every officer and soldier absolute confidence in the ability of the regiment to take care of itself under any and all circumstances." [2]

Although officers agreed on the importance of training their troops, their views on how that task should be accomplished varied considerably. At the core of the debate were their impressions of the black soldiers. Those who had high regard for blacks treated them like men, developed them as soldiers, and eventually were able to delegate sundry responsibilities to them, whereas those who believed in racial stereotypes, such as that blacks were childlike and ignorant, had limited expectations of their men and received little in return.

All officers had to devote considerable time to the training of their troops, but some who saw in black soldiers tremendous promise went above and beyond that. Rather than attempt to carry responsibility for everything on their shoulders, to oversee all aspects of military duty within their commands, these officers sought black soldiers whom they could train to perform a variety of supervisory functions, as did noncommissioned officers in white units. They worked with these men, taught them tactics, regulations, and in many cases reading and writing, so that they were capable of fulfilling all the duties of noncommissioned officers. Officers placed their confidence in these men, and they in turn felt an obligation to fulfill their roles and assignments satisfactorily.[3]

Commands raised in the North had an immense advantage over units with Southern blacks, because of the reading and writing skills of the men. Civil War armies ran on paperwork, and without literate troops the burden of this labor rested with the officers. It took one officer four days of constant work, from rising in the morning until bedtime, to prepare all the muster rolls and returns of clothing and camp and garrison equipage for his company, and he had to perform this work every three months. Along with the day-to-day paperwork, this was a heavy load. Training an enlisted man to do this work freed an officer to devote more time to the men. Equally important, it spread responsibility for critical jobs to a few black troops and gave everyone a sense of satisfaction that black soldiers were contributing substantially to the development and administration of the unit.[4]

Officers who recognized black soldiers' potential for development frequently adopted a more positive and progressive training program than did their peers. Instead of berating troops and punishing them vigorously for minor errors, they were much more willing to work with the men to overcome difficult aspects of soldiering and to use incentives to promote achievement. While some officers doled out sets of sergeant's and corporal's stripes immediately, others withheld them to award at a later date to men who merited the positions. As a lieutenant announced to his family, "I have the honor and pleasure of appointing my non-commissioned officers and of giving them their stripes   I tell you they feel proud of it." Incentives, these officers learned, spurred efficiency better than any other means of training. At Camp William Penn, a rendezvous site for Northern black units, standing policy was that as men completed guard duty they were to discharge their loads at a target. The best shot won a forty-eight-hour pass, and any soldier whose gun did not discharge because it was dirty had four more hours of guard duty. An even better incentive was the one instituted by Lt. Col. Robert Cowden. Each month his regiment had a drill competition, judged by impartial officers, and the winning company received a rosette that its members wore on the left breast of their dress-parade jacket. Although the award was trifling, it became a badge of honor for the troops, and it brought out the best in the men. Cowden's contest promoted the concept of teamwork and fostered esprit de corps within companies.[5]

On the other hand, many officers had little confidence in the potential development of their black soldiers. With small hope of progress, their entire approach frequently fostered a self-fulfilling prophecy. They treated their men like children, and the troops responded accordingly. Black soldiers in their commands did the work sloppily, failed to listen to instructions, and for the most part made life miserable for their officers. In return, such behavior vindicated the prejudices of these officers, and they began to view their jobs more as those of baby-sitters than of commanders in the U.S. Army. While troops became lethargic, officers grew more and more frustrated until command became a constant chore and at times a hellish experience. Repeated bad performance on review drove one disillusioned captain to complain, "It seems very hard to make anything of these men, I am about discouraged." The difficulty of teaching troops how to fire weapons caused a lieutenant to lose his temper, call one soldier "a wooly headed nincompoop, aim his gun correctly for him again, and tell him if he did not do it right the next time I would kill him." For another officer the frustration became so intense that he was "ready to quit the business of teaching 'Unbleached Americans.'" He then concluded, "I would rather swing a scythe all day than to endeavor to teach a squad of recruits any of the motions of the Manual of arms." Fortunately he remained in the USCT and became a fine officer, but many others found the work intolerable and damaged the morale of the men.[6]

Often these officers had an unenlightened approach to command. There were no incentives or rewards for achievement, just punishment for mistakes. Rather than instruct the men patiently, "They strike the men with their swords and jog and punch them in their side to show them how to drill," complained a private in the 43rd U.S. Colored Infantry. They found noncommissioned officers through trial and error, yet they made little effort to work with their appointees. In one month the 65th U.S. Colored Infantry reduced thirty-two noncommissioned officers to the ranks and filled their slots with new men. Worse conditions, though, prevailed in the 45th U.S. Colored Infantry. In late September 1864, promotions and demotions affected thirty-three soldiers, and twenty-one more within the next six weeks. Matters reached such a point that regimental headquarters had to warn company commanders, "It is detrimental to the good discipline of the service to reduce non com officers with the same facility with which a guard detail is named in a company." He then warned that if other companies did as Company B, it would not be long before every member of that unit at one time held the rank of sergeant or corporal twice! The regimental commander then urged all company commanders "to test the qualities of each man before promotion, that none may be made hastily." Nevertheless, this warning did not prevent officers from awarding fifty-six promotions on a single day in March 1865, with an almost corresponding number of official reductions. Such wholesale replacements created instability within units and wreaked havoc with the morale of the troops.[7]

To help simplify the training of black soldiers, Maj. Gen. Silas Casey, head of the examining board in Washington, D.C., and the author of the infantry tactics manual, prepared a new version specifically for the USCT. Despite Casey's good intentions, the entire notion was absurd and demeaning. Casey's goal was to make infantry tactics as elementary as possible to aid black troops in mastering them. "The tactics are about as simple as they can be made now and require but little intelligence in the individual in the ranks," Casey wrote of his new manual for black troops. "I dont see how they can be simplified more without destroying the efficiency of the system." The problems, however, were numerous. Black and white Union infantrymen were not using the same tactics manual, which could lead to a catastrophe in battle. For another, Casey had the USCT training with a more elementary manual simply because black soldiers, with presumed inferior intelligence, composed those commands. Finally, the entire effort at simplicity for the sake of black soldiers was ridiculous. Throughout its entire history, the United States Army had never prepared a tactical manual that fulfilled the needs of its enlisted men, because not enough of them were literate in English. According to the best authority, during the forty years before the war, between one-third and one-fourth of enlisted men were incapable of signing their own names on enlistment papers. In addition, during the 1850s a clear majority of the enlisted population were immigrants. Although many of them may have been literate, it was not in English, and in any event, they were not necessarily literate enough to comprehend a tactics manual. Though Casey's

simplified version for the USCT merely eliminated a few tactical
movements, it was not more readable. Furthermore, Regular Army
troops had to depend on their officers to teach them infantry tactics,
just as most black and many white soldiers did during the war, so
that tactical manuals were in reality issued for officers' use. The
officers of the USCT, as Casey well knew, had demonstrated their
knowledge of tactics and other subjects, including reading and writing, and were just as capable of mastering either manual and explain-
ing it cogently to their troops as any officers in the service.[8]

There were no shortcuts in drilling the troops. Soldiers learned
different tactical formations and maneuvers only through long and
arduous hours of practice. "The men are willing and easy to drill,"
a colonel authoritatively stated to Adjutant General Lorenzo Thomas,
"but only constant attendance and indefatigable energy on the part
of the officers will make these regiments do Justice to the Uniform
they wear." Officers labored with the men on the drill field hour
after hour to pound the information into their heads. Yet despite
its complex nature, most troops absorbed the training rapidly. Some
officers argued that their troops' ability in drill was innate, derived
from their love of music and dance, but more accurate was the
opinion of a lieutenant who thought black soldiers were successful
because they "pay better attention and take more pride in it than
white soldiers do." [9]

Instruction for guard duty required personalized attention, which
over the course of a few weeks became extremely tedious. Night
after night officers had to take a handful of new troops out to serve
as pickets and explain their duty. On picket or guard duty, their
job was to halt anyone from entering camp except those with the
proper password, which changed daily. Because many black soldiers
could not read, troops had to memorize the password, and after
several hours at their posts, especially at night, some inevitably
forgot the key words or phrase and caused a mix-up. Moreover,
many troops had difficulty staying awake during those late-night
hours, and officers had to check up on them continually to test
their vigilance. As with drill, officers met with both failure and success. A captain found one of his sergeants asleep and discharged
the soldier's weapon near his head to frighten him into performing
his duty. Another officer, however, instructed his men in the art
of guard duty, and despite their total lack of experience, "The tour
went on more satisfactorily, if any difference, than it would have
done with the more experienced soldiers." In fact, one lieutenant
thought black soldiers were more alert than white troops, because
again they took greater pride in their labors. "They are good for
pickett," he boasted, "the 'Johny's' [Confederates] will have to be
sharp to surprise them." [10]

One of the most critical areas of training, and also one of the most neglected, was firing weapons. Strangely enough, few white units devoted much time to target practice, and in black commands, because owners often prohibited bondsmen from using firearms, many of the black troops had never learned to use a musket. Thus, while most officers in white units thought they could omit this aspect of training and depend on the general familiarity with weapons in society, officers in the USCT avoided such assumptions.[11]

Though artillery shot and shells were expensive, and batteries could do little live firing, in black infantry and cavalry commands, regular target practice was rather common. Regimental commanders made a point of training the men with blanks and live cartridges as frequently as possible, and depending on their other responsibilities some worked on marksmanship four times per week. Of course, duties dictated training, but when opportunity availed itself, many officers viewed marksmanship as an integral component of their training program. During the Petersburg Campaign in Virginia in 1864, one brigade commander had all his troops fire four rounds per week at targets and directed his officers to work on marksmanship techniques off the range. The regimental commander of the 45th U.S. Colored Infantry had company commanders submit weekly reports on target practice, including the number of rounds fired per man, the distance, the ratio of hits on the target per one hundred rounds, the ratio of hits within six inches of the bull's-eye per one hundred rounds, and the three best marksmen in each company. Often commanders assigned the premier marksman among the officers to supervise the training, indicating in some small way how highly the officers valued this practice.[12]

One officer described in detail how he trained the men in his regiment to shoot. He erected a wooden target, about six feet high and twenty-two inches wide, and covered it with a sheet that had a big black bull's-eye in the middle of it. In front of the target he had the troops dig a trench deep enough to conceal a man, who was to serve as the spotter. The spotter received a stick with a flag on one end to signal a cease-fire and a disk on the other to point where the round hit. Some two hundred yards away the lieutenant set up a tripod of sticks, supported by a sack filled with dirt. He went through training individually, resting each soldier's rifle on the sack and tripod and sighting the target. Soldiers had to repeat the process until they understood how the sight worked, with the lieutenant frequently having to aim at the target several times before troops mastered the technique. Troops then loaded and fired. The lieutenant believed that after one week of instruction "these fellows would have been doing some very good shooting." Unfortunately, a battle interrupted their training.[13]

As evidenced by this effort to teach soldiers marksmanship, the experience of instruction in the USCT taught the lesson that a motivated officer corps went a long way, but other factors also dictated the effectiveness of the training process. For one thing, the amount of time officers had to devote to training was extremely important, particularly in the USCT. Superior officers assigned black units to an inordinate amount of fatigue labor, which drastically reduced officers' ability to train their men. With evident disgust, a major whose first assignment with his new regiment was to dig trenches complained, "How in the name of sense we are to bring the instructions of the regiment up to what it should be, is difficult for any one but a row of incipient I.G.'s [inspectors general], to see." Unfortunately, the situation did not change much. After twenty-five of twenty-eight months in the USCT performing fatigue duty, the lack of training time was wearing down Col. Thomas Morgan: "I prefer service in the field in command of fighting men, to service in garrison in charge of laborers, as *a profession.*"[14]

Another factor that had a significant impact on training was the number of officers who were able to work with the men. Even when commands made time to instruct the troops, officers were at a premium, due to detached service and other duties and illness and death. To help provide better individualized attention, several officers sought a more favorable ratio of officers to enlisted men in black units, at least in the early stages, to train the men more rapidly. Major General Banks called for companies with fifty instead of one hundred enlisted men, so that new officers "might render wholly uninstructed troops available in the shortest possible time." These units could then serve as a cadre for regiments expanded to full strength. Brig. Gen. John P. Hawkins thought an additional lieutenant alone would make a substantial difference in the rate of training black troops, while a colonel preferred white drill sergeants, temporarily assigned for the purpose of teaching the men, as sufficient. In every case, these officers agreed that to improve the rate of training, the troops needed more individual and small-group instruction.[15]

Finally, knowledgeable officers were a key to effective training. With rare exceptions, in inspection after inspection blame for the poor condition of black units rested with the officer corps. One inspector found the 56th U.S. Colored Infantry "unsoldierlike." The regiment, he insisted, had "good material, and its bad condition is the fault of its company officers." The prognosis for the 57th U.S. Colored Infantry was almost identical. It had good troops and incompetent officers. The worst case, however, was that of the 63rd U.S. Colored Infantry. After twenty months of service, the inspector found its condition "disgraceful" and its officers and men "grossly unmilitary and ignorant of their duties." Troops on picket duty dropped their rifles to salute and the first sergeant opted to "take off his hat and making [sic] a low bow" rather than salute. Officers did not know commands and the troops did not know tactical movements. Evidently the officers had made no effort to work with the men because they knew nothing themselves.[16]

From a psychological standpoint, it was also essential that blacks have knowledgeable officers in whom they could believe. With prejudice everywhere around them, black soldiers knew how important it was that they perform all duties well and that their officers train them properly. In addition, most troops had little faith in the white race, based on their past experience. To win the confidence of the men, white officers had to prove their ability to train troops and lead them in battle. Those officers who demonstrated incompetence, no matter how supportive they were of the black race, "ain't for truss," or were not trustworthy, according to the troops.[17]

Although most officers in the USCT had passed a competency examination, too many knew nothing of military duties. They had depended on their general education to pass before the board, and when they stepped into command they had to teach themselves first, or learn by working with the men, confusing them as they confused themselves. For others, prolonged absence from duties had made them rusty in their knowledge of commands and tactical formations. To ensure that officers knew their business, numerous units instituted mandatory classes for them. They usually met from three to five times per week, with separate classes for company-grade and field officers. They had homework, usually the study of Casey's tactics manual, and classes consisted predominantly of recitation. In Nashville, however, Col. R. D. Mussey tried something different. Drawing on the Free Military School for Applicants for the Command of Colored Troops in Philadelphia, Mussey took a major step toward professional development when he opened his own school for USCT officers. He obtained the aid of experts from the various branches of service to lecture once or twice per week on topics of military importance. The lectures were open to all. Mussey also encouraged officers in the Nashville area to set up their own quiz groups to improve their military knowledge.[18]

In the end, the rate at which black troops learned the art of soldiering impressed most white officers. One captain wrote his wife, "I have been drilling mine for a few days, and they learn very fast, faster than any white men I ever saw." The reason, so explained a lieutenant, was their motivation: "New uniforms guns in their hands and the stamp of the government upon them seemed to give them self respect and consciousness of manhood and power so that the rapidity of the transformation was marvelous." Simply put, blacks learned faster than whites because they cared more about soldiering. For most whites, military service was a duty; for most blacks, it was an honor and a privilege.[19]

Training, though, was only part of the preparation for battle. Success and survival demanded that troops know how to be soldiers, how to execute various tactical maneuvers with skill and speed, but they also required discipline to utilize this knowledge. Amid the horror and confusion of combat, officers needed to have disciplined troops who remained at their positions and executed orders instead of disintegrating into a mob in the face of the enemy. And just the right amount of discipline worked wonders on troop morale. Rather than serving as a divisive element within the command, discipline helped to bond the men together because it enabled them to accomplish tasks as a team. It was the glue that held everyone in the unit together.

Yet in the black units, discipline was even more important. Deep down, most white officers were a bit uneasy about commanding black soldiers. For them it was absolutely critical that they maintain control of their troops and dominate the relationship with the men at all times. Because they perceived their black troops to lack self-discipline and to have mercurial temperaments, white officers perpetually feared that their men would cast aside all restraints and embark on a rampage, killing and destroying everything in their path. If these officers were going to work closely with black soldiers, they insisted on dominating them, keeping shackled that "latent savagery" of the black race. Under these conditions, inexperienced white officers had to forge a policy of discipline that was effective in punishing transgressors and discouraging others from undertaking such misbehavior. At the same time, they sought to control the relationship between officers and men while enhancing troops' regard for their officers and one another—a difficult but nonetheless critical proposition.[20]

In most cases, the lessons in discipline that white officers had learned in their volunteer units were inapplicable to commands in the USCT. Northern blacks, like whites, had at least a notion of military discipline and structure, whereas freedmen had no concept of army rigidity unless they had previously been camp followers. More important, in spite of prejudice, Northern blacks had tasted freedom. Many Southern blacks went directly from slavery into the USCT, and it was in this regimented environment that these black soldiers explored the limits of their newfound freedom. Just as freedmen had learned to create their own space in an oppressive atmosphere such as slavery, so they tested the boundaries of the military system, mainly by trial and error. In the course of time, these black troops learned that many of the techniques they had employed successfully in slavery were useless in the military world, while others proved even more effective than in the past. The problem was that neither the patience of the officers nor the exigencies of the war permitted blacks to feel their way through this new experience. According to a white officer, had he lived strictly by army regulations, "My time would have been mainly occupied in preferring charges against these men and getting them into a military prison, thereby depleting the ranks of the regiment equal to the number of convictions secured. It was more men we wanted; we had none to spare." Thus, white officers had to devise means of discipline that would ensure them control of their troops, prepare the men for the brutality of combat, and encourage efficiency—all without constant punishment.[21]

Of course, not all officers were sensitive to the prior experiences and current motivations of their black soldiers. Some white officers reacted harshly to the slightest transgressions, utterly convinced that only the most vigorous punishment would have the proper effect on blacks who had endured slavery. One argued, "If a man does not obey me I am at liberty to punish him as severe as I may think fit & as they have been used to very severe treatment, why any light punishment is of no account whatever." Unlike many of their fellow officers, who hoped that military experience would uplift the downtrodden race, the only goal of these sorts of officers was to exact a certain level of performance from their troops. They had little confidence in black soldiers' ability to learn right from wrong through instruction and encouragement, and instead resorted to physical pain to force compliance. To coerce their men into behaving according to their standards, even over trivial matters, such officers were quick to buck and gag soldiers—tie them up in a crouched position and leave them for several hours, which resulted in muscle cramps and almost unbearably aching joints—or tie them up by the thumbs for hours, so that only their toes touched the ground, which sometimes resulted in dislocated thumbs. As one officer stated authoritatively, "It is useless to talk about being lenient with them for if you give them an inch they will take a mile." Other officers entered the USCT with better regard for blacks, but over the course of time their patience for the work wore thin and punishments were swifter and more severe. After nine months in command one exasperated officer told his brother, "I no longer wonder slave drivers were cruel. I am. I no longer have any bowels of mercy." [22]

Such harsh treatment and petty attention to minor errors of the troops frequently irritated subordinate officers as well. The work of one overbearing superior officer had the uncanny ability of nullifying the excellent rapport that other officers had labored for months to establish. A lieutenant complained that his colonel was very disagreeable and the lieutenant colonel suffered from "an immense amount of old maid, or grannyism." Between the two of them "the patriotism of the whole regiment [is] neutralized, and the government weakened." He believed the colonel kept the regiment out of combat, "probably knowing that his own men will shoot him at their first opportunity." When another colonel mistreated his regiment and then refused to listen to the complaints of the line officers, a lieutenant wrote sarcastically that his commander "is trying his best to make an ass of himself, and he don't have to try very hard either." On still another occasion an assistant surgeon, despite retaliatory threats, intervened on behalf of a soldier whom the colonel intended to punish too harshly. This, however, was rare, as subordinates had few means of protecting their men from tyrannical superiors.[23]

Even worse were the officers who went a step beyond that and insisted that the only way to discipline the men was to instill fear in them. It was fairly common practice to humiliate criminals by parading them before their comrades with placards stating the offenses they had perpetrated, or to line up troops to observe executions, in the hope that such awful scenes would discourage others from committing serious crimes. Nevertheless, some officers were so terrified by the thought of losing control of their black troops that they made it their express policy to frighten them into proper conduct. One officer informed a superior that his troops knew he would shoot every one of them to maintain discipline. "It is only fear," he explained, "which will keep this class of men in their place, and make good soldiers, and the moment they find an officer is afraid of them they will overrun him and put him down."[24]

No doubt, excessive leniency did undercut discipline, as some USCT commanders learned to their own regret, but many officers discovered that compassion blended with firmness was the best means of disciplining black troops. There was a difference, these officers realized, between harsh and effective discipline. By resorting to severe punishment for any misconduct, a number of officers compelled the troops to behave as they wanted, but they also erected a barrier between themselves and the men that inhibited their ability to command well. Effective leadership demanded good communications between officers and enlisted men, and martinets usually alienated their troops. After the war, Colonel Higginson recalled, "Inexperienced officers often assumed that, because these men had been slaves before enlistment, they would bear to be treated as such afterwards. Experience proved to the contrary. The more strongly we marked the difference between the slave and the soldier, the better for the regiment." Any punishment resembling that meted out by overseers caused irreparable damage to morale. And the same was true for blacks from free states. They, too, had suffered from unfair treatment, albeit not so brutal, and while they understood the importance of discipline in the military, they were also very sensitive to mistreatment.[25]

Above all, both Northern and Southern blacks respected officers who were just. "I find no harm in being mild," wrote one fine young officer to his mother, "if I am at the same time firm. My men will like me much better for it. But they find me stern and unyielding when obedience and military discipline is required." A black corporal corroborated this belief. He boasted that his colonel "has three noble traits as a commander, justice, humanity and firmness in all his orders to both officers and men." Officers who insisted that their soldiers must first develop a sense of self-respect, and then pride in the unit, proved extraordinarily successful in maintaining effective discipline, because the troops did not want to disappoint commanders who were fair. "As soon as they find they are not to be circumvented or cheated, and treated like dogs, their grateful hearts respond by words and acts," a captain declared.[26]

Over time, most white officers realized that punishment, regardless of the severity, was only a partial deterrent. Additional means were readily available to help them maintain effective discipline and prevent troops from committing infractions.

One sensible approach was for white officers to explain to their troops what illegal acts were and what punishments they warranted. According to army regulations, officers were supposed to read the Articles of War twice a year, but many commanders never did it while others merely paid lip service to the requirement, without any concern for the troops' comprehension. The Articles of War was a lengthy list of offenses and possible punishments (twenty-one pages' worth in *The Regulations for the Army of the United States*), and no soldier was going to understand them while standing for hours in the hot sun of summer or the cold of winter as an officer plowed through article after article in a monotone. Moreover, because of the inadequate reading skills of most black soldiers, this was not something they could study in their spare moments. Only through more regular readings, thorough explanations, and insistence that all officers follow regulations to ensure that troops consistently received their rights could officers properly disseminate the information among the men. Black troops regarded this as one of the fundamental differences between discipline in slavery and the military. "Our old masters would get angry with us and sometimes punish us almost to death, and we not understand why," said a private in a black infantry regiment. "But here if we are punished, we know why for the officers tell us our duty and never punish us unless we disobey." [27]

Even better were officers who announced specific punishments for crimes of a more minor nature. An artillery battery commander, for example, established specific punishments for minor crimes, had them read to the men often, and posted them for all to see and understand. A soldier who left camp at night without authorization would be bucked and gagged for two hours, and anyone who talked back to a guard had to stand on a barrel for one day. Thus, before a soldier committed an offense, he knew exactly what the consequences of his action would be. Repeat offenders suffered expanded sentences, which the commander also clearly stated. The result was a diminution of both petty and serious offenses, according to the captain. [28]

A second step was to insist that all white officers had to serve as role models for their troops. It was absurd to expect black soldiers to accept discipline when their white officers lived according to lesser standards. In many instances where discipline broke down within black commands, the white officers had perpetrated a wide assortment of offenses. The 38th U.S. Colored Infantry, for example, suffered a total collapse of discipline as the result of crimes committed by dozens of its officers. The lieutenant colonel withheld bounty payments for some troops and exacted loans from incoming subordinate officers, who in turn pressured enlisted men to lend them money. Other officers undertook a variety of enterprises, such as watch repair and the sale of tobacco, to make money off their troops at exorbitant rates. To rectify matters, the War Department had to dismiss several officers and bring in a new commander. Nevertheless, it took months to get the regiment in order. [29]

Another practical policy was proper enforcement of regulations for both enlisted men and officers. Whether from the North or South, blacks had always suffered from double standards, and in the service whites were again in positions of authority. To ease tension and improve discipline among black soldiers, it was imperative that the same code of behavior apply to blacks and whites and that violators suffer punishments. According to a lieutenant, the salutary effect of cashiering an officer, tearing off his shoulder straps and buttons with several black regiments bearing witness, was tremendous. Everyone who viewed such an event realized that officers as well as enlisted men were culpable for their misconduct. [30]

Those officers who structured the day with worthwhile duties and properly supervised their men discovered that they had far fewer disciplinary problems. A colonel explained, "If men see that they are watched and kept to their duty, punishment will rarely be necessary." Most offenses, he insisted, were the result of officers' negligence: "It is the officer's duty to prevent the possibility of such misdemeanors by never allowing smaller ones to go unchecked." The problem was that a few careless officers, or a depleted number as a result of detached duty or illness, made such oversight difficult. Commands with well-trained sergeants and corporals were able to offset the shortage by laying considerable responsibility on their shoulders and having them supervise duties, but too many officers never worked with their noncommissioned staff and therefore could not depend on them.[31]

Finally, when officers punished troops, they had to act promptly and without passion or vindictiveness. For one thing, it was important that officers warn transgressors and their comrades that all such violations would merit similar penalties. As a regimental commander elaborated to his officers, "Men must be made to feel that it is law and orders that have been violated when an offense is brought to punishment, not merely the directions of the individual officer." For another reason, dispassioned assessment of penalties helped to reduce the number of excessively harsh and abusive punishments, a major problem in the USCT. With powerful predilections for prejudice, white officers were much more prone to institute unnecessarily brutal punishments with black than with white soldiers.[32]

Many black soldiers no doubt resented the authority of their white officers. On the one hand it was natural for enlisted men to object to individuals who had power and control over their lives. Their officers often felt the same way during duty in white volunteer units, even toward people they had known and liked during the prewar years. On the other hand, for many black soldiers, the military structure, with whites over blacks, was too reminiscent of the relationship of master and slave. Freedom, they had perceived, was a shield from the dictates of whites, yet in military service they were again subject to the whim of the white race. Time after time, black soldiers resisted the authority of white officers for racial reasons. A private who got into an argument with his lieutenant insisted "he was no slave to be driven," and another private who refused an order exploded in rage, "I am as good as any white man, and I'll be damned if I will be bossed over by any of them." Sensitivity to such matters was keen, and frequently it took only a series of trivial affairs to instigate the outbursts. "It is time we took our own part," a private urged his comrades after an officer ordered him to fill canteens. "We have been run over by our officers long enough; if we don't take our own part, nobody else will take it for us." [33]

There were numerous instances of mistreatment of black soldiers at the hands of white officers. The most famous case involved Lt. Col. Augustus W. Benedict of the 76th U.S. Colored Infantry, whose conduct was at times ruthless. As punishment for a soldier, Benedict had stakes driven into the ground, tied the man with his arms and legs spread apart, and applied molasses to his face, hands, and feet. He left the man in that condition for an entire day and did it again the next day. On other occasions, he struck one soldier and severely whipped two drummer boys. When it appeared to the troops that Benedict would go unpunished, they rioted. A court-martial dismissed Benedict from the service, but it also executed two soldiers for mutiny and imprisoned six others. Another officer, a lieutenant, abused his troops so regularly and for such trifling reasons that his superiors felt obligated to press charges against him. In the course of his brief tenure, the lieutenant had tied up four soldiers for prolonged periods of time, one of them for complaining to the regimental commander that he had no rations. While trying to implement an unlawful punishment, he clubbed a private with his revolver three times and punched him once, and he struck another man during battalion drill. [34]

Unfortunately, other instances of violent attacks by white officers against their black soldiers went unpunished. The colonel of the 62nd U.S. Colored Infantry rebuked his officers for striking and kicking the men for petty offenses and warned them that an officer who could not control his temper was unfit for command, but did not press charges. A chaplain who accompanied the 73rd and 92nd U.S. Colored Infantry on a scouting expedition witnessed officers cursing at troops and beating and kicking them. Both of these officers equated such conduct with that of slave drivers and called for an immediate halt. In the 32nd U.S. Colored Infantry, the frequency of abuse reached such a level that one of its black soldiers threatened to eliminate officers in his company: "I know that some of us have left our homes, only to be abused and knocked about; but one consolation is left us, we have their own clubs that they gave us, to break their own heads with; and, in short, they are making a trap to enslave themselves in." [35]

Despite the illegal nature of such attacks, they were by no means the greatest bone of contention black soldiers had with the disciplinary system in the USCT. There were other, legal penalties, such as bondage, that black soldiers found particularly humiliating. Reminiscent of the days of slavery and extremely degrading to both Northern and Southern blacks, nothing instigated trouble within the

USCT like tying up black soldiers. Time after time black troops protested such punishment, yet few of their white officers listened. A handful did object to the severity of tying men up, and Brig. Gen. John P. Hawkins, a Regular Army officer with a rigid view of discipline, outlawed all such practices in his division of black troops, but he was the only high-ranking officer to intervene on behalf of the troops. Finally, with no other recourse available, black soldiers began to cut their comrades loose. A private in the 38th U.S. Colored Infantry who freed one buddy and attempted to cut another loose insisted, "No white son of a bitch can tie a man up here" and kept an officer at bay with a bayonet. After a captain in another regiment tied up a private, two soldiers cut him loose and immediately went to the commanding officer and demanded to know why the private had been abused that way. Pvt. Henry Bird of the 27th U.S. Colored Infantry tried to free a prisoner, and an officer struck him with a sword. Bird responded by pulling a knife and threatening to kill the officer if he ever tried that again. The sad part was that these episodes frequently escalated into small- and large-scale mutinies, with executions or long-term jail sentences as a result.[36]

Outright mutinies and charges of mutiny were much more prevalent in the USCT than in white units, as was the severity of the punishments. Despite the fact that fewer than one of every thirteen Union soldiers was black, nearly 80 percent of all soldiers executed for mutiny were black, in addition to dozens and dozens of black troops who received lengthy jail sentences for the offense. Had these soldiers erupted in wild and violent uprisings the sentences would have been more justifiable, but the most unfortunate aspect of these crimes was that many of them were non-violent protests for legitimate reasons. In several units black soldiers stacked arms peaceably and refused any further military service until the government paid them the same as white troops, and in another regiment a company of troops passively resisted because their company commander had searched and discarded their belongings when they were on duty.[37]

Time after time, officers were too fearful of losing control of the men and overreacted to the situation, which in turn converted a minor affair into a major controversy. In the 2nd U.S. Colored Light Artillery, an officer ordered a noncommissioned officer tied up, which had never been regimental policy. When a sergeant sought to speak to a captain about the matter, the officer simply ordered him to his tent. Later that day, the captain went to the sergeant's tent to tie him up for his attempted protest, and the sergeant resisted. In a Northern black unit, the 11th U.S. Colored Heavy Artillery, a company protested unequal pay by refusing en masse to answer for monthly inspection. The major went to the men and explained that

their act was mutiny, a grievous offense punishable by death, and
the men then assembled for duty. Instead of letting the matter drop,
the major foolishly inflamed the situation by preferring charges of
mutiny against the noncommissioned officers and twenty privates.
After a court convicted and sentenced them to prison, the troops
again erupted in mutiny, this time threatening to kill the white
officers, and a lieutenant shot one soldier on the spot to regain
control of the men.[38]

In many of these instances, black soldiers had no idea that their
act was a serious offense. The commander of the 21st U.S. Colored
Infantry, whose troops protested unequal pay, blamed the affair
on incompetent officers and insisted the men did not know they
were doing wrong. When good officers explained their obligations
as soldiers, *"all at once entered willingly to their duties."* A sergeant
from that regiment, whom a court found guilty of mutiny and ordered
his execution, stated during his trial, "Never, since the organization
of the company, have the 'Articles of War' been read to us nor any
part of the 'Regulations' even." The same was true for a company
in the 49th U.S. Colored Infantry, which stacked arms because its
captain had searched their personal property and thrown out food
and many items, such as candles, the troops had in their tents.
As one soldier explained to the secretary of war, they merely wanted
better treatment from their captain, and "at the time of doing this
we were not aware what the consequences of Mutiny would be."
An officer involved in the affair seemed to agree when he wrote his
father, "They had got an idea in their head that as they were free
that they could do as they wished without fear of punishment but
this idea is being driven out of their heads fast." A court ordered
two soldiers executed, gave life sentences to seventeen more, and
still another had to wear a ball and chain for the duration of his
term of service as punishment for the passive protest.[39]

In part, the overreaction of white officers to the protests of black
troops was racially motivated. As one black soldier attested in his
trial, white officers "feared that they were facing a general mutiny,
and were ignorant of the next movement that might be made by
the excited crowd before them." Although in most cases the troops
were not acting violently, it appeared to the white officers that they
were losing control of their men, and they reacted vigorously to
restore their dominance.[40]

Yet it was somewhat more complex than that. Earlier in the war,
officers had tolerated such outbreaks, and in a few instances future
USCT officers had participated. In one white regiment the troops
refused to respond to roll call because the commanders had promoted
a corporal who had political connections to second lieutenant over

a sergeant whom the men had elected to that rank. Despite a filled guardhouse and repeated lectures on the hazards of mutiny, the men would not budge and the officers eventually backed down. Shortly after its organization, the 8th Kansas Infantry rioted when a West Point graduate tied a man up by his thumbs. The drunken troops grabbed their rifles, cut the soldier free, and drove all the officers from the camp. Eventually, authorities arrested twenty-six men, but "all the officers were glad to let the matter drop." In the 83rd Pennsylvania Infantry, when officers used troops to quell a barroom brawl and numerous soldiers suffered gunshot and bayonet wounds, the troops got so mad that they refused to turn out for roll call for several days. Future officers in the USCT participated in each incident. Yet these offenses occurred when troops looked on the war as a gigantic game, an event not to miss.[41]

As the casualties mounted and the hardships endured by the troops seemed ceaseless, their attitudes toward the war and the military experience hardened. They no longer viewed it as a game but as serious business. One reason why the Northern troops and public tolerated blacks in military service was that the war had toughened them, that their experiences had forced them to rethink their entire approach to the war and consider possibilities that had been extremely unpopular earlier in the struggle. Black troops were committing acts no less serious than many of their white officers had done in earlier stages of the war, yet such conduct was now intolerable.

To try soldiers for offenses, the military had general and regimental courts-martial. General courts-martial were for serious crimes or cases in which officers were defendants, while regimental courts-martial were for lesser offenses, had restrictions on the punishments, and did not permit witnesses from outside the unit to testify.[42]

Commanding officers, usually at division and brigade level, created general courts-martial from time to time to handle serious cases. A court consisted of at least three officers and usually six or seven, with one sitting as president of the court. Another officer served as prosecutor, or judge advocate, and defendants frequently served as their own counsel but had the right to select anyone in the command. These courts had the power to assess any punishment allowable by the Articles of War, including the death penalty by a two-thirds vote.[43]

If trials for black troops before general courts-martial were indicative of anything, it was inconsistency. At times, courts proved exceedingly severe. When thirteen black soldiers slipped past the guard one night to go hunting for Rebels, and a few of the group entered the home of a white family, robbed it, and murdered a woman, a court sentenced everyone to execution. A superior officer commuted the sentence of three of them to five-year jail terms, but authorities hanged the others. On other occasions, courts-martial demonstrated genuine sympathy for the defendant. When 1st Sgt. William Jackson deliberately shot and wounded a slave named Fisher, the court acquitted him because of the "deadly and unpardonable offense given by Fisher." Fisher had intercepted and destroyed letters from Jackson to his wife, convinced Jackson's wife that her husband was dead, and coaxed her into having sexual relations with him. The court did not approve of Jackson resorting to violence, but it sympathized enough with his plight to exonerate him completely: "A man that wantonly violates the domestic relations of a soldier by seducing his wife while he is absent in the service of his country, deserves the heaviest punishment known to law." There was, then, no definite pattern to court decisions. Maj. Gen. Quincy A. Gillmore blamed the discrepancies in verdicts and punishments on the "unofficer-like familiarity on one hand, and extreme harshness on the other." More likely, the reason for such erratic behavior of judges was that service in general courts-martial was a temporary duty assignment and legal expertise was unnecessary.[44]

As demonstrated by the number of black soldiers whom courts executed for crimes during the war, race was often a factor. Twenty-one percent of all soldiers executed were black, even though they composed less than 8 percent of the entire Union Army. A disproportionate number of black soldiers were executed for rape, along with mutiny, and all of the victims were white women. Yet an examination of nearly all the transcripts of trials that resulted in executions indicates a surprising degree of fairness. Although many of the crimes were against whites, many of the victims were also black, particularly in murder cases. Moreover, in almost every trial the evidence of guilt was overwhelming. Only in two cases does the evidence appear inconclusive. In Kentucky a black soldier shot and killed a white resident. He claimed that the man drew a pistol on him, and an officer testified that the victim's son admitted his father had pulled a pistol on the soldier. A court, which had no representatives from the USCT, decided to support the testimony of family members, including the son who now denied the existence of the weapon. In Carrollton, Louisiana, a court with five of seven judges from the USCT convicted a soldier of murder. A brawl occurred between a couple of white citizens and a black soldier, and in the melee the soldier stabbed a citizen. Several whites testified, as did a black woman, against the private. The evidence, however, seems to indicate that the motives of the white men were questionable.

Apparently, a black woman was begging for money from the soldier, hassling him, and he finally pushed her away. A crowd of white residents then provoked the altercation, calling out, "Knock the d___d nigger in the head. He's a d___d nigger soldier anyhow   he's got no law here." Another one yelled, "There is no law for him" and struck the soldier with a stick, which instigated the fight.[45]

To prevent unfair treatment of black troops, authorities made an effort to place some officers from the USCT on courts trying their men, but in a world of prejudice, with untrained men operating the system, this was not enough. Few soldiers from the USCT were convicted without adequate evidence, but black troops appear to have received stiffer penalties than whites, mainly because officers from the USCT sat on the courts. Evidently, a number of their white officers were unusually harsh on purpose, to send a message to their enlisted population that misconduct would result in severe punishment. And in at least one instance, a court gave a harsher sentence to a black soldier who committed a crime against a white than one who robbed a fellow black. The same court that found Pvt. Cage Heath guilty of theft when he stole $280 from a white soldier and sentenced him to two years at hard labor with a ball and chain convicted Pvt. James Johnson of stealing $65 from a black noncommissioned officer and drunkenness in camp and gave him one year at hard labor with ball and chain. Technically Heath committed the exact same offense as Johnson, plus the court convicted Johnson of drunkenness, yet Heath received a jail sentence twice as severe.[46]

Despite the greater notoriety of general courts-martial, they actually did not have that much impact on the everyday life of soldiers. Officers handled most offenses arbitrarily, by confining soldiers in the guardhouse or ordering them to perform extra fatigue duty or taking them before a regimental court-martial. This court, usually composed of three officers from the unit, handled cases involving such minor offenses as neglecting one's duty, getting drunk, leaving camp against orders, gambling, and petty theft. In the 119th U.S. Colored Infantry, for example, the number of prisoners ranged from a high of twenty-four to a low of three, and nearly every one was the result of a regimental court-martial. Because they had strict limits on the type and length of punishments they could direct, including a maximum fine of one month's pay and imprisonment or hard labor for one month, such problems as unfair rulings and severe punishments were not quite as evident in regimental courts-martial. For giving army rations to a woman, Cook Robert Harris received twenty days' hard labor and a one-dollar fine. In the same regiment, a court convicted two privates of thievery and imposed a fine or extra duty and had the culprits "posted on a bank in a conspicuous place maning a board three feet long & one foot wide having the word '*Thief*' in long letters." Clearly court members were creative in their design of punishments, to compensate for the restrictions, yet even they could be unnecessarily severe. When a court convicted two privates of conduct prejudicial to good order, it had them staked to the ground from reveille to noon and then stand on a barrel head till tattoo for seven days. For two weeks more, they had to stand on a barrel head from reveille to tattoo.[47]

Despite the excesses of some officers, discipline more than any single thing converted a mob of black males into soldiers in the United States Army. It acted as the bond that linked the men together and enabled them as a team to accomplish goals that would otherwise have been impossible. Without discipline, the endless hours of training were worthless, but together, they produced some gratifying results. One captain wrote home, "We are doing a great work in driving away prejudice against the negro by making him a proficient soldier," and another exclaimed, "I am more contented with the service than with any work which I had tried before it." A colonel boasted that his troops were so impressive on dress parade, "Even the N.Y. Cavalry in the street forgot to say 'Nigger.'" Their troops learned rapidly, in some cases so quickly that despite the limited training time they impressed officers and inspectors. One command, the 68th U.S. Colored Infantry, overcame the seemingly constant duty as laborers to be selected by Maj. Gen. N. J. T. Dana as the best-drilled regiment in the department.[48]

Gradually the troops began to feel and act like soldiers rather than civilians. A lieutenant knew his men were learning the business of soldiering, sometimes too fast: "There is hardly a man in the company who cant run a guard equal to a veteran of the Army of the Potomac, and as to foraging, though officers havn't been able to get boards for flooring, most of the mens tents are neatly floored." In complete contradiction to the stereotypical view many whites had of the black race, his troops were becoming self-reliant. The troops were hardening from the training and discipline, doing for themselves and one another the essential things that their government was not helping them to do. When the War Department issued a company rifles, the bayonets did not fit. Mysteriously, a few months later, "They fit very nicely."[49]

7

Proving Their Valor

*B*oth officers and enlisted men in the USCT knew that no matter how they conducted themselves, no matter how hard they labored on fatigue duty, no matter how handsomely they paraded, it was insignificant in the eyes of friend and foe. Only on the field of battle could these black soldiers prove beyond any doubt that they earned the same rights as whites. For them, combat was a great opportunity to demonstrate to all others their willingness to lay down their lives on behalf of their country, for the restoration of the union and the termination of slavery. Equally important, it was an arena in which to dispel misgivings that whites had about the character of the black race.

Throughout Northern white society, there were doubts about the ability of blacks to cope with the rigors of combat, which in turn reflected on the policy of enlisting blacks in military service. Many whites argued that because blacks lacked the character to sustain themselves in battle, attempts to convert them into soldiers were preposterous. Others, while not quite so vocal certainly needed convincing. They argued that blacks did not have the fortitude to withstand the stress of combat and conduct themselves properly, and although military training and discipline might improve their self-reliance and control their latent savagery, they also might desert them in times of crisis. Only the black population had full confidence in their race; nearly all their white friends shared some skepticism, too. Such moderate newspapers as the *New York Times*, for example, supported the use of black troops cautiously. "Whether negroes shall or shall not be employed as soldiers," argued its editors in February 1863, "seems to us purely a question of expediency, and to be solved satisfactorily only by experiment." Yet its editors preferred to withhold judgment until after those few commands in service had performed in battle. Until then, they advocated caution in the enlistment of blacks, fearing that an expansion of recruitment efforts at this time would merely be "adding it to the cause of dissension already existing in the country at large." [1]

From the very beginning, though, black soldiers conducted themselves well in combat. Big Jim Lane's black regiment boasted the first baptism by fire. In October 1862, several months before the government accepted his troops for service as United States volunteers, Lane had sent them into Missouri, where they skirmished with a large force of Confederate guerrillas. Their performance was so encouraging that a newspaper reporter claimed the fight had resolved the entire debate: "It is useless to talk any more about negro courage. The men fought like tigers, each and every one of them." [2]

Several months later, Higginson's 1st South Carolina Infantry, later called the 33rd U.S. Colored Infantry, embarked on a raid up the St. Mary's River in Georgia and Florida and also passed the test. It got into a nasty skirmish with some Confederates at night, and while steaming home, withstood fire on several occasions. In fact, the troops were so game for combat that Higginson had considerable difficulty keeping his men below decks, as everyone scrambled to take shots at the guerrillas. First they pleaded their case to the colonel, and when he refused to let them land and go after the Rebels, the troops sought the intervention of the surgeon, begging him to convince Higginson "to let we spill out on de sho' an' meet dem fellers in de brush." In the official report, Higginson declared the experimental use of black soldiers in battle an unqualified triumph:

No officer in this regiment now doubts that the key to the successful prosecution of this war lies in the unlimited employment of black troops. Their superiority lies simply in the fact that they know the country, while white troops do not, and, moreover, that they have peculiarities of temperament, position, and motive which belong to them alone. Instead of leaving their homes and families to fight they are fighting for their homes and families, and they show the resolution and the sagacity which a personal purpose gives.

One month later they had "mo chance for shoot dem bucra mens," as the troops had hoped, this time at Jacksonville, Florida, and again the men were reasonably cool under fire. [3]

In early April the 2nd Louisiana Native Guards, later designated the 74th U.S. Colored Infantry and one of the black militia units that Butler called into federal service, made a reconnaissance to Pascagoula, Mississippi, to disrupt a Confederate staging ground and to divert troops in Mobile from going to Charleston. Almost immediately after their landing, Confederate infantry and cavalry struck, and the party of 180 black troops repelled four assaults from superior forces in a four-hour running battle. On learning that Rebel reinforcements were en route, Federal commander Col. Nathan W. Daniels ordered his men back on the transport to be evacuated. While on the wharf, a United States gunboat that accompanied the expedition mistakenly assumed the forces were Confederate and fired one shell into the black troops, killing four and seriously wounding five more. Otherwise, Daniels lost two men killed and eight wounded in the sharp skirmish, and he claimed to have inflicted at least twenty Confederate casualties. Again, the black troops proved themselves capable of enduring the rigors of combat. The performance of the men, Daniels argued, demonstrated "the oppression which they have heretofore undergone from the hands of their foe, and the obloquy that had been showered upon them by those who should have been friends, had not extinguished their manhood, or suppressed their bravery, and that they had still a hand to wield the sword, and a heart to vitalize its blow." Equally important, these troops had black officers through the rank of major, and their conduct was "cool and determined throughout the action," with Maj. Francis E. Dumas, Capt. Joseph Villeverde, Lt. Joseph Jones, and Lt. Theodore A. Martin singled out for their outstanding performance.[4]

Yet in each instance these were skirmishes, and while at least Higginson's expeditions received widespread coverage in Northern journals, they were not utterly convincing. The Northern white public wanted to see how they would handle themselves in major engagements before they were willing to commit, even halfheartedly, to such an undertaking as the general enlistment and use of black soldiers. By the end of July 1863, however, it had ample evidence upon which to ruminate.

The first major engagement in which black soldiers participated was an assault on Port Hudson, Louisiana, in late May 1863. Control of the Mississippi River had long been a goal of the Union Army, and by the spring of 1863 it had secured the river's entire course, except for Confederate bastions at Vicksburg, Mississippi and Port Hudson, Louisiana. To cut off the Confederates in the Trans-Mississippi West and provide Midwestern farmers with a water route for the shipment of their crops, the War Department determined that a command under Maj. Gen. U. S. Grant was to capture Vicksburg, and Maj. Gen. Nathaniel P. Banks, head of the Department of the Gulf, was to seize Port Hudson.[5]

For months the Confederates had been fortifying Port Hudson, particularly to the south and west, taking full advantage of the choppy terrain to erect an ominous defensive position. The occupation force consisted of some six thousand Confederates under the command of Maj. Gen. Franklin Gardner, a gritty officer and talented engineer who hailed originally from New York.

In late May portions of Banks's Nineteenth Corps converged on the area around Port Hudson, and after some intense fighting the Federals took a horseshoe-shaped position around the Port Hudson garrison, with flanks nestled near the river. Among Banks's besiegers, filling in at the northern edge of the Union line and closest to the Mississippi River, were the 1st and 3rd Louisiana Native Guards, later the 73rd and 75th U.S. Colored Infantry, a little over one thousand black soldiers in number. The 3rd Louisiana Native Guards consisted of former slaves who had white officers. Originally, the regiment had black line officers, but efforts by Banks to purge the Louisiana Native Guards of all black officers had already driven them from the service, regardless of qualifications or competence. The 1st Louisiana Native Guards, though, were free blacks, with black captains and lieutenants who for the time being were unwilling to buckle under Banks's pressure. According to its white colonel, the regiment had some of the "best blood of Louisiana," the offspring of sundry white politicians, as well as numerous prominent and wealthy free blacks from New Orleans.[6]

One of its officers was Capt. André Cailloux, a man of great intellect and property, a pillar in the free black community of New Orleans. Educated in Paris and fluent in both English and French, Cailloux was honored to be a member of the African race, declaring with evident pride that he was the blackest man in New Orleans. By the time the war broke out, he was a legitimate success story. He had achieved wealth, raised a wonderful family, and had earned the respect of blacks and whites, all before the age of forty. Yet, like his fellow blacks, the indignity of discrimination and slavery bore heavily on his shoulders. Thus, when the "Crescent City" fell to the Union Army in early 1862, Cailloux immediately announced his support for the Federal cause and was one of the first men to raise a company of black soldiers. With his troops he was firm yet just, and he whipped his company into an outstanding unit, barking out orders in English and French for all to understand.[7]

Also among the officers' ranks of the 1st Louisiana Native Guards, but not very well known, was a young second lieutenant named John H. Crowder. His mother, originally Martha Ann Spencer, was a free black who grew up in Kentucky. His father was Jacob Crowder, also a free black, and they married in Louisville in 1844. Shortly after John's birth in 1846, his father ran off with the United States Army to Mexico and never returned. After waiting in vain for two years, John's mother divorced Crowder and moved to New Orleans, where she had some old friends. There in 1850 she married Thomas Stars, who was a steward on a steamboat that ran between New Orleans and Louisville. According to friends of the family, Stars proved to be "a worthless man," thriftless in conduct and "habitually addicted to drunkeness." Even worse, he "contributed little at best towards the support of his wife and stepson John Crowder" and "wastefully squandered in drink and drunkeness" the small earnings Martha had acquired by taking in sewing. By 1861, Stars had abandoned his family financially.[8]

Out of necessity, young John took work as a cabin boy on steamboats on the Mississippi River at age eight, earning five dollars per month. Over the next four years, John gradually worked his way up to steward at twenty dollars a month, all of which he gave to his mother for household expenses. He then took employment for a man named Tyler as porter at a jewelry store for twenty-five dollars per month. In early 1862 John quit that job for a position with a Rebel officer, which he found unsatisfactory and left several weeks later.[9]

All was not misfortune for John Crowder, though. Since childhood his mother had known John Mifflin Brown, a brilliant black man who eventually rose to the position of bishop in the African Methodist Episcopal Church and was a trustee of Howard University. When Martha moved to New Orleans, she became a member of Brown's congregation. The clergyman took an interest in the boy and taught him at every opportunity. As a result, despite extensive labors from an early age, John became a reasonably well-educated young man.[10]

By dint of ability and intelligence, Crowder secured a position as lieutenant in the 1st Louisiana Native Guards. He concealed his age and "joined the Army to serve his country and also because his mother was very poor, and he had to do something for her support," he explained to a woman one day in camp. At sixteen he may have been the youngest officer in the Union Army, and he once queried his mother, "If *Abraham Lincoln* knew that a colored Lad of my age could command a company, what would he say[?]"[11]

Regrettably, not everyone was happy with an underage black officer who showed them up repeatedly in leadership, drill, and general efficiency. Rumors reached his mother's ears that he had been arrested and had caused the death of one of his closest friends. Other tales "said that I was married and I was cashered for marrying a contraband," both of which he categorically denied. Six weeks later, the rumor mill was again at work, this time accusing young John of drinking alcohol and smoking tobacco. As he bluntly stated to his mother, "You know That I never touch licquor and farther more i never smoke." [12]

One black captain in his regiment, Alcide Lewis, was trying to drive Crowder out of the service. An older woman named Mrs. Marsh had taken a liking to the youthful lieutenant, and when he came down with a bad fever, she nursed him back to health. Such preferential treatment infuriated Lewis. Some days later, Captain Lewis was talking to Mrs. Marsh, when a soldier from Lewis's company took "from his pantloons his privates and shook them at her." Both Mrs. Marsh and Lewis saw the vulgar display, yet Lewis did nothing about it. When Crowder found out about the incident, he had the soldier arrested, which made Lewis look derelict in his duties. "I remember your first lesson, that was to respect all females," Crowder wrote his mother, especially ones who had shown him kindness as had Mrs. Marsh. Livid with rage, Lewis then made efforts to "get me out of the regt, and he has said to persons that he thought would not tell me, that he would get me out if he had to tell *Gen. Banks* that I was not of age." [13]

In addition, most white soldiers found any black officers disturbing, let alone one so young and proficient as Crowder. Whites insulted black officers, protested vigorously to authorities and folks at home, and threw every impediment in the path of these blacks. But despite pressure to squeeze them out of the army, Crowder determined to "stay in the service, as long as there is a straw to hold to," or as he forcefully declared to his mother several days later, "I do not intend to resign, nor will I resign unless I am the only black officer in the Service, as long as there is a button to hold to I will hold to it." [14]

On the evening of May 26, 1863, Cailloux, Crowder, and other men in the two black regiments occupied their position in the Federal line for the attack the following morning. According to Banks's plan, these black regiments were just a small component in a major assault. All around the horseshoe line the Federals were to attack, pressuring the defenders everywhere and, Banks hoped, breaking through at various locations where the Confederates were weakest. Yet for Cailloux, Crowder, and their comrades in the 1st and 3rd Louisiana Native Guards, the attack had a special significance. The assault on Port Hudson offered them the first opportunity to demonstrate to all witnesses that the black race could measure up to any white troops in prowess on the battlefield. [15]

The next morning, when they assembled in position to begin their advance, no one in the Federal Army had examined the terrain. Several days earlier, as Banks's forces approached Port Hudson from various directions, they had caught the Confederates by surprise. Gardner and his men had expected an attack from the south and possibly from the east, and they had devoted nearly all their time to fortifying their defenses in those areas. An advance in part from north of Port Hudson had caught them unprepared, and the Confederates had to throw up works hurriedly. To their great advantage, though, the terrain suited their designs superbly. The black regiments were north of Foster's Creek, and before they could do anything, they had to pass over a pontoon bridge to get at the Confederates. South of the creek, a thoroughfare called the Telegraph Road led to Port Hudson. The problems for the attackers were that a bluff ran parallel to the road on the Federals' left, and the Confederates had positioned riflemen there to harass troops as they crossed the pontoons and attempted to move along the road. It was virtually impossible to get at these Confederates, because the area between the road and the bluff was choppy and filled with underbrush and fallen trees. To make matters worse, a Confederate engineer had skillfully tapped into the Mississippi River and drew backwater directly through that strip between the road and the bluff. On the right side of the road was a huge backwater swamp of willow, cottonwood, and cypress trees. To the front of the advancing troops was a bluff, well defended by Confederate infantrymen and supported by artillery. As if the Confederate defenders needed more help, the backwater cut across the pocket between that main Rebel line and the end of the bluff that ran alongside the road, shielding the Confederate artillery from possible assaults. Had an officer with authority and any sense examined the Confederate position, the charge of the 1st and 3rd Louisiana Native Guards would never have taken place.[16]

The first assault came from troops to the east of the two black regiments, and once those blue columns failed to pierce the Confederate defense, the burden shifted to the blacks. Around 10:00 A.M. they began crossing the pontoon bridge over Foster's Creek. Immediately a few Confederate sharpshooters peppered them with rifle fire as a warning for what was to come, but despite their losses, the black troops retained their composure. They quickly deployed as skirmishers and worked their way along the right side of the road, trying to use the timber as cover, although the swamp and felled trees delayed their advance and some Confederate artillery shells depleted their ranks.[17]

The black regiments had hoped to rely on artillery and some white troops as support in their attack. All they got, though, were two artillery guns, which proved no help at all. After their crews hurled one round, Confederate artillery promptly silenced them with a barrage, and for the remainder of the fight they contributed nothing to the battle. Success in that sector, then, depended solely on the black troops.

Some six hundred yards from the main Confederate works, amid the timber, the black regiments shifted to their left and formed two battle lines consisting of two rows each, with the 1st Louisiana Native Guards in the lead. They emerged from the woods advancing rapidly, although once clear of the trees, fire from the Confederate riflemen on the bluff alongside the road now struck them in the flank and created gaps in the ranks. As they reached a point some two hundred yards from the main works, the Confederates opened with a hail of canister, shells, and rifle fire that ripped through the lines of black troops. By dint of sheer determination, the men pressed onward to their slaughter. When the sheets of Confederate lead staggered the first regiment, the 3rd Louisiana Native Guards joined the fray, yet their entry into the assault merely compounded the casualties.[18]

Because of the confusion on the battlefield, it is unclear how many times the two black regiments charged the Confederates. The *New York Times* eyewitness claimed that he saw six separate attacks, while both the Union and Confederate commanders on the scene counted only three. Nevertheless, the black troops demonstrated dash and courage in the face of overwhelming odds. Some soldiers attempted to wade through the backwater to get at the Confederates, and a handful of others tried to scale the bluff where the riflemen had posted themselves, to no avail. In fact, never did the black troops seriously threaten to break through the Confederate lines, regardless of their grit.[19]

In defeat, these black troops demonstrated an inner strength comparable to that of any soldiers in the Union Army. Several months earlier the regimental commander of the 1st Louisiana Native Guards had presented the colors and directed, "Color guard, protect, defend, die for, but do not surrender these flags." In response, Color Sgt. Anselmas Planciancois of the 1st Native Guards vowed, "Colonel, I will bring these colors to you in honor or report to God the reason why." In the lead of his command, Planciancois was struck down by a missile, and two corporals grabbed at the regimental flag, stained with their sergeant's blood, and wrestled for it, one of them sustaining a wound in the process. Nor were Planciancois and the corporals the only heroes that day. A captain saw a black soldier limping away from the hospital and toward the battle. When he asked the man where he was going, the soldier replied, "I been shot bad in de leg, Captain, and dey want me to go to de hospital, but I guess I can gib 'em some more yet." According to a hospital steward in the 3rd Louisiana Native Guards, a shell took off the leg of a soldier below the knee. His captain, standing nearby, went over to comfort the soldier and tell him they would return to care for him. "Never mind me take cair of yourself," the soldier advised his captain. He then pulled himself on a log and "Sat With his leg a swing and bleeding and fierd thirty rounds of Ammunition." A few days later, the soldier died.[20]

After several charges, it had become apparent to everyone on the field that renewed attempts to take the Confederate position were insane, and eventually the troops fell back to the woods for good. Nearly two hundred black troops were casualties, some 20 percent of the two regiments, and to highlight the utter futility of the assault, they had inflicted no casualties upon the Confederates. Among those who never returned was Lt. John H. Crowder, who suffered a critical wound, was borne to the rear, and died that day. His grieving mother gave him a pauper's funeral, which was all she could afford.[21]

Also dead was Capt. André Cailloux. He had survived much of the battle, although a rifle ball had shattered his arm below the elbow, and it hung lifelessly at his side throughout the rest of the fight. Around 1:00 P.M., just before the final retreat, Cailloux was still at the head of his company, his voice hoarse and his body weak, leading his men onward, when a shell struck him down permanently. A truce to collect the dead and wounded did not apply in the sector where the black troops had fought, and Cailloux's body lay on the field for six more weeks until the Port Hudson garrison surrendered. In late July thousands of New Orleans black mourners came out for his funeral, carrying miniature flags or tastefully affixing them to their clothing. As one New Orleans newspaperman wrote, "The cause of the Union and freedom has lost a valuable friend." [22]

Despite the terrible defeat, the Battle of Port Hudson marked a turning point in attitudes toward the use of black soldiers. A lieutenant in the 3rd Louisiana Native Guards told a captain, "My Co. was apparently brave. Yet they are mostly contrabands, and I must say I entertained some fears as to their pluck. But I have now none." And another officer noted, "They fought with great desperation, and carried all before them. They had to be restrained for fear they would get too far in unsupported. They have shown that they can and will fight well." From a more official viewpoint, Banks announced to Maj. Gen. Henry W. Halleck, "The severe test to which they were subjected, and the determined manner in which they encountered the enemy, leaves upon my mind no doubt of their ultimate success." In concurrence, Brig. Gen. Daniel Ullmann, who was in the process of raising a black brigade in Louisiana, informed Secretary of War Stanton, "The brilliant conduct of the colored regiments at Port Hudson, on the 27th has silenced cavilers and changed sneers into eulogizers. There is no question but that they behaved with dauntless courage." The *New York Times,* which had cautiously endorsed the limited use of black troops on a trial basis just four months earlier, now declared the experiment a success:

> Those black soldiers had never before been in any severe engagement. They were comparatively raw troops, and were yet subjected to the most awful ordeal than even veterans ever have to experience—the charging upon fortifications through the crash of belching batteries. The men, white or black, who will not flinch from that will flinch from nothing. It is no longer possible to doubt the bravery and steadiness of the colored race, when rightly led.[23]

Maybe the finest tribute to the valor of the black soldiers who charged the Confederate works that May day, though, came a year later. One evening, a white chaplain heard some strange noises near his tent and went out to investigate. There, almost exactly upon the spot where the black soldiers had sustained such heavy losses the previous year, sat a freedman and his wife at a fire. They were trying to read the Bible, and although neither of them was very proficient, together they stumbled along passably. As the chaplain listened closely he realized that the sentence they were deciphering was, "I am the resurrection and the life," a fitting memorial for the black soldiers who had lost their lives a year before. From those sacrifices sprouted hope for their race.[24]

Barely ten days after the fight at Port Hudson, black troops were again in the midst of a battle, also along the Mississippi River, and it proved to be one of the most vicious engagements in the entire war. Confederate Maj. Gen. Richard Taylor, former brother-in-law of President Jefferson Davis, sent a division of five thousand troops to weaken the Federal holds on Vicksburg and Port Hudson and to eliminate fledgling black units that were protecting freedmen on cotton plantations near the river. In all cases the black troops were part of Adjutant General Lorenzo Thomas's attempts to organize black regiments among the freedmen, drawing officers primarily from the enlisted ranks of Grant's army at Vicksburg, and the most experienced of these commands had only three or four weeks in Union uniform.[25]

Reports of substantial Confederate forces nearby reached Federal district commander Brig. Gen. Elias Dennis, and he ordered a battalion from the 10th Illinois Cavalry and black troops in the 5th U.S. Colored Heavy Artillery—at the time called the 9th Louisiana (Col-

ored) Infantry and stationed at Milliken's Bend with other black
units—to reconnoiter in the direction of Richmond, Louisiana, to
ascertain the strength and objectives of the Confederates. Under
orders from Col. Herman Lieb, commander of the black regiment,
two of his companies mounted mules and took the advance, while
the infantry trailed in the rear.[26]

Such an assignment met with the utter dissatisfaction of the
Illinois cavalrymen. Not only did they have to serve with black soldiers, but these black troops were completely inexperienced. Yet
the events of the next two days demonstrated that although the
troops were green—many had had only two days of target practice—
the men were eager to fight their first campaign.

In the lead, the mounted black soldiers soon encountered some
Confederate cavalry, and in a bloodless assault they drove off the
Rebel horsemen. By this time the black infantry had come up, and
as they were about to continue the advance, Colonel Lieb spotted
a substantial force of Confederate cavalry trying to conceal itself in
a cluster of trees, with the object of circling around to the Federal
flank. Lieb immediately reversed his command and began to fall
back, with the mounted black soldiers covering the rear.[27]

Meanwhile, the Illinois troops rode to the sound of gunfire to
rescue their inexperienced comrades in blue. As they passed through
the lines of the rear guard, with the black troops off to the side of
the road, some Illinois cavalrymen sneered, "A man ud be a dam
fool to try to make soldiers out ah niggers. . . . Any one ought to
know a nigger wont fight; they'r running now, before they seen a
reb. . . . We will show them how it is done if we find any of them."
The company commander of the mounted blacks peered back at
his troops, and they all dropped their eyes. "They thought their
officers were making a cowardly sneak while they themselves were
itching for a fight," he explained. The troops were sulking. Casually,
the lieutenant slipped back in line and encouraged them to move
across the bridge. Then, "If they hit us we will have a fair show."
At once the troops' spirits lifted. Several minutes later the Illinois
horsemen raced past in retreat, pursued closely by the Confederates.
The black company then rose up and delivered a volley that drove
the Rebels back and saved the day.[28]

Lieb quickly recognized the seriousness of his situation and continued to retreat rapidly to Milliken's Bend. In addition, he sent a
dispatch to Brigadier General Dennis, alerting him to the size of
the Confederate force in the area and calling for reinforcements.
To assist Lieb, Dennis sent some soldiers from the 23rd Iowa Infantry, slightly over one hundred men, and the gunboat *Choctaw*. Thus,
on the morning of June 7, Lieb had four under-strength black regi-

ments, with only a few days of training and antiquated Belgian rifles, and two under-strength companies from the 23rd Iowa Infantry, some one thousand strong in all. The detachment from the 10th Illinois Cavalry, although posted nearby, "took no part in the action." For artillery Lieb had to rely solely on the gunboat.[29]

Fortunately for him, the terrain provided some compensation for his command's inadequate size and lack of experience. Because the water level on the Mississippi River was low, the riverbank was high and quite steep, but it was serviceable as natural earthworks for the Federals. Beyond that was a flat open area, some 150 yards long and a quarter mile wide, where the black units had established their camp. At the western border of this area was a levee, some six feet high, covered with sod. The top of the levee was wide enough for horseback riders to use, and on the opposite side of the levee was a road for wagons. There Federals laid logs, brush, and other obstacles to impede passage from that direction. The road was some sixty feet wide, bordered by a huge orange osage hedge. This proved to be of great advantage to the Union troops, because it was impassable except through the gaps locals had carved in it. Foolishly, some Federal officer with a poor eye for terrain had his men cut down some hedges on the extreme left of the line on the previous day. He realized his error and put a halt to the work, but only after he had created a one-hundred-foot gap. In addition, some one thousand yards west was another hedgerow, and beyond that a third one. Other hedgerows ran perpendicular to the levee. The anchor on the extreme right of the Union line was heavy timber and an old cross-levee that ran down to the riverbank. Lieb fortified this with cotton bales. A manpower shortage rendered the left flank open, but another cross-levee and the hedges channeled attackers into an open field, where the defenders had a clear shot at them.[30]

Once Lieb reached camp, he promptly doubled the pickets and placed some mounted troops well outside the line for early warning. He also directed the black troops to take positions behind the levee, and after the 23rd Iowa infantrymen arrived, they also occupied the line. On the extreme left was the 9th Louisiana Infantry (5th U.S. Colored Heavy Artillery), and next to it was the 1st Mississippi Infantry (51st U.S. Colored Infantry). In the center Lieb placed the 13th Louisiana Infantry (63rd U.S. Colored Infantry) and the 23rd Iowa Infantry, and on the far right he positioned the 11th Louisiana Infantry (49th U.S. Colored Infantry).[31]

A brigade of Confederates fifteen hundred strong, under Brig. Gen. Henry E. McCulloch, pursued the retreating Federals vigorously and began driving in the pickets before 4:00 A.M. McCulloch quickly deployed his column some three-quarters of a mile from the Federal line and struck with a vengeance. Attackers cried, "No quarters for white officers, kill the damned Abolitionists, but spare the niggers," and during the course of the battle they executed at least two white officers. Union commanders enjoined their men from firing too soon, and despite their inadequate marksmanship training, the first volley, delivered with the Confederates some two hundred yards away, stunned the attackers momentarily, but they drove onward.[32]

At this point inexperience played a crucial role. Under the enormous stress of the assault, untrained black soldiers were unable to reload rapidly enough, and this enabled the Confederates to get a foothold on the levee. They poured through gaps in the hedges, and rather than re-form into battle lines, they simply charged the Union defenses. Since most Confederates had yet to fire, they discharged as they came over the top, and for the next few minutes a vicious hand-to-hand fight ensued. A captain in the USCT insisted, "It was a horrible fight, the worst I was ever engaged in, not even excepting Shiloh." He personally suffered two bayonet wounds, and his men "met death coolly, bravely; not rashly did they expose themselves, but all were steady and obedient to orders." His young cook begged for a weapon when the Confederates began their advance and fought valiantly, suffering a gunshot and two bayonet wounds. A second black man, a new recruit in his company who had almost no familiarity with a rifle, was found dead after the battle with his bayonet broken in three pieces.[33]

In reserve Lieb had stowed away two under-strength companies, and they now joined the melee. Their commander knew that because his troops were green, they would most likely shoot high in the excitement, and he ordered them to load their weapons but not to fire unless the muzzle was against a Confederate. Their primary weapon was the bayonet. Once he unleashed them, they struck with a fury, reviving the embattled Federals. One of his men, "Big Jack" Jackson, smashed so many people that his rifle butt shattered. In the hand-to-hand fighting Jackson sustained multiple bayonet wounds but continued to struggle until a ball struck him down permanently.[34]

For a few moments it seemed that the Federals might hold. Then, just as suddenly, the tide shifted when the Confederates seized a position on the extreme left portion of the levee and "poured a murderous enfilading fire along our line," according to Lieb. This stampeded the two companies of Iowans from the field, or, as Confederate General McCulloch described it, "The white or true Yankee portion ran like whipped curs almost as soon as the charge was ordered," while the blacks resisted with "considerable obstinacy," yet they could not hold the levee. Outflanked, nearly all the Federals had to fall back to the riverbank, except for the troops on the extreme right behind the old cross-levee and cotton bales, who managed to repel repeated assaults.[35]

Several times the Confederates attempted to drive the black troops into the river, but they could not gain a toehold on the riverbank. After a long march, an early-morning advance, and several hours of vicious fighting, unanticipated by the Rebels, they were too exhausted to mount an effective charge, or as an officer in a black regiment crowed, "Those negro bayonets had got on to their nerves." This gave the black troops a moment to catch their breath and regain some composure. Behind the riverbank they could load their weapons standing, without fear of being shot, and deliver their fire almost completely protected, so that "our men cooled off and shot with greater care," commented a lieutenant.[36]

With the troops along the riverbank, the gunboat was now able to join in the fray. As low as the water level on the river was, the gunboat's crew could not see the battle. Now, with a full view of the Federal position, they could open fire without worrying about striking down their comrades in arms. Later two more gunboats arrived, and they also hurled shells blindly over the bank.[37]

Stung by Federal resistance and unable to advance in force after several hours of toil, the Confederate commander decided to withdraw. McCulloch had requested additional manpower, and the division commander had positioned one brigade to help McCulloch if he needed it, but for some reason the two failed to coordinate properly. With no help coming, McCulloch decided that continuing the attack was futile. The Battle of Milliken's Bend, one of the most desperate in the entire war, had ended.[38]

Casualties in the fight were staggering. McCulloch lost 44 killed and 131 wounded, and he also admitted that an unusual proportion of the wounds were severe. For the Federals, losses were much worse. When Acting Rear Admiral David Dixon Porter arrived on the scene of battle a few hours after it had ended, he noticed, "The dead negroes lined the ditch inside of the parapet, or levee, and most were shot on the top of the head." Among the black units, 35 percent of the troops who participated in the fight had been killed or wounded. Well over two hundred more were missing, although Lieb believed that many of those troops wandered off sometime after the battle and were not present at roll call. In the 9th Louisiana Infantry (later the 5th U.S. Colored Heavy Artillery), nearly 45 percent of its men were killed or mortally wounded, the highest proportion in a single battle throughout the entire war, nearly 17 percent higher than figures for the next nearest regiment, the 1st Minnesota Infantry at Gettysburg.[39]

Only one black regiment did not act superbly in the battle, and that was because its commander and several other officers removed themselves from the view of their men. When the troops saw no officers, they felt deserted and some left their posts. Otherwise, the valor exhibited by these black troops was impressive. The commander of the 1st Mississippi Infantry African Descent recorded, "Many of the severely wounded voluntarily returned to the ranks after washing their wounds. One soldier whose jaw was so severely shattered that utterance was impossible would not leave his post, until peremptorily ordered by his commander to the rear." He died shortly after the battle.[40]

The performance of the black troops impressed everyone who witnessed the battle or had knowledge of its aftermath. "I never more wish to hear the expression, 'The niggers wont fight,'" declared a captain in the engagement. Another captain who was not in the USCT but observed the black soldiers in action that day announced to Maj. Gen. Ulysses S. Grant, "The capacity of the negro to defend his liberty, and his susceptibility to appreciate the power of motives in the place of the last, have been put to the test under our observation as to be beyond further doubt." And Charles A. Dana, a prominent New York Republican and Secretary of War Stanton's "eyes and ears" in the Mississippi Valley, declared with pleasure that "the sentiment in regard to the employment of negro troops has been revolutionized by the bravery of the blacks in the recent Battle of Milliken's Bend. Prominent officers, who used in private sneer at the idea, are now heartily in favor of it." [41]

In both engagements, Port Hudson and Milliken's Bend, the conduct of black soldiers had been genuinely impressive. On one occasion they had advanced courageously despite a hopeless situation, and on the other black troops proved to be stalwart defenders even without adequate training. Serving either as officers or enlisted men, free Southern blacks and former slaves had fought valiantly, and this had reassured their supporters and swayed some doubters. Yet prejudice did not yield easily, and it took a grand assault at Fort Wagner, South Carolina, by a Northern black regiment, the 54th Massachusetts (Colored) Infantry, to convince that large contingent of skeptics that Afro-Americans were a powerful weapon in the hands of the Federal government.

Few Civil War regiments attracted the interest of the Northern public as did the 54th Massachusetts (Colored) Infantry, the brainchild of Massachusetts Governor John Andrew and the dream of thousands of blacks and whites throughout the North. Although it was a state volunteer regiment, a majority of its men actually came from other states. The regiment attracted some of the finest young black men the North had to offer, including two sons of the prominent black abolitionist Frederick Douglass. Its officer corps, too, consisted of outstanding young white men. Andrew handpicked its colonel, the talented and likable Robert Gould Shaw, and Shaw gathered around him men of real ability for command. Among his original officers were the Hallowell brothers, who had been abolitionist soldiers in Wendell Phillips's army, and a cluster of Massachusetts bluebloods, nearly all of whom had previous military service.[42]

Andrew received permission to form the 54th Massachusetts at the end of January 1863, and from that moment a mob of one thousand black civilians transformed rapidly into a unit of soldiers. Within a few months the ranks filled, and by the end of April authorities issued the men Enfield rifled muskets. They trained rigorously just outside Boston, at Readville, and there Andrew presented the regiment with its flags. With the troops in line and dignitaries in attendance, Andrew announced to Col. Shaw, "I know not, Mr. Commander, when, in all human history, to any given thousand men in arms there has been committed a work at once so proud, so precious, so full of hope and glory as the work committed to you." Ten days later they paraded through Boston as huge crowds lined the streets to cheer. There they boarded a steamer bound for the South Carolina coastal islands, and by early June they were in the war zone.[43]

The first expedition for the 54th Massachusetts was a raid on Darien, Georgia, that resulted in the burning of the town and embarrassment for the entire regiment, although it was an unwilling participant in the conflagration. Shortly afterward, the 54th Massachusetts was again on the move, this time on a major campaign to seize Fort Wagner and other bastions that protected Charleston, South Carolina. Again it seemed that the authorities had relegated the regiment to a minor role. They helped to lead a feint on adjacent James Island while other Federals slipped ashore at Morris Island in quest of the prized Fort Wagner. Yet, while helping to hold the line at James Island, a portion of the 54th Massachusetts had its baptism by fire. One night a large Confederate force struck three companies of Shaw's command on picket duty, and in a heated exchange the black troops held the line long enough for soldiers in the 10th Connecticut Infantry to retreat and reinforcements to advance to the front. As one of the Connecticut troops wrote to his mother, "But for the bravery of three companies of the Massachusetts Fifty-fourth (colored), our whole regiment would have been captured. As it was, we had to double-quick in, to avoid being cut off by the rebel cavalry. They fought like heroes." Word of the conduct of these three companies spread quickly throughout the Federal ranks, and white troops now cheered the black regiment.[44]

Meanwhile, Shaw had been scheming to participate in the upcoming fight at Fort Wagner. At the time his regiment was part of a brigade under the command of Col. James Montgomery, a Kansan and the officer who had ordered the burning of Darien, Georgia, but Shaw preferred to serve under Brig. Gen. George C. Strong. Strong was a Massachusetts man, a West Point graduate who had established a reputation as a skillful officer. For a brief while Shaw's regiment had been under Strong's overall command, although the campaign separated the black regiment from Strong. In parting, Shaw planted a seed in Strong's head by writing him a letter expressing his disappointment that the 54th Massachusetts was being left behind and telling him how much the officers and men desired a prominent role in the campaign against Fort Wagner as part of Strong's command. When Strong's brigade received the assignment to lead the assault on Fort Wagner, its commander requested the transfer of the 54th Massachusetts, fresh from its outstanding performance on James Island, to head the attack. Although Strong and the officers and men of the 54th Massachusetts regarded the offer as an honor, division commander Maj. Gen. Truman Seymour assented to the request for another reason, telling overall operations commander Maj. Gen. Quincy A. Gillmore, "Well, I guess we will let Strong lead and put those d____d niggers from Massachusetts in the advance; we may as well get rid of them one time as another." [45]

Fort Wagner rested near the northern tip of Morris Island. The bastion was valuable because it protected Battery Gregg, at the very edge of Morris Island and overlooking the entrance to Charleston Harbor. With Battery Gregg in Federal hands, they could shell Fort Sumter in the middle of Charleston harbor into capitulation, which would close the harbor completely to Confederate blockade runners and pave the way for an attack on Charleston. [46]

An engineering marvel, Fort Wagner extended across the entire neck of the island. Along its western side was Vincent's Creek, and to the east was the Atlantic Ocean. At high tide the surf washed right up to its eastern wall. About 150 yards outside the walls, an impassable marsh projected down from the creek to the east, so that at high tide there was only a 25-yard wide strip over which attackers could advance on the fort, something the Federals had overlooked. Because the main approach was from the south, Confederate engineers had constructed two walls made of sand, turf, and palmetto logs. The southeastern and southwestern corners of the fort projected outward, which enabled the defenders to fire on attackers from front and flank, and sometimes both flanks, simultaneously. Seventeen hundred troops and seventeen artillery guns defended the fort from all directions, and between them they swept the southern approach superbly. For added insurance, the Confederates had prepared a moat three feet deep just outside the first wall and a rifle pit two hundred yards beyond that.[47]

Around 9:00 A.M. on the morning of July 18, Union artillery and naval vessels began shelling Fort Wagner to soften its defenses for the attack at dusk. Several Confederate guns returned fire, while other artillerymen shielded their weapons with sandbags and weathered the storm in bombproofs with most of the infantrymen.[48]

Early in the evening, the 54th Massachusetts (Colored) Infantry, some 630 officers and men, arrived at Strong's headquarters. The regiment had been in motion for much of the last two days, and the troops had eaten nothing since breakfast. Nevertheless, Strong fed them merely some words of encouragement and pushed them forward. The plan called for the black troops to strike first, succeeded by regiments from Strong's brigade. In the event these troops did not carry the works, Seymour had two more brigades to throw into the fight, but he viewed them as a precaution. The Federal high command greatly underestimated the strength of Fort Wagner and the size of its garrison and anticipated a swift success.[49]

As the men in the 54th Massachusetts (Colored) Infantry advanced into position, some Confederate gunners began hurling shells overhead, which startled a few troops until Lt. Col. Edward Hallowell restored order. Shaw planned to have his regiment attack in column in two waves, five companies across his front. Once they got in position with his right flank on the edge of the surf, approximately one mile from Fort Wagner, he had the men lie down to give other regiments a chance to get in position. Officers gave no specific assault instructions to the men. They simply ordered the troops to load their weapons but not to place the percussion cap on the firing nipple. This was to be a bayonet charge, with close support from other regiments.[50]

When it appeared that succeeding regiments were nearly in place, Strong rode up to give some parting words of encouragement. After some platitudes, he reminded them, "Don't fire a musket on the way up, but go in and bayonet them at their guns." He then asked who was going to carry the regimental flag if the color-bearer fell, and Shaw, removing a cigar from his mouth, replied calmly, "I will," to the delight of the men.[51]

As Strong rode away, Shaw began to wander up and down the lines and spoke briefly to his troops. Like his men, he too had an inkling of the hazards of the attack, and a little while earlier Shaw had even unloaded some personal papers to an old friend to send to his family in the event of his death. At this stage, though, there was little for him to say. In an affectionate tone that surprised the troops, he simply called on the soldiers of the 54th Massachusetts to "prove themselves as men" that day.[52]

After a wait that seemed interminable to officers and men, Shaw gave the order for his command to stand up and begin their advance. He decided to lead the left wing and positioned himself next to the regimental flag, while he directed Hallowell to head the men on the right. The troops tried to march quickly, but the projection of the marsh on the left and the high tide on the right created congestion as the column approached within a few hundred yards of the works, and those men on the extreme right were forced out into the ocean and had to churn their way through the surf.[53]

Confederate batteries on adjacent islands opened fire as soon as they observed the advance, but the troops at Fort Wagner waited until the black troops packed tightly into the pocket between the swamp and ocean. Suddenly, powder flashes lit up the wall and Confederate shot and shell tore huge gaps in the Federal columns. "Not a man flinched," wrote survivor Sgt. Maj. Lewis Douglass, "though it was a trying time. A shell would explode and clear a space of twenty feet, our men would close up again." The black soldiers pushed on intrepidly, sustaining heavy casualties yet increasing speed until they were on a dead run. Through the waist-deep ditch they poured and clambered up the outer embankment. Some Confederate troops now came out from their protection and lowered their aim to strike down the black attackers as they mounted the first slope.[54]

Shaw had swung past the salient in the southeastern corner and driven directly into the center, where Confederates blazed away at the attackers from three directions. Considering his position at the head of the assault, it was miraculous that he even reached the Rebel works, although he had sustained multiple wounds. As Shaw reached the top, he called upon the men to move forward, when a ball crashed into his chest and toppled him backward dead. Despite the loss of the regimental commander, the color bearer planted the flag on the parapet and some black soldiers penetrated into the Confederate works and battled them hand-to-hand. The Confederates, with manpower superiority, were able to drive them back outside the inner wall and began dropping hand grenades and lighted shells on the assailants.[55]

On the right, Hallowell went down with a severe groin wound, but a small portion of his men struck the fort in the southeast corner. There some unnerved North Carolinians abandoned their defenses, and for a moment it seemed that the first assault might succeed, until Confederate reinforcements arrived to drive back the attackers. Had Shaw concentrated on this portion of the Confederate line, the outcome of the battle might have been more in doubt. As it was, the Federals here were too few in number to make a difference, and the Confederates stymied them, as they had Federals farther to the left. In addition, the supporting blue columns had been too slow. By the time they arrived on the scene, the Confederates had completely repulsed the assault of the 54th Massachusetts. And like Shaw's regiment, they suffered the same fate, albeit without such severe losses.[56]

Those survivors in the 54th Massachusetts who were able to retreat began to fall back over the ground where Confederates had struck down scores of their black comrades. Several hundred yards to the rear, a junior captain and the temporary regimental commander collected these men and placed them in rifle pits where they supported other Union troops in the attack.[57]

As night fell, some men in the 54th Massachusetts crawled away or bolted across open ground and managed to return to Federal lines. One of those men was Sgt. William H. Carney, who grabbed the national flag as its bearer fell and planted it on the Confederate works. There he sustained a wound in each leg—one in the chest, and another in the right arm—yet he managed to carry the flag back in retreat. Others who refused to run the gauntlet or had suffered wounds became prisoners of war. Among them was First Sgt. Robert J. Simmons, who had his arm shattered by a Rebel ball. Unknown to Simmons, three days earlier in New York City a draft protest had turned into a race riot, and a mob had terrorized his mother and sister and stoned and clubbed to death his seven-year-old nephew. In one of the great tragedies of the war, Simmons had his arm amputated and died several weeks later in a Charleston hospital, having fought for those very same people who murdered his young nephew.[58]

Well over 40 percent of the men in the 54th Massachusetts were casualties in the assault on Fort Wagner. Confederate officials sent the wounded to Charleston hospitals, and after considerable indecision the prisoners of war went to camps, where some died and others were exchanged. The Confederates interned the bodies of two officers in separate graves, but they laid Shaw to rest in a pit with his men, or as a Confederate supposedly explained when the Federals sought his body under a flag of truce, "We have buried him with his niggers!" Clearly the Confederates had intended to insult the sensibilities of whites; instead, it became a rallying cry across the North and helped to immortalize Col. Robert Gould Shaw. One month later, when Shaw's father learned that Gen. Gillmore was attempting to secure the remains, he requested that his son's body lie with his men: "We hold that a soldier's most appropriate burial-place is on the field where he has fallen." [59]

Two weeks after the battle at Fort Wagner, a black sergeant wrote his company commander, at home recuperating from a wound, "I still feel more Eager for the struggle than I ever yet have, for I now wish to have Revenge for our galant Curnel and the spilt blood of our Captin. We Expect to Plant the Stars and Stripes on the Sity of Charleston." Rather than undercut their commitment to the cause, the defeat at Fort Wagner enhanced the desire of the men in the 54th Massachusetts (Colored) Infantry to see the war through to its successful conclusion.[60]

Taken in conjunction with the outstanding performance of black soldiers at Port Hudson and Milliken's Bend, the assault on Fort Wagner challenged contemporary racial stereotypes. Blacks had demonstrated a willingness to stand up and fight against the Confederacy, something few Northern whites had considered possible, and this in turn helped to lay the foundation for the tremendous expansion of blacks in the military service over the next two years. Prejudice was too deeply rooted for the Northern white population to cast it aside, but the conduct of blacks in these battles impressed them enough to give serious consideration to the widespread use of black soldiers. Slowly yet steadily the Northern public began to warm to the idea that blacks could contribute significantly to the war effort. If the black troops had misbehaved under fire in these three battles, the results would have been catastrophic for the black race and the USCT. Fortunately, they fought with the courage of veterans, and that opened the door for over one hundred fifty thousand more blacks to enter the military service.

Some eight months after the assault on Fort Wagner, the 20th U.S. Colored Infantry, raised throughout the state of New York, paraded through the streets of New York City, the same place where a mob had murdered Sgt. Simmons's nephew. Now, thousands of people, both white and black, lined the avenues to cheer these blacks in Union blue. In part the draft had made the enlistment of black soldiers more acceptable to whites, because blacks filled manpower quotas as did whites. But there was more to it than that. Whites had come to realize that these one thousand black soldiers were fighting for the same government and causes as were white troops, trying in some small way to help win the war. The change in Northern attitudes, noted the *New York Times*, was startling:

Eight months ago the African race in this City were literally hunted down like wild beasts. They were shot down in cold blood, or stoned to death, or hung to the trees or to the lamp-posts. . . . How astonishingly has all this been changed! The same men who could not have shown themselves in the most obscure street in the City without peril of instant death, even though in the most suppliant attitude, now march in solid platoons, with shouldered muskets, slung knapsacks, and buckled cartridge boxes down through the gayest avenues and busiest thoroughfares to the pealing strains of martial music, and everywhere are saluted with waving handkerchiefs, with descending flowers, and with the acclimations and plaudits of countless beholders.

It was truly a "prodigious revolution which the public mind everywhere is experiencing," the editors concluded. The performance of a few thousand black soldiers on three different battlefields made all that possible.[61]

8

Leaving Their Mark
on the Battlefield

Despite the outstanding performance of black soldiers at Port
Hudson, Milliken's Bend, and Fort Wagner, there was still a
sense of uneasiness about blacks in combat. Their conduct had
certainly not convinced everyone, and just because the Northern
white population was coming around to the viewpoint that blacks
in uniform could contribute to the war effort did not mean that
they were willing to stand alongside black soldiers and slug it out
against the Confederates. In addition to Rebel soldiers, black commands were battling generations of racial prejudice, and the lingering doubts were by no means easy to dispel. Thus, throughout the
war, the USCT was under the spotlight of the Northern public, both
in and out of military service.

Even among the white officers, nearly all of whom had previous
combat experience, there was considerable consternation. The bulk
of these commands had not devoted enough time to training, and
in the back of their minds they were still unsure that the black
race had the fortitude to stand up to the fire of the Confederates.
Despite widespread acceptance of the notion of the innate savagery
of the black race, Southern whites were held somehow to have sub-
dued them, and some officers thought black soldiers might flee in
the face of their former masters. As one lieutenant in the USCT
recalled, "For so many years had the black man cowered beneath
the lash of the oppressor, that his spirit was thought by all to have
been crushed." [1]

Yet many white officers had good reason to dread risking their lives with such raw troops. On the eve of his first campaign with black soldiers, one lieutenant was the only officer in his company, and his regiment "had never fired a shot" in anger or on the practice range. Understandably, he was worried: "I was scared good and sure and would of given most any thing to of been at home with my dear Mother." Even units that had time to drill were not ready for combat. Too many white officers trained their men for parades to win the kudos of superiors and inspectors, but flashy drills did not prepare them adequately for battle. "Our regiment has been drilled too much for dress parade and too little for the field," a lieutenant complained, while a major in another regiment admitted his troops were able-bodied, muscular, and highly motivated, but the commander drilled them "more in what makes a good show, than in what will be needed in a fight." Indeed, very few officers entered their first engagement alongside black soldiers and had no apprehensions that they would perform well.[2]

Among those white officers and black soldiers who had no combat experience, there were shared sentiments of eagerness and anxiety. On the one hand, the prospects of combat excited them, as it had white soldiers earlier in the war. Although they knew of the tremendous losses the war had inflicted, they still yearned for the opportunity to prove themselves on the field of battle, to see if they had what it took to stand up against enemy fire. In the 43rd U.S. Colored Infantry near Petersburg, when the troops received word to prepare for battle, everyone excitedly threw their gear together in anticipation of an immediate march. Then a seemingly interminable wait occurred, and a young, inexperienced soldier began to grumble, "I don't believe we are going to move at all." To that a veteran who had felt the same eagerness before his first battle replied that the soldier and his young comrades would "sing a different tune" in twenty-four hours, and he was right. At the same time there was a big question mark: what if the individual did not have the inner strength to act properly in combat. A new lieutenant revealed his doubts to his father when he wrote, "I have never yet been under fire. I do not want to prove a coward, and yet I am afraid I shall. I shall go into it, realizing all the importance and danger of my position; and I shall trust in strength other than my own."[3]

With black troops, especially freedmen, this sense of anxiety was not quite so powerful. Many of them had already demonstrated unusual fortitude in their escape from slavery. As Colonel Higginson noted of his troops, "There were more than a hundred men in the ranks who had voluntarily met more dangers in their escape from slavery than any of my young captains had incurred in their lives."

More importantly, they had motivations that enabled them to overcome these doubts better than did white soldiers. While whites
fought for an impersonal restoration of the union, or even for the
freedom of people they had never known and regarded as inherently
inferior, blacks entered combat in search of freedom and justice
for themselves and their families. One black sergeant commented
that what his comrades lacked in military knowledge, at least early
in their service, they compensated with commitment: "they had
been to the armory of God and had received weapons of the heart,
that made them daring and dangerous foes—men to be really reckoned with." For black soldiers, this was a crusade for the rights of
themselves and their race, and the passions these goals generated
helped them hurdle the obstacles of fear and doubt.[4]

Despite the lack of preparedness, these black units nonetheless
found themselves in the thick of combat. The commander of the
39th U.S. Colored Infantry complained that the government threw
his men into the field with almost no training whatsoever. Many
of the men did not even know how to use their weapons. Some
troops believed the ball went into the barrel first; others thought
putting in two rounds was proper; and still others fired without
taking aim, because no one had taught them. In the 8th U.S. Colored
Infantry, a lieutenant wrote his sister that in the battle around
Jacksonville, Florida, his troops had had so little rifle training that
they could not defend themselves adequately, yet they held their
ground. "We have had very little practice in firing, and, though
they could stand and be killed, they could not kill a concealed enemy
fast enough to satisfy my feelings." When they fell back on order,
the men naturally bunched together and made an even easier target
for the Confederates. The most amazing instance, however, was a
company of recruits for the 52nd U.S. Colored Infantry. Confederate
infantry and an artillery battery attacked them, and although the
men had not been mustered into service, they begged their lieutenant
not to surrender. The lieutenant vowed that they would "fight as
long as there was a man of them left," and for three hours they
somehow held the Confederate forces at bay.[5]

Naturally, there was a great deal of rhetoric around camp about
what combat was going to be like and how individuals were going
to perform, but as one enlightened soldier said to his comrades,
they were all flapping their jaws: "You don't know notin' about it,
boys. You tink you's brave enough; how you tink, if you stan' clar
in de open field,—here you, and dar de Secesh? You's got to hab
de right ting inside o' you. You must hab it 'served [preserved] in
you, like dese yer sour plums dey 'serve in de barr'l; you's got to
harden it down inside o' you, or it's notin'."[6]

Just as the sage soldier had predicted, all the campfire nerve did them no good as they approached battle for the first time. To reassure his comrades when they first heard the roar of battle, a sergeant who knew about combat from his previous service as a teamster told them, "You yeres dat music? How you likes it? It's to hear dat, and not to be skeered by it dat de guv'ment feeds you fer; dat's what dey gib you dese bu'ful shiny guns fer; no skulkin' now! Doan' ye dar to flinch!" Officers, too, tried to instill some confidence in their men. Like Colonel Shaw before the assault on Fort Wagner, most commanders tried to speak to their men about doing their duty just before a battle. And when both black and white troops were participating in the fight, officers in the USCT had an additional motivator. At Petersburg in 1865, Capt. Marshall Harvey Twitchell told his troops that they were fighting alongside the Sixth Army Corps, the best in the Army of the Potomac, and this was an opportunity to prove to the entire world whether they were men or fit only to be slaves. During these tense moments before coming under fire, a joke frequently worked wonders. While entering combat for the first time, a major in the 30th U.S. Colored Infantry instructed the men, "Now just imagine you are hunting for coons, and keep your eyes open." To this a soldier cracked, "Pears like 'twas de coons doin' de huntin' dis time," and the line erupted in laughter.[7]

After a few encounters with Confederates, Higginson felt his troops advanced into battle calmly but once they were under fire they became more and more excitable. In support of this view was the statement of an officer in the 1st U.S. Colored Infantry. During their first battle the men performed well, but "many of them got so excited and earnest that they would stand right up on the rifle pits regardless of exposure." On the other hand, a colonel reported that his troops froze at first. After they received a few rounds, however, the men settled down and fired with "the steadiness and deliberation of veterans." A lieutenant had similar experiences. He confessed feeling "pretty dubious" about his men, and they "went in rather skeary, but after a while when they could distinguish the enemy, they got perfectly reckless." Overall, the lieutenant was "delighted" with their performance and crowed to his brother that black troops were "the equal of the best soldiers that ever stepped for Soldiers."[8]

Clearly, the key was the sense of confidence troops had in one another and their officers. It took a sort of mystical chemistry that some officers were able to create during training while others needed actual combat experience, which pitted all the men together under the same adverse circumstances, to forge it. When troops felt they could rely on their officers and one another for support, they began to feel a bit more at ease in the combat arena. Often it was just

DARK ARTILLERY; OR, HOW TO MAKE THE CONTRABANDS USEFUL.

When fighting broke out between the Union and Confederacy, most white Northerners agreed with the decision of the Lincoln administration to enlist only whites. Prejudice in the Northern states was powerful, and few whites believed that blacks had the character to endure combat. This racist cartoon in a popular Northern periodical clearly depicts the lack of regard most whites had for the military potential of blacks. (Library of Congress)

After sixteen months of fighting, with tens of thousands of casualties and enlistments down to a trickle, the Lincoln administration reconsidered its position on blacks in the Union regiments. This cartoonist for a Southern periodical ridicules Lincoln's decision to use black soldiers, who he believed would run at the first sign of battle against their former masters. (Library of Congress)

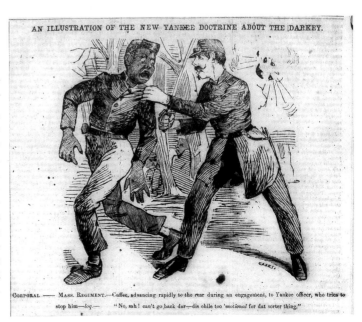

AN ILLUSTRATION OF THE NEW YANKEE DOCTRINE ABOUT THE DARKEY.

CORPORAL —— MASS. REGIMENT.—Cuffee, advancing rapidly to the rear during an engagement, to Yankee officer, who tries to stop him—loq.—   "No, sah! can't go back dar—dis chile too 'motional for dat sorter thing."

COME AND JOIN US BROTHERS.

PUBLISHED BY THE SUPERVISORY COMMITTEE FOR RECRUITING COLORED REGIMENTS
1210 CHESTNUT ST. PHILADELPHIA.

Desperate for manpower, the Northerners made a virtue of necessity, repressing their prejudice, in order to actively recruit black soldiers. Note the tidiness of the black troops (with their white officer beside them in this recruitment poster) to make them as tolerable as possible to the Northern white populace. With few exceptions, the Lincoln administration insisted upon white officers to supervise black troops. (U.S. Army Military History Institute)

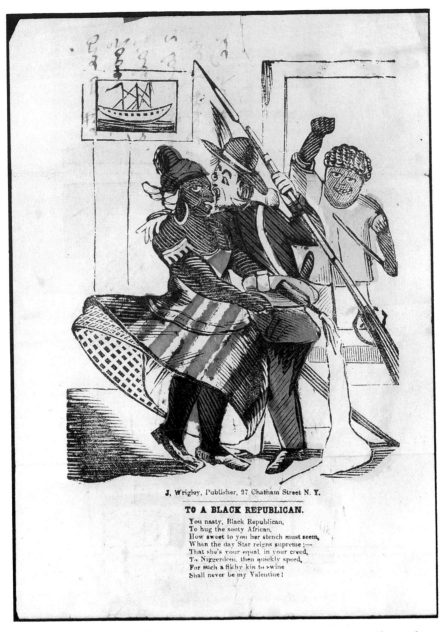

J, Wrigley, Publisher, 27 Chatham Street N. Y.

TO A BLACK REPUBLICAN.

You nasty, Black Republican,
To hug the sooty African,
How sweet to you her stench must seem,
When the day Star reigns supreme ;—
That she's your equal, in your creed,
To Niggerdom, then quickly speed,
For such a filthy kin to swine
Shall never be my Valentine !

Nevertheless, many whites opposed blacks in the Union Army throughout the war. Here a political cartoonist for the Peace Democrats, better known as Copperheads, tries to sway voters from the Republican party by playing upon the racist fears of Northern whites. (Browne Family Papers, Schlesinger Library, Radcliffe College)

Throughout the final ten months of the war, the benefit of black troops was most apparent, particularly in the Virginia Theater. During the siege of Petersburg, blacks forces composed one-eighth of the Federal Army. The first photograph shows two black soldiers, with rifles aimed, performing picket duty; the second one shows black troops living in dugouts in August 1864. (Library of Congress and MOLLUS-Massachusetts Collection, U.S. Army Military History Institute)

During their military service, black troops received a disproportionate share of fatigue labor. No doubt, the most disagreeable assignment was burial detail. Here black soldiers are re-interring bodies at the Cold Harbor battlefield in April 1865. (National Archives)

Military service offered an unusual opportunity to teach blacks to read and write. According to historian Bell I. Wiley, this is a group of black soldiers and their Northern officers and teachers in South Carolina. (Library of Congress)

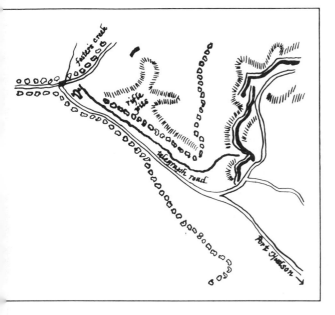

On May 27, 1863, black troops participated in their first major engagement. At the Battle of Port Hudson, the 1st and 3rd Louisiana Native Guards, composed of free blacks and former slaves, and holding ranks ranging from private to captain, crossed a pontoon bridge under fire and drove along the west side of Telegraph Road. There they launched several valiant assaults on a commanding Confederate position. (Taken, with permission, from *The Guns of Port Hudson*, by David C. Edmonds)

Less than two weeks after the Battle of Port Hudson, nearly one thousand black soldiers repulsed a vigorous assault by a larger Confederate force at Milliken's Bend, Louisiana. Despite being in military service for only a month, the black troops fought a vicious hand-to-hand battle with the Confederates and held on even after white Union soldiers had fled from the field. (This map, taken from the *Official Records*, shows the battle from the perspective of the Confederate attackers.)

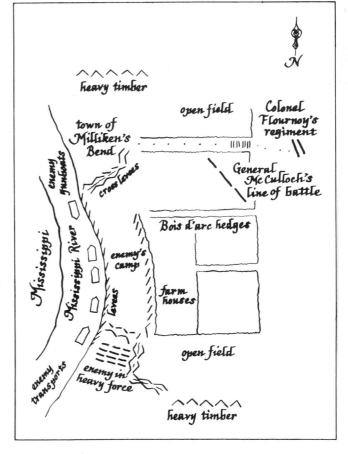

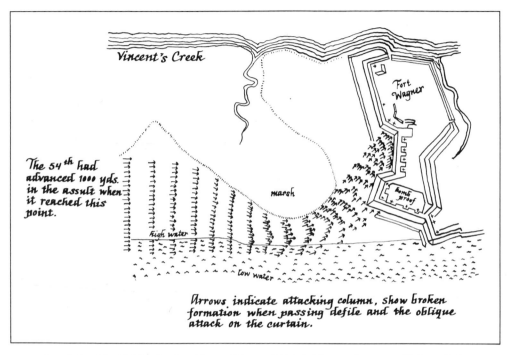

On July 18, 1863, the highly publicized 54th Massachusetts (Colored) Infantry led an assault on a Confederate bastion named Fort Wagner. Led by its intrepid commander, Col. Robert Gould Shaw, who lost his life in the battle, the 54th Massachusetts stormed the Confederate position. Probably more than any other engagement, this daring attack by the 54th Massachusetts convinced Northern whites that black soldiers were capable of contributing significantly to the Union Army. (The map is derived from one prepared by a participant, Capt. Luis F. Emilio, for his book, *A Brave Black Regiment*.)

one or two soldiers whom an individual could count on in desperate moments that gave him this self-assurance, and occasionally these bonds of comradeship crossed racial boundaries. After the war, an officer in the 19th U.S. Colored Infantry admitted, "I always found comforting in battle the companionship of a friend, one in whom you had confidence, one you felt assured would stand by you until the last. I can well remember our fight at Hatcher's Run. I had a sergeant, tried and true, who was at my elbow always. True, he was black; he was a pure African. No drop of white blood ever coursed his veins, but a hero in every sense of the word." The captain had regarded the man as reliable, and at the Battle of Yellow Tavern he sent him on a dangerous mission, which the black soldier successfully accomplished. That night, while trying to sleep on the picket line, the captain overheard an enlisted man tell the soldier that he would not thank the captain for sending him on such risky missions, that he would wind up dead. The soldier replied, "The captain will never send me where he thinks I will be killed, but if he would order me to go through hell, I'd die trying!" The next day the captain promoted the man to sergeant, and the bonds between them grew stronger with each passing day.[9]

Eventually, the sense of interdependence, of supporting one another in times of crisis, became so overwhelming that individuals felt an obligation to be with the unit in desperate times. Regardless of the inherent danger of combat, time after time they left their sickbeds to be with comrades for battle. A lieutenant in the 36th U.S. Colored Infantry, excused from duty for lameness, volunteered to charge through a swamp at the head of his company in the battle near New Market, Virginia, and suffered a breast wound. Another lieutenant, this one in the 5th U.S. Colored Infantry, was ill but wanted to be with his company for an assault. He fought alongside the men, and immediately after the battle he collapsed. Nor were things different with the enlisted men. One astonished officer noted in his diary that when the bugle sounded and the troops assembled for their first battle, "the sick list deserted the doctor," the opposite of what he had expected. "We have not had such full ranks since they fell in for pay," he quipped.[10]

Like most of their white counterparts in blue, the more battles they fought and the more losses they incurred, the stronger was their desire to see the war through to the finish. The allures of battle no longer enticed them; it became a matter of ensuring that their comrades had not died in vain. A black sergeant with exceptional writing skills explained the concept effectively when he asserted, "We had tasted of the dangers of battle, and this taste brought out the desire that we should fight to the finish. Some of our dear friends had laid down their lives already, and we reasoned that if it should be necessary for them to give such a sacrifice, that we were no better than they. So in our judgment, we were becoming calm, and in our determination, we were becoming more and more fixed." [11]

As the drum pounded or the bugle blared to alert the men to a coming battle, nearly all had a wrenching feeling in their stomachs. They rushed about, gathering gear and forming in position, while fear and bolts of panic raced through them. One veteran officer revealed to his parents, "That is a time when thought is active and for a little time my nerves refuse control but I soon become cool and I think I should then be prepared to act with coolness & deliberation." For those who were attacking, at least they knew roughly when the battle was going to begin. Defenders simply had to wait, and that was often the greatest agony. [12]

Once the battle began, most men settled into their work. Like their enemies, the Confederates, black soldiers had their own version of the Confederate attack cry, the "Rebel yell" that one officer termed "horrible howls." It had the twin psychological benefit of unnerving the defenders and releasing tension among the attackers. [13]

As the deafening roar and brutal scenes of the battlefield bombarded the troops' senses, they selectively tuned out much of the combat experience for psychological survival. Hours seemed like minutes. They performed their jobs almost mechanically, and after it was all over they had great difficulty recalling many of the specific events or feelings. In the attack on Petersburg in 1864 an officer who never cursed learned from those around him that he "swore all the way through the fight," but he did not remember it. "For myself," a lieutenant recorded in his diary after a battle, "I can truly say, I was oblivious of all danger. I had given up the hope of returning alive from this 'very Jaws of death,' and thought that it was only left for me to die facing the enemy." Many of them, particularly officers, were so preoccupied with their own duties that they saw very little. After a successful assault, a captain recalled that his command advanced across an open cornfield and charged the enemy works with a yell, but "I was too busy to see much beside the work before me." During the course of the battle he suffered an injury that made him partially lame, although "The Excitement of the charge & the work to do made me Entirely unconscious of it." The time to mourn losses was after the conclusion of the battle. During the fight, each man had an obligation to fulfill certain duties, and the survival of others depended upon it. Even though comrades fell, they had to keep at their posts. [14]

With the effective range of rifled muskets, the standard Civil War infantrymen's weapon, and the quality of field fortifications that troops learned to construct in the latter half of the war, most experienced soldiers preferred to fight on the tactical defensive. From behind breastworks, defenders were able to compensate for inadequate training or manpower inferiority, and it seemed logical that Federal authorities would use black units that way, especially considering the level of experience of their Confederate foe. Nevertheless, aside from the battles at Milliken's Bend, the infamous Fort Pillow, Wilson's Wharf, and a few other relatively minor engagements, the USCT seldom fought on the defensive.

Federal authorities much preferred to use black units as storming parties, or shock troops, to assault Confederate lines and punch holes through them. Most senior officers believed that employing black troops in charges was merely an effective utilization of their manpower. Because black units had not received enough training, from a tactical standpoint they were more capable of conducting assaults than anything else. Moreover, such attacks took advantage of white preconceptions of the black race. Permitting them to storm the enemy works and destroy everything in their path utilized what whites perceived as the greatest fighting quality of blacks, their innate savagery, to its fullest potential. "The most unbiased opinion," wrote the editors of the *New York Times*, "seems to be that they are best for a sudden *dash*, but are not good in a great disaster—not having the moral stamina to see long the horrible affects on the human body which shell or round shot produce." [15]

Nevertheless, military authorities did not consciously throw away the lives of their black troops on prejudiced grounds. Certainly many of them cared less for black than white lives; as one general officer wrote, "I shall feel less regret over the slain than if my troops are white," but in only one instance, at Fort Wagner, was there evidence that expendability was an issue. Commanders drew upon the forces they had available and employed them as they saw best. If they ordered black troops to make frontal attacks, it was an attempt to utilize their assets effectively, not to waste black soldiers for personal reasons. [16]

Even their own officers saw the value in using blacks for such assaults. They had doubts that black soldiers could stand up under sustained fighting, but in a short burst, an assault, they regarded their troops as excellent. In a sense, they viewed their men as wild and undisciplined in battle. "He rushed into a charge with terrible fierceness," described one of their officers, "but his impetuosity was apt to yield in long continued struggles." Another officer wrote to his wife, "I confess I am surprised at the dash and courage of these men. I have never felt *sure* of them before and even now I fear they would not have that steadiness under fire that many have but for a charge they cannot be beat." He compared their ability to assault with Thomas Meagher's Irish Brigade, notorious for its bravery, although many thought the courage of the Irishmen derived from their ignorance.[17]

The most famous charge involving black troops was the Battle of the Crater, or the Petersburg mine assault. Federals dug a long mine beneath the Confederate works and loaded it with dynamite. On July 30, 1864, after one abortive attempt to light the charge, the mine exploded, creating a huge crater on the Confederate line. The original plan called for a black division to lead the assault, but for fear of political repercussions if the endeavor failed and black troops sustained huge losses, Maj. Gen. George Meade had a white division head the attack. As a result of mismanagement, Confederate obstinacy, and the difficulty of crossing the huge crater, the white troops soon bogged down and the Federals sent in the black division to exploit the break in the Confederate line. At first the black troops made good headway, but the Confederate artillery fire became so heavy that they could do nothing but hug the ground. Confederates then sealed off the breakthrough and fired on the attackers from the front and the flank. For the Federals, it appeared too dangerous either to retreat or advance, and throughout much of the day the black and white troops could do little more than hold their place. Eventually, the Confederates gathered enough forces to launch a counterattack, and most Federals, rather than surrender and risk their fate with their enemies, "after desperate resistance broke, and fell back in perfect disorder, [and] horrible slaughter," concluded an officer in the USCT. As the black commands rallied by units to tabulate losses, one officer wrote a friend, "I felt like sitting down & weeping on account of our misfortune." One regiment, the 29th U.S. Colored Infantry, entered the fight with 450 troops and exited with 128. In total, the black commands suffered more than 40 percent of the fatalities and 35 percent of the casualties, despite a preponderance of white soldiers in the engagement.[18]

At the battle of Chaffin's Farm near Richmond, Virginia, in late September 1864, Lt. Gen. Ulysses S. Grant used white and black troops in an attack to prevent Confederate reinforcements from being sent elsewhere in Virginia and also to weaken the garrison at Petersburg. Here again black units had to charge over difficult terrain against strong Confederate works. After working their way through a maze of felled trees, troops from the 4th and 6th U.S. Colored Infantry had to wade a swamp as they approached the Confederate fortifications. Officers had instructed troops to fix bayonets and not to fire, but as their advance slowed to a crawl in the swampy area and Confederates began to shoot down the attackers, the black troops could not resist firing back. When they stopped to reload, Confederates cut them down in huge numbers. Their brigade commander, among the wounded, praised the tremendous bravery his men exhibited that day: "Ah! give me the Thunder-heads & Black hearts after all. They fought splendidly that morning, facing the red tempest of death with unflinching heroism." One company lost over 87 percent of its men in the assault, and one regiment had 209 casualties out of 377 men who entered the battle. Another brigade of black troops, attacking near the 4th and 6th U.S. Colored Infantry, also had to traverse a swamp and had problems with their troops firing in the open, yet they drove the Confederates from the defensive position. Their losses, however, were staggering. The black brigade entered the battle with 1,300 men and had 455 casualties. The worst instance, though, occurred when Brig. Gen. William Birney ordered four companies to charge a Confederate fortification that an entire regiment probably could not have taken. Despite heavy fire the troops advanced to a deep ditch outside the fort, but every time they hoisted soldiers to the top, blasts from the Confederates knocked them back. Rebel forces then began to lob hand grenades and short-fuse shells into the ditch, and the survivors all had to surrender. In the end, although black units comprised only a small portion of the Federal force in the battle, they suffered 43 percent of the casualties.[19]

Probably the most audacious assault by the USCT occurred at a railroad bridge over the Big Black River in Mississippi in late 1864. Confederate Lt. Gen. John Bell Hood had just begun his invasion of Tennessee, and by a roundabout railroad route he was able to draw supplies from southern Mississippi and Alabama. By destroying this railroad bridge, Federals would cut his supply line. The problem was that the railroad bridge was situated in an almost impenetrable swamp, and the only way over it was the railroad ties and trestles. At both ends of the span, some twenty-five feet high, the Confederates had erected a stockade and had allocated a large infantry force, estimated by one Union officer as "at least one regiment," to protect it. Although two previous attempts by the Federals with much larger forces had failed, authorities sent Maj. J. B. Cook and his 3rd U.S. Colored Cavalry to try his hand. Cook, who had to move rapidly as Confederates closed in on his raiding party, sent a dismounted company into the swamp on each side of the track with orders to work their way up near the bridge. "The men waded waist deep in mud and water a great part of the distance, which rendered progress extremely slow and tedious," an officer who commanded one of the companies in the swamp recorded. To occupy the attention of the defenders, Cook had his men advance toward the bridge, discharging a few rounds, and then fall back, luring the Confederate forces out of the near stockade to fire at the distant Federals. Eventually, the two companies worked their way to the riverbank, concealed themselves in thick underbrush, and awaited a bugle blast that signaled them to fire. The two companies caught the Confederates completely unprepared, and after they routed the Rebel forces outside the stockade, they peppered the portholes to keep the Confederates inside from returning fire. Meanwhile, Cook's forces assaulted the stockade by charging along the narrow railroad tracks, and after a hand-to-hand battle, they drove the Confederates out. From the other side of the bridge, however, Confederates again poured a heavy fire into the 3rd U.S. Colored Cavalry, and after attempts to silence that stockade with musketry fire failed, Cook boldly led three companies in an assault over the narrow ties of the bridge and drove the Confederates into some woods on the other side. Planning ahead, Cook had directed one company to bring oil in its canteens, and the troops doused the bridge and piled on timber and brush as Confederates continued to harass them with fire from the woods. When some black troops lit the bridge, the entire structure went up in flames. Cook then had his men destroy part of the railroad track by lifting up the ties and hurling the entire structure, ties and rails, down the slope and into the swamp. As a reward for such outstanding service, Maj. Gen. E. R. S. Canby promoted Cook to lieutenant colonel and declared this "one of the most daring and heroic acts of the war" in a general order published throughout his military division.[20]

In fact, there were dozens and dozens of instances of brilliant performance by men in the USCT during combat. The most famous cases were Sgt. Anselmas Planciancois of what became the 73rd U.S. Colored Infantry, who promised his commander to carry the regimental colors in the assault on Port Hudson and return with them or explain why he failed to God; Sgt. William H. Carney of the 54th Massachusetts (Colored) Infantry, flag bearer who planted his colors on the Confederate parapet at Fort Wagner and carried them back despite wounds in his legs, breast, and arm; and Sgt. Maj. Christian A. Fleetwood of the 4th U.S. Colored Infantry, who saved the regimental colors after Confederates had shot two color guards and carried them heroically throughout the rest of the battle. Both Carney and Fleetwood were Medal of Honor winners, and deservedly so, along with thirteen officers and fourteen other enlisted men, yet there were many acts of bravery performed by men in the USCT that passed with little acknowledgment. At Chaffin's Farm,

Orderly Sgt. William Strander, "scarce 20 years of age and as brave a boy as ever wore the diamond [the corps badge]," refused to seek medical attention despite a serious wound and insisted on continuing the fight. According to his commander, "with the blood streaming from his neck [Strander] followed me over the enemys works." During the Red River Campaign of 1864, acting First Sgt. Antoine Davis of the 92nd U.S. Colored Infantry suffered wounds in the head and breast but refused to leave the field. Not until a Confederate cavalryman felled him with a shot in the groin were Federals able to remove him from battle. Five days later, Davis died in a New Orleans hospital. After the 33rd U.S. Colored Infantry conducted a raid, a company commander reported that one soldier, wounded in the neck and shoulder, still carried two muskets from the field. Another man, with three wounds, one of which was in the head, refused to seek medical attention until his officers forced it upon him. And in the most unusual case, a soldier who had a bullet in his shoulder neglected to report to the surgeon and even performed guard duty until someone discovered his wound.[21]

What made the performance of the USCT so unusual, though, were the widespread and consistent levels of audacity and grittiness. Time after time black units as a whole acted bravely, because they were so afraid of accusations of cowardice. They fought aggressively, even recklessly, and no one could challenge their valor or commitment to the war. Black soldiers knew full well what was at stake, and they were willing to take greater risks in hopes of postwar rewards. *"Dat's just what I went for,"* replied a soldier who had suffered two wounds when Higginson asked if a recent battle was more than he had bargained for.[22]

Of course, there were occasions when black units performed poorly and officers and men exhibited cowardice. At the Battle of Guntown, Mississippi, in June 1864, twenty-one of seventy-seven soldiers from a company in the 59th U.S. Colored Infantry threw away their rifles in the retreat. That same month back east, an officer went into combat twice with some unassigned recruits and had a mixed evaluation: "Some of our men acted very bravely last night and others acted very badly and even cowardly." The most serious case of cowardice involving black forces was when the commander at Fort Athens, Georgia, surrendered the entire garrison of over six hundred men, well fortified, without firing a shot, yet this was not the fault of the troops or even of subordinate officers.[23]

Most of the time, though, acts of cowardice were isolated instances. A major in the 34th U.S. Colored Infantry conveniently fell ill before two battles and left his place, even though the surgeon pronounced him fit for duty. In the 68th U.S. Colored Infantry, almost the exact

same thing happened. A lieutenant colonel claimed he was ill, although the surgeon insisted that there "wasn't a d___d thing the
matter with him." The regimental commander let him go to the
rear, but not until he extracted a promise that if fighting began
the lieutenant colonel would return to duty. During three days of
combat, he was nowhere to be seen. A general court martial later
dismissed him from the service, but the lieutenant colonel used
his personal connections with two U.S. senators to get the decision
overturned. In Virginia a court convicted a major of cowardice and
tore off his insignia, broke his sword, ripped off his buttons, and
drove him out of camp on an ox cart to the tune of the "Rogue's
March" with all the troops present. And some cowards were not
always so obvious. According to one officer who suffered a wound
in the Battle of the Crater, among the patients in Chesapeake Hospital at Fort Monroe, Virginia, there were heroes, "But I see also some
others here that I am sure *will* be sufferers all their life time—from
cowardice."[24]

Nor were enlisted men immune. A private in the 5th U.S. Colored
Infantry fled to the rear in the face of the enemy three times. A
court ordered his head shaved, had him wear a placard that stated
"Coward," and fined him ten dollars per month for six months. In
the first battle of the 6th U.S. Colored Infantry, a captain had a
big impressive man for his color sergeant. As they advanced in battle,
the sergeant began to falter, and the captain first pushed him forward
and then struck him with the blunt end of his sword to shame
him. Eventually, the soldier could no longer advance, dropped the
flag, and literally crawled on his hands and knees to the rear.[25]

These acts of cowardice, however, were rare. In fact, one of the
most significant problems USCT officers had was restraining their
men in battle. With inadequate training, and a burning desire to
prove themselves on the battlefield, officers had great difficulty con-
trolling their men. A lieutenant at the Battle of the Crater thought
his men "were brave in their charge, but as a body, wholly unmanage-
able." Before the American Freedmen's Inquiry Commission, Higginson testified that "the most difficult thing in regard to them might
be, for instance, to restrain them in such cases where they are
required to charge with energy up a hill side," and sundry fights
proved him right. In a skirmish at Vidalia, Louisiana, in 1864,
the 6th U.S. Colored Heavy Artillery, fighting as infantrymen, broke
up a Confederate assault, and only forceful action by the regimental
commander "prevented them from breaking ranks to follow the enemy, their anxiety being great to do so." The eagerness of black
troops in the battalion held in reserve was so "irrepressible" that
the commander and all his line officers "were obliged to place them-

selves before their men with drawn swords, and threaten summary punishment to the first man who would attempt to quit the ranks to join their comrades fighting in the front." [26]

For Confederates, the prospect of fighting black soldiers was a bit frightening. Like their Northern enemies, Southerners cloaked their fears of slave violence with stereotyped descriptions of laziness, ignorance, and joviality. They had argued vociferously that slavery was good for blacks, that the institution was paternalistic, not cruel, yet deep down many knew that blacks despised enslavement. Nothing brought shudders to Southerners like the thought of armed slaves. For centuries they had kept blacks in a debased state, and now, in Union blue, blacks had a chance to strike back and destroy the oppressive institution. From the very beginning of black enlistment, the concept of fighting black soldiers worried Confederates. "I have talked with numbers of Parolled Prisoners in Vicksburg," wrote one Union officer to his mother, "and they all admit it was the hardest stroke that there cause has received—the arming of the negrow. Not a few of them told me that they would rather fight two Regiments of White Soldiers than one of Niggers. Rebel Citizens fear them more than they would fear Indians." [27]

In part as an outlet for their frustration that blacks aligned with Union forces and in part as a means of intimidating blacks in uniform, to ruin the prospects of blacks developing into good soldiers by destroying their self-confidence and the regard Northerners had for the prowess of black troops, Confederates made a special effort to harass and abuse the USCT at every turn. A commander of a black regiment commented that Confederates fired at his troops regularly all night. They "seem to have a great animosity towards the colored soldier," he wrote. Maj. Gen. E. O. C. Ord informed Grant that in Virginia "the rebels on Warren's front called out to our men that they were going to shell Burnside's Niggers and they (Warren's men) must not mind it. They have shelled every morning since." In Louisiana a lieutenant reported that Confederate troops attacked their outposts and killed two black troops, then mutilated the bodies as a warning: "They were found in the morning with their ears cut off, and scalped and burned to a crisp." And the attack had the desired effect. Within a week the officer was complaining that his troops were "seeing Rebs where there were none" and shooting at cows and inanimate objects: "They get skeered and fire." [28]

Wartime atrocities against the USCT were commonplace, as Confederates first hoped to discourage blacks from enlisting and later sought revenge for their contributions to the Union Army. Initially they were frequent yet isolated incidents. In Louisiana after the

Battle of Milliken's Bend a Confederate deserter reported that they had executed an officer and a few enlisted men, and not long afterward some Rebels beat some black troops and hung two others. Similar executions also occurred in Kansas and North Carolina.[29]

But as the war dragged on and Confederates became more and more frustrated, atrocities in battle escalated. In Arkansas at Poison Springs in 1864 Confederates struck some twelve hundred Federals from front and flank and forced them to give ground. Many of the wounded from the 79th U.S. Colored Infantry (New) fell into the hands of the Confederates, and "I have the most positive assurances from eye-witnesses that they were murdered on the spot," charged a Federal colonel. The black regiment suffered nearly twice as many troops killed as wounded, a rarity in the Civil War. At the Battle of the Crater, a Union officer ordered all troops in the crater to surrender, and a few kept up their firing. In retaliation, some Confederates began to bayonet wounded black soldiers, which in turn prompted blacks to counterattack with bullets, bayonets, and rifle butts. Eventually, a Confederate major managed to restore order, and he guaranteed adequate treatment for all prisoners, but if they resisted, he promised all would die. On the urgings of the Federal officers present, everyone then surrendered. In early October 1864 in the Battle of Saltville, Virginia, some fledgling black soldiers in the 5th U.S. Colored Cavalry launched a brilliant charge on Confederate works and drove their adversaries back. For two hours they held their position, but without support, authorities withdrew them at dusk. During the battle Confederates executed numerous black troops who fell into their hands, and wounded black soldiers insisted that their comrades take them in retreat. Despite efforts to collect everyone, some remained on the field, and over the next two days two separate parties of Confederate troops entered hospitals and executed seven wounded black soldiers in their beds.[30]

Without doubt, the most famous series of atrocities in the war occurred at Fort Pillow, some forty miles north of Memphis, in April 1864. There a force of 1,500 Confederate cavalrymen under the command of Maj. Gen. Nathan Bedford Forrest demanded the surrender of the fort, manned by some 550 Federals, nearly half of whom were black soldiers. When the Union commander refused, Forrest's forces stormed the fort and killed, wounded, or captured almost the entire garrison. Some two-thirds of all black soldiers at Fort Pillow lost their lives, while Confederates killed 36 percent of all white troops. After the fight, Federals charged Forrest's command with committing all sorts of atrocities against black soldiers who surrendered. Forrest and Confederate authorities claimed that no such thing occurred, that only black soldiers who continued to fight or tried to escape lost their lives. Eventually, the U.S. Congress's Committee on the Conduct of the War investigated the affair and concluded that Forrest's men had butchered black troops. Southerners, on the other hand, argued that the report was sheer propaganda, and that Forrest and his command had done nothing wrong. Testimony from both Federal and Confederate troops and civilians on the scene, however, indicates that Forrest's men did execute some black soldiers. No one will ever know how many men from the USCT lost their lives after they had surrendered, nor will anyone satisfactorily determine Forrest's role in the massacre.[31]

Southern guerrillas, too, proved to be a problem. Some Confederates and partisans surrounded a foraging party of twenty men from the 51st U.S. Colored Infantry under a lieutenant and forced them to surrender. They then murdered and mutilated the Federals, shooting the lieutenant through the mouth and leaving him for dead, although he lingered on for another ten days. In Kentucky some guerrillas attacked a guard of ten men from the 108th U.S. Colored Infantry, killed three of them, and then butchered their bodies. Six weeks later in Georgia, guerrillas killed three black troops from the 40th U.S. Colored Infantry and split their heads open with an ax. Such acts of violence did little for the Confederate war effort and only served to infuriate Federals.[32]

In his report after the battle at Fort Pillow, Forrest expressed hope that the "facts will demonstrate to the Northern people that negro soldiers cannot cope with Southerners." On the contrary, such atrocities solidified Northern support for the USCT and hardened attitudes toward Confederates within black units. They fought with a little more vigor, and they also decided that wartime atrocities was something "*at which two can play*," so wrote Brig. Gen. August Chetlain. At times they fought under the black flag, which warned the Confederates that they would neither take prisoners nor ask for any mercy for themselves; in other engagements, they acted without warning. An officer in the USCT wrote his wife that some troops in his regiment trapped ten Confederates and gunned down five of them. "Had it not been for Ft Pillow, those 5 men might be alive now. 'Remember Ft Pillow' is getting to be the *feeling* if not the word. It looks hard but we cannot blame these men much." During a scouting mission in Louisiana, a company of black cavalrymen discovered a party of guerrillas. The colonel of the expedition instructed his black soldiers to "Remember Fort Pillow," and the black horsemen captured and executed seventeen prisoners. In South Carolina a Confederate general complained that one of his privates had fallen into the hands of the 26th U.S. Colored Infantry. When the Confederates retook the ground, they found the private with six or seven bayonet wounds in him. A Maine cavalryman informed a friend at home that he had witnessed black troops executing a number of Confederates after they surrendered: "We had 200 niggers soldiers with us it did not make eny differance to them about the Rebs surrendering   they would shoot them down   the officers had hard work to stop them from killing All the prisoners   when one of them would beg for his life the niggers would say rember port hudson   it was the Same regiment that the rebs took part of and hung them over the walls." And in an assault at Fort Blakely, Alabama, where black units charged without orders, their conduct was not much different from the behavior of Forrest's command at Fort Pillow. According to a lieutenant in the USCT, when the black troops attacked, "the rebs were panic-struck. Numbers of them jumped into the river and were drowned attempting to cross, or were shot while swimming. Still others threw down their arms and run for their lives over to the white troops on our left, to give themselves up, to save being butchered by our niggers   the niggers did not take a prisoner, they killed all they took to a man." Many of their white officers simply overlooked such retaliation, while others did not endorse such conduct but proved incapable of putting a halt to it. In fact, the problem of blacks executing Confederates became so widespread that black chaplain Henry M. Turner complained publicly about these atrocities.[33]

Under such circumstances, both sides were extremely hesitant to surrender to one another, even when the situation demanded it. In a Federal attack along the Darbytown Road near Chaffin's Farm, Confederates had dug gopher holes and manned them with marksmen. They held their positions "until the inmates saw that we were black & close on them when they dropped all and ran." Black troops captured several South Carolinians in the fight, "who were badly scared lest the darkies should kill them," an officer wrote home. "Indeed all the rebels who fall into my hands remind me strongly of the fugitives who used to call at our house for aid— except that now the master begs favors from the slave and gets them too." During the extended siege of Petersburg, thousands of Confederates deserted to Federal lines, but very few came to the black units for fear of mistreatment. When they did accidentally surrender to commands in the USCT, both white officers and their black men enjoyed observing the "terrified" look once "they found out they had thrown themselves into the hands of the avenging negro."[34]

For black outfits, the possibility of execution if they fell into the clutches of the Confederates was an incentive to fight even more aggressively. Nevertheless, sometimes it was a question of surrendering or being annihilated, and then their officers opted to place their own lives and those of their men in the hands of the Confederate foe.

Needless to say, black prisoners of war had nowhere to hide, and they were exclusively at the mercy of the Rebels, who sometimes committed atrocities and other times treated them as ordinary prisoners. For their white officers, though, it was not always so obvious whom they commanded, and occasionally they had opportunities to protect themselves when captured in large battles by claiming they served in white units. In a fight in Tennessee in November 1864, two officers from the 44th U.S. Colored Infantry told their captors they served in their original white volunteer regiments and the scheme worked temporarily, but Confederates later executed them. At the Battle of the Crater, numerous officers in black units refused to acknowledge their service with the USCT, and their black troops covered for them. Some, however, had consciences that would not let them lie, or they were too proud of service alongside black soldiers to conceal it from anyone. After several whites provided false information to Confederate interrogators, one lieutenant indignantly barked out, "Lemuel D. Dobbs, Nineteenth Niggers, by ————." Dobbs as well as others who admitted service in the USCT received bad treatment at the hands of the Rebels, but it was no worse than any other Union soldier who surrendered at the Crater. Other times, soldiers in gray intended to teach USCT officers a lesson, but their own officers refused to tolerate such conduct. When Lt. Joseph K. Nelson surrendered and told his captors that he was an officer in the 111th U.S. Colored Infantry, a Confederate soldier shoved a revolver in his face and said, "You are one of those G____ d____ nigger officers, are you?" Fortunately a Confederate officer intervened and ordered the man away before the soldier could do anything.[35]

Like all soldiers who entered combat, officers and men in the USCT had to deal with the prospect of death, and they appeared to cope with it well. White officers and Northern blacks had made a conscious decision to enter the USCT, well knowing the increased risks, and many former slaves, with religion as their anchor, had long ago adopted the view that God would repay them for all sacrifices and hardships on earth with rewards in heaven, and this belief continued to sustain them throughout their military careers. One officer thought a number of his men "were perfect fatalists in their confidence that God would watch over them, and that if they died, it would be because their time had come." Along similar lines, a lieutenant explained to his mother that Confederate threats to hang white officers did not worry him: "If a man is born to be hung he

will not be shot." Others claimed no insight into fate. They merely
regarded the goals of the war as worthy of the risk to their lives.
"If I fall in the battle anticipated," a black sergeant wrote a friend,
"remember, I fall in defence of my race and country." In a dramatic
scene that left a lasting impression on the commander, a lieutenant
told his troops prior to an advance, "Boys, it may be slavery or
Death to some of you today," to which a black soldier replied, "Lieutenant, I am ready to die for Liberty." Moments later, a ball pierced
the soldier's heart.[36]

Statistically, during the last two years of the war black troops
suffered one-half the fatalities in combat per one thousand men
that white volunteers did, but this information is misleading. Because military authorities assigned black commands to peripheral
duties and reserved the combat jobs in main armies for white soldiers, black troops fought in comparatively few major battles, even
in 1864. But when they did have an opportunity to fight, they almost
always battled tenaciously. On numerous battlefields black commands suffered proportionately higher casualties and performed
as well, if not better, than more experienced white units. No doubt
part of the reason for advances of black troops beyond those of
whites, and higher casualties, was inexperience. One advantage veteran troops had was to recognize when attacks were hopeless and
when retreats were essential for survival. Veterans learned to con-
serve their own lives to fight the next day. Yet black troops had to
prove to whites that they were inferior to no one, and combat served
as the primary arena. They consciously took on extra risks, and
lost many lives because of it, in hopes that their labors on the battlefield would reap benefits to the survivors, their families, and future
generations. As an officer in the 100th U.S. Colored Infantry explained after the Battle of Nashville, it was sad to walk over the
battlefield and see hundreds of bodies of black and white men, clad
in blue, killed in battle; but in a peculiar way, the sight was also
uplifting, because "the blood of the white and black men has flowed
freely together for the great cause which is to give freedom, unity,
manhood and peace to all men, whatever birth or complexion." No
doubt, amid the tragedy of combat sprouted hope among black soldiers, so alluded a sergeant and former slave at the end of 1864:
"The bones of the black man are at present time whitening the
battle-fields, while their blood, simultaneously with the white man's,
oozes into the soil of his former home." [37]

Given their aggressive conduct in battle, officers and men in the
USCT certainly suffered their share of wounds. Varying in seriousness from nicks to those that inflicted fatal injuries, wounds were
at times the most harrowing experience of war. One captain in com-

mand of a skirmish line during a Confederate attack sustained a
wound in his left forearm, then in the right shoulder, and finally
in the right forearm, which pierced an artery. For nine hours he
lay on the field with no water or medical care and bullets and shells
flying all around him. All he could think about was home and the
possibility of being a cripple for life. He prayed for water to ease
his thirst and for nightfall, when his comrades could come out and
rescue him. For another officer, the agony was even worse.[38]

At the Battle of Olustee in Florida, an officer in the USCT sustained
a serious wound. A ball entered the back of his right side, deflected
off his shoulder blade, and lodged against his spine, paralyzing
his legs. That night, due to the pain, the officer babbled considerably,
most of the time in his native German. By the next morning, he
was "more like himself," so wrote a surgeon to the officer's wife,
and he knew his death was impending. He died the following day.
Other times, the injuries were mere scratches that did not amount
to "a hill of beans," so wrote an officer to his father, or soldiers
sustained one fairly serious wound but had so many near misses
that they left the field feeling fortunate. A soldier in the 14th U.S.
Colored Infantry had a spent ball strike him in the head. The ball
had enough force to cut through his scalp, but it could not penetrate
his skull and passed around his head and exited on the other side.
After the fight his comrades chided him that when the ball struck
him, it "sang out 'too thick' and passed on." Then there were the
soldiers who always seemed to get wounded, yet they were present
for the next fight. A private in the 30th U.S. Colored Infantry, for
example, received a grapeshot to the head at Petersburg, a leg wound
at Hatcher's Run, a shoulder wound at Chaffin's Farm, and a wrist
wound at Fort Fisher. After all that, he confidently announced to
his lieutenant, "I don't reckon I'se gwine to get killed in dis wah!,"
and he survived it. In combat areas, no one was immune; so learned
a private who was "attending to a call of nature" next to his captain
when a ball struck him in the back. The wound, however, was not
serious, and it proved more embarrassing than anything else.[39]

In most cases wounded soldiers received medical attention right
near the front line. As units assembled for battle, it was the duty
of operating physicians within a brigade or division to assemble a
surgeon's booth, some three hundred yards to the rear, and prefer-
ably in a protected area, where they removed balls, stopped the
bleeding, and dressed wounds temporarily. They also administered
morphine as a pain killer and some whiskey as a "stimulant." Ambu-
lances then transported the wounded to "flying" or field hospitals,
where they received more thorough medical attention. Providing
they were able to travel, patients with injuries that were likely to

keep them from duty for more than ten days then went to a base or general hospital.[40]

Combat units regarded it as critical to have at least two physicians. One had to set up the surgeon's booth, hang out a lantern, and then send a messenger to the front to guide the stretcher-bearers to the operating area. The other physician went to the front to give water and sometimes whiskey to the wounded and have the stretcher-bearers remove the injured men from the field of battle. This was an important job, particularly in the USCT, as a surgeon stated: *"I know what will become of the white troops who fall into the enemy's possession, but I am not certain as to the fate of the colored troops."* Yet it was also a dangerous duty that cost the USCT numerous physicians. Although one assistant surgeon tried to reassure his wife that he would not be "rushing into battle" because "I am one of the biggest cowards in the world & then my province is not to fight," there were considerable risks. Another surgeon more candidly explained to his mother that he did his best not to expose himself recklessly, not only because he feared injury but also because he was not "doing his full duty to my men if I expose myself, when my services may be exceedingly necessary to them." Nevertheless, he had a three-pound shot pass just over his head, "much disarranging my ideas & causing me to skedaddle swiftly." [41]

Stretcher-bearers were usually musicians and any noncombat personnel a unit could assemble. Their tool of the trade was a canvas sheet stretched over a wooden frame to carry the wounded back to the surgeon's booth for medical care. According to a surgeon, one could recognize a veteran unit most easily by examining its stretchers. The experienced units had the canvas "literally dyed in blood." Throughout the battle, stretcher-bearers made trip after trip, exposing themselves considerably and at times becoming casualties themselves, in hopes of hauling wounded troops to the rear for medical attention.[42]

For operating surgeons, the work was frantic. After one battle a surgeon wrote home that he had attended two hundred wounded and performed thirty-five to forty "capital" operations,—that is, leg and arm amputations, at all possible spots,—besides as many more resections." He even had to remove about one-half of a soldier's upper jaw without chloroform because he feared the man would swallow too much blood and choke. Another surgeon, whose regiment suffered two hundred killed and wounded in one day, wrote, "For the last sixty-four hours I have had but ten hours sleep. I worked twenty-two hours yesterday." Serving with a combat regiment in Virginia in 1864, he labored so intensively that, he confessed, "It is rarely I sleep nights I am so nervous." One month later, the pressure of surgery and overwork resulted in dizzy spells.[43]

With elementary equipment, the most prominent item being a saw, and little understanding of sanitation and sterilization, these surgeons operated on their patients in desperate hope of saving lives. Huge, soft chunks of lead inflicted horrible wounds, and clothing and dirt introduced with the projectile produced infections and gangrene. One surgeon told his father, also a doctor, that out of one soldier's back he removed "a piece of shell weighing a pound, completely embedded in the flesh." Many surgeons were quick to sacrifice limbs to save lives, while others agonized over the decision, particularly with arms, because some men could lose a considerable amount of bone and still retain use of the limb. Miscalculation with amputations, however, often resulted in the death of patients from infections and hemorrhage. In search of lead and bits of clothing, surgeons sometimes cut substantial holes in patients and poked and pried until they secured the foreign objects. At times, patients could not decide whether the injury or operation was more painful. "The fact is I've lain now seven days," complained an officer, "wounded in both thighs by the enemy & wounded in the rear by the surgeon who cut a ball out—by the rear." Other times, because of the location of the ball, surgeons could only remove clothing fragments and dress the wound. One such instance occurred when a ball entered the left shoulder of a man and pierced his lung. Miraculously, he recovered, although he carried the ball around, lodged in him permanently.[44]

One of the least visible and most private injuries in the Civil War was combat stress. Fighting in relatively compact formations, with buddies all around to help ease the tension and buoy the confidence, combat stress seldom afflicted black troops, just as it was rather uncommon in white volunteer units. But for white officers in the USCT the situation was different. As models for black soldiers, these whites had to try to suppress their very natural fears and uncertainties concerning both their troops and themselves and portray a sense of confidence and composure. Worse yet, they entered combat under the added pressure of fighting with troops whom they regarded as inexperienced, improperly trained, and not wholly trustworthy. And because they felt a keen sense of isolation, surrounded by dozens and dozens of blacks, many of them had no viable outlet for their emotions. The night after the Battle of Chaffin's Farm, a captain who led thirty-two men into the fight and returned with only three others, all black, began to feel depressed. "I experienced a tingling, prickly sensation, as though a thousand little needles were jagging my flesh. The air seemed oppressive, and I breathed with difficulty." The captain realized he was in trouble and sought help from the

regimental surgeon. That night the surgeon drugged the captain
to enable him to sleep and the next day sent him to the corps hospital
for ten days. Although doctors diagnosed his problem as intermittent
fever, the captain knew better: "The strain on me was so great
through the day, that when the excitement passed over and quiet
came, my nervous organization broke down temporarily. That was
all." Ten days of rest, along with a liberal amount of quinine, "toned
me up again," and he returned for duty. Another officer, this one
in the 54th Massachusetts (Colored) Infantry, also suffered from
combat stress after the attack on Fort Wagner, and his regimental
surgeon did a much better job of determining his problem: *"His
brain has been seriously affected by isolation and exhaustion
during the recent field operations on James* [Morris] *Island so that
an absence from the department is necessary to prevent permanent
disability."* A third officer also experienced some combat stress,
yet doctors refused to acknowledge his problem. As a foreigner who
had just joined his unit before the Virginia Campaign of 1864, he
had not integrated into the command. Exposure to the scenes of
battle several days after they had taken place horrified him, and
the officer soon found service with black troops unrewarding. With
the added burdens of fighting, regular campaign duties, and some
homesickness, he became so depressed that he could not get up
out of bed. When he finally sought medical attention, the doctor
found nothing physically wrong with the officer and ordered him
back to duty. That evening the officer vented his spleen in his diary,
"The meanness of the medical department in the army here, no
assistance, no sympathy, no help." Three weeks later he admitted
that joining the USCT had been the greatest blunder of his life
and even mentioned suicide as an alternative.[45]

Despite the temptation to compare the combat performance of
black and white units in the Union Army, such efforts are utterly
unfair. By the time the Federal government decided to enlist black
soldiers, hundreds of thousands of white troops already had substantial battlefield experience, and as fledgling black soldiers "saw the
elephant" for the first time, they faced a veteran Confederate Army.
Most high-ranking Union officers preferred to use black troops for
fatigue and noncombat duty and rely on the veteran white commands
for combat. Thus, black units had little time for drill and were often
relegated to rear-area occupation duties or secondary and tertiary
campaigns. While black soldiers had powerful reasons for military
service, such as the elimination of slavery, revenge for generations
of bondage, and a chance to demonstrate to whites the fallacy of
prejudice, they also suffered the humiliation of unequal pay and
bounties and virtually no promotions to the officer corps. Along

with shouldering the additional burden of the welfare of their families in the transition from slavery to freedom, it is a tribute to their commitment to the war effort that the desertion rate of black soldiers in the Union Army was almost identical to whites.[46]

On several occasions, the performance of black commands outshone that of white volunteer units. In South Carolina the 7th U.S. Colored Infantry came to the rescue of a veteran white regiment that had run out of ammunition. As the black troops marched in behind the line, veteran white soldiers broke and fled under the weight of a Confederate assault. The men of the 7th U.S. Colored Infantry turned toward the Confederates and advanced boldly, with white Federal troops pouring through their formation, and filled the gap in the Federal line to repulse the attack. At the Battle of Brice's Crossroads in June 1864, Forrest's command routed a Federal force and black troops blocked the Confederates while their white comrades escaped. With almost no assistance from white volunteers, two black infantry regiments and a black light artillery battery battled the advancing graycoats for three days, sometimes in hand-to-hand combat, and even ran out of ammunition, but saved the command of Brig. Gen. Samuel D. Sturgis. Out of 1,350 men, the black brigade suffered well over 800 casualties. On yet another occasion, the 600 recruits who composed the 5th U.S. Colored Cavalry were so raw that a black sergeant admitted he did not even know the names of his men when they first entered combat. En route to Saltville, these troops silently endured insults, harassment, and derogatory remarks about their lack of fighting prowess from the white volunteers. In the battle, of the 400 black soldiers who saw combat, the Confederates killed or wounded 118, and the black regiment penetrated deepest into the Rebel works. According to a captain in the 13th Kentucky Cavalry, a regiment that so opposed the enlistment of blacks that some of its men nearly murdered a recruiting officer for the USCT, he and his comrades "never saw troops fight like they did. The rebels were firing on them with grape and canister and were mowing them down by the Scores but others kept straight on." The captain admitted he "never thought they would fight till he Saw them there." In support, Col. James S. Brisbin wrote, "I have seen white troops fight in twenty-seven battles, and I never saw any fight better" than his black soldiers. Brisbin also noted that "On the return of the forces[,] those who had scoffed at the colored troops on the march out were silent."[47]

As they earned more and more combat experience, those raw recruits were transformed in attitude and performance into veterans. They neither shunned battle nor craved it; combat became an obligation. Black troops still regarded it as a great opportunity to prove themselves to whites on both sides of the line, and they continued to fight aggressively, yet their previous battlefield experience had taught them warfare's serious side and they acted a bit less recklessly. More importantly, they learned to cope with dangers and fears of combat, and confidence in their own ability to handle its rigors grew. When a Confederate army approached Fort Pulaski, Tennessee, manned by the 14th U.S. Colored Infantry, a black soldier told his regimental commander, "Col'nel, dey can't whip us; dey nebber git the ole Fourteenth out of heah, nebber." Several weeks later, in Virginia, another black regiment got into a nasty fight as most of the men fired two hundreds rounds at the Confederates. Unfortunately, the residue from all the black gunpowder they used got the muskets so dirty that troops were unable to ram down charges and had to clean them while under heavy fire. Nevertheless, they retained their composure, which thoroughly impressed one of their officers: "the men however, coolly sat down, dismounted their pieces and cleaned them, after which they resumed firing." [48]

Before the American Freedmen's Inquiry Commission, Higginson stated what nearly all whites held to be fact. If the black troops "lose their officers the effect will be worse upon them than upon white troops—not because they are timid but because they are less accustomed to entire self-reliance." Time after time, as black soldiers gained more and more combat experience, they proved Higginson and others wrong. In the 1st U.S. Colored Infantry, Company C lost all its officers and two sergeants in a skirmish and an assault, and command of the company in battle fell to a corporal. Sgt. Reddick Witchel of the 61st U.S. Colored Infantry commanded a company during the entire campaign for Eastport, Mississippi, in 1864, and he won the respect and admiration of several officers, including his regimental commander, for a "splendid" job. During the battle of Chaffin's Farm all the officers in four companies were either killed or wounded, and command devolved on black sergeants who "led them gallantly and meritoriously through the day" and earned Medals of Honor for their conduct. And on an expedition to the Rappahannock River in Virginia, a party of black soldiers ran into some Confederates. With no officers present, the troops seized the initiative and attacked, killing, wounding, or capturing every Confederate except one who escaped. Thus black soldiers had good reason to clamor for the promotion of noncommissioned officers into the commissioned ranks. [49]

Once they fought alongside white troops and demonstrated their combat prowess, black soldiers went a long way toward neutralizing the distrust and disdain whites had for them. After the garrison at Paducah, Kentucky, held off Forrest's larger force, the post commander confessed, "I have been one of those men, who never had much confidence in colored troops fighting, but these doubts are now all removed, for they fought as bravely as any troops in the Fort." Nothing could have felt better than to hear the three hearty cheers some white troops gave to the 14th U.S. Colored Infantry after their stellar conduct at Decatur, Alabama, or the reception three black regiments received after their successful assault on the works outside Petersburg in June 1864. "You ought to have heard the 'Bully for you's the Cavalry (Kautz's) favored the boys with," an officer wrote his wife. When Hancock's Corps from the Army of the Potomac arrived and relieved his regiment, these veterans congratulated the black soldiers and treated them with respect. "A few more fights like that," predicted the officer, "and our Cold [Colored] boys will have established their manhood if not their Brotherhood to the satisfaction of even the most prejudiced." [50]

In the late stages of the war, the USCT really began to make its presence felt. Nearly one in every eight soldiers in the siege of Petersburg was black, and at the Battle of Nashville, where Maj. Gen. George H. Thomas's troops crushed the Confederate Army of Tennessee and put a halt to Lt. Gen. John Bell Hood's Tennessee invasion, black forces played a major role despite their comparatively small size. On the first day of fighting, the two black brigades attacked the Confederate right to draw resources away from the main Federal thrust on the Rebel left flank, which was successful. During the second day, black and white troops swarmed up the slick slopes of the Confederate position on Overton Hill. "I can hear the voices of the officers as they called out, 'Close up those ranks,' " recalled an officer in the USCT, "as great gaps were made in them by howitzer and grape shot guns loaded to the muzzle." Although they did not break the Confederate line, these troops again forced the Confederate high command to transfer men to its right, which weakened the left and facilitated its fall to Federal attackers. Black units sustained 630 casualties out of 3,500 men in the victory. [51]

An even better example of black troops acting decisively in a major engagement was the Battle of Fort Blakely, Alabama, in April 1865. There a division of black troops occupied the extreme right of the Union line, and in the late afternoon, because of Confederate inactivity, they received permission to advance their skirmishers. Although Confederate troops fought vigorously, Rebel skirmishers fell back quickly into their own trenches. According to one officer in the USCT, "As soon as our niggers caught sight of the retreating figures of the rebs the very devil could not hold them their eyes glittered like serpents and with yells & howls like hungry wolves they rushed for the rebel works   the movement was simultaneous   regt.

[regiment] after regt. and line after line took up the cry and started until the whole field was black with darkeys." Similar in some respects to the famous Union assault up Missionary Ridge near Chattanooga, Tennessee, in October 1863, the black troops seized the opportunity and pursued the Confederates so closely that the defenders could not fire on them without fear of hitting their own men. Moments after the unscheduled charge, Federal troops around the line launched a planned assault, although word had never reached the black division, and the Federals carried the Confederate works everywhere.[52]

These and other outstanding battlefield performances by the USCT appeared to open new avenues to the black soldiers. In Virginia, where black units did some of their best fighting, an officer may have exaggerated a bit when he wrote his daughter that white troops "say the Darkies are Bully fellows to fight and all the prejudice seems to be gone," but he nevertheless conveyed the changing attitude among white volunteer units toward the USCT. Another USCT officer who had just come to Virginia from service in South Carolina and Florida also noted the more liberal racial atmosphere: "The colored troops are very highly valued here & there is no apparent difference in the way they are treated. White troops & blacks mingle constantly together & I have seen no single Evidence of dislike on the part of the soldiers. The truth is they have fought their way into the respect of all the army." Elsewhere progress was slow albeit steady. White troops were looking at black soldiers in a completely different light than they had some two years earlier.[53]

Such changes boded well for the future. Both white officers and their black soldiers believed that no one would ever again doubt the combat abilities of the black race. "The long contended point of negro fighting qualities is now forever settled," wrote one officer in the USCT. "They have proven themselves good soldiers, as well as ardent fighters." In fact, a few antiblack stalwarts now insisted that they "fight too well," noted Brig. Gen. Daniel Ullmann. Some of these individuals had actually recommended to Ullmann that "We must not discipline them, for if we do, we will have to fight them some day ourselves." Moreover, black troops and some white officers had reason to hope that a new era of race relations and civil rights was dawning, with blacks attaining all the rights and privileges of the white race. "The future of the colored soldier seems open more and auspiciously, both for himself and the country," concluded a chaplain. Such elevation, argued a captain, would also have a positive effect on white society: "They have raised themselves and all mankind in the scale of manhood by their bold achievements for I hold that, as water seeks a common level, so does the raising of a certain class of the people *must* of necessity raise the whole community!"[54]

9

Prejudice in the Service

*B*lack soldiers quickly learned that donning the uniform of the United States Army and fighting in battle for their country was an uplifting experience, but it was also a transitory sensation. Just as important was whether the United States government and the United States Army treated them the same as white soldiers. With good reason, blacks were skeptical. Before the war the white race had enslaved blacks in the South and discriminated against them in the North. Now, they wanted to believe that the government and military would regard them like all other soldiers, yet they had witnessed firsthand the seemingly unshakable power of prejudice and needed some demonstration of good faith. Unfortunately, such equal treatment was slow in coming.

When the War Department first authorized the enlistment of black men into the Union ranks, it had every intention of paying these soldiers the same as white troops. Brig. Gen. Rufus Saxton received instructions to recruit up to five thousand black soldiers with "the same pay and rations as are allowed by law to volunteers in the service," and when the state of Massachusetts advertised for recruits for the 54th and 55th Massachusetts (Colored) Infantry, it offered thirteen dollars per month, rations, and clothing, the same as white regiments, plus a bounty of fifty dollars upon signing and an additional one hundred dollars on muster out of service. In fact, in early 1863 an army paymaster gave each soldier in the 33rd U.S. Colored Infantry and the Louisiana Native Guards the standard pay for all soldiers, from thirteen dollars for privates to twenty-one dollars for sergeants, as well as proper pay for officers. According to a company commander, it was a jubilant day as "a steady stream of men" came to his tent, "some bringing money to be deposited for safe keeping, others wishing it sent to their wives, mothers, and sweethearts, and some wishing to pay debts contracted with me and with the sutler." To his great consternation, payday celebrations were a long time in coming again.[1]

Upon consultation with Solicitor William Whiting, the War Department announced on June 4, 1863, that the Militia Act of July 17, 1862, which approved the enlistment of blacks into military units, specified that pay was to be ten dollars per month, three of which was for clothing, the same pay as black government laborers, regardless of rank. This dictum touched off a storm of protest within the USCT, both from enlisted men and officers, that struck at the very core of the concept of equal standing for black soldiers. They had enlisted under an agreement, sometimes assumed but other times under written authorization, that as United States volunteers they were to receive the same pay and emoluments as other volunteers. Now, without forewarning, the government was rescinding part of its obligation, without giving black troops an option to leave the service.[2]

Because they were in the United States Army during wartime, the forms of protest available to men in the USCT were highly restricted, and their best course of action was to refuse payment under the inferior status. As men in the service of the volunteer army, the government called upon them to perform all the duties of soldiers, and the troops rightly insisted on being paid as soldiers. Seldom did black troops accept payment at seven dollars per month. In the 54th and 55th Massachusetts (Colored) Infantry, the paymaster mustered the troops seven times, and seven times they refused to accept the money. The government owed the men up to eighteen months' salary, yet they remained steadfast in their refusal to accept inferior pay for equal work. When Massachusetts Governor John A. Andrew, who both sympathized with their plight and felt an obligation to rectify the matter because he had unwittingly enlisted these troops under false pretenses, attempted to redress the injustice by providing the monetary difference from the state treasury, the troops reacted indignantly. Money had little to do with it. The issue, according to a great friend of the USCT, was whether "a colored man shall be acknowledged a man by even the U.S. Govt." or, as the commander of the 54th Massachusetts (Colored) Infantry explained to the governor, "They feel that by accepting a portion of their Just dues from Massachusetts and a portion from the United States, they would be acknowledging a right on the part of the United States to draw a distinction between them and other soldiers from Massachusetts, and in so doing they would compromise their self respect."[3]

Soldiers in the USCT also wrote letters to friends and family, newspapers, and government officials complaining of the discrimination. A sergeant in the 2nd U.S. Colored Infantry informed a family friend that he enjoyed the service except for the unequal pay: "I am willing to bee a soldier and serve my time faithful like a man but i think it is hard to bee poot off in sutch a dogesh maner as that." Another black soldier found it perplexing that "the Gobermant of whom We habe faithfully Serbid With the Humblis obedience for one Round year it has failed to Gibe the Reward that our Loss and Labours Has and now Dose demand, and for Reasons yet unowen [unknown] to us." The sufferings of their families at home were so great that "its Enough to demoralize all our fiting qualities." Still another black enlisted man indicated disgust with the entire affair: "Martha we have not our Pay yet and I never think we will   Oh for Shame on Such Equality   Such a Government as this dont Suit me. Oh for a Lodge in Some lost Wilderness   any where but here." In a letter to the editor of a prominent black newspaper, an outraged soldier who had just returned from battle wrote forcefully, "Do we not fill the same ranks? Do we not cover the same space of ground? Do we not take up the same length of ground in the grave-yard that others do? The ball does not miss the black man and strike the white, nor the white and strike the black. But sir, at that time there is no distinction made, they strike one as much as another." And to Abraham Lincoln, who received numerous missives from black troops on the issue, the simple yet powerful logic of their arguments was inescapable: "Now your Excellency, we have done a Soldier's duty. Why can't we have a Soldier's pay?"[4]

The most disconcerting aspect of the fight for equal pay was that the ones who suffered most were the soldiers' families. Black troops could decline to accept unequal pay and preserve their self-esteem because they received rations and clothing from the government, but they did not bear the brunt of the money shortage. Their families, however, lived in an environment in which money was essential for survival, and when the men refused to accept the unequal pay, their families lost a major source of income. In the South, compensation for the loss was virtually unattainable because families of freedmen had great difficulty obtaining work, as a soldier notified his president: "The most of the inhabitince perticular the welthey portion are so prejudice against the famely of colored soldiers in the US servise that they wont even give them employment for no prise to sustain if possible the old hipocrittical idea that free colored people wont work and of cours the soldiers families have to suffer." Nor was it much better in the North. A Northern black enlisted man, bemoaning the hardships the families were enduring, insisted that when they "consider the Horible Suferings of our deer Sufering familys at a Distant Home its Most more than our Manhood Can Beare." To complicate matters, Northern prejudice prevented many of these families from drawing upon aid from local charities. An officer in the USCT wrote to a politically active friend on behalf of his troops that "The wives of the men are, they say, often refused the almshouse for their color, and are reduced to degradation that drives the husbands almost crazy." Two weeks later a soldier complained that his comrades "more or less have familys and 2 thirds have never recieved anny State Aid." He then concluded on a sarcastic note, "and how do you think men can feel to do there duty as Soldiers?" Out of pity for the families, a number of their white officers encouraged the men to continue the fight yet take the money. Most of the troops, though, remained unyielding in their refusal to accept inferior pay.[5]

The Lincoln administration and the more liberal elements in Congress made a serious judgmental error on the issue of equal pay. When it became apparent that the law as it existed did not provide black and white soldiers with the same pay, politicians dragged their feet in seeking a solution, in the hopes that discriminatory pay would make the concept of black soldiers more tolerable to the Northern public. In fact, it appeased no one. Whites who opposed black enlistment recognized unequal pay for what it was, a sop, and the issue merely infuriated blacks and Northern whites who endorsed the policy of the USCT.

To make matters worse, blacks had no real political influence to redress their grievances. When a white soldier perceived an injustice, he notified his parents who in turn could bring the matter to the attention of some politician in power. Southern blacks had no influence, and Northern blacks, because of their small numbers, had little leverage with federal authorities. One politician who made a genuine effort to right the wrong was Massachusetts Governor John A. Andrew. Andrew felt the government's stand on unequal pay was absolutely ridiculous: "For fear the uniform may dignify the enfranchised slave, or make the black man seem like a free citizen, the government means to disgrace and degrade him, so that he may always be in his own eyes, and in the eyes of all men, 'only a nigger.'" He mobilized numerous supporters on behalf of black troops and spoke publicly and privately of the injustice, yet Lincoln and Congress approached the issue with timidity.[6]

The best spokesmen for the black troops were their own officers.

From generals down to lieutenants, officers affiliated with the USCT regarded the issue as outrageous. Major General Butler, commander of the Department of Virginia and North Carolina, could see no reason why black troops received less pay. "The colored man fills an equal space in the ranks while he lives and an equal grave when he falls," he argued. Col. James Montgomery wrote Sen. Henry Wilson, chairman of the Committee on Military Affairs, that his troops were second to none in efficiency and "their loyalty and fidelity might put to the blush some who boast of white skins." They deserved the same pay from their original date of enlistment. In a group letter, the entire officer corps of the 21st U.S. Colored Infantry pleaded to Adjutant General Thomas that most of its troops had given up positions in the quartermaster or commissary departments for double or triple the pay, just to serve in the ranks, and the inequality was grossly unfair. One lieutenant even announced that if Congress did not address the pay inequality question, he intended to resign: "I did not enter this service from any mercenary motive but to assist in removing the unreasonable prejudice against the colored race; and to contribute a share however small toward making the negro an effective instrument in crushing out this unholy rebellion." In his eyes, unequal pay was a slap in the face to those combating racism.[7]

With black families suffering and troops growing more and more indignant over the blatant discrimination being committed by the federal government, trouble was inevitable. When the paymaster paid white troops in the vicinity, the men in the 79th U.S. Colored Infantry, who had received no money for ten months, grew irritable and insubordinate. To stifle the unrest, their commander shrewdly removed the troops from their construction duties and devoted full time to drilling them and improving their discipline, which probably prevented mutiny. The 21st U.S. Colored Infantry, however, was not so fortunate. Sgt. William Walker decided that because the government was not fulfilling its end of the enlistment agreement, the contract was null and void and he no longer had to perform the duties of a soldier. Evidence indicates that Walker did not attempt to incite mutiny or encourage violence. His was a passive brand of resistance. Nonetheless, military authorities tried, convicted, and executed him for mutiny. Governor Andrew provided the most fitting epitaph for Sergeant Walker when he wrote, "The Government which found no law to pay him except as a nondescript and a contraband, nevertheless found law enough to shoot him as a soldier."[8]

From these experiences black troops quickly learned that resistance, either violent or passive, to the discriminatory pay policy served no purpose. Military authorities cracked down hard on such misbehavior, and in the process the troops also alienated their most vocal and influential supporters, their white officers. The better course of action was the one that some of their officers had been pursuing—seeking change in the political arena by writing to military officials and politicians and attempting to generate public support through the newspapers. Officers such as Col. Alfred S. Hartwell, commander of the 55th Massachusetts, officially called on the government to redress the unequal pay grievance or muster out of service for nonfulfillment of contract those regiments that had received promises of equal pay. At the same time officers explained clearly to the men the steps they were taking and warned them, "Nothing can be more certain than that mutinous conduct or refusal to do duty would result in the extreme penalty of the law to the ringleaders, and the probable disarming of the entire regiment and their employment at hard labor on Military works during the remainder of their term of service." [9]

At this stage, black troops had finally gained some leverage. Along with the support their cause had generated in the public sector and the military, U.S. Attorney General Edward Bates gave his opinion that black soldiers should receive equal pay and reminded the president of his constitutional responsibility to see that all laws were faithfully executed. Second, the government had obviously violated the terms of the enlistment agreement with numerous black units, and a court would be hard pressed to endorse its position. The government would then have to muster these troops out of service at a time when military commanders were clamoring for more manpower. Third, because of unequal pay, the provost marshal general ruled that blacks could not serve as substitutes for whites, which infuriated many Northerners. [10]

Under pressure from several fronts, in mid-June 1864 Congress authorized equal pay for all soldiers from January 1, 1864, and back pay to the level of white soldiers holding the same rank, providing the black soldiers had been free on April 19, 1861. Thus, only prewar free blacks received equal pay for 1862 and 1863. It was another insult to the black race. To skirt the ruling, the commander of the 54th Massachusetts, Col. Edward N. Hallowell, devised a "Quaker Oath" to ensure full and equal pay for his men. As evidence of freedom before the war, the government accepted a sworn statement. Hallowell prepared an oath none of his men could oppose: "You do solemnly swear that you owed no man unrequited labor on or before the 19th day of April, 1861. So help you God." They unanimously swore the oath and later received full pay, retroactive to the day of their enlistment. This, however, was a temporary solution. Again supporters of the USCT picked up their pens and demanded equal pay for ex-slaves as well. As it did before, Congress moved slowly, but in early March 1865 it approved a law that granted equal pay from enlistment date for all black troops who had been mustered into service under the assurance that they would receive the same pay as white soldiers.[11]

Unfortunately, the equal pay issue had some negative long-term results. Many of the black troops considered the affair another instance of unfair treatment and solidified their opinion that blacks simply should not trust the white race. As black Sgt. Isaac Hill wrote of the controversy, it was just another example of the willingness of blacks "to comply with the wrong teachings of strange gods, especially when they come from white men, and this is the reason we cannot be a united nation." For the relationship between the white officers and their black soldiers, the results were mixed. Nearly all the white officers supported their men, in conscience if not in deed, and the black troops recognized the efforts on their behalf. Yet those black soldiers who witnessed the vigorous and unnecessarily harsh methods that some white officers used to quash protests suffered nearly irreparable damage to the confidence and esteem they had for these white men.[12]

In addition, the controversy created fissures in the ranks of black soldiers. As Congress stalled, frustration among the troops increased, which in turn bred dissension in the ranks as they disputed among one another over the best course of action. Some—particularly the officers and men of the 54th and 55th Massachusetts— continued their barrage of letters to friends, Congress, and the press, yet others preferred a different tack. Whereas some black soldiers insisted they must fight for equal treatment whenever confronted by discrimination, others believed that success in the army would result in attitudinal changes that would lead to equality. They had enunciated their views on the pay issue, and now it was time to get back to their work as soldiers, through which they could win lasting equality. These troops were particularly fearful of acquiring a reputation as complainers and thereby nullifying any goodwill blacks had already earned in the army and the North. Chaplain Garland White thought, "Those few colored regiments from Massachusetts make more fuss, and complain more than all the rest of the colored troops of the nation. They are doing themselves and their race a serious injury. I sincerely hope they will stop such nonsense, and learn to take things as soldiers should. It is not that they are undergoing any more than we are." In response to this and similar charges from freedmen, one Northern sergeant in the USCT warned his black opponents to mind their own business: "In future, then, please pay a little more attention to yourselves, and not quite so much to us boys from the North, who came out to fight and not to play." Eventually, a black soldier from the 11th U.S. Colored Heavy Artillery tried to diffuse the situation by calling for peace among the various segments of the black population. "I hope that there will be more union among colored troops than there has been," he commented, "as my opinion is, that we have been disunited long enough." Unfortunately, the proposal did not come soon enough to prevent a level of resentment from developing.[13]

Another major area of discrimination against blacks was appointments as officers. In late summer 1862, when Butler called the Louisiana black militia units into federal service, he appointed a mixed lot of officers, some white and others black, "precisely as I found intelligence." These units came predominantly from the free black population of New Orleans, noted for its education, wealth, and tradition of military service, and Butler had no problem obtaining men with leadership skills. He appointed some seventy-five blacks as captains and lieutenants, along with Maj. Francis E. Dumas, whom he intended to compliment by saying, "He had more capability as Major, than I had as Major General, I am quite sure." All other field-officer posts Butler reserved for experienced white soldiers. Around the same time in Kansas, Jim Lane, who needed no authorization to recruit a black regiment, also felt he need not seek permission to appoint a qualified black man as captain. Together these events boded well for blacks as officers in the Union Army.[14]

Yet the pendulum rapidly swung in the opposite direction. Early the next year, when Massachusetts Governor John A. Andrew was trying to raise Northern black regiments, he sought permission to appoint a few "plainly competent" blacks as line officers (captains and lieutenants), assistant surgeons, and chaplains, which would facilitate recruitment. Secretary of War Stanton, unwilling to take a position because at the time Congress was considering a bill that would decide the matter, refused Andrew's request. Out west, the War Department accepted Lane's black regiment into federal service, but not its black officer, despite attestations from twenty-one officers in the unit who insisted the captain was "among the most thorough and efficient officers in our organization; in every sense of the term, drilled, disciplined, and capable." To the south, the War Department replaced Butler with Maj. Gen. N. P. Banks, who immediately began the systematic elimination of all black officers and their replacement by whites, "being entirely satisfied that the appointment of colored officers is detrimental to the service." Banks insisted, "It converts what, with judicious management and good officers, is capable of much usefulness, into a source of constant embarrassment and annoyance. It demoralizes both the white troops and the negroes."

Initially Banks tried to challenge these black officers on grounds of competence, which proved fruitless in many cases, particularly since they knew tactics and regulations as well as most white volunteer officers and had proven themselves very capable of command during combat. Much more effective was slighting and sometimes blatantly humiliating these officers until their pride no longer permitted them to endure such insults and they resigned.[15]

Again, at the heart of the matter was race prejudice. The Lincoln administration was struggling to convince the military and public to accept black units. Having black officers was a step beyond that. Whites had great difficulty dealing with blacks on an equal basis, let alone one of inferiority, a condition that would be created by the appointment of blacks to officers' rank. When men in the 70th Indiana Infantry passed the 15th U.S. Colored Infantry, the white troops were silent until they spotted a black with lieutenant's shoulder straps. Then cries of " 'jerk them off, take him out, Kill him' resounded all along the line." Had the white troops not been in the line of march, according to one of their officers and a future major in the USCT, they "would have dealt severely with him." In Maryland a group of six physicians threatened to resign after they learned that their commander was a prominent black surgeon. In a letter of complaint to Lincoln, they expressed dismay over the situation:

> When we made application for position in the Colored Service, the understanding was universal that all commissioned officers were to be white men. Judge of our surprise and disappointment when, upon joining our respective regiments, we found that the Senior Surgeon of the command was a Negro.
>
> We claim to be behind no one, in a desire for the elevation and improvement of the Colored race. . . . But we cannot in *any* cause, willingly compromise what we consider a proper self respect.

They requested that this "degradation . . . may in *some way* be terminated."[16]

Moreover, most whites had serious doubts about the leadership ability of blacks. Chaplain John Eaton, who was later a colonel in the USCT and did great work with freedmen throughout the war, felt that only whites could handle the job of commanding black soldiers because "the work of putting these men into soldiers, is altogether so new, that its success will depend entirely upon the officers in charge." Brig. Gen. Rufus Saxton, another friend of the black soldier, honestly believed they preferred white officers because "they have been brought up to have a special respect for the guidance of white men." Despite their warm feelings for the race, neither of them could envision black soldiers with enough character and good judgment to train and lead a company or a regiment in battle.[17]

Others argued that blacks did not have enough educated men to fill the officers' slots in a regiment. The enormous amount of paperwork involved in a Civil War command demanded officers with good reading and writing skills, and few blacks had attained that level. In fact, few white soldiers in the Union Army, officers or enlisted men, possessed the writing fluency of Sgt. Maj. Christian Fleetwood of the 4th U.S. Colored Infantry or Sgt. Maj. Louis Douglass of the 54th Massachusetts, the son of black abolitionist and former slave Frederick Douglass, to name just two. Nor were all Union officers as literate as some men supposed. The arguments of black illiteracy, however, were so prevalent in the army that when Adjutant General Lorenzo Thomas began to organize black units in the West, he appointed whites not only to all officers' positions but also as quartermaster sergeants and first sergeants, jobs that also required extensive paperwork. His plan was that these positions would serve as a replacement pool for officers' vacancies in the units and, once black troops became literate, the best ones could take over those duties. The problem was that white soldiers usually accepted these noncommissioned officers' positions with the goal of receiving promotion to a lieutenancy. When vacancies did not develop, they failed examinations for officers' commissions, or a few received promotions and the commander filled the first-sergeant openings with blacks, as Thomas had intended, the remaining white sergeants became disgruntled and damaged the morale of the units. And, from the standpoint of black soldiers, these whites blocked the elevation of competent black troops even to high levels in the noncommissioned officers' ranks.[18]

Throughout their service black soldiers complained bitterly over the lack of opportunities for advancement into the officers' ranks. A former lieutenant in the Department of the Gulf who fell during the Banks purges argued forcefully that "this privilege our fathers enjoyed in 1812 & 1815 and as the late battles of East Pascagoola Miss & Port Hudson has proved that the colored officers are capable of commanding as officers." The best way to spur enlistments, he argued, was to permit blacks to serve as officers. Another former black officer insisted that free blacks in Louisiana "are naturally ambitious, and of course would like a show for promotion. With white officers we have not that chance." Enough black soldiers had proven leadership skills and military knowledge sufficient to drill the 54th Massachusetts splendidly without the aid of officers. As one sergeant who acted as a company commander that day wrote, "All that we ask is to give us a chance, and a position higher than an orderly sergeant, the same as white soldiers, and then you will see that we lack nothing." In response to arguments that blacks preferred white officers, one black soldier flatly stated that was sheer drivel. Northern whites were fighting for the Union while blacks were fighting for liberty, "and if we heave to fight for our rights let us fight under Colored officers for we are the men that will kill the Enemies of the Government." To locate competent blacks for officers' commissions, Sgt. Maj. Louis Douglass maintained, the government need not look farther than its noncommissioned ranks in the USCT. "In regard to the capability of colored men to perform the duties of commissioned officers, we would respectfully suggest that there are hundreds of non-commissioned officers in the colored regiments who are amply qualified for these positions, both by education and experience." Black soldiers were not asking for any special favors. As a man in the 7th U.S. Colored Infantry requested, "Let the Board at Washington be opened for the examination of colored men, and I have no fear for the result." [19]

In the end, a number of blacks did receive commissions as officers. Governor Andrew promoted Sgt. Stephen A. Swails of the 54th Massachusetts to the rank of second lieutenant in early 1864, on the basis of his military record and nomination by regimental commander Colonel Hallowell. Unwilling to rock the boat, Maj. Gen. John G. Foster, commander of the Department of the South, negated the decision by refusing to muster Swails out of service to accept the commission, and the secretary of war promptly endorsed Foster's position. Andrew, noted for his perseverence in these matters, nevertheless kept working on Swails's behalf, and by January 1865 he finally convinced Stanton to direct that Swails receive the appointment he richly deserved. This opened the door for others and, over the course of the next six months, ten blacks received commissions for command in the infantry and artillery. [20]

Among this group performance was generally good. Five more lieutenancies went to enlisted men in the 54th and 55th Massachusetts who, like Swails, had earned promotions through tireless and effective leadership in camp and on the field of battle. Both white officers and black enlisted men believed these six had merited the advancement and throughout their tenure treated them with all the courtesy and respect of white officers. Two others, Maj. Martin Delaney and Capt. O. S. B. Wall, received commissions in the 104th U.S. Colored Infantry to assist in recruiting, which they did well, and authorities later employed them successfully in the Freedmen's Bureau to aid ex-slaves in their adjustment to freedom. Only the three black officers in the Independent Battery, U.S. Colored Artillery (Light), had command problems. Originally designed as a battery of black officers and troops, the trouble began when authorities violently pressed men into service. According to a circular letter signed by fifty-three enlisted men:

> many of us were knocked down and beaten like dogs, while others "were dragged from our homes in the dead hour of [night] and forced into a Prison without Law or Justice   others were tied and thrown into the river and held there until forced to subscribe to the Oath   Some of us were tied up by the thumbs all night   we were starved beaten kept out all night untill we were nearly frozen and but one alternative to join the service or nearly suffer death.

To compound the dissatisfaction, a lieutenant died three months after the battery's organization, and its commander lacked good administrative skills and borrowed large sums of money from his troops. Conditions within the unit became so poor that the post commander endorsed a proposal to muster the entire battery out of the army, stating, "They Are of No Service to the Govt at all." [21]

Blacks had greatest success in obtaining commissions as regimental chaplains. Other than those men in the three Louisiana Native Guards regiments, records indicate that thirty-two blacks received commissions, thirteen of which went to chaplains. Candidates for chaplaincies had to present a certificate from some ecclesiastical body, or testimonials from five ordained ministers, verifying that the candidate was an ordained clergyman for a certain denomination and recommending him for the position. Company commanders and field officers then elected the candidate, and the regimental commander appointed him. The procedure offered mixed results for black clergymen. On the one hand they were able to bypass the War Department, but on the other their appointment was subject to the racial attitudes of white officers. As a result, when Sgt. Francis A. Boyd of the 109th U.S. Colored Infantry wrote to Butler late in 1864 and requested an appointment in his regiment as chaplain, since he met all the qualifications and was already performing the duties, Butler obliged him. Once Boyd tried to assume his duties officially, however, the white officers turned on him. "I have been coolly and contemptuously treated by the Officers of this Regiment with some exceptions, prejudices are Dark, and Bitter, and I feel that my life is in peril," he complained to Butler. Shortly afterward, the War Department replaced Butler with Maj. Gen. E. O. C. Ord, who had the War Department revoke Boyd's commission and reduce him to the ranks. Because the officers of the regiment had not elected Boyd, ruled Ord, the appointment was illegal. One year after the controversy began, however, the officers in the regimented voted

Boyd chaplain, but by then the regiment's strength was too low for authorities to muster him into service, and Boyd served as a private for the remainder of his military stint.[22]

Like the performance of other black officers, that of the chaplains was mixed, with most of it quite good. Officers and men of the 54th Massachusetts paid tribute to Chaplain John R. Bowles for his excellent services, as did the officers of the 28th U.S. Colored Infantry to Chaplain Garland White, whom they praised by declaring, "In him we find all the elements of true manhood." Those who fared well in the eyes of the men went out of their way to comfort and aid soldiers. Black Chaplain George Washington LeVere, for example, voluntarily took on the unappealing duty of informing a prisoner that authorities planned to execute him in three and one-half hours. Together they kneeled and prayed for forgiveness, and LeVere accompanied the prisoner to the spot of execution and again offered prayer before the fateful act of punishment. Other times, black chaplains failed to fulfill the basic needs of their troops. One black enlisted man claimed his chaplain, William H. Hunter, "who Should be ar Best freind & to Looke out for our wellfear has Even gone intou Buisness of Speculation," while a pious white assistant surgeon charged that Chaplain Benjamin Randolph "is not energetic enough for an army chaplain. An Army chaplain has got to work as well as preach, he must knock arround with zeal & business like energy." He blamed the problem on Randolph's youth and lack of forcefulness, although ten months later he stated, "Perhaps the greatest fault of ours was Laziness and self conceit, too proud to do many of the little things which as a chaplain he might do for the comfort of the men." [23]

In fairness to all blacks who took on the job of chaplain, it was no easy task. The war, with its inherent risks, bred immorality in the ranks, and without support from high-ranking officers, most good works changed little if anything. More important, these clergymen were usually the only black officers in their regiments and were at times the victims of racial slights. The officers in the 1st U.S. Colored Infantry asked Chaplain Henry M. Turner to preach to them before he held services for the enlisted men, which he agreed to do, "but disliking some misconduct, exhibited by men [officers], whose character should be exemplary, I stopped immediately" and left to preach to the enlisted men. The thick-skinned Turner did not consider this misbehavior of officers "personally insulting"; rather, he stopped "because I considered their conduct very ungrateful to God." In the case of Chaplain Randolph, he was in a regiment in which a number of officers paid little heed to morality, which sent a bad signal to the enlisted men and undercut his efforts.

Moreover, the assistant surgeon, who was his greatest critic, commented to his wife, "It is hard to find a black man smart enough and every way qualified to be a chaplain," which beneath the racial remark indicated that he believed the job of being a chaplain was much more difficult for a black man than a white because of racial attitudes among the officers.[24]

By the end of the war, approximately one in every two thousand black soldiers had made it into the officers' ranks, a minuscule ratio compared to whites. Other than those commissioned under the auspices of Butler, most were chaplains and some physicians, although a few, by dint of their extraordinary skill and the persistence of superior officers and the occasional politician, received commands in infantry or artillery units. For most black soldiers, this was a hollow victory, however, because so many more blacks who genuinely merited promotions were never seriously considered for them.[25]

Another area in which the government openly discriminated against black soldiers was in the amount of fatigue duty, or military labor, that senior officers assigned to them. From the outset, nearly all high-ranking officers preferred to detail black units to manual labor and "save" their white commands for combat. An assistant inspector general noted in October 1862 that Lane's Kansas black regiment performed fatigue duty rather than soldiered, even though authorities promised "they were to fight, not work as common laborers." Brig. Gen. Daniel Ullmann, who supervised the organization of the Corps d'Afrique in Louisiana, complained some seven months after its formation that officers used his troops as "diggers and drudges" and that "months have passed, at times, without the possibility of any drill at all."[26]

In part, the argument some whites put forward had validity. Combat was the single most important aspect of soldiering, and nearly all the white troops had seen action before. Senior-ranking officers felt more comfortable relying on soldiers who had demonstrated their ability to stand up in battle. Yet racism played a powerful role in the way officers employed their men. Many of them assigned black soldiers to fatigue labor because they regarded it as inferior duty, while others doubted whether the black race could endure the rigors of combat. Officers made feeble arguments to justify their insistence on the disproportionate amount of fatigue work that black commands performed, such as their "industry and docility," or that they "are easily handled, true and obedient" and "stick to their work patiently, doggedly, obediently, and accomplish a great deal"—depicting the black race as possessing characteristics naturally suited to manual labor. Some tried to argue that blacks were better at such labor because the climate was unsuited to whites and illnesses ran disproportionately high among the white units. Butler, lawyer turned major general, shrewdly pointed out to Secretary of War Stanton that such views would inevitably "establish the necessity for exclusive black labor, which has ever been the cornerstone of African slavery," an argument Stanton promptly adopted. In addition, illness statistics disproved the claim.[27]

All eyes were on these black units, particularly early in their deployment, to see if they could measure up to the standards of white commands. Among the criteria whites used for their evaluation were the ability of these black units to drill effectively and perform well on the march and in combat, none of which they could do while digging trenches or constructing fortifications. In the Department of the South, Maj. Gen. John G. Foster blamed the poor performance of black troops during a raid on excessive fatigue duty, which made the men "unused to marches and active movements." Numerous officers complained that constant fatigue duty deprived officers of time for drilling their men, and thus the troops had difficulty performing the various tactical movements when thrust into battle. To make matters worse, constant fatigue labor wore out clothing more rapidly and gave the troops a dirty, unkempt look that diminished their appearance to outside observers and fortified prejudicial assertions that blacks could not care for themselves. Occasionally military inspectors recognized the cause of their shabbiness, although most assessed blame for their untidiness on the officers and men. And because of unequal pay, those who could least afford it had to replace their clothing more regularly than other troops.[28]

For the black soldiers, this was another disillusioning aspect of military service. A private in a Louisiana swamp protested to the president, "Instead of the musket It is the spad[e] and the Wheelbarrow and the Axe," and a sergeant wrote his commander, at home recuperating from a wound, "We are slaves to hard fatigue work and bone labor." In the eyes of many black soldiers, they were merely chattels in Union blue, performing labor constantly. Pvt. T. D. Freeman insisted, "Instead of Elevation it Seems more like Degradation. . . . [W]e can never be Elevated in this country while Such rascality is Performed[.] Slavery with all its horrors can not Equalise this for it is nothing but work from morning till night." One soldier went so far as to refuse to perform any more fatigue duty, because he had enlisted to serve as a soldier, not as a laborer. An unsympathetic court-martial extended his hard labor for two more years, this time in a military prison.[29]

Among their white officers, dissatisfaction over excessive fatigue duty was widespread. It was absurd to subject USCT officers to rigorous examinations, many of them in the field of tactics, only to have them supervise gangs of uniformed laborers, and it was patently unfair to call on the black units to perform fatigue duty on behalf of white soldiers. One major so much disliked serving with troops that performed labor "more than *three fourths* of the time and do the dirty work for White troops" that he sought a transfer to another department. In a letter to his brother, Maj. Daniel Densmore made clear his views on fatigue duty:

> We have been discussing the propriety of going back to the former nomenclature, as being much more in Keeping with our business, to wit: Col. to be *"Ole Massa,"* and the remainder of us to be *"bosses"* numbered 1,2,3 & c for convenience,—Squads to be "gangs," and all sentences of courtmartials to be in terms of "lashes." Such an organization and terminology would better fit us as "Nigger drivers."

Speaking on behalf of his officers, the colonel of the 92nd U.S. Colored Infantry wrote that

> the Slur and Stigma of *inferiority* is what displeases so many officers and makes it so difficult to keep our best officers for they *will* not command troops that the Government allows *inferiority* to become attached to, for they say if the Government wants bosses or overseers let them be so employed from those who want the position but while they bear commissions they want only their *fair share* of fatigue but will do any amount of fighting.

As morale declined and fatigue duty extended over prolonged periods, the officers grew despondent and the pride they once had in service in the USCT waned, which again affected the efficiency and appearance of these units. For many white men with ambition, service as an officer in the USCT became a dead end, due to the extremely limited opportunities in which to shine in either battle or drill. Nor were they likely to continue to attract good men into the USCT as officers, as Lt. Col. Thomas Morgan explained: "The class of men who are willing to take hold with all their energies to drill and discipline a body of soldiers will not for any consideration consent to become overseers for black laborers." [30]

For both the officers and their men, some of these assignments, and the demeaning nature in which they had to perform them, were simply outrageous. Around Petersburg, some white troops made an unsuccessful assault on Confederate works. After the dead bodies baked in the hot June sun for ten days, military authorities called in a black regiment to serve as the burial detail. Because they had to perform the duty within range of Confederate guns, they had to do the work at night, groping around for their bloated comrades in blue amid the stench of decomposition and burying them quietly. On a raid with black and white units, the commander assigned all fatigue work to the USCT, and "No white troops lifted an ax or a spade." In South Carolina, a furious Col. James C. Beecher of the 35th U.S. Colored Infantry found the practice of using black soldiers to lay out and police the camps, or pick up the garbage, of white troops absolutely inexcusable:

> They have been slaves and are just learning to be men. It IS a draw-back that they are regarded as, and called "d___d Niggers" by so-called "gentlemen" in uniform of U.S. Officers, but when they are set to menial work doing for white regiments what those Regiments are entitled to do for themselves, it simply throws them back where they were before and reduces them to the position of slaves again.

The departmental commander immediately checked the practice, but the humiliation that both officers and men bore could not be erased so easily.[31]

Complaints were so rampant, and senior-ranking officers were so lackadaisical in their efforts to redress the grievances, that Adjutant General Thomas had to step in and forbid an unequal use of black troops in fatigue duty to provide black units with more time to train for combat. The intention of his Order No. 21 was admirable, and some abided by it, but like so many other dicta that attempted to strike at racial prejudice in the military, whites found ways to circumvent the regulation. Much to his credit, one young officer on inspection duty found that black soldiers performed labor eight hours per day while "there are several Regiments of white Infantry at this place who have not yet been required to work a day since receipt of this order." The officer furnished brigade headquarters with another copy of Order No. 21. Yet few inspectors were willing to stand up to Maj. Gen. George Meade, commander of the Army of the Potomac, when he relieved a division of black soldiers "to use these troops in the construction of Warren's redoubts, as they work so much better than the white troops, and save the latter for fighting."[32]

Because so many high-ranking officers had so little regard for black soldiers, the USCT frequently received the worst matériel the federal government issued to its troops. Of course, in some cases they fared no worse than white troops. Both white and black units occasionally received faulty gunpowder, "shoddy" uniforms and knapsacks, shoes that wore out prematurely, and inedible rations. Yet when officers in the USCT squawked about the quality of weapons and animals their commands received, the complaints were usually legitimate. Here military authorities clearly discriminated against black troops, providing them with matériel that they never would have issued white troops at this stage of the war.[33]

Many of the officers in the USCT felt it was critical to provide black troops with quality weapons. For one thing, many Northerners were watching the performance of black troops very closely, hoping for a military catastrophe that would prove indisputably that blacks could not stand the rigors of combat. One small step the federal government could take to prevent that was to provide its black soldiers with good weapons. A second reason, as one officer told the secretary of war, was: "Besides adding much to the efficiency of the Regiment, we believe that it is good policy to show the colored men of the North that the Government puts into their hands the best arms." Unfortunately, a government that adopted unequal pay, blocked opportunities for advancement, and demanded excessive fatigue duty from its black troops cared little to impress them with the quality of weapons it gave them.[34]

In some instances, black units received excellent weapons, such as the 29th Connecticut (Colored) Infantry, whose colonel managed to get them brand-new Springfield rifles. Most of the time, though, the complaints over inadequate weapons were valid. When the 4th U.S. Colored Heavy Artillery received its guns, they were unusable without extensive repair. In April 1864 an inspector condemned 340 muskets in the 2nd U.S. Colored Infantry, which the government replaced with Springfield rifled muskets. Yet the government did not provide rifles for the six companies of men who had antiquated smoothbore muskets, which had an effective range approximately five times smaller than that of rifled muskets, as the inspector also had suggested. Over the next eleven months its officers filed repeated requests for five to six hundred more rifled muskets, all in vain. Along similar lines, a brigadier general complained that an entire black regiment under his command had smoothbore muskets, and in light of the massacre of hundreds of black troops by Confederates at Fort Pillow, the government should give them Spencer repeating rifles.[35]

On a few occasions, it was not the quality of the weapons that disturbed inspectors, as well as the officers of those commands, but the hodgepodge of them. An inspection of the 54th U.S. Colored Infantry, one of a number of regiments with this problem, determined that troops not only had three different types of rifled muskets but also that they fired three different calibers of ammunition. In moments of battle, such complications could easily lead to disaster.[36]

The worst aspect of this sort of discrimination was that several black regiments with inadequate weapons saw extensive action. An

inspector reported two different rifled muskets, with different calibers, in the 79th U.S. Colored Infantry (New): "The arms and accoutrements were old, worn and in indifferent firing order." Nevertheless, he continued, "This regiment has performed hard service. It
was soldierlike in its appearance and is said by every one to have
fought gallantly in several battles where it has been engaged." In
late 1864 the 107th U.S. Colored Infantry, a new unit, occupied a
position on the line around Petersburg with 40 percent of the men
armed with imitation Enfield rifled muskets, made in Philadelphia,
which had a defective mainspring and could not fire. The saddest
case, however, was the 3rd U.S. Colored Cavalry, which needed 285
carbines, 403 sabers, and mounts for the men. It had "remarkably
good" officers and "the reputation of the regiment for fighting qualities is high." The inspector, a former regular officer now Maj. Gen.
N. J. T. Dana, then stated: "This regiment is thought by good judges
to be about as good cavalry as we have. It is a pity they should not
be immediately completely armed and mounted and put to active
service." [37]

Still another aspect of discrimination—the least publicized yet
most critical in the military service—was in the area of medical
care. Even though black units fought infrequently in major battles,
they did participate in 449 different fights, and their aggressiveness
in combat resulted in exceedingly high losses. Moreover, illness took
a much heavier proportionate toll on the USCT than it did on white
volunteer units. Many of the black troops had no previous exposure
to the diseases that roared through military camps, and authorities
assigned black commands to the most unhealthy locations, mainly
to perform occupation duties, because they assumed blacks were
immune to all tropical diseases. As weeks and months passed in
garrison, camp sanitary problems invariably compounded, and the
ensuing illnesses inflicted fearful losses on blacks in Union blue.[38]

According to official medical records, which significantly under-
stated the workload, the surgeons and assistant surgeons in the
USCT cared for over six hundred thousand cases of illness among
enlisted men, not to mention illness in the officers' ranks, ranging
in degrees of seriousness from headaches to extremely deadly diseases such as typhoid fever and cholera. In addition, physicians
in black units had more than ten thousand wounded enlisted men
to treat, plus an undetermined number of officers. All these cases
were the responsibility of several hundred physicians.[39]

From the very beginning, the War Department had great difficulty
procuring competent physicians for the USCT. Throughout the
North there was a limited number of properly trained physicians
who were physically able to handle both the strain of army life and

its professional demands. Black commands had to compete with white volunteer units, which had organized earlier and therefore had first crack at qualified physicians. In addition, like the rest of Northern society, not everyone wanted to serve in the USCT. Black units offered few attractions for physicians already in the volunteer service, and regimental officers could certainly block attempts by doctors to transfer to the USCT on the grounds that medical personnel were indispensible to their commands. To facilitate the process of obtaining physicians for black units, the surgeon general ordered the formation of permanent boards for the examination of candidates for appointment as medical officers in the USCT in a number of large cities—Boston, New York, Washington, Philadelphia, Cincinnati, and St. Louis—as well as temporary boards in various other locations "as the exigencies of the service demand." He insisted that "qualifications of Medical Officers of Colored Troops should be equal to the standard required for those serving with other Troops." [40]

Such efforts alone did not provide enough surgeons and assistant surgeons to keep pace with the rapid rate at which the government was organizing black units. Departmental commander after departmental commander complained of the shortage of medical personnel in the USCT, and all the head of the Bureau of Colored Troops could say was "there are no candidates available for appointment," and "great difficulty is experienced in obtaining medical officers." [41]

Another viable pool to tap was black physicians. Although there were not that many qualified black physicians in the United States, these men understandably had an interest in serving in the USCT. But at the same time prejudiced whites had a powerful desire to keep them out of the service. During battle, surgeons and assistant surgeons treated patients brought to them regardless of unit, and many feared the reaction when white volunteers went to a black surgeon. Even in the USCT, black physicians would also have to treat officers, something a little extreme for the sensibilities of these whites. In the case of Dr. Alexander T. Augusta, a black man who went to Canada for his medical education, the board in Washington was loath to appoint him until Augusta made clear his hope to serve in a black regiment. Then, after Augusta demonstrated his medical competence to the board, white surgeons found it insulting to serve under, let alone alongside, a black physician. Through most of the war Augusta performed his duty on detached service, at a rendezvous camp for black troops, rather than with his regiment. In mid-1864 in the 54th Massachusetts, black hospital steward Dr. Theodore J. Becker cured an officer when no one else could help him. As a result, some officers circulated a petition seeking Becker's promotion to a vacancy as assistant surgeon in the regiment. Everyone signed it except one captain and two lieutenants, who admitted Becker was a smart man and understood his medicine, but he was also black. Instead of submitting the petition and revealing prejudice in the 54th Massachusetts, Colonel Hallowell tore it up in disgust, and Becker remained a hospital steward throughout the war.[42]

In the end, at least eight black physicians served in the Union Army, but they had to meet standards that were well beyond many other physicians. Dr. William Powell had a degree from Pennsylvania Medical College in 1856, Dr. John De Grasse graduated with honors from Bowdoin Medical College and was the first black man admitted to the Massachusetts Medical Society, and Dr. Charles Burleigh Purvis attended Oberlin College and graduated from Wooster Medical College (later to Western Reserve Medical School), to name just a few. Prejudice barred all except three from admission into the USCT. Within that group, only De Grasse, whom authorities cashiered for drunkenness on duty, and Powell served with their regiments.[43]

In the meantime, commanders of black units had to have someone to care for their sick and injured troops, and they usually assigned anyone with medical knowledge to the post of acting assistant surgeon. Frequently these were men who had served as hospital stewards. The problem here was that a few hospital stewards received the appointment because of some medical or pharmacological knowledge, but most were merely recuperating patients who had demonstrated intelligence and could handle light duties. Men like Lt. Herman W. Dickinson, who had been a temporary hospital steward during his stint with the 23rd Michigan Infantry, began his service in the USCT as an assistant surgeon in a regimental hospital, a terrible ordeal for Dickinson and his patients. In the Department of the Gulf, the practice of appointing "hospital Stewards of low order of qualifications" to posts as surgeons and assistant surgeons became so widespread that complaints flooded Major General Banks's office about the "inhumanity of subjecting the colored soldiers to medical treatment and surgical operations by such men." Even more forceful were officers from white volunteer units, who complained "upon the ground that in the exigencies of battle any officer might be subjected to the necessity of surgical treatment by this class of officers."[44]

To prevent a full-scale scandal from blooming and to provide these black commands with the competent medical care they deserved, several prominent officers took some decisive steps. Banks, a Massachusetts politician before the war, drew on his extensive personal contacts and arranged a deal with some of the best medical schools in New York and New England to get their finest students into black units in his department. Adjutant General Thomas also acted along similar lines. First, he sent a medical officer to New England to induce physicians to appear before the medical board for commissions in the USCT. Later, he arranged an early graduation program with selected medical schools for those who agreed to enter the USCT immediately after successful completion of the college's oral examination and written thesis. In Tennessee, Colonel Mussey appointed anyone who "can procure a diploma from some recognized medical school." Implicitly, the advantage was that the physician would not have to appear before the medical board unless he exhibited such gross incompetence as to warrant the examination. Nor did they neglect other viable sources. They began to scour the army in search of contract surgeons, physicians who signed a one-year agreement to work for the military, and medical cadets, who were medical trainees employed by the War and Navy Departments. Both of these groups were attractive because they had an understanding of military structure and experience in the types of injuries and illnesses they were likely to encounter in the USCT.[45]

Most of these efforts resulted in the acquisition of competent doctors, but some physicians in the USCT, like their comrades who held commissions as field and company-grade officers, were patently incompetent. A surgeon wrote his wife, "You speak about the rank of surgeon. I have seen more confounded fools in the service with that rank that I care but little about it," and his opinion was hardly unique. A fellow surgeon regarded one of his colleagues as a "simpleton," while another had an assistant surgeon whom he tactfully described as "not a brilliant man," based on the consistency of his diagnoses. Every case was either rheumatism or pneumonia, and "his treatment for them is one and the same, viz. Dover's Powder frequently repeated till death or recovery ensues."[46]

Fortunately, in these instances a very competent physician was on hand to correct the blunders, but this was not always the case. In Arkansas a surgeon who ran a hospital for black soldiers "did not evince much Knowledge of his duties," according to the inspector general, and twice as many black soldiers died from disease as did patients in a nearby white hospital. A soldier stationed in Texas accused the three surgeons at Brazos Santiago of being "murderers" because of their lack of skill and callous disregard for black troops. The most outrageous instance of incompetence, however, occurred when a surgeon let the hospital buildings fall into disrepair, failed to remove a dead body from the hospital for more than forty-eight hours, and neglected to care for the health and comfort of the patients in general.[47]

A white physician in the USCT complained, "Very few surgeons will do precisely the same for blacks as they would for whites," yet a number of medical officers in black units were utterly brutal in their treatment of black soldiers, obviously the product of racism. Two physicians lost their positions for whipping black soldiers who were serving temporarily as nurses. After the doctors berated the nurses for leaving the hospital ward while on duty, the nurses responded in turn with "unbearable insolence," so the physicians flogged the men with a leather strap. One nurse then tried to leave the hospital again after the beating, and the doctor had a soldier chain him at the ankles. Had the nurses been white, these whippings would never have taken place. Worse was the complaint of a black sergeant that the medical staff treated patients as "brutes" and the hospital stewards, who were also black, robbed deceased patients before they reported them dead. Protesting physical mistreatment, a black soldier from Massachusetts wrote home, "If a man Says he is Sick it is the Doctors Priveledge to Say yes or no if you cannot work then you are Sent to the Guard House Bucked, Gagged and Stay so till they See fit to relieve You and if you dont like that Some white man will Give you a crack over the Head with his Sword. [N]ow do you call this Equality[? I]f so God help Such Equality." Early in the war this sort of thing occurred in white volunteer units, but by 1864 white veterans never would have endured it.[48]

In Texas complaints of abuse from medical officers were rampant. In part a result of overwork, such outrages were nonetheless inexplicable on any grounds other than racism. A soldier insisted that a surgeon had bucked and gagged a black comrade for feigning illness. That afternoon the doctor sent the victim to the hospital, where he died the next day. On another occasion a surgeon kicked a sick soldier for leaving his tent to relieve himself, and that night the soldier died. One surgeon cursed a dying man who was moaning in pain, yelling, "God damn him if he was going to die and dont [make] So much fuss about it."[49]

Other times, physicians were utterly callous in response to human needs. A surgeon in the 30th U.S. Colored Infantry refused to care for a wounded soldier because it was late, cold, and rainy and he was eating his supper. Instead, someone had to get a surgeon from another regiment to come treat the soldier. Along the same lines, although a much more serious case, a surgeon in the 5th U.S. Colored Infantry failed to attend to the needs of a black soldier whose foot had been partially severed by a shell because he was conducting sick call. In his defense at the general court-martial, the doctor argued that "a man with a part of his foot cut off by a piece of shell was not suffering much pain." The division commander, outraged by the abuse of his soldier, responded to the explanation by stating, "While the Brig. Genl. Comdg. [Commanding] regrets extremely that a medical officer in this Division should be found so ignorant of his profession as to set up such a defense, he much prefers it to be so than to think any officer could be so grossly inhuman as to leave a wounded man to suffer." [50]

The most incomprehensible case of abuse, though, was the butchery of the body of a deceased black soldier who collapsed unexpectedly. Under the ruse of a postmortem examination, a surgeon in the 23rd U.S. Colored Infantry carved up the body shamelessly. The surgeon removed the heart, the liver, a kidney, the small intestines, and the spleen, without securing the proper arteries and veins, and blood poured all over the floor. He also unintentionally cut the jugular vein, which exacerbated the mess. The surgeon then severed the head from the body and in its place affixed a bottle with an old blanket wrapped around it. Being late in the evening when the surgeon began the autopsy, he put the organs and head in a sack and placed them under a bench for the night. The body and mess remained in the regimental dispensary where he had conducted the autopsy and where enlisted men entered regularly. Later that night, fearful "that something might happen [to] the head and other viscera, animals such as dogs being in the camp, and no person remaining with the body," he returned to the dispensary and brought the sack to his tent. Excited by the investigation, and unable to sleep, he "proceeded at once to remove the scalp" in preparation for the removal of the brain. By this time the regimental commander learned of the "autopsy" and heard rumors that the doctor had offered an enlisted man one dollar to spend the night with the body, and he directed the surgeon to return the head, by that time slashed horribly, to the body. The regimental commander argued vigorously to the corps commander "that such actions as these known to enlisted men being permitted to pass unnoticed will demoralize troops and destroy all confidence and discipline is beyond doubt: especially among men of Such Supersticious cast of mind as these Colored Men." The Corps Medical Director concurred: "A proper post mortem would have been interesting and of importance to the profession, as showing the nature and course of disease; but it should have been made at a *proper* time, a *proper* place, and in a professional *manner.*" He then concluded, "This case was not a Post Mortem examination, or a dissection; it was a mutilation of the body not justifiable." No doubt, had the soldier been white, this desecration would never have taken place. A court dismissed the surgeon from the service, but through his political contacts he won reinstatement, only to be cashiered later for refusing to appear before a medical board.[51]

Unfortunately, despite these instances of overt racism, soldiers in the USCT received their best care in these regimental hospitals. There were, of course, limitations on the number of physicians who treated troops as well as the extent of the facilities, but the physicians who received commissions in the USCT were for the most part competent. With the entire command stationed nearby, soldiers had direct channels for their complaints and regimental commanders could oversee the hospital organization and rectify problems as they developed. And while some physicians were insensitive in their conduct toward sick or injured black troops, regimental surgeons served in the same command as the troops they treated, and most of them were truly devoted to the art of healing and sensitive to the miseries of the men. As a result, regimental hospitals tended to be designed and maintained rather well and earned high marks from inspectors.[52]

By comparison, post or general hospitals, which cared for seriously ill patients, regularly had separate and grossly unequal facilities for blacks and whites. Time after time, post or general hospitals for black troops were understaffed and poorly policed, and death rates were dramatically higher than in adjacent or nearby facilities for whites. At Fort Smith, Arkansas, in the black hospital "there were evidences of habitual neglect of proper police regulations. The kitchens, out buildings and grounds were filthy in the extreme, and the medical officer in charge did not manifest much efficiency in the discharge of his duties." Out of 343 patients, 92 died. At Pine Bluff, Arkansas, there were also separate and unequal facilities: "the police of the wards in the hospital for white soldiers was fair but the police of the negro hospital was filthy in the extreme." Hospital linen was "tolerably clean in the white hospital but not so in the negro ward." In Vicksburg, after six months in service, the black hospital had treated 646 patients, 197 of whom had died, some 30.5 percent, while the white hospital had 415 deaths out of 2,963 cases, or 14 percent. According to the inspector, the black hospital had a good location, but "neither the General police or the beds were in as good order as in the other hospitals [white]. The sinks were old, and in bad police." At the nearby black smallpox, or "pest," hospital, as contagious disease hospitals were called, the tents were "old and badly pitched, no floors and no drainage." The mortality rate was over 30 percent. Of all the military hospitals in New Orleans, by far the worst one was the Corps d'Afrique Hospital. "The police of the hospital and grounds was bad, the floors and bedding were dirty, and there seemed to be a lack of system and discipline." The previous day, the inspector had examined Sedgwick General Hospital in New Orleans, for whites, and considered it a "model hospital," in "most perfect condition." One of the worst hospitals for black troops was in Helena, Arkansas, which "was the dirtiest place inside and the filthiest place out side it was fallen to my lot to inspect," wrote a colonel. "The sick men are dirty their beds filthy and uncomfortable. The police about the hospital, kitchens & c [etc.] disgraceful. Not a thing about the whole establishment could I find to mention in favorable terms." [53]

Hospital care was somewhat better to the east, but that was because black commands were more frequently part of an organized military structure and thus had brigade or division hospitals. Nevertheless, they had their share of problems with proper medical care as well. One officer lamented to himself and posterity, "Our treatment in hospitals [is] worse than a criminals in penetentiary." In fact, complaints among the troops were so rampant that a regimental commander sent a medical officer to investigate the conditions of a small pox hospital and then notified brigade headquarters that "the colored soldiers in the Small Pox Hospital are neglected, that the rooms they occupy are unventilated and unclean." [54]

Probably the worst assortment of hospital facilities for black soldiers existed in Nashville. Since before blacks had entered the service there had been remonstrations about Nashville hospitals, and when authorities had to establish hospitals for black troops, they were inferior, even for these substandard institutions. Protests from officers such as Capt. Josiah V. Meigs, who claimed that the pest house that cared for some of his men was "completely disorganized, men lay in the filth of their disease without change of clothing from the time of entry until they deserted or died," passed unheeded. As a result authorities made no improvements, and in the aftermath of the Battle of Nashville in December 1864, the system for black soldiers all but collapsed. Within one week Colonel Mussey complained, "Hospital accommodations here for colored Troops are very insufficient." Several weeks later, after Adjutant General Thomas received a complaint from a captain about the treatment of sick and wounded in his company, he inspected a black hospital and the sight appalled him. Men were wearing the same clothing they had donned in the battle one month earlier, bloodstains and all, and had never changed them. One amputee complained that no one had bathed him and he still suffered from lice bites; another had no shirt because ten days earlier he had to discard it because of filth. "Had these been white soldiers," barked Thomas indignantly to the officer in charge, "think you this would have been their condition? No!" Nevertheless, in February, Mussey continued to uncover inadequacies, including a shortage of two hundred beds.[55]

As a result of such woeful and discriminatory medical care, nine times as many black troops died from disease as on the battlefield, and compared to white volunteers, two and one-half times as many black soldiers per one thousand died of disease. Over twenty-nine thousand died from illness, with pneumonia, dysentery, typhoid fever, and malaria taking the heaviest tolls on the black ranks. Within specific commands, the number of deaths was sometimes staggering. A black heavy artillery regiment lost over eight hundred men, and one infantry regiment, in service less than one year, had 524 deaths, nearly 50 percent of its strength. "The mortality in our Regt. beats anything I ever saw," wrote a lieutenant stationed in Louisiana. "They frequently drop dead in the streets, and in two or three instances have been found laying dead in the weeds some distance from camp." He had just ordered his men to build one dozen coffins and pondered in disillusionment, "How long do you suppose they will last the old Dr.?" [56]

If anything positive developed from prejudicial government policies toward the black units, it was that for the most part the mistreatment drew the black troops and their white officers closer together. No one knew better than their white officers how the unequal pay hurt black soldiers and their families physically and psychologically, how lack of opportunities for promotion wrecked morale, how excessive fatigue duty and inferior equipment cost lives needlessly and stifled chances of proving their prowess on the field of battle, and how inadequate medical care depleted the ranks of enlisted men and officers. By the same token, although white officers seldom fought for the promotion of blacks to the officer corps, black soldiers were well aware that their white officers helped lead the struggle for equal pay, constantly battled high-ranking officers for better arms and equipment and less fatigue duty, so that they could train the men properly and lead them in combat successfully, and complained about the medical care. In many respects, once these white men accepted commissions in the USCT, their interests and those of their black soldiers converged.

Yet these were not the only obstacles of prejudice that black units encountered, nor did they have the most impact on the relationship between the white officers and their men. This type of mistreatment came from some faceless policymakers or general officers. It was the personal abuse and discrimination, from both outside and inside the military, that affected the white officers and their men most and served to bind them together tightest.

Upon completion of its organization in November 1863, the 2nd U.S. Colored Infantry had to pass through Philadelphia to catch a train to New York, and as they marched through the streets, an angry mob pursued them. One black soldier knocked down a civilian for calling an officer a "white nigger," and the regimental adjutant also decked a man who insulted him. En route to New York, "our car was stoned," according to Col. Stark Fellows who, along with everyone else, resigned himself to the abuse: "Such is our life. But we are all proud of our regiment." The trip through New York and by ship to Key West, Florida, was uneventful. Upon arrival, though, they learned that the citizens had petitioned the government to have the command removed, "simply for the reason that it is a colored regiment." The regimental chaplain noted, "The people here seem to hate these soldiers simply because they are black. The officers of the regiment have been treated with such contempt and contumely." Their duty was to replace the 47th Pennsylvania Infantry as the force of occupation, which also abused the black troops. According to Fellows in a letter home, the Pennsylvanians were "very much opposed to us. They used every sort of epithet against me, as did also the citizens." After Fellows died from disease, the new commander, far less tolerant than his predecessor, filed a complaint to military authorities over the misconduct of the Pennsylvania troops: "After our arrival not a night passed but some of the officers or men of this regiment were struck by stones, &c.," until those white troops left. Although the experiences of the 2nd U.S. Colored Infantry were more striking than those of most black units, they nevertheless illustrate clearly the widespread prejudice these commands encountered.[57]

Opposition to black units in Southern states, where slavery had (or still) existed, was at least anticipated. The prejudice and violence in the Union states, however, was very disturbing. Hostility among certain segments of the population toward blacks was evident in New York City during the draft riots of July 1863, which swiftly became race riots and resulted in the death of over one dozen black residents and the sacking and burning of an orphanage for black children. Unfortunately, this was no isolated instance of racial violence. In the nation's capital during the spring of 1864, for example, a captain in the 27th U.S. Colored Infantry expressed dismay about "Secesh white[s] spitting at us" as they passed through the streets. Six months earlier a black sergeant took some prisoners from Virginia to Washington, D.C. One prisoner broke loose, and after the sergeant apprehended him, a crowd of citizens and soldiers "stoned him, struck him, and besides insulting him in every way, took his sword" and turned it over to the provost marshal. The sergeant had to flee for his life. Somehow, he obtained a rifled musket for self-defense and headed to the provost marshal's office. There some soldiers threw him in the guardhouse without a hearing. Eventually sympathetic witnesses interceded on the sergeant's behalf and convinced authorities of his innocence, but by then the prisoner had escaped.[58]

Nor were black officers safe from racist mobs. Surgeon Alexander T. Augusta, traveling in uniform from his home in Baltimore to Philadelphia, had quite an experience. He arrived at the train station safely, but shortly after he sat down two men attacked him and tore off his officer's insignia and an angry mob quickly gathered and threatened his life. Fortunately, some provost guards arrived and conducted him safely to the provost marshal's office, where Augusta proved his rank by providing a copy of his commission from the president. The officer in charge, a lieutenant colonel, was very cooperative and sent Augusta back to the train depot with an armed guard to arrest the culprits and ensure Augusta's safe passage. En route Augusta spotted one of the men who ripped off his insignia and had him apprehended, along with another man who "emerged from the market and assaulted me." With two men in custody, they continued their walk to the train station when a man suddenly stepped out to block Augusta's way and punched him in the face, which "caused the blood to flow from my nose very freely." This man they also seized, and with revolvers drawn the party worked its way to the train. There Augusta met an officer on Maj. Gen. Joseph Hooker's staff, who agreed to accompany Augusta to Philadelphia in case any more trouble erupted. The entire affair was particularly galling to Augusta, even though he had "always known Baltimore as a place where it is considered a virtue to mob colored people," because "I had only volunteered to bind up the wounds of those colored men who should volunteer, as well as those rebels and copperheads whom the fortune of war might throw into my hands."[59]

Abuse of black units within the military started near the top and filtered down through the ranks, often manifesting itself in violence. Such men as Brig. Gen. John P. Hatch, who constantly referred to his black soldiers as "Niggers," Maj. Gen. Lovell H. Rousseau, who asserted that "no female shall be arrested by a Negro soldier," and Maj. Gen. William T. Sherman, whose views against black soldiers disseminated throughout his army and beyond, served as poor examples for subordinate officers and men. Far too many soldiers viewed these attitudes of their superiors as a license to abuse black troops and their white officers. According to some black enlisted men in the 73rd U.S. Colored Infantry, Col. William H. Dickey "cursed our Regt and Said we wer the dam Smart Nigers" in public. Dickey later denied the charges. An even more blatant case was that of Col. John L. Wolford of the 1st Kentucky (Union) Cavalry, who went on a campaign against black soldiers, with public speeches and accusations of tyranny against the president, which resulted in his dishonorable dismissal from the service. Black soldiers on detached assignments, where they were without comrades and their officers could not protect them, were particularly susceptible to such verbal assaults. In one case when an officer in the USCT learned of the problem he preferred charges against the culprit, and in another instance a colonel recalled his black soldier and refused to detach any more of his men unless he received assurances that they would be treated as U.S. soldiers.[60]

These problems also extended to the white officers of black troops. At Fort Pickering in Tennessee some Regular Army men and black soldiers were performing guard duty. That night a regular decided to let some of his buddies slip out of the fort. A vigilant black soldier spotted them, however, and he notified his officer, who promptly arrested the regulars after a brief scuffle. The officer in the USCT then took the prisoners to their commanding officer, a major, who was so furious that "Nigs should arrest his men" that he preferred charges against the officer. Later, when the major's temper cooled, he realized his foolishness and dropped the ridiculous charges.[61]

Even more absurd was the experience of Capt. Josiah V. Meigs. One day in May 1864 he went to the penitentiary to check on two of his troops confined there. A white soldier named Spofford told him "they had no 'niggers' here belonging to a 'nigger' Battery." When Meigs replied that such statements could get the soldier in trouble, the soldier again said, "they have no niggers belonging to any dam'd nigger Battery and if they had they would not keep them long." Meigs then rode away, pistol in hand, amid "cries of derision and laughter." He admitted afterward, "My patience was sorely tried at this insult to the livery which I wear and to the cause in which I am espoused, and I felt very much like using my pistol." [62]

On a number of occasions, whites committed offenses ranging from thievery to murder against officers and men in black units. During the summer of 1864 troops in the 56th New York Infantry plundered the camp of the 26th U.S. Colored Infantry. One assistant surgeon alone lost seventy-five dollars' worth of property in the ransacking. Much worse was the inhuman treatment a private in the 45th U.S. Colored Infantry received at the hands of some white soldiers. In the field in Virginia during the winter of 1865, the private was out hunting for some firewood with permission when some white soldiers marched up and discharged their weapons wildly at a target. One ball struck the private in the chest. After he was hit, the private called out that they should "look out who they were firing at," to which the white troops replied, "Get out of the way, you damned black son of a bitch," and fired a few more rounds. The whites then marched off and left the private to die.[63]

As one lieutenant in the USCT remarked, there was considerable hatred between black units and "unprincipled white ones," which they seemed to encounter everywhere. The solution, so said several high-ranking officers, was to restrict the freedom and rights of black soldiers by confining them to camp at all times, thus avoiding confrontations. Such a policy was so blatantly discriminatory and such an unnecessary burden on their white officers, who had to perform all duties away from camp, that even strongly racist commanders had to rescind these directives. Others called for segregation and, where black and white units came together, "keep the colored troops in the back ground." Yet this situation was also demeaning and impossible to maintain under all circumstances.[64]

Most friends of the USCT preferred regulations that compelled all officers in military service to treat black and white soldiers equally, and "until that is done," insisted Maj. George L. Stearns, "they will be at the mercy of any officer, from Colonel up, who chooses to vent his spite or air his prejudice on them." In Louisiana the commander at Port Hudson warned his troops that any abuse of black troops "will be punished with unrelenting severity" and prohibited disparaging remarks toward the USCT by his white men. Major General Butler announced that he would punish with "severity" any officer, soldier, or citizen who shall "insult, abuse, ridicule or interfere with" black soldiers on the grounds of obstructing recruiting. To shield officers and men in black units from further abuse, Butler required that all courts-martial involving men in the USCT must have a majority of court members from the USCT, which was contrary to regulations but he believed essential for justice in those cases.[65]

But not everyone in the USCT could live with those solutions. Some white officers found the prejudice more than they were able to cope with and decided that service in black units was too embarrassing to admit to outside camp. One former officer in the 4th U.S. Colored Cavalry claimed that his colonel, a political appointee, denied he commanded a black unit during a trip through several Northern cities. When three officers in the 3rd U.S. Colored Heavy Artillery went into Memphis, they represented themselves as officers in an Ohio battery. A general court-martial dismissed one of them from the service for "acting as though he thought it was a disgrace in belonging to a Negro regiment."[66]

A much more common response was for black troops and their white officers to fight back. In the streets of Nashville black soldiers brawled with white troops from Tennessee (Union) and U.S. regulars. After some Philadelphia soldiers tried to tear the sergeant's stripes off the sleeves of Prince Rivers, a freedman with "remarkable executive ability" and an impressive physique, they "found it wiser and safer to leave him alone," so stated the regimental surgeon. In yet another instance, a black soldier in Norfolk, Virginia, shot a drunken sailor after he caused a public disturbance and insisted he "wont be controlled by a damned nigger." Butler fully supported the conduct of his soldier and warned the commodore in command, "When men get drunk, and are violent and outrageous in a garrisoned place policed by armed guards under my command, they will not be treated with rose water."[67]

Nor were white officers in the USCT passive in the defense of their men. Overhearing a lieutenant in a white regiment order two of his black soldiers to carry a personal trunk, a lieutenant in the USCT announced that "United States soldiers were not to be called upon to do menial service." In Louisiana black soldiers in the 51st U.S. Colored Infantry and their families endured repeated abuses from nearby white troops, and despite numerous complaints, the ranking officer of the white troops did nothing to put a halt to them. The commander of the black troops, Col. Isaac Shepard, became so fed up with the problem that when an incident occurred that could have resulted in the execution of the white soldier, Shepard took matters into his own hands and had his men flog the culprit. A court of inquiry later refused to censure Shepard for his actions. In Virginia a notorious Confederate supporter and slaveholder gave some slave women a whipping. When an officer in the 1st U.S. Colored Infantry found out, he had the man tied to a tree and permitted Pvt. William Harris, a former slave on this man's plantation, to administer fifteen to twenty lashes, "Bringing the blood from his loins at every stroke," and then had the beaten women deliver a few more cracks of the whip for good measure. The most incredible episode, though, was when Maj. Jeremiah B. Cook and twenty-one line officers in the 3rd U.S. Colored Cavalry hanged a civilian. On board a steamer on the Yazoo River the civilian told Cook and several other officers that Confederate Maj. Gen. Nathan B. Forrest had been right to massacre black troops at Fort Pillow. Later on the trip, the civilian threatened to cut the throat of a black sentinel for talking to a black woman. Even more galling to the officers was the fact that the civilian was making money by speculating in cotton under the protection of black troops. They held a court, convicted the civilian for his death threat, and hanged him. The division, corps, and departmental commanders all wanted the officers dismissed from the service, but the regimental commander, who had been absent when the event transpired, stood by his subordinates by insisting they were some of the best officers in the Union Army, and the government retained them. In each of these cases, the esteem that the black soldiers had for their officers must have risen dramatically.[68]

If the United States Army did not treat its own black commands properly, there was little hope that the Confederates would do so. Most Southerners regarded the conduct of blacks who enlisted in the Union Army as traitorous. In their eyes, they had raised these men from barbarism to a far-more-advanced level, and in return they demanded labor and loyalty, neither of which they were receiving. Deep down, however, they felt that the black race, though less civilized and therefore more savage, nonetheless resented enslavement. Their greatest nightmare was a slave uprising, and in a very real way, blacks in Union blue were a fulfillment of that horror scenario. The Federals took in slaves, provided them with a new suit of clothing and weapons, and then sent them into the South to overthrow the Confederate government.

Late in 1862, Confederate president Jefferson Davis attempted to deal with the issue of black soldiers and their white officers by directing that government forces turn over any captured men from the USCT to state authorities, which would try them for insurrection or inciting insurrection. Every Confederate state had laws that mandated the death penalty for both those crimes. Despite this proclamation, various questions arose, such as what to do if the soldier was a free black, especially a Northern free black, or if he was a former slave whose master wanted him back. In late April and early May the Confederate Congress merely confused military authorities when it passed a joint resolution calling for the death of white officers for "inciting servile insurrection" and the reenslavement of black soldiers. To complicate matters even more, these were disturbing features of the war to Europeans, whom Confederate authorities were courting for recognition and military succor. Officers proposed to avoid the problem by not taking prisoners, but in the end, although the Confederate authorities did not endorse these proposals, Confederate commands did occasionally fight under the black flag, a signal that they would give no quarter, against the USCT.[69]

For the bulk of the black population, military service was their great opportunity. While some slaves remained loyal to their former owners, most blacks, in both the North and South, felt considerable animosity toward Southern whites. Yet the ruthless revenge that Southern whites feared appeared only in retaliation for the murder of black soldiers. Most blacks preferred to vent their violent anger on the institution of slavery and its remnants; thus, a fairly common sight was black soldiers chopping down whipping posts and burning slave pens. As one white officer in the USCT noted while observing some troops in his regiment furiously hacking away at a whipping post, "It seemed as though they were cutting at an animate enemy & revenging upon him accumulated wrongs of two centuries." Toward their former owners collectively, black soldiers felt resentment over the demeaning and debasing existence these whites had forced on them, but they did not resort to savagery as whites had imagined. Some hated specific owners who had mistreated them, just as others had warm regard for kindly masters, but most blacks in uniform concentrated their animus on the concept of ownership rather than on individuals. When black soldiers captured former masters or guarded them as prisoners of war, there was rarely unprovoked violence. The emotional and psychological victory of overseeing the conduct of their former owners was satisfaction enough. Very revealing was the dream a black private divulged to a surgeon. He wanted to put on an officer's coat with shoulder straps, arm himself with a pistol, and have his photograph taken with a terrified Confederate prisoner at his feet. The private proposed to send the picture to his old master. As a smile stretched across his face, the soldier described how the master would throw the picture to the ground in a rage and grind it into the dirt with his foot. For this private and many others, that was enough to satisfy them.[70]

There is little evidence that the Confederate threat of enslavement or even execution deterred any blacks from military service. Blacks realized that they had an obligation to fight for freedom, not just for themselves but also for friends, relatives, and strangers. In fact, public disclosure of this policy may have been a boon for black enlistees, because it helped harden them psychologically much more quickly.[71]

For their white officers, the threat of death for inciting insurrection was a consideration, and it may have kept some from entering service in the USCT. From that standpoint, however, it had a positive function—to serve as a screen that weeded out those white men whose commitment to service with black troops was shakable. According to a captain in a black artillery battery, "The officers who accepted the command of colored troops were old soldiers in almost every instance. Death in their country's service was what they had been facing for years, and this threat of the rebel congress added no terrors sufficient to restrain them." Many of them had formulated a fatalistic view of warfare, as a Connecticut sergeant explained to his folks after deciding to accept a commission in the USCT: "I thought nothing of the extra danger for in war I don't see much difference in the danger. A man in the least dangerous spot may be killed & one in the most dangerous spot may not be." [72]

Nevertheless, it was important to both the white officers and their black troops that the Federal government enunciate a policy of retaliation for the execution or enslavement of United States soldiers. In April 1863 the War Department issued "Instructions for the Government of Armies of the United States in the Field," which stated,

"No belligerent has a right to declare that enemies of a certain class, color, or condition, when properly organized as soldiers, will not be treated by him as public enemies," and also, "The law of nations shows no distinction of color, and if an enemy of the United States should enslave and sell any captured persons of their Army, it would be a case for the severest retaliation, if not redress." Three months later, Lincoln reaffirmed this policy by proclaiming that the Union would retaliate man for man for executed soldiers, and for each enslaved soldier the government would place a Rebel prisoner at hard labor on the public works.[73]

This stymied Confederate authorities quite effectively, but it did not prevent subordinate officers and guerrillas from committing brutal acts against Union prisoners of war. In most cases Federal officers responded on their own initiative, rather than seek advice on how to retaliate from Washington. When Confederates murdered a black soldier from the 79th U.S. Colored Infantry (New), its commander executed a Confederate prisoner in return. To deter North Carolina guerrillas from murdering black troops they had captured, Brig. Gen. Edward A. Wild seized the wives and families of officers of the guerrilla band as hostages, which he found highly successful: "We learned that they grew disgusted with such unexpected treatment. It bred disaffection—some wishing to quit the business—others going over the lines to join the Confederate Army." Unfortunately, it was often difficult to isolate the culprits, especially when they were guerrillas, yet Maj. Gen. Lovell H. Rousseau adopted an ingenious means of retaliation. After partisans near Springfield, Tennessee, murdered Assistant Surgeon Eli M. Hewitt, Rousseau assessed and collected five thousand dollars from the local population to compensate Hewitt's family for the unnecessary loss. These were all effective techniques that either prevented Confederate atrocities or forced the Rebels to pay a heavy price for such acts.[74]

The Confederate policy of executing white officers and enslaving black troops had a positive effect on relationships within the USCT, too. Black troops, always wary of whites, realized that these white men were voluntarily placing their lives in grave jeopardy by serving in the USCT. And the white officers, recognizing the perils of surrender, had to depend even more on the performance of their troops in battle, which forced them to work a little harder to improve the fighting ability of the men. Even though many Confederates eventually respected the rights of white officers and their black soldiers as prisoners of war, some did not, and many officers in the USCT were unwilling to risk the possibility of execution by surrendering. These circumstances demanded a degree of interdependence between officers and men in the USCT that rarely existed in white volunteer units. The commander of the 83rd U.S. Colored Infantry (New) called Davis's order a "godsend" because of its impact of binding the white officers and their black soldiers together, and Col. Higginson wrote, "We all felt that we fought with ropes around our necks." Some officers, such as the commander of the 82nd U.S. Colored Infantry, deliberately used this argument to bond the men to their officers:

> You have Officers who have faith in your manhood. They have left their homes and come among you, knowing that they are liable of being hung by the rebel govt should they be taken prisoner and why? Because they instruct you to be soldiers. Because they teach you how to fight for liberty they would wish you to enjoy. Respect those Officers, obey them and help them, and be grateful to them.

In the end, the Confederate policy toward prisoners from the USCT gave both white officers and their black troops a foundation on which they were able to build a powerful relationship.[74]

Just as most Northerners and Southerners regarded blacks as inferior and discriminated against them, so the Civil War military experience of black units exemplified that inferior status and prejudicial treatment. The Northern government consistently treated blacks as second-class soldiers, while white troops abused both black soldiers and their white officers on sundry occasions. Confederate authorities, motivated by prejudice and fear of retaliation by blacks for more than two centuries of enslavement, also discriminated against prisoners from black units. White officers were subject to execution for inciting insurrection, and at times Confederates executed or returned to slavery black soldiers whom they captured.

Nevertheless, all was not bleak for the USCT. At the same time countervailing forces were working to enhance the position of black units. In a strange way, the discriminatory treatment of black troops as prisoners of war legitimized their use in the Union Army and enhanced their reputation among white soldiers. Regulars and volunteers slowly began to realize that men in the USCT were fighting on the same side and for the same causes they were, yet these white officers and black troops were incurring greater risks. Obviously, even strongly racist white soldiers noticed their commitment to a vigorous prosecution of the war and their dedication to victory at all costs. Their foe evidently regarded black units as the most detested element in the Union Army, and under those circumstances, no firmly committed unionists could help but regard the USCT more highly as comrades in arms.

Equally important, Northern Peace Democrats, nicknamed Copperheads by their opponents, advocated an immediate termination of hostilities and an independent Confederate nation, in direct contrast to the stated war aims of the president. In their attacks, Copperheads were most vocal against the use of black soldiers. Playing on the racial attitudes of the Northern public, and frequently concentrating their efforts on immigrant groups that would suffer economic competition from an enlarged free black population, they attacked abolitionism and the USCT at every opportunity to discredit the Lincoln administration.

The black soldiers and their white officers retaliated with their own venom. One black sergeant sought to rally all blacks against the Copperheads when he urged them, "When I say, resist, I suppose you will ask, Against whom? I answer, those cowardly copperheads of the North." Even more telling was the banner of the 11th U.S. Colored Heavy Artillery newspaper, which read, "Freedom To All. Death To Copperheads And Traitors." A lieutenant colonel commented to his mother, "It amuses me to see these insane old Copperheads keeping up their parrot cry of 'abolition bolition bolition bolition.' Why slavery's dead & they don't know it—there's nothing to abolish." When the parents of a captain mentioned to their son that they heard no one respected officers in the USCT, he retorted, "A class known as the 'Peace Democrats'" may not respect them, "But by all true lovers of country and who wish the downfall of slavery it is different." [75]

Also aiding in their defense was Lincoln himself. To a congressman who opposed blacks in the ranks he chided, "You say you will not fight to free negroes. Some of them seem willing to fight for you." Even more forceful was his letter to the editor of the *Frankfort Commonwealth* in 1864, in which Lincoln argued that anyone who stood for reunion should also support the USCT:

> And now let any Union man who complains of the measure, test himself by writing down in one line that he is for subduing the rebellion by force of arms; and in the next, that he is for taking these hundred and thirty thousand men from the Union side, and placing them where they would be but for the measure he condemns. If he cannot face his case so stated, it is only because he cannot face the truth. [76]

As Copperheads launched more and more vociferous attacks against a continuation of the war and the use of black troops, Union soldiers who believed deeply in the war began to align themselves with the USCT and to defend the use of blacks in the military. Copperhead protests cast the war issue in very stark terms. As Federal troops viewed it, Northerners were either for the war and everything that assisted reunion, or they opposed it and demanded an immediate cessation of hostilities. Since the USCT clearly aided the war effort, attacks by Copperheads forced many white soldiers to defend the enlistment of blacks, something that had been unthinkable two years earlier. By mid-1864, the tune of white soldiers toward black troops was clearly changing, so argued a soldier who was debating an appointment to the USCT, and Peace Democrats were simply out of step with the Union Army: "The copperheads of the North need not complain of them being placed on an equal footing with the white soldiers, since the white soldier himself does not complain. After a man has fought two years he is willing that any thing shal fight for the purpose of ending the war. We have become to[o] familiar with hardships to refuse to see men fight merely because their color is black." Others had looked more favorably on emancipation and the employment of black soldiers as a consequence of the war and its terrible hardships, but now Copperhead challenges helped to enhance the stature of the USCT by forcing them to support it publicly. A surgeon in a black artillery regiment described the process of change accurately when he wrote his wife that in the 1850s many people considered the expression "Rabid Abolitionists" as a "term of reproach; but now, if you will substitute the adjective earnest, which is all that was meant *then* by *'Rabid'* it is a title of honor. *We are all Abolitionists,* unless we are copperheads, which is *now* the contemptuous epithet." [77]

Thus, despite all the prejudice and discrimination, white officers and their black troops began to win a place in the Union Army. The attitude both in and out of the military toward the USCT began to change slowly and stubbornly yet steadily.[78]

Times were changing. One captain in a black regiment claimed that fellow officers in the volunteer units ostracized officers in the USCT at first, but later in the war "officers received every respect from their associates in the regular and volunteer service." [79]

As the first anniversary of the Emancipation Proclamation approached, an officer in the USCT queried his wife, "Do you remember how it was with the Emancipation Proclamation? How many tho't 'twould be the ruin of the nation and all that? Yet who so blind today, as not to see that it has done great good?" The Emancipation Proclamation, he continued, had not only freed slaves but put blacks in uniform, and that converted a bleak future into a bright one. "That Proclamation did not destroy the Nation did it—on the contrary I am inclined to think under the Providence of *God* it *saved* it in spite of the Copperheads of the North." More and more, unionists and their troops were hesitantly casting aside much of their racial blinders and viewing black units on much fairer terms.[80]

10

Army of Occupation

Nearly everyone in the USCT viewed the reelection of Abraham Lincoln in 1864 as the last nail in the coffin of the Confederacy. Clearly the momentum had shifted dramatically in favor of the Union that summer, and despite some tense days and weeks ahead, the fall of Atlanta in early September marked the beginning of the end of the fighting. All that Union supporters needed was a continued commitment to the war effort, something a Lincoln victory at the polls would provide.

To ensure success in the upcoming presidential election, men in the USCT did all they could for their candidate. Black soldiers, few of whom had the sacred ballot, flooded black newspapers with letters urging family and friends to do all in their power for Lincoln's campaign. White officers, too, relied on voice, pen, and vote to make known their selection. Early on, they proclaimed their choice to loved ones back home. "Do you think I am in earnest in staying in the army or just in [for] fun?" an officer sarcastically queried his wife when she asked him for whom he intended to cast his ballot. "I shall vote the Union ticket if I live and am permitted to vote at all." Another officer urged his brother, "Do all you can for the reelection of old Abe & you will do the best thing you can for the country's good." Democrats, too, crossed over to the Republican camp, justifying their switch very easily. "You say I have departed from the 'faith of my fathers,'" responded a captain to his aunt's teasing about his abandoning the Democratic party. "God knows I have not, and could my father this day rise from his grave it would only be to

207

rebuke the hypocracy and *treason* that stalks through the ranks of the party he once honored." Indeed, very few officers in the USCT could cast their vote for the Democratic presidential candidate, George B. McClellan, in good conscience. "What few McClellan men there are," explained an officer in the 4th U.S. Colored Infantry, "I notice are those thick-headed, ignorant men, who vote the Democratic ticket because they have always voted it, and can give no reasons for their choice." [1]

In those final months of the war, as the Confederacy collapsed and Rebel stronghold after Rebel stronghold fell into Union hands, the USCT played the role of avenging heroes to thousands and thousands of joyous blacks. Marching into Wilmington, North Carolina, in March 1865, "They stepped like lords & conquerors," boasted their commander. "The frantic demonstrations of the negro population will never die out of my memory. Their cheers & heartfelt 'God bress ye's' & cries of 'De chains is broke; De chains is broke,' mingled sublimely with the lusty shouts of our brave soldiery that welled up as they caught sight of the 'Old Glory' floating again over the dwellings of the loyal citizens." After the fall of Mobile that same month, the 51st U.S. Colored Infantry traveled by boat to the Alabama state capital, Montgomery, and freedmen lined the riverbank and cheered, danced, sang, and saluted the black troops with hats and handkerchiefs. Again, when the Confederate defenses at Petersburg fell, blacks came out to greet their rescuers, and in the race to occupy the Confederate capital of Richmond, it was black troops who entered the city first. As a Northern black regiment marched victoriously through those city streets, an old woman forced her way through the throngs of rejoicing blacks in search of Chaplain Garland H. White of the 28th U.S. Colored Infantry, who she knew had run away in Washington years before and escaped to Canada, and who was rumored to have resided in Ohio at the outbreak of the war. A black soldier overheard the woman and brought her to see his regimental chaplain. The woman proved to be White's mother. [2]

In their euphoria over the surrender of Lee's army and the end of the war came the tragic news of Lincoln's assassination. Soldiers of long service had identified closely with Lincoln, because, like them, he had borne the hardships, frustrations, and calamities of four years of war. Over that time Lincoln had been such an unyielding voice for reunion and freedom that he had come to symbolize those goals. Almost one year after the Emancipation Proclamation went into effect, an officer in the USCT and future United States congressman recognized this association when he wrote his wife, "Do you know Lydia that I am getting to regard Old Abe almost as a *Father*—

to almost venerate him—so earnestly do I believe in his earnestness, fidelity, honesty & Patriotism. I begin to look upon him some as the ancient Jews did upon Moses—as a chosen instrument of God for the deliverance of the Nation." His assassination, mourned a lieutenant, was a catastrophic loss for all downtrodden people: "Alas the *friend* of the *oppressed*, the *'Liberator'* is, no more!" [3]

Within the USCT, Lincoln's death was particularly devastating. The black units were Lincoln's creation, and their men thought the loss was a bit more personal than that of most other Federal troops. "I cannot paint to you the grief and indignation that our officers feel," a lieutenant wrote to his sister. "With us of the U.S. Colored Army the death of Lincoln is indeed the loss of a friend. From him we received our commission—and toward him we have even looked as toward a Father." [4]

The black soldiers revered Lincoln as the "Great Emancipator," and his death was a severe blow. "We have looked to him," wrote a black chaplain, "as our earthly Pilot to guide us through this National Storm and Plant us Securely on the Platform of Liberty and Equal Political right." Yet among the black troops there was a sense that Lincoln, like Moses, had done his job by establishing the course, and it was now time for others to see his policies through to their conclusion. One black infantryman insisted that "I shed not a tear for him. He has done the work that was given him, and today sings the song of redeeming love." Lincoln had positioned them on the track of equality, and for this he had earned a special place in the hearts and minds of Afro-Americans. "Although he is taken away from us," wrote a black sergeant, "his acts of kindness and deeds of philanthropy will live through all eternity." [5]

It was, in a sense, the debate over the direction of this course that began to unravel the bonds between the white officers and their black troops. With the war's end, the great link between them had disappeared. The Federal Army had restored the union, and the Thirteenth Amendment to the United States Constitution had abolished slavery. Now the public had to determine the relationship between the two races, a very ticklish proposition in a racist world. To make matters worse, this debate took place while the USCT endured the tension, hostility, and frustration of service as the army of occupation.

Within a few months of Lee's surrender, the government instituted a policy of rapid demobilization. The expense of maintaining an army of one million men was bankrupting the government and both the citizen-soldiers and the Northern public clamored to bring the troops home as soon as possible. The problem was that the government needed an occupation force to help implement the reconstruction program. The solution, however, seemed to be a simple one: Muster out all the white veteran commands as rapidly as possible and retain a disproportionate number of black units for reconstruction duty. In most cases these white troops had served longer and, after all, they also had the vote. Black units composed of freedmen had to return to the economic chaos of the South. By keeping them in the service, these black soldiers would have three meals per day, shelter, and pay, and this would ease their transition from slavery to freedom and from wartime to peacetime.[6]

Yet reconstruction duty was by no means an easy assignment. Despite a gradually shrinking force, the army of occupation had an obligation to assist Southern blacks in this shift from slavery to freedom—a complex and at times frustrating endeavor. In addition, as representatives of the federal government, they had the unenviable chore of imposing reconstruction programs on an unreceptive Southern white population. This was particularly difficult for blacks in uniform, whose mere presence infuriated the bulk of the white population. To complicate matters further, both Lincoln's successor as president, Andrew Johnson, and Radical Republicans in Congress had different approaches to reconstruction, and both sides tried to use the army of occupation as a pawn in their political struggle.[7]

The centerpiece of the reconstruction program to assist Southern blacks during their first turbulent years of freedom was the Freedmen's Bureau. Designed in the final months of the Lincoln administration, the Freedmen's Bureau operated under the auspices of the War Department. Its original job was to help reunite black families separated in slavery, assist them in obtaining fair employment, protect whatever rights the federal government granted them, and coordinate relief and developmental activities, especially education, for the freedmen.[8]

Naturally, ties between the Freedmen's Bureau and the USCT were strong. The bulk of the black troops, as former slaves, had a vested interest in any sort of program that supported and uplifted Southern blacks. Northern black soldiers, too, benefited indirectly from such a program. Many of their relatives had won freedom during the war, and improvements among Southern blacks helped to elevate the stature of the entire black population. Even the white officers had powerful ties to the Freedmen's Bureau. Merely by serving in the USCT, many of them had staked their interest in uplifting the black race. And the head of the Freedmen's Bureau, Maj. Gen. Oliver Otis Howard, had links to the USCT. His own brother and several members of his staff during the war held commissions in the USCT. Thus, when Howard sought people to work in the Freedmen's Bureau, he relied heavily on officers in the USCT. They had considerable experience supervising large bodies of men, extensive knowledge of blacks and the problems that confronted them, and enough concern for the condition of the downtrodden race to risk their lives fighting alongside black soldiers.[9]

Those officers in the USCT who served as agents in the Freedmen's Bureau quickly learned that the position demanded a wide range of talents, few of which military service had taught them. "My work here is very hard," complained one officer. "I could not endure the labor & anxiety of my present duty were it not for the interest I feel in the work." First, they had to explain clearly to ex-slaves what privileges and responsibilities freedom and citizenship entailed and what their relationship was to former owners. Second, they had to oversee the preparation and fulfillment of labor contracts. Third, agents had to settle disputes between new freedmen and their old masters. Finally, they aided a variety of philanthropic organizations in establishing schools for the Southern black population.[10]

The most rewarding aspect of the job, according to an officer in the USCT and a Freedmen's Bureau agent, was to deliver addresses to huge audiences of freedmen and planters and other Southern whites. "You should have seen that crowd, that sea of eager faces," announced an ecstatic captain in the 73rd U.S. Colored Infantry working in Alabama. "You might imagine somewhat of the feelings which take possession of one standing before thousands of people to tell them that *They were free* & of the new duties & responsibilities that come with this gift of freedom." Another commander of black infantrymen attempted to disabuse freedmen of the belief that they could rely on the government for more than immigrants received. He told them in the "plainest terms that it would only protect them in their freedom—that it would not keep them in their idleness, and that it could not give them land and personal property that belonged to others." The lieutenant then urged them to "cultivate habits of industry, frugality, and temperance, assuring them that [this] was the only course that would secure to them comfort and happiness." [11]

Many officers found the preparation of labor contracts a difficult chore. These agreements established the working relationship between whites and blacks for an entire year, and very few of the officers had the legal skills or knowledge to prepare sound ones. After having been away from the private sector for several years, they had difficulty determining fair wages for civilians and struggled to ensure that both parties lived up to the contracts. And compounded by hundreds and hundreds of such documents, agents shouldered huge caseloads.[12]

Accustomed as these officers were to mountains of army paperwork, though, the preparation of contracts was never their primary
concern. The major problem that confronted these officers was shap-
ing the new relationship between freedmen and Southern whites.
After generations of subservience, freedmen insisted on decent treatment while whites, who had regarded blacks as inferior creatures,
considered such demands outrageous. "Their old masters grant their
freedom grudgingly," explained an officer to his wife, "and in many
cases beyond the eye of the military, they are but little better than
slaves yet." In concurrence, another officer told his parents, "The
greatest difficulty I have to contend with is the persistency of the
planters in continuing their old habits of punishing or spooking
those who in any way offend them." After hiring freedmen as laborers,
whites attempted to use the lash to discipline the work force or
hire drivers to perform the task. Others withheld payment, complaining that the work was sloppy or in some way inadequate. Mostly,
though, whites refused to recognize the rights that new freedmen
had gained through the Federal victory. "It seems that they are
determined to defeat the policy of the government," complained an
officer.[13]

In this atmosphere disputes and controversies were inevitable,
and again these officers stepped in as Freedmen's Bureau agents
to adjudicate the issues. Sitting as "a Kind of Freedmans Court,"
officers listened to witnesses from both sides and ascertained who
was at fault in these quarrels and determined the proper solutions,
including fines and compensations. The mere presence of these
courts, and the way they conducted business, galled Southern
whites. As one officer explained to his wife, "It comes very hard for
some of these elders of aristocracy to be brought up before me at
the instance of the 'niggers' and then be confronted by their sable
countenances as witnesses—very hard indeed, a great infringement
of their 'Constitutional rights.' " Yet it was also a monumental experience for blacks and the white judges. One of the most striking proofs
of freedom, recalled an officer, was the first time he heard a case
between a white man and a black woman, and he decided on the
merits of the black woman's testimony.[14]

Of course, Southern whites were not about to accept the decrees
of Freedmen's Bureau agents voluntarily, and here the army of occupation played a critical role. Traditional channels for resolving disputes and apprehending and punishing criminals, such as the court
system and local constabularies, were utterly ineffective, as few
Southern whites were willing to take a public stand and declare
neighbors guilty of abuse against blacks. Any justice that blacks
received, then, derived from decisions of the Freedmen's Bureau

and their enforcement by the army of occupation. The government had created the Freedmen's Bureau to see that "justice was done between the Freedmen and the whites," a colonel in a black regiment instructed one of his captains, and "if they call upon the military authorities at any garrison to carry out their mandates, guards should be furnished them to act *under their instructions.*" [15]

In a number of instances, the mere presence of the army of occupation helped to ease tensions between the two races. Even with black commands, a number of officers noticed that after the initial shock, attitudes of Southern whites began "softening." It was apparent, according to a captain in the USCT, that the presence of armed forces was working:

> These bayonets are reflecting a great deal of light into the surrounding country—*moral* light, I mean, such as reaches the minds & consciences of men. The Colored people are now holding schools & religious meetings all around here. Many of the employers are coming to the conclusion that these people are after all really free and can earn something besides their mere food and clothing. I know of some very sudden conversions of that kind lately—almost as sudden as Pauls—caused by the light spoken of above.

"The fact is," wrote black Chaplain Henry M. Turner, "when colored Soldiers are about they [whites] are afraid to kick colored women and abuse colored people on the Streets, as they usually do." [16]

Other times, however, the only remorse that Southern whites felt was for the fact that they had lost on the battlefield. Although their army had been defeated in combat, the Union had not conquered them, and they were unwilling to treat blacks with any dignity. They continued to strut through the streets in Confederate uniforms, passed laws that abrogated or circumscribed the freedom of blacks, and tried to elect ex-Confederate officers and politicians, including the vice president of the Confederate States of America, to the United States Congress. Southern whites made vigorous efforts to undercut the work of the Freedmen's Bureau and intimidate its agents, and they committed acts of violence against blacks in untold numbers. After several months of duty in the Freedmen's Bureau, an officer in the USCT wrote his mother in dismay that Southern whites were "a poor ignorant superstitious people, and they think no more of killing a man than we would of a dog if he *offended us.* So it is, all through the South." In Texas, for example, whites justified murdering blacks on such grounds as the victim "failed to remove his hat" or "wouldn't give up his whiskey flask." One white claimed he "wanted to thin out the niggers a little" and another decided it would be fun "to see a d___d nigger kick." [17]

No doubt, Southern whites resented the presence of any Federal soldiers, yet their hostility was particularly keen toward men in the USCT. Not only did they regard black troops overseeing the conduct of whites as outrageous—a complete reversion of their proper roles—they also considered the existence of black troops an impediment to a resurgence of white supremacy. Blacks throughout the United States viewed the USCT as a great achievement. Its troops had become heroes throughout the black population, and its presence among freedmen encouraged blacks to demand that whites respect their newfound rights. Because of this leadership role, the USCT was especially odious.[18]

Thus, white Southerners tried in every way to impugn the reputation of the USCT. Some "taunted and jeered" black troops in an attempt to instigate trouble, while others accused them of plundering white homes and inciting trouble among freedmen. Whites in Texas and Louisiana went so far as to commit all sorts of crimes against other whites, disguised as USCT men "with blackened faces and in the Uniform of United States Soldiers, this to get an order issued for the removal of the only reliable troops (the colored)," wrote a captain. They tried to place the onus for nearly all controversies on the shoulders of black troops and their white officers, and through collaboration among Southern whites, the burden of proof in fact rested with the accused. In Tennessee, when a white man attacked a black, and the police promptly arrested the black, a crowd of blacks assembled to demand their friend's release. About that time Lt. Frank Baird of the 111th U.S. Colored Infantry came along and tried to defuse the situation, but the blacks nevertheless broke open the jail and set the prisoner free. In retaliation, three whites tried to discredit the USCT by accusing Baird of drunkenness and instigating the riot. Fortunately, two enlisted men and a captain were eyewitnesses to the event and testified on Baird's behalf at his court-martial, which exonerated him.[19]

Nor did Southern whites hesitate to resort to violence to intimidate or drive out black troops. In several instances, whites provoked a dispute, and fighting erupted when black soldiers refused to endure the abuse. One evening a Memphis policeman said to a black sergeant, "I wish I could get a chance to kill all the Damned Nigger Soldiers." The sergeant replied that he could not kill *him*, and the policeman charged at the soldier and began striking him with his nightstick. Soon a second policeman arrived and joined in the beating, clubbing and kicking the sergeant several times. On another occasion, when six enlisted men entered a bar in Baton Rouge and ordered a beer, the owner refused to serve them, and a patron then insulted them and punched a sergeant in the group. A brawl eventually ensued, with white customers drawing revolvers and soldiers grabbing up brickbats from out on the street. In the melee the sergeant suffered a leg wound. Even more striking was the general harassment of black soldiers of occupation in Memphis, which eventually resulted in a tragic race riot. When the troops refused to let whites bully them any longer, white mobs tried to show the blacks who was master by sacking the black community and murdering forty-six blacks, twelve of whom were former soldiers.[20]

Other times, though, black soldiers were merely passive victims of racial assaults. Three whites with knives attacked Sgt. Elijah Marrs, home on a furlough in Kentucky, just for being a black man in the Union Army. Marrs grabbed a stick and battled his assailants in retreat, back to his father's house and safety. A gang in Raymond, Mississippi, fired on three black soldiers simply for walking around town in uniform, killing one and driving the others into hiding. Several months later, a black private was strolling along a street in Columbus, Georgia, when he heard a white man say, "God damn son of a bitch." The soldier glanced at him and continued walking. Suddenly he heard a pistol fire, and a ball passed through his hand. Moments later, two more shots followed, a ball striking him in each arm. And in Virginia, a white resident tried to poison the camp well, vowing to kill every black soldier if only he could find a way to accomplish it.[21]

Officers, too, were victims of such violence. In Louisiana some white citizens grabbed a lieutenant and executed him. The lieutenant begged for his life for the sake of his wife and children, but his pleas fell on deaf ears. He was "nothing but a d___d Nigger officer any how," the assassins later insisted. One evening in Walhalla, South Carolina, Lieut. J. T. Furman of the 33rd U.S. Colored Infantry stepped out of a hotel onto the front porch. A former Confederate soldier approached him, and the man began chatting, telling Furman how glad he was that Federal troops were there to bring law and order to the town. After a minute of discussion, the two men began a casual stroll around the town. They had walked only a few steps when the civilian pulled a pistol from his pocket and shot the lieutenant in the back. As Furman lay prostrate on the ground, the man discharged his pistol into the officer's head and fled. A month later, when the odds were in their favor, several men were brazen enough to boast of their part in Furman's murder to a colonel in the USCT and ask him what he planned to do about it. Helplessly outnumbered in that instance, the officer could do nothing.[22]

The only major conspiracy to eliminate a sizable number of officers and men in the USCT occurred in South Carolina. There Federal authorities had sent the 33rd U.S. Colored Infantry under Lt. Col.

Charles T. Trowbridge to occupy and keep the peace in Pickens and Anderson counties. Trowbridge knew he was in for a rough tour of duty when he learned that Anderson County alone had voted almost unanimously for secession and had had 1,800 of its men killed or wounded in the Confederate Army. Much to the colonel's delight, his stint was brief, and the regiment received orders to return to Charleston via train for mustering out of the service. Before leaving for the coast, South Carolina politician James L. Orr, whom Trowbridge had befriended, warned the colonel that locals had a plan to annihilate the entire regiment. To ensure safety, Trowbridge ordered his most trusted enlisted man, Sgt. Fred Brown, to take four privates, ride on the engine, and shoot the engineer if anything strange happened. As darkness fell the train moved along nicely until it reached a high trestle bridge, some one hundred feet above the water. Near the middle of the bridge someone pulled the coupling pin and the engine sped on while the rest of the train, carrying the officers and men of the 33rd U.S. Colored Infantry, slowed to a halt, suspended above the water. Volleys of musket fire then began crashing into the cars, as locals tried to pin down the regiment and set fire to the span. Trapped inside, the troops could neither return effective fire due to the darkness nor abandon the cars. After a few moments, though, their sense of desperation ended. Above the rattle of musketry they heard the engine backing over the trestle. When the two sections connected and someone replaced the pin, Trowbridge noticed that Sergeant Brown had his pistol cocked and nestled up against the back of the engineer's head. Apparently Brown had threatened to blow the man's brains out if he did not back the engine up immediately, and his swift action had saved the entire regiment.[23]

To compound the entire problem, when fanatical whites were unable to attack black troops, they went for the next best thing, their families. This was particularly upsetting to the men, who felt that their families were innocent victims in the struggle between Southern whites and the federal government. Whites plundered the homes of black soldiers, occasionally attacked family members, and, most commonly, forced families from their homes for non-payment of rent, which soldiers provided irregularly as a result of the infrequency of army pay.[24]

Solutions to these attacks on men in the USCT and their families were difficult to formulate. Many officers permitted parties of troops to return home to gather their families and bring them to the army, settling them adjacent to camp. Others relied on the Freedmen's Bureau to ensure the safety and well being of soldiers' families. And some, such as Capt. Will Story, used vague threats that Story termed a "friendly warning" to the former owner of one of his men. When the soldier learned that his wife and children were being forced from their home, he called the matter to Story's attention, and the captain wrote the landowner and offered to have the soldier pay a reasonable rent. Story then pointed out that the government was about to open a Freedmen's Bureau Court in that area because of the large number of complaints from blacks there, and he did not want to see the white man suffer worse than he had already: "Be wise and do not commit yourself by any act that will cause you to loose more, when it can be avoided by a *manly straitforward* course with those of your blacks that are yet with you." [25]

To prevent further harassment of officers and men in the USCT, though, military authorities never developed an effective policy. They were, in effect, attempting to put down a guerrilla war, yet the peculiar legal status of Southern whites stripped from the military their more aggressive and controversial options. The best they could do was advise subordinate officers, as did the commander of the 119th U.S. Colored Infantry: "In all cases you must exercise great discretion and especially to avoid collisions with the people but firmness must be evinced in the execution of duty." Some officers tried to keep their men apart from Southern whites, or placed their reliance on the inadequate court system. Others banded together and tried to ease racial tensions within the community, if necessary by intimidation, such as several officers in Winnsboro, South Carolina, who "visited the editor of the paper here and advised him not to publish pieces against negro troops." None of these approaches, however, resolved the problem.[26]

Inevitably, black troops took matters into their own hands when authorities failed to deal with the problem satisfactorily. In Louisiana, troops in the 20th U.S. Colored Infantry retaliated against locals, and an inspector general defended their behavior to authorities. He argued that these were Northern blacks, mostly from New York. Unaccustomed to such abuse, they "will not submit now." To avoid further difficulties, the War Department promptly mustered the regiment out of service. At a Florida train station, a civilian remarked that "all the niggers should be in _____." Immediately twenty soldiers from the 3rd U.S. Colored Infantry leveled their rifles at the man, and one soldier fired, grazing the speaker's cheek and alerting him that the shooter could just as easily have killed him. Still another time, after a barroom brawl between black troops and white civilians, a regimental colonel destroyed all the liquor in the saloon, but the company commander of the black soldiers predicted that if his superior officer did not punish the civilian culprits, "the men will by stealth execute the law themselves and I wont blame them one bit."

Moreover, avenging abuses that Southern whites committed against blacks served to drive a wedge between the enlisted population and their white officers. Southerners, especially ex-Confederates, harassed black troops, and when the men retaliated, military authorities punished them. The officers were simply trying to maintain discipline, but it infuriated black soldiers that their own officers penalized them, who had labored so hard in the war, while their enemies walked away, apparently unpunished.[27]

Even more upsetting, Southern whites were not the only ones who abused blacks during occupation duty. In South Carolina twenty soldiers from a white regiment mobbed five black civilians for no reason other than race, and along the Mississippi River an engineer on the steamer *Idaho* refused to let a black soldier arrest him and shot and killed the man. An even worse case was in Cairo, Illinois, where the 125th U.S. Colored Infantry encamped. According to an inspector general, locals there "took every opportunity to annoy them by personal violence, *while in the performance of their duties*, as well as upon every other occasion. The Civil Authorities of the Town are as bitter as the populace, often arresting the Soldiers while passing from Barracks to the Post, at which they are detailed for duty."[28]

Along with implementing orders from agents of the Freedmen's Bureau or enduring harassment from whites, other occupation duties for black units proved disillusioning. The USCT tended to receive such assignments as reinterring dead from major battles, a ghastly chore, or occupying the most remote and unhealthy places. There medical care was in short supply, pay was rare, and living conditions were wretched.[29]

Probably the worst location for occupation service was Texas. During the war France had invaded Mexico and seized control of the government, in violation of the Monroe Doctrine. While the fighting between the states was going on, the Federal government was preoccupied, but as soon as the Confederacy collapsed, Grant sent hard-charging Maj. Gen. Phil Sheridan to the Texas-Mexico border with a substantial army in the event of an American invasion, but primarily as a show of force. To support Sheridan, Maj. Gen. Henry W. Halleck, the new commander of the Department of Virginia, decided to send all his black units to Texas. According to Halleck, the entire Twenty-fifth Corps was "poorly officered and in bad discipline, and altogether unfitted for the military occupation of Virginia," although Grant had found them entirely suitable to assist in the defeat of Lee's army. Halleck promptly merged all black commands in his department into the Twenty-fifth Corps and shipped it to Texas.[30]

Many of these black troops, however, reacted violently to the move. Nearly all the black soldiers had come from Northern states or the Chesapeake region, and many of the families of ex-slaves were in refugee camps nearby. Just before they were to set sail, authorities terminated the rations to these families, based on the logic that black soldiers now had equal pay and were able to support their own families. In response, a number of these troops mutinied because they had no means of caring for their families while they were a thousand miles away in Texas. They had not received pay for eight to ten months and had no money to provide for their families' welfare.[31]

Men in another regiment, the 29th Connecticut (Colored) Infantry, also mutinied, although the root of their problem was a failure of the officers to communicate properly to the troops. Wild rumors spread throughout the regiment that the officers intended to take them to Cuba and sell them into slavery. In both cases, inadequate planning and poor communication on the part of officers prompted the revolts.[32]

Nor did the problems stop there. In transit from Virginia to Texas, troops suffered so badly from fever, poor sanitation, and spoiled or insufficient food that men in one regiment, the 115th U.S. Colored Infantry, died at a rate of twelve per day. Disgruntled with the trip and their destination and woozy from seasickness, the troops landed at Brazos Santiago, where no one had made any preparations for them. Both officers and enlisted men pitched tents on the beach and tried to endure the scorching summer sun as best they could. For a while, fresh water was in such short supply that soldiers received only one pint per day, and men were selling water for one dollar a mouthful. At the end of June, though, a tremendous storm struck, overturning the flimsy tents of the enlisted men and soaking them thoroughly. Yet, much to their delight, the wind increased in force and ripped up the officers' tents too, which "left them to take the Storm with us," recorded a sergeant. Several days later they trekked to Brownsville, on what an officer termed "a horrible march" through thick mud, for garrison duty.[33]

At least at Brazos Santiago, troops could swim and fish. In Brownsville life was terrible. One officer described the town as "rather the best place I have seen in all Texas—thus far, and even the most wretched hamlet of our most miserable districts of the north would be perfection compared to this place." Another officer complained that "The climate does not suit me & besides we are kept in constant fear of lying down on a venimous reptile or insect of some description." Apparently tarantulas, rattlesnakes, and mosquitoes infested the area. Food shortages required troops to go on half rations, and when a supply ship did arrive, it contained seeds to grow their own food—of course too late for use that year.[34]

Although these hardships were severe, they were at least tolerable. The most awful part of occupation duty in Texas was a massive outbreak of scurvy, still another manifestation of the woeful planning of military authorities. By 1861 physicians mistakenly attributed to all fruits and vegetables the power to check scurvy, rather than to selected edibles with Vitamin C. Yet efforts to diversify the diet and include fresh fruits and vegetables had helped considerably, so that in late 1862 the surgeon general boasted that "Scurvy has been almost entirely prevented" within the army. There were some cases of scurvy, as well as other undiagnosed illnesses due to deficient diets. According to physicians, though, these were more the fault of individual soldiers who failed to consume their rations in full or bad foraging during campaigns than anything else.[35]

During the last few months of the war in Virginia, black soldiers began to show signs of scurvy and other dietary ailments. A surgeon complained that his troops had not received vegetables in five months and "Scorbutic Diathesis [scurvy] prevails strongly," and another surgeon levied a protest about scurvy in his regiment to the Twenty-fifth Army Corps Medical Director, but "My *representations were disdainfully spurned, and no attention paid to me or them.*" After Lee's army surrendered and the Twenty-fifth Army Corps left for Texas, scurvy reached epidemic proportions. En route via ships, cases of scurvy became more and more frequent, and within one week of their arrival at Brazos Santiago the situation was critical. A post hospital with beds for only eighty had five hundred patients, and these were the worst cases. Medical officials sent hundreds of troops to New Orleans for care, yet there was no checking the problem. One surgeon wrote that soldiers became dejected and physically listless, and they lost interest in providing themselves with good shelter and caring for themselves generally. The troops' gums swelled so badly from scurvy that they completely hid patients' molars, bicuspids, and canine teeth. During the summer of 1865 the medical inspector in Texas estimated that 60 percent of the Twenty-fifth Army Corps had scurvy. Physicians and their staffs worked frantically, but to little avail. A surgeon insisted that many troops were "actually begging to be left with their comrades to die in the regt. rather than be sent to the place where neither sufficient attendants, nor food can be obtained." Another surgeon distributed all the canned tomatoes and pickles he had on hand and wrote his father despondently, "We have no fresh vegetables, except a few from the 'sanitary arm,' all antiscorbutic medicines exhausted—and discouragement *everywhere*. Men are taken down one day—& the next are in unmarked graves." To aid his men, a surgeon even traveled south into Mexico to purchase barrels of onions and tomatoes, but Mexican authorities would not permit such a large quantity of vegetables and fruit to pass over the border. By mid-August, fresh vegetables and fruits began to pour into Texas, and within two weeks a surgeon announced ecstatically that the sick list had declined 40 percent as a result of recoveries. Nevertheless, angry medical officers insisted that the entire affair was inexcusable and hoped that military authorities would punish commanding officers for the "wilful neglect or culpable ignorance" of their failure to provide the men with fresh vegetables and fruit, but prosecutions were not forthcoming.[36]

Along with the hazards of racial conflict with whites and the awful conditions that black soldiers endured, the most striking feature of reconstruction duty was the seemingly endless hours of boredom. During the war much of the work was routine and often tedious, but military service was a new and uplifting experience for blacks, and they felt a sense of contribution toward the goals of reunion and freedom. With the war at its end, life in the army was no longer a novelty for most black troops, and soldiers felt they could make better progress outside the military structure. According to one officer, "Inactivity and idleness breed discontent from which a long train of evils follow." Boredom and frustration converted into all sorts of trouble, as public drunkenness was on the rise and "loathsome diseases of a private nature have spread fearfully," complained a regimental commander.[37]

Among the officers there were problems as well. Many decided that their jobs had ended with the war, and they lost interest in military service. With large blocks of free time on hand, they too suffered from outbreaks of public intoxication and loose moral behavior. A handful of others, thinking about their postwar lives, began scheming to defraud black troops of their money, and several got away with the entire savings of their men, which only served to increase the mistrust black troops had for their white officers.[38]

To counteract the bad effects of free time and uninterested officers, a number of other officers tried to impose rigorous discipline on the men. They began to drill troops vigorously and penalize them for slight offenses in hopes of reviving the sagging morale and upgrading moral conduct. Yet the bulk of the black soldiers reacted unfavorably to such efforts. They were hardened veterans who had grown accustomed to the more relaxed discipline that existed in combat zones. Now, they believed their extensive service and trustworthiness during the war had won them a little more freedom within the military structure and a continued easing of regimentation. To be sure, this was an adjustment problem that both white and black commands faced, a normal experience in the transition from wartime to peacetime that pitted officers against enlisted men, but in the USCT racial factors exacerbated the issue.[39]

It was disturbing, as one enlisted man complained, that superior officers had asked black soldiers

> to forget old grudges and prejudices, and fight like men for a common cause, meaning for us not to let the cruel and unjust treatment of the officers to the men, influence us to disregard for our duty to our common country. But now there is nothing of the kind to fear, the officers feeling that they have nothing now to fear from stray bullets, are exercising all the arrogance and despotism that their power gives them, and what appeals has an enlisted man if he applies for redress to the superior officer?

The harsh punishments and inconsiderate treatment that most black soldiers had endured during the war was utterly intolerable now, and complaints were on the rise. One soldier attempted to arouse public support by writing to a black newspaper about the various forms of punishments his regiment suffered, such as tying men up by the thumbs and bucking and gagging. The "most cruel of all," though, was called a sweat box. It was a fully enclosed wooden crate five feet in height, two feet in width, and two feet deep, with a one-inch hole bored in the top for air, which soldiers occupied for hours. Others fired off dozens of letters of protest to government officials, in particular Secretary of War Stanton, accusing officers of all sorts of mistreatment. One soldier in the 44th U.S. Colored Infantry, who refused to sign his name, even warned Stanton, "Col Johnson if he Don't look out he will get apple cart tumble he has been kicking some of the Boys but the[y] say the[y] will stop that or stop his life."[40]

Part of the spoils of victory for blacks was freedom, and in the days of reconstruction they were especially sensitive about their rights. As a result revolts against the authority of officers were on the upswing, and general courts-martial convicted dozens and dozens of black soldiers of mutiny. And with few exceptions, these troops were responding to abusive treatment.[41]

In the 109th U.S. Colored Infantry, an officer tied two soldiers up by their thumbs and the troops rebelled. "These officers think they can do just as they have a mind to with us now the war is over," complained one mutineer, "but we will show them, if we have to kill every one of them!" Another private insisted that "he would not allow any white man to run over him, he never allowed his master to!" He then continued, "The damned white sons of bitches think they can do as they please with us. They have lied long enough." Yelled still a third private, "We will see if these officers are agoing to tie up a colored man. We are free, our Colonel told us so, and we will fight before they shall keep our men tied." A fourth soldier, a corporal, put the situation in very clear perspective when he protested, "We came from home to get rid of such treatment as this." A court convicted all four of mutiny and put them to hard labor.[42]

The 117th U.S. Colored Infantry had an enormous revolt, the result of a new commanding officer who, in his own words, "put on the screws." The mutineers' plan was to gather under arms at midnight, storm the guardhouse and free all prisoners, and then force concessions from the regimental commander and a particularly severe captain. Unwittingly, the lieutenant colonel in charge of the regiment brought tensions to a head when he punished an entire company for sloppiness on dress parade. This excited the rebellious troops, and they cast aside their plot in favor of an armed uprising as soon as possible. A mob of two hundred black soldiers then advanced on the parade ground and rescued their comrades from punishment. Recognizing the crisis immediately, the lieutenant colonel called out the rest of the regiment, and before anyone realized what he was asking them to do, they formed a square around the mutineers, with officers outside the square under announced orders to shoot anyone who left his place or permitted rebellious men from breaking free. He then offered rewards to anyone who identified the ringleaders and sought assistance from other regiments nearby. Despite the pressure, no soldiers cracked, and the regimental commander then gagged and bound two soldiers as punishment. When reinforcements arrived, it was clear that the armed protest was a failure, and by 1:00 A.M. he had twenty-two leaders under arrest for inciting mutiny and a variety of other charges, among them one white officer who was partial to their cause and had failed to make a vigorous effort to suppress the uprising.[43]

The most shocking mutiny, however, occurred in Jacksonville, Florida, in October 1865. There Lt. Col. John L. Brower tied up a soldier by the thumbs, and the troops revolted. Incited by the words of Pvt. Jacob Plowder, who insisted it was "a damned shame to tie men up" and "he would be damned if he would not be one to cut the man down," a cluster of armed troops advanced on Brower, who panicked and started shooting into the crowd. Troops then returned the fire, and an officer and an enlisted man were wounded in the melee. After battling for some time, the officers gained control of the situation and arrested scores of troops. Military authorities executed five men in the regiment, but most others served little time in prison because authorities mustered the regiment out of service several days later and they could not get witnesses to testify against their comrades.[44]

These mutineers were certainly not representative of black soldiers, but their disillusionment with harsh discipline and military service in general was indicative of a deep-seated desire to move on to a new chapter in their lives. They had fought the war, helped to achieve victory, and now wanted to enjoy the fruits of their labor among family and friends. According to one sergeant who spoke for himself but whose views expressed the wishes of thousands, during that final year of army life he longed for the day when "no man can say to me come and go, and I be forced to obey."[45]

As an alternative to boredom, declining morale, and misconduct, some perceptive officers in the USCT intensified their long-standing programs of religious study and education. In the eyes of most Northerners, particularly officers in the USCT who had strong ties to evangelicalism, religion was not only the vehicle to eternal salvation, it also fostered the development of morals that were the cornerstone of citizenship in a participatory government. Officers in the USCT were unsure what sorts of rights Northern and Southern blacks were going to possess in the postwar world, but there was no doubt that their status would improve as a result of the war, and military authorities had an obligation to help prepare them for that responsibility. Education buttressed religion by allowing individuals to study the Bible and learn the moral lessons of Christianity. Moreover, white officers believed that education would provide both Northern and Southern black soldiers with essential skills for the postwar world, to earn a decent living, protect those things they cherished, and properly utilize their rights in a free society. Together, religion and education were the basis of the free society in the North. "The permanency, and success, of a Republican form of Government," insisted a chaplain, "will depend upon the virtue and Intelligence, of the great masses of people."[46]

Of course, those most in need of religious and educational instruction were the freedmen. Contrary to the claims of Southern whites, most Northerners believed that slavery had stunted the development of the black race and had intentionally imposed on Southern blacks a condition of immorality that prevented them from becoming civilized and therefore helped to justify enslavement. Despite the conviction among Northern whites that blacks were innately inferior, they implicitly assumed that by removing the obstacle of slavery and providing proper religious instruction and education, Southern black soldiers would adopt those same qualities that their Northern benefactors possessed and improve their condition dramatically.

The more Southern black soldiers studied the Bible, and the better they learned to read and write, the sooner proper character, represented by morality, thrift, industry, and striving for perfection, would take shape among these new freedmen. In turn, this would help to uplift the entire South.[47]

By the time of the war, however, blacks in slavery were no heathens. They had well-established views on Christianity and were unwilling to yield to the dogmatic or paternalistic approach to religious education that many chaplains and officers offered. Because of the excitement and emotionalism in black religious services, most whites assumed that the prayers of black soldiers lacked substance or that, as a chaplain claimed, their religious notions "consist more in emotional exercises than a consciencious performance of duty and trust in God." As a result, these whites preferred to challenge or ridicule the views and practices of blacks in an effort to discredit them and made little headway in religious conversion or improving the moral climate of the command.[48]

Those few clergymen and officers who worked with black soldiers and acknowledged the existence of black ministers within units, who tried to act more as coordinators of religious services than as sole arbiters of proper religious dogma, were the ones who had the greatest impact on the religious and moral conduct of their men. Successful chaplains attempted to appeal to their audience and encouraged black ministers to take a lead in prayer meetings, as did a clergyman who oversaw a major revival in his regiment: "Not thinking it best to constrain them, exclusively to modes of worship that prevail with whites, I have endeavored to accommodate the services somewhat to their tastes and habits." Others such as one effective chaplain stood in the background during prayer meetings, and when they were about to break up, he then injected one brief idea that he asked the men to consider before the next gathering or reminded them to incorporate the lesson from the prayer meeting into their everyday lives. When chaplains preached on Sunday, they had to bridge the gap between black and white expectations, but again with care they could accomplish this goal and actually find the experience more rewarding than any of their previous assignments. As missionary-turned-colonel James C. Beecher wrote to his wife, "I never enjoyed speaking more intensely[.] I never preached to so appreciative an audience."[49]

In the end religious endeavors had no more impact on black soldiers than they did on whites. Although a number of regimental commanders made service attendance compulsory, only one or two hundred black troops per regiment were active in religious affairs, and if moral conduct was better in the USCT, it was more the product of infrequent and inferior pay than the absence of temptation. Apart from family and friends and the coercive aspects of peacetime society, and enduring hardships regularly, moral opposition to some vices seemed to lack force to soldiers when certain comforts were available. Theirs was a high-risk world, and the temptation was to live for today rather than an uncertain tomorrow. A black enlisted man summed up the situation well when he wrote that in military service, "The devil is ever on the alert to carry your mind away from every thing that is good."[50]

Much more effective were efforts to teach black soldiers reading, writing, and arithmetic. White officers in the USCT viewed education, like religion, as essential for success in a free society. However, black soldiers also shared a passion for the white man's brand of literacy. Unavailable in much of the South before the war and deficient for blacks in the North was education. Soldiers in the USCT knew it was the key to self-improvement, and they clutched at the opportunity that the United States Army provided. During the war, other demands consumed the time of the troops, and although literacy was a high priority among officers in the USCT, especially since they had to carry the burden of doing almost all the paperwork, most commands were not able to devote as much time to studies as both officers and men wanted. Once the amount of duties tapered off during reconstruction, though, nearly every commanding officer of black troops incorporated formal education as part of their daily regimen.[51]

In some cases black units hired civilian teachers and paid them from company funds, but most of the time the chaplain, who had responsibility for educating soldiers and their families in the Regular Army, in conjunction with a few officers, headed the program. Northern benevolent associations or officers' families provided the essential materials such as books and blackboards, and officers and literate blacks served as teachers. In the early stage, most schools concentrated on those who already had some reading and writing skills, so that they were able to act as teachers for the less proficient students. This enabled teachers to hold very small classes and devote more personal attention to the soldiers. After students mastered the alphabet, they moved into reading and writing, and from there on to arithmetic, geography, history, the Bible, and even Casey's tactics manual. Shrewd regimental commanders aided the program by instituting awards for educational achievement and assessing such punishments for minor military infractions as learning a spelling or reading lesson.[52]

The advancement that some black soldiers made in the course of their military service was truly remarkable. A chaplain began to work with a corporal who was totally illiterate. In two days the soldier could write his own name, and by the end of five months he prepared company reports and read the Bible and the infantry tactics manual. More important, his case was not that unusual. After six months of instruction, more than five hundred ex-slaves in a brigade could "read and write very well." A company commander boasted that after six weeks all his troops knew the alphabet and many of them were able to read, when previously only "four or five could read a little." In Co. C, 44th U.S. Colored Infantry, only nine men were literate when they enlisted, yet all of them could read and write by the time authorities mustered them out of service. The 43rd U.S. Colored Infantry, composed of Northern blacks and freed slaves, had only seventy men who could read, and few of them could do that well. After seven months of work, over one-half could read and many "attend to their own correspondence." [53]

Overall, black soldiers made tremendous strides combating illiteracy during service in the army of occupation. The military structure provided a good atmosphere for instruction, and although other duties sometimes upset the academic schedule, the desires of black soldiers and commitment of their white officers more than compensated for the interference. In fact, by the time black soldiers left the service, their reading and writing skills most likely surpassed the general black population, despite extensive efforts on the part of Northern philanthropists to educate black civilians. Equally important, once given a fair opportunity, they had demonstrated an ability for self-improvement on a widespread scale, and this elevated their sense of self-accomplishment and self-worth. [54]

With their wartime contributions and evident ability to improve themselves when provided an opportunity, black soldiers felt that the government had an obligation to give them full and equal rights with whites in the postwar world. "We want two more boxes besides the cartridge box—," announced Sgt. Henry Maxwell several months after the war, "the ballot and the jury box." These veterans were well aware of the power of racism, and they also knew that a sizable portion of the Northern white population regarded them as inferior, but surely this victorious nation had an obligation to reward the black population for the service of nearly 180,000 of its sons who had sacrificed for several years, and more than 36,000 of whom had given up their lives, all in military service for their country. In their eyes, they had earned equality. [55]

Thus, black soldiers made appeal after appeal to the white population to grant them the equal rights that they deserved and needed to prosper in their homeland. They hammered away at each argument Northerners put forward to deny them their just rewards, highlighting the contradictions and absurdities with exceptional skill. "With the nation we have suffered, and as part of this nation, we must rise with it," wrote a black private. "Why did the colored man leave his quiet home, and forsake the dear ones there? It was that he might establish for himself and his successors a home in the land which the Author of every good and perfect gift saw fit to give unto him." The federal government had terminated slavery, argued a Northern black infantryman, but it had not granted the key to freedom, which was the vote: "Let not the thousands who have stood the storm of battle and suffered the privations of the march for the glory of their country, be excluded from the ballot box. He that has defended the nation with the sword, will also defend it to the same advantage with the ballot." If blacks were going to succeed in freedom amid white hostility—as demonstrated by the conduct of many Southerners in the early stages of reconstruction—they must have the sacred franchise, insisted Chaplain Garland H. White: "We soldiers ask the nation to grant us the right to vote, that we may, by that bestowment, be enabled to protect our families from all the horrors that prey upon a disfranchised people." Those who argued that only literate citizens should possess the vote, according to a sergeant in the 27th U.S. Colored Infantry, confused education with stupidity and overlooked good moral character as the most important criterion for participation in the election process. "I wonder, as the Southern black man has got sense enough to fight for this country, if he ain't got sense enough to vote, whether he is educated or not," he penned thoughtfully. "It seems to me, if he knew where to strike with his steel and firearms, he will also know where to strike with his vote."[56]

No doubt, black troops knew that their white officers took considerable pride in the contributions of the USCT to the war effort; therefore it came as a great shock when black soldiers learned that the bulk of their officers opposed proposals to grant blacks equal rights, including the vote. After all that effort, it stunned them that so many officers, with whom they had endured so much, the same individuals who had left white volunteer units several years earlier to battle alongside black soldiers, now hesitated to fight for what their race had earned, full and equal rights.

Yet the bulk of their officers viewed things differently. True, some 178,000 blacks had joined the Union ranks and contributed significantly to the war effort, but that alone did not convince the white officers that blacks were capable of living up to the responsibilities of full citizenship. Throughout the war they had supervised the black troops, and many of these officers felt entitled to much of the credit for the achievements of the USCT. None of them doubted that blacks deserved their freedom and as free men needed certain civil liberties, such as the rights to own property, have full access to the judicial system, and to an education for themselves and their families, but whites in the USCT had very mixed opinions on whether blacks deserved full equality—more specifically, the franchise.[57]

Some officers called for the vote to aid the Republican party in dominating national politics, while others argued that it would be much easier to educate blacks and prepare them as full citizens with the right of suffrage, than it would be to "infuse loyalty into the hearts of those lately in armed rebellion." Southern whites, they observed, were not about to treat blacks properly, and they must have the vote as part of an arsenal to protect themselves.[58]

Most, however, had little regard for the intelligence and character of blacks, particularly freedmen, in their current condition. "I have come to the conclusion," a lieutenant wrote his father, "that the present race of black men will not be of any account; the next generation educated in the midst of freedom will be worth three of the present." Another officer who was working in the Freedmen's Bureau complained in a moment of frustration, "Many of them are so Ignorant that they do not understand why they are free and have to work for a living." Among the white officers, some were willing to let blacks who could read and write cast the precious ballot, but as one officer in the USCT wrote, "I am utterly opposed to the indiscriminant voting of negroes." Others agreed with an officer who believed blacks should receive the vote eventually, and "The time may be coming but if so it is far distant." He considered the idea of giving blacks the vote then "dangerous folly." Still others steadfastly refused to commit themselves to the enfranchisement of blacks. In the end, the arguments of blacks won out and they received the vote, but more as a means of Northern whites ridding themselves of the nasty problem of reconstruction than on the merits of the case.[59]

For black soldiers, reconstruction service was a bitter pill to swallow. Amid the danger and unpleasant duties, they witnessed the breakdown of the bonds between themselves and their white officers. In part an inevitable result of the transition from war to peace and the reassertion of discipline that combat troops had seldom experienced since their initial months of training, it was also a by-product of the differing aspirations of the white officers and black troops. With the end of the war and the passage of the Thirteenth Amendment that abolished slavery, blacks and whites in the USCT had fulfilled their mutual goals, and their paths now diverged. It was becoming increasingly apparent that blacks could count on very few of their officers to fight alongside them for equal rights; instead, they must stand together and rely on one another for future victories. This lesson far overshadowed the great success black soldiers gained in the area of education.

11

Life After the USCT

As soon as the war ended, a number of officers in the USCT thought they should be able to leave the service. They were citizen soldiers who had joined the army to suppress the rebellion and terminate slavery. That accomplished, it was time to get back to the "real" world. Moreover, nearly all of them had served three or more years, longer than most soldiers in white volunteer units, and by right of longevity they deserved to go home. Once the federal government made it clear that it planned to muster most white commands out of service and retain the bulk of the black troops for occupation duty, officers flooded the War Department with requests for discharge. According to one surgeon who summarized the sentiment well, "every body has *resignation on the brain.*—and I am becoming infected." [1]

Black soldiers, too, wanted to rid themselves of blue uniforms. Many of them, as Sgt. Maj. Christian Fleetwood stated, had enlisted to "assist in abolishing slavery and to save the country from ruin," and this they best accomplished in Union ranks. Yet their ultimate goal had been equal rights with whites, "and it strikes me that more could be done for Our welfare in the pursuits of civil life." Fleetwood knew that most Americans regarded a peacetime army as a useless organization and an unnecessary drain on tax dollars. In an army of occupation, "No matter how well & faithfully they may perform their duties they will shortly be considered as 'lazy nigger sojers.' " The problem was that, while officers could resign, enlisted men had only five ways out of the Army—desertion, death,

231

dishonorable dismissal, medical discharge, and being mustered out—and only one was an appealing prospect.[2]

A considerable number of officers and men, however, thought it was sensible to remain in the service as long as possible. They anticipated no more loss of life, and the pay was good for officers and at least assured for enlisted men. A doctor told his wife he was not coming home when his salary was $150 per month, with a strong possibility of promotion and a pay increase to $200. Another officer who entered military service with assets of $1,000 left the army in early 1867 worth $4,000 through a program of careful saving and shrewd investment. Compared to civilian salaries in the North, such as $2 per day for a carpenter or a farmhand during harvest season, even a second lieutenant made out much better, and in the South no one was sure how high wages would be or when jobs would be plentiful. Others decided to wait until the inevitable postwar economic tumult eased. "There will be a great many wild men turned loose in the country before long (I mean soldiers)," wrote an officer in late May 1865 to his parents. "They will get to work and their numbers will tend to decrease the price of labor, and I imagine that there will be a stagnation of business for some time after things are settled: Therefore I *think* I will stay."[3]

After one year of reconstruction duty, though, nearly all of them wanted to return to civilian life. The work was unenjoyable and at times hazardous, and both officers and men thought valuable time was passing them by and that they were missing all sorts of personal and occupational opportunities. Army life was abnormal for them, and they yearned for the freedom of being private citizens. And as each day passed, they missed their families and friends more and more. "I want to go home so bad . . . ," complained a black soldier. "It Seems to me that I have been gone from home 70 years & longer." One lieutenant wanted to get out of military service so badly that he intended to commit some act that would warrant his dismissal, unless authorities mustered out his regiment soon: "I shall think it quite as much of an honor to be *dishonorably* dismissed from a service which I deem disgraceful as to be *honorably* dismissed [from] an honorable service."[4]

Finally, orders would arrive to muster a regiment or battery out of the service, producing a flurry of emotions. Almost to a man, soldiers in the USCT were glad that they were going home, but it was also cause for reflection. Invariably they thought about comrades who had died, as well as the friends they would never see again. "Another epic [epoch] in my life has been reached," mentioned an officer in his twenties. For him and others, though, leaving the service was the start of a new era. The War Department had plucked many of them from civilian life before they had got their adult lives in order, and now it was time to begin careers, several years late.[5]

Army regulations required that commands muster out of service at the same location that they mustered in, which meant that most units had to travel extensively before they were free of the service. It struck one soldier as odd that, after surviving more than three years of war, with all its hardships, death, and disease, the idea of a trip home instilled terror in his heart. "All there is bettween us now is the time it will take to go & the dangers of the trip; but now the dangers of the trip seem a hundred fold greater than they did when I *came* here. My anxiety is indiscribable." Such fears were not unwarranted. En route from Brownsville, a vessel carrying the 43rd U.S. Colored Infantry sprang a leak in heavy seas. The pumps failed to remove water rapidly enough, and the flood extinguished the fire in the engine. Troops had to throw horses and goods overboard, and for nearly two days they bailed water to stay afloat. Fortunately, they ran aground on a sandbar near the mouth of the Mississippi River and a tugboat towed them to New Orleans. Rather than risk further catastrophe, the company sergeants on behalf of the men requested that the colonel let them travel the rest of the way by train, and if necessary they were willing to bear the cost of the railroad tickets.[6]

Despite this nightmarish experience, everyone returned home alive. That was not the case with the 56th U.S. Colored Infantry, which suffered one of the war's great tragedies in August 1866, an outbreak of cholera. Cholera is a virus, spread primarily through water and bodily discharges, that releases a toxin in its host's small intestines. Those afflicted with the illness begin to suffer from acute diarrhea and vomiting, which dehydrates the body and causes severe muscle cramps. The disease enervates its victims until they lapse into shock and, with a collapse of their cardiovascular system, die horribly, sometimes within twenty-four hours. At the time cholera was untreatable and claimed the lives of one-half its victims.[7]

The regiment was traveling by two steamers from Helena, Arkansas, to St. Louis, Missouri, to be mustered out of service. On the way several soldiers died of an undiagnosed illness, and when the command reached Quarantine Grounds near St. Louis, the regimental commander, Col. Charles Bentzoni, had a surgeon inspect the men and found *"no cholera among them."* The regiment continued on to the port of St. Louis, arriving at night. Fortuitously, Bentzoni elected to keep all the troops on board instead of permitting them to roam around town. The following morning, a doctor reported *"a clear case of cholera,"* and Maj. Gen. William T. Sherman immediately ordered the vessel back to Quarantine Grounds. Within a few weeks 178 enlisted men and 1 officer died from cholera in the regiment. Had Bentzoni let his men into St. Louis on their arrival that night, the results could have been as devastating to the city as they were to the 56th U.S. Colored Infantry.[8]

On the final day troops received their back pay, any bounty owed them, and their discharge papers, and in return surrendered all equipment they did not wish to purchase. Some Northern black regiments were fortunate enough to have a dress parade with crowds out to cheer them; most Southern black units enjoyed no such celebration. Then they assembled for one last time, and the unit commander spoke to the men. Col. John Holman told the 1st U.S. Colored Infantry that they had overthrown slavery and earned the right of full citizenship. He warned them of problems with Southern whites and insisted that they must not let their hatred lead to violence. As soldiers, they had learned industry and forbearance, and now they must act as leaders among the black community and teach these qualities to all other freedmen. The commander of the 62nd U.S. Colored Infantry sagely advised his men to buy land with their money. A family did not need a lot of acreage to live adequately, and "it is a great deal better for you to live upon your land, than to hire land from another, or to work for another." Lt. Col. James Brisbin of the 6th U.S. Colored Cavalry also told his men to "Save your money, buy property, and educate your children" and assured them the government would protect their rights. In conclusion, he ordered them, "Go now, black soldiers, to your houses, & become orderly, sober & industrious citizens," and reminded them, "The flag that now floats over us is as much yours, as it is mine, and, you must at all times be ready to defend it."[9]

After the talk, the men broke ranks and shook hands all around. One officer, Capt. Joseph Forbes of the 43rd U.S. Colored Infantry, was fortunate enough to receive a gold Twenty-fifth Army Corps badge and pin from his troops with the inscription, "Presented to Capt. Forbes, Co. E, 43d U.S.C.T., by his Company for his bravery and impartiality in command," a touching memento. Soon, though, the grounds were quiet, as everyone scattered to their homes to pick up their lives.[10]

Not surprisingly, some men in the USCT enjoyed military service and joined the Regular Army. The government decided after extensive debate to create six regiments, four infantry and two cavalry, for black soldiers under white officers in the expanded force after the war. Several years later, as a result of further reductions in the Regular Army, the War Department cut the number of black infantry regiments to two, and it remained at that level until World War I. There were no black artillery batteries because the War Department thought artillery was too complicated for the black race, even though there had been numerous light and heavy artillery batteries composed of black men that performed well in the war. Despite this slight, black veterans quickly filled the ranks of these Regular Army regiments, and although personnel changed over the next few decades, these units remained near full strength and had a desertion rate four to six times lower than did white regiments. For black soldiers, pay was low but equal and guaranteed, with meals and housing included, and compared to most members of their race, these soldiers endured far less discrimination.[11]

Quite a few white officers also sought commissions in the Regular Army. Some had wanted to be army officers all along, and this offered them an opportunity, while others had discovered the appeal of a military career during their service with black troops. With numerous new regiments, including six for black soldiers, there were plenty of officers' slots, particularly for men who had experience commanding black soldiers. In awarding these commissions, political contacts certainly worked wonders, as one officer in the USCT commented when a regimental major received a second lieutenancy and a captain retained his grade: "Maj Moore was better qualified for a Colonel than Ward was for a 2 Lt, but such is the luck. Influential friends often give an ordinary man a great start. Merit is often lost sight of entirely." [12]

Yet the list of officers in the USCT included some talented men who rose to positions of importance in the United States Army. Henry C. Merriam commanded the 73rd U.S. Colored Infantry, won the Medal of Honor for leading the successful assault on Fort Blakely, and after the war accepted a major's commission in a black infantry regiment. Merriam retired as a major general. Another ascending star in the U.S. Army was William F. Spurgin, the West Point dropout who had offered his services to the Confederacy at the beginning of the war. Spurgin was a lieutenant in Merriam's regiment after the war and made brigadier general in 1902. The cobbler's son, Adolphus Greely, had an extraordinary life after his tour in the USCT. Greely struggled from second lieutenant to captain by 1886, and the next year he became a brigadier general and chief of the Signal Corps. Interestingly, after his retirement Greely helped to found the National Geographic Society and was the second man to win the Medal of Honor for service in peacetime.

The two most famous officers in the USCT who remained in the army after the war were William R. Shafter and Henry C. Corbin. Shafter, a young man from Michigan, served brilliantly in Virginia and won a Medal of Honor. He then took command of the 17th U.S. Colored Infantry and led it superbly. In a letter of recommendation for a commission in the Regular Army, Maj. Gen. George H. Thomas wrote, "Colonel Shafter is one of the most successful Officers who has ever held position in the Colored Regiments. He has given his whole attention to the subject of their improvement and his command has attained to a degree of discipline and soldierly bearing, which is not only creditable but very remarkable." Shafter became lieutenant colonel in a black regiment and commanded the invasion force in Cuba during the Spanish-American War.[13]

Henry C. Corbin, the adjutant general during the Spanish-American War, ran the war with President William McKinley from a room in the White House. Corbin had served in two different Ohio regiments before entering the 14th U.S. Colored Infantry, where his military career nearly came to an end. Corbin's regimental commander was Col. Thomas J. Morgan, an effective leader with deep religious convictions that he continually attempted to force on the officers and men in his regiment. Eventually Morgan and Corbin had a falling out, and Morgan accused Corbin of cowardice before the enemy in the after-action report of the Nashville Campaign. A general court-martial not only vindicated Corbin of the charge, but in an unprecedented move it rebuked Morgan for attempting to take notes on the testimony of previous witnesses for the prosecution, obviously with the intention of verifying those statements, and accused two officers who were close friends of Morgan's of "misrepresentation and falsehood" under oath. This resounding victory in court won Corbin a promotion and a career in the U.S. Army.[14]

Those who left the army permanently, as nearly all did, noticed a dramatic change in themselves. In military service they had grown up, and the war and its effects had hardened them or stripped away their youthful outer layer. The intensity of war had crammed decades of living into months or years, forcing young men to accept responsibilities that were alien to other generations of individuals their age. One officer noticed that he had gone away a "bashful boy," and thirty months later he was commanding a company of men. Wartime experiences had peeled off much of their exuberant view of life, portraying it instead in stark forms. Another soldier told his wife that he was glad he had married before the war, because "Uncle Sam has so completely taken the romance out of me that I don't believe that I shall ever have the inclination to make love to another woman." He now found little glamour in life; its highlights were human relations.[15]

The war also offered men an opportunity to measure themselves against their peers in the most difficult circumstances. They saw man in his basest condition, developing insights into the human behavior that they never forgot. "I have learned a great many things,

a great deal of human nature," wrote a young officer to his mother.
A slightly older man elaborated further:

> The service aged me mentally, but it also broadened my outlook
> on life, and gave me a confidence in taking hold of the problems
> of civil duties that could not otherwise have been reached in years.
> I learned to know men; men stripped of veneer and hypocrisy,
> whose real worth or worthlessness stood out clear in camps, on
> the march or on the battlefield.[16]

After several years of discipline and structure, with individuality
downplayed and unity and teamwork encouraged, soldiers yearned
to be free of the military service. "How happy we were that we should
be permitted to breathe the fresh air again and to tramp through
the country as free men," recalled a black sergeant. "I never felt so
much like a *free man* before in my life as I did when I got my
Discharge," concurred a former captain, "and though I haven't got
so much pay in *money* since, yet I have got a good deal more in
something else Viz: *health* and *happiness!*"[17]

One lieutenant joked to his wife that his troops "get fits if they
don't toe the line with me. Expect I shall be just so when I get
home—better be preparing." In fact, his return to peacetime was
relatively uneventful. Yet many soldiers had serious difficulty making
the adjustment from the military to the civilian world and suffered
from mental and emotional problems for the rest of their lives.[18]

Certainly most black soldiers underwent a dramatic change after
the war in the transition from slavery to freedom. This, in conjunction with sketchy or unreliable medical records and other statistical
evidence on the condition of blacks after the war, prevents an effective
evaluation of their readjustment to the peacetime world. No doubt
the military experience created or increased emotional distress for
some soldiers. During the war eleven black enlisted men committed
suicide, and a small number received treatment for "nervous depression," most likely combat stress.

But for most black soldiers, psychological adaptation to a peacetime environment seems to have gone quite smoothly. Despite the
war's hardships and traumas, it was a very special time for blacks,
and the allure of freedom helped ease their way into postwar society.
Available evidence indicates that black veterans divorced rarely, exhibited few signs of mental problems, and avoided opium addiction,
all indicators of relative stability. In fact, only alcoholism was a
problem in the postwar world, and even then a very small proportion
suffered from it. It afflicted both black officers and men, and in at
least one instance excessive drinking wreaked havoc on a family.
"He spent all his money on liquor, and he beat me so I could not

stand it," complained the wife of an ex-soldier after she abandoned him. "He drank a great deal, got intoxicated and then beat me." [19]

A major reason why black soldiers adjusted well to peacetime life was the support they received at every step throughout the war from one another and the black masses. They fought sporadically, and in combat they maintained compact formations, with comrades literally alongside them, which reduced the sense of isolation on the battlefield and inhibited the development of combat stress. Although they endured all sorts of abuse from whites during and after the war, this was nothing new, and the excitement of freedom, the vision of genuine equality, and the enthusiastic response of the black population for their work easily offset that trauma.

Although it is impossible to link many of the problems specifically with military service, tendencies among the white officers seem to indicate considerable difficulty in the readjustment process. The divorce rate of officers may have been as high as four or five times above the national level, and alcohol and opium abuse and suicides were serious problems. A number of men died from excessive drinking or "delerium tremens," as one doctor termed it, while alcoholism and drug addiction plagued many others for the remainder of their days. [20]

In most cases this was symptomatic of other problems that experts never treated, but even when professional care was available, it was seldom worthwhile. Postcombat stress was a closet ailment, one to which neither ex-soldiers nor officials admitted publicly or privately, and therefore no effort was made to understand or devise a treatment for it. Thus, a lieutenant in the 28th U.S. Colored Infantry who never seemed to readjust to the postwar world floundered repeatedly in society until his wife had him committed to an insane asylum for an epileptic seizure, melancholia, and some beer drinking. An initial examination also diagnosed him as "addicted to masturbation." After lengthy care, his doctors maintained that "epilepsy was the predisposing cause of his insanity; that the exciting cause was inebriety and abuse of sexual functions." With no real treatment, however, he never regained his mental health. [21]

Just as tragic was the suicide of a former captain and a prominent engineer in Washington, D.C., "while suffering from a temporary aberration of mind." After extensive combat service, the government had hired him to prepare the national cemeteries for the burial of Union soldiers who had died during the war, a job that alerted him to the real costs of the fighting and the sort of gruesome work that psychiatrists after World War II determined was a frequent cause of postcombat stress. By most standards, though, his postwar career was a success, and at the time of his death he had amassed

$25,000 worth of money and property. Yet shortly before the suicide, the ex-captain was laid off from a project because government funds had run out. Most likely this was the stressful event that triggered the act of violence. For several days before the suicide, witnesses had noticed that he had been restless and excited, but no one paid much attention because his family life was good and he had been prospering. Late one morning he simply locked his office door and shot himself in the heart.[22]

Even more perplexing was the suicide of a young officer while in military service. He had grown up on an Illinois farm and cultivated his father's fields and taught school before the war. During his army stint he had fought in several major battles and then received a captain's commission in the USCT. Extremely intelligent, with tendencies toward perfectionism and fortified by a deep religious commitment, the captain admitted being "blue" occasionally, but he showed no signs of serious problems. In late September 1864 he led a work detail into the woods to cut shingles, most likely the only white man in the group, and when he returned, the captain was "acutely despondent." What triggered the depression is unclear, but possibly it was the result of his sense of isolation, being the only white among black soldiers, an experience of which numerous white officers complained during the war. He told the chaplain that although he could have been more devout, he had "never deviated from the cardinal principles of virtue and morality as inculcated in the Bible." In his late stages, he thought he was "a fool or crazy" and complained of light-headedness. The doctor noticed that he was unable to complete a train of thought and witnessed several tearful outbursts, although the captain suffered from no fever, as they had originally thought. Late the next evening, the captain closed his tent, placed a pistol in his mouth, and fired.[23]

In a number of serious cases the connections between the officer's problems and military service were evident. During the war a physician diagnosed a captain in the 20th U.S. Colored Infantry as suffering from malaria, when in reality his "nervous irritability" indicated a breakdown, the result of personal and professional anguish. After the regiment boarded a ship to travel from Texas to New Orleans, the captain "exhibited symptoms of insanity—which were soon developed into a raving madness." They confined him to his stateroom, but the instant his nurse looked away, he threw himself out his window and into the Gulf of Mexico and drowned. The regimental surgeon blamed the suicide on "despondency from pecuniary embarrassment arising from non receipt of his pay for some months, harsh and abusive language from the Col. of his Regt. and the excitement and confusion attendant upon the embarkation and removal of the Regt. all occurring at the same time" and in conjunction with physical debilitation and nervousness.[24]

Another former officer lived a troubled life until he committed suicide in 1879. To recapture the excitement of his war years, he joined the army and gained a reputation as a heavy drinker, gambler, and opium user. He took his life after a gambling excursion in which he lost a large sum of someone else's money and had a short time to repay it.[25]

The most famous individual in the USCT who developed disorders in part because of military service was Col. James C. Beecher of the 35th U.S. Colored Infantry. The family renegade in his youth, Beecher had settled down before the war and served effectively as a missionary for seamen in China. He returned for the war and served first as a chaplain in the 67th New York Infantry, which fought on numerous battlefields, and then as a lieutenant colonel in the 141st New York Infantry, where there was considerable infighting that caused him terrible distress. To make matters worse, his wife had an alcohol problem and was apparently unfaithful. He overworked and could not sleep, and he began to have "insane imaginings or morbid religious impressions." Gossip charged that he developed a drinking problem himself, but the evidence indicates he became addicted to opium after frequent use as the only means to obtain some rest. One night after he took chloroform and someone administered morphine, he attempted suicide. "That I fully intended to commit suicide," he told his brother, "I've no doubt, & of course, none as to the fact of my being entirely crased." He finally resigned and his family took him to New York, where he underwent mental treatment. His doctor described the characteristics of his disorder as "irresolution, incapacity to determine for himself, and the kind of depression usually known as moodiness." [26]

After several weeks of care, his symptoms abated, and he decided to reenter the army. Because of his wife's drinking problem, he could not return to the pulpit, nor would his religious views permit him a divorce. By joining the army again he was able to keep apart from his wife, and secretly he admitted that "my hope, for the last four or five yrs. has simply been that Annie or I might die." Command of the 35th U.S. Colored Infantry and the death of his wife offered Beecher a second chance.[27]

Unfortunately, the stress of command led to a return of his problems. Every decision caused him anxiety, and he began to sense that his officers were nullifying all he did. According to his regimental surgeon, he began "laboring under the delusion that there was a conspiracy among the officers of the regiment to his detriment." He became so paranoid that the physician "scarcely permitted him out of my sight." Beecher told Brig. Gen. William Birney "more than once, in effect, that he wished to die honorably in the first battle." Birney was giving serious consideration to relieving Beecher when authorities called the regiment into active service, where Beecher exhibited "courage, intelligence and energy." At the Battle of Honey Hill, Beecher suffered a serious wound and his tensions eased, but on his return four months later came the old conspiratorial delusions.[28]

After the war he began preaching again, but his unsoundness led him to abandon the ministry and move into isolation in the Catskill Mountains of New York, where he "lived the life of a hermit," according to a doctor. For six and one-half years he endured profound emotional and religious swings, until family and friends persuaded him to take over a church in Brooklyn. Under this stress, he grew even worse, burdened by his own perceived imperfections and fearful only in his mind that two friends were going to bring charges against him for immorality. He resigned and fled from "place to place to escape spies." He spent the last years of his life in and out of asylums. In 1882 he was still experiencing "painful apprehensions and dark hallucinations" and admitted to his second wife, "I don't understand these nervous elations and depressions any better than when they first came upon me." By 1885 he started hinting to his wife that suicide was the only solution: "I cannot endure the life that is passing." Less than one year later, he committed suicide. His wife explained to their children that after four and one-half years of suffering, insanity overcame him and he was "perfectly unconscious of the act." The Pension Office, after a thorough investigation, ruled that army life was a major factor in his emotional decline: "Col. Beecher was exposed to all the vicissitudes of army life, which, in my opinion, are amply sufficient to render unstable the equilibrium of a mind such as that under consideration."[29]

Not only was treatment for mental anguish related to the war haphazard and ineffective, but afflicted veterans found little comfort within society. According to a captain who had suffered from combat stress during the war, he had repeated attacks and received no attention in the postwar world:

> I was young and strong, and had never suffered from any sort of dissipation, which was all in my favor. But I have suffered more or less every year of my life since from that day's experience. Over work, physical or mental, would bring me back to the place where I was that September night. On three different occasions, if not four, I have been brought to where I was that September night in Old Virginia, and have borne it all with a mighty small amount

of sympathy from those about me. Soldiers have lost a leg or an
arm and never suffered as much as I have done from the breaking
down of my nervous system there at Fort Harrison.[30]

Thus, as officers in the USCT, they were at times pariahs in their
own army, ridiculed by some white volunteers and separated from
their enlisted men by racial, cultural, and military barriers. As representatives of the white race, they felt an obligation to act as models
of behavior, especially in combat. Outwardly they portrayed the brave
and unflappable officer, while beneath the facade they experienced
the same wrenching emotions of fear and uncertainty as did others
who entered battle. Any comfort they received during the war came
from supportive family and friends and one another. Under the enormous stress of military service in the USCT, and amid their sense
of isolation, a number of these men suffered debilitating psychological effects from the war. For years and years afterward they bore
its emotional scars, and seldom did they receive care or even compassion for their injuries.

Much more prevalent than the mental problems was the poor
physical condition of the officers and men in the USCT. By the
time the government had mustered them out of service, many of
these men were physical wrecks, and it took months of care before
they were able to work regularly. Still, many resumed employment
immediately, but over the years they lost days and weeks battling
recurrent bouts of malaria or chronic diarrhea. Others fell victim
to some disease they had contracted during the war. Soldiers who
recovered from illnesses, such as ex-Privates Henry Walker and William Boyce, who survived scurvy, nevertheless bore its effects—the
loss of their teeth—for the rest of their lives. And as a result of
extensive service and its hardships, many aged well beyond their
years. Before ex-Private John Mixon was sixty, his arthritis was so
bad that "I was ordered to leave the house and was Called all Sort
of names Called a Cripple and a Dam Son of a Bich and Was Told
to go to the Dam Soldiers Home and Stay There" by his wife, which
was exactly what Mixon did.[31]

Those who had sustained injuries suffered terribly too. Approximately ten thousand black soldiers received wounds in the war, as
did an untold number of their white officers, and thousands more
were victims of accidents that left them no better off than many
bullet or shell victims. William Blanchard sustained four wounds
in the war and could no longer work regularly, but the government
took care of him. They gave him ten dollars per month as a pension,
beginning in 1889. Likewise, ex-Major Frank Holsinger suffered a
severe wound to his arm. After the war, the good-natured Holsinger

The best tool for enlistment was success, as this Northern recruitment poster for blacks indicates. Recruiters stressed the opportunity for blacks to prove their worthiness of full and equal rights. They also emphasized the valor of ex-slaves at Port Hudson and Milliken's Bend. By implication, Northern blacks had to prove that free society engendered greater character in the black race than did the institution of slavery. (Chicago Historical Society)

Across the North there was substantial opposition to the enlistment of blacks. Nowhere was this more evident than in New York during July 1863, when a draft protest turned into a brutal race riot. After the excellent performance of black regiments at Port Hudson, Milliken's Bend, and Fort Wagner, though, Northern whites began to appreciate the USCT. Eight months after the riot, the 20th U.S. Colored Infantry received its colors amid much fanfare in Union Square in New York. (Library of Congress)

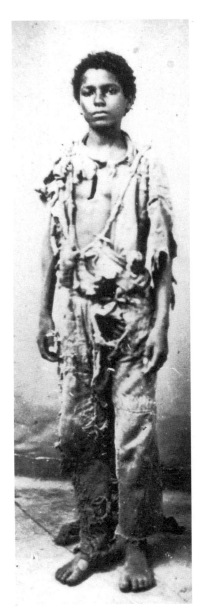

Approximately 144,000 of the 178,000 blacks who served in the Union Army during the war came from the slave states. For most, especially ex-slaves, service in the Union ranks was a great opportunity to prove that blacks merited full citizenship. In the eyes of blacks and whites, the Union uniform elevated the status of these freedmen from chattel to man. For a young man named Jackson, the transformation was striking. The first picture is Jackson as a slave, working as a servant in the Confederate Army. The second photograph is Drummer Jackson of the United States Colored Troops. (MOLLUS-Massachusetts Collection, U.S. Army Military History Institute)

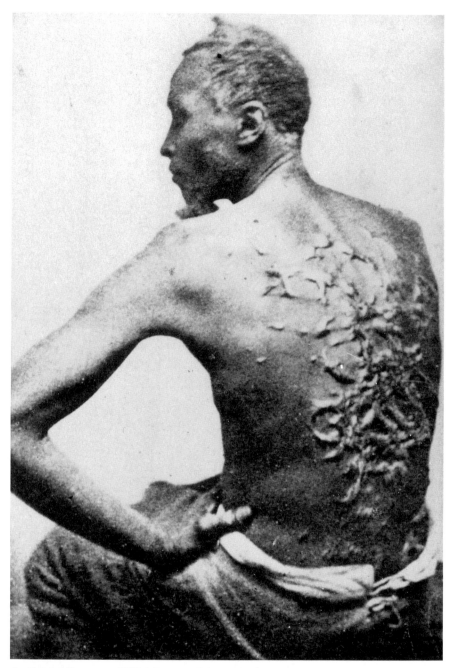

Assistant Surgeon T.W. Mercer of the 47th Massachusetts Infantry sent this photograph of a former Mississippi slave named Gordon with a message to a colonel: "I have found a large number of the four hundred contrabands examined by me to be as badly lacerated as the specimen represented in the enclosed photograph." According to other descriptions in the USCT, such evidence of brutality was not uncommon. (MOLLUS-Massachusetts Collection, U.S. Army Military History Institute)

Black recruits usually assembled at specific camps until they filled up a regiment or an artillery battery. There they received clothing and equipment, took the oath to serve and defend the Constitution, and frequently learned the most elementary aspects of drill. One of those camps, where the 5th United States Colored Infantry formed, was located in Delaware, Ohio. Here a company from that regiment posed on Sandusky Street in Delaware. The regiment, composed primarily of Northern blacks, served in North Carolina and Virginia and boasted four Medals of Honor among its enlisted men. (Ohio Historical Society)

Discipline was an essential component of military service. Most white officers believed in the racial stereotype that blacks had tendencies toward savagery and required strict control. Here, two soldiers outside the Provost Marshal's guard house in Vicksburg, Mississippi, ride the wooden horse as punishment for some minor offense. Although innocuous looking, hours seated on the wooden horse caused great discomfort. (MOLLUS-Massachusetts Collection, U.S. Army Military History Institute)

In an effort to retain control, whites levied unusually severe punishments on black soldiers. Whereas one in every twelve soldiers was black, one in every five soldiers executed for a crime was black. Even more striking, 80 percent of all soldiers executed for mutiny were black. This is purportedly the execution of a black soldier named Johnson in front of Petersburg, June 20, 1864. (Library of Congress and MOLLUS-Massachusetts Collection, U.S. Army Military History Institute)

Mustering out of service was a joyous event, especially for ex-slaves, because this was their first opportunity to enjoy their hard-earned freedom. Shown is a sketch of black soldiers mustering out in Arkansas. Friends and family have come out to cheer the heroes of the black community. (Library of Congress)

In the postwar years, whites conveniently forgot the real contributions that the USCT made throughout the war. An International Drill Competition in 1887, organized by former Union Army soldiers, created a stir when they barred black units. A cartoonist ridicules the decision by depicting the black soldier, on the right, as being denied entry by a superior and having the soldier respond with an allusion to "dem times," on the left, when the colored troops fought for the Union at Wagner and Petersburg. Pressure eventually forced the organizers to rescind their ban. (Library of Congress)

joked that the limb was practically useless, but it never failed to draw him a pension.[32]

These physical injuries often had psychological ramifications that exacerbated the problem. A black private received two nasty wounds, one in the left shoulder and another through the jaw. Surgeons removed the ball in his shoulder and left the one in his jaw, which "would swell up as large as an egg and burst open." He continued, "The excrutiating pain would almost drive me insane. I often thought of committing suicide. I suffered a thousand deaths, and often wished the bullet had passed through my heart or brain, which would have ended it all." For years he had to live on gruel, milk, and soup, until he could afford false teeth. Although not nearly so painful, a cannon recoiled and ran over an officer, ripping his abdominal muscle and causing a severe hernia. By 1910 his testicles had stretched to twenty-three inches in length.

For the white officers, military experience had a mixed effect on their postwar careers. One officer complained that it was not until he sought employment that he realized how badly five years of service had hurt his life:

Entering the army at nineteen, with neither education completed nor trade learned, and coming out at twenty-four without trade or profession or capital, and with a wife to support; with habits of spending formed in the extravagance that prevailed in the army, bringing as almost the sole advantage from those years a sense of self-reliance, I feel increasingly the extent of the sacrifice made by myself and so many thousands of other youth who gave their years of seeding time to their country."

Others, however, viewed the war as a godsend. Years in the military enabled an officer to realize that since he started his own farm, he had worked too hard physically and had not cultivated his mind. "I think if I had continued much longer as I was," he told his brother, "I would never have amounted to anything except as a farmer or laborer." The war served as a means of breaking him away from his prewar occupation. With the money he saved in the service, he decided to go to college. "O, it is a sad thing to grow up in ignorance while so much remains to be known," he explained to his mother. Rubbing elbows with college graduates in the USCT convinced him and a number of others that education was the ticket to success.[34]

No doubt wartime experiences shattered many dreams of independent farming. As officers, they had relied predominantly on their brains, and they found that much more appealing than working with their hands. "Having spent four years without performing manuel labor to any extent I do not feel able or willing to go back to it if I can help it," insisted a captain. Others had no alternative but to give up working with their hands. According to a former officer, the war had so sapped his strength that he "must rely on my pen for a living." Those who had lost limbs or health in the service could only perform nonmanual labor, and since virtually everyone knew soldiers who had to make this occupational adjustment, the disdain many people had held for such jobs began to disappear. Communities banded together to aid disabled veterans by appointing them to government positions or using political influence to obtain post offices or similar jobs for them. Most important, the war had changed the American economy, accelerating the rate of industrialization in the North and laying the groundwork for the huge corporations that developed in the postwar years. With them came jobs that involved managing men, which officers in the USCT had been doing for several years, often under the most adverse circumstances. In the end, as many as one in every five officers in the USCT shifted from manual to nonmanual employment after the war, whether by choice or necessity.[35]

A sizable portion of these officers also made the leap into professional positions, mainly as a result of their wartime experiences. "The army is a grand school," explained a young officer who had left college to command black soldiers. "I have got more business ideas and forms in my head than I would in a commercial college in two years. I have learned what it is to be held responsible for what you do and think." Doctors honed their skills in military service while numerous white hospital stewards converted their experience into postwar medical positions. An officer who had attended the Free Military School for Applicants for Commands of Colored Troops claimed that the knowledge he acquired there "advanced my very limited education more in my judgement than that of any two or perhaps three years of my prior schooling," and that enabled him to become a lawyer after the war. A considerable number of others found work with the less fortunate a rewarding experience and went into the ministry. In the aftermath of the war, evidence indicates that the number of doctors, lawyers, and clergymen more than doubled among officers in the USCT. As one lieutenant who was about to leave the service for a career as a physician advised a former officer, if we can manage it, we might as well *fall on our feet*, no matter how high they throw us."[36]

After sacrificing for so many years, a considerable number of officers in the USCT gave some thought to getting rich quickly, and the South was a very tempting investment opportunity. Everywhere around them was economic chaos, and few Southern whites had access to capital to rebuild. White officers, on the other hand, had plenty of money stowed away, and they also had a supply of labor within their enlisted ranks. Quite a number tried to capitalize on their funds and source of workers by purchasing land and signing contracts with enlisted men. Within several years the bulk of these ventures failed, and the Yankees came home. Those few who did succeed, however, made quite a fortune. One former officer, raised in Ohio with little schooling and a runaway at twelve, returned from Mississippi after four years with enough money to buy a nine-teen-thousand-dollar farm, the same one that had hired him at fifty cents per day in 1861 just prior to his enlistment.[37]

Blacks, too, benefited from the war. Young Private Junius B. Roberts saved approximately four hundred dollars from his military career to use for education to become a minister. The war taught an Ohio soldier one important lesson. The key to his success and that of his children was for him to acquire a skill and for his children to receive an outstanding education. He learned to be a bricklayer, and with his pay he financed the education of his four children through graduation at Fisk University. With some hard work, a sergeant in the 128th U.S. Colored Infantry converted his meager savings into nearly two thousand dollars' worth of property by 1870, and when Thomas Higginson returned to scenes of the war in the late 1870s, he found that two of his former soldiers had parlayed their funds into assets of at least three thousand dollars.[38]

One trend among former black officers and men was clear. In most instances, blacks who obtained a thorough education labored in some philanthropic way on behalf of their race, whether they received the schooling before or after the war. A number of the officers, for example, worked in the Freedmen's Bureau, while others devoted considerable time after their military stint to work for the benefit of the black population. William H. Holland attended Oberlin College after his tour of duty and then returned to his native Texas, where he taught school. An ardent Republican, Holland eventually entered state politics, and in the Texas state legislature he helped to establish Prairie View Normal School, currently Prairie View A & M, and the Texas Institute for Deaf, Dumb, and Blind Colored Youth, which he ran for fourteen years. In the nation's capital, two black ex-army surgeons, Alexander T. Augusta and Charles B. Purvis, worked in hospitals that catered to blacks and served as faculty at the Howard Medical School for many years, including hard financial times when they received no remuneration for their teaching. Their commitment to a multiracial medical profession led them to form the National Medical Society, when the local affiliate of the American Medical Association refused their admission on the basis of race. Purvis also fought charges of black inferiority within the scientific community.[39]

In freedom some Southern blacks also drew on their army experience in determining their vocation, while for many others the Union victory merely cleared obstacles from their path. Sgt. Elijah Marrs, who had learned to read and write in slavery, concluded after his military service that he would "labor for the development of my race," sharing his talent by opening a school and later becoming a minister. Others, such as Henry Butler, had had the dreams for some time, but the results of the war provided an opportunity for their fulfillment. As soon as he left the army, "I immediately set out to obtain an education," Butler explained. "A determination I possessed, partly because of my own volition and partly because of what my father had told me. That was to educate myself if I had the opportunity." He entered grade school and did odd jobs after hours, and gradually he progressed through high school and attended Washburn College in Topeka, Kansas. There he majored in English: "My purpose was to become a teacher and assist my race to improve their station and to become more useful men and women." Upon graduation, he took a position as a steam engineer for four years and then began teaching blacks. "I exerted my best efforts to advance my race," he asserted proudly in old age.[40]

A much more common means of benefiting from military service was through the acquisition of land for farming. For most black soldiers, the advice of their officers was unnecessary, since they had fully realized the value and independence that land ownership would give them. As early as 1863 black troops in the 33rd U.S. Colored Infantry had organized a building association, to pool resources and acquire property, with Sgt. Prince Rivers as its head. According to Rivers, the acquisition of land was essential for blacks: "Every colored man will be a slave, and feel himself a slave until he can *raise him own bale of cotton* and *put him own mark upon it* and say *Dis is mine!*" The problem for most black soldiers was that pay was inferior for much of the war, and it was difficult—particularly for soldiers with families—to save two hundred dollars or so at seven to thirteen dollars per month. A sensible solution that several individuals proposed was to pool resources and purchase a huge tract of land. That way blacks could own enough land to support families and benefit from being part of a black community. An old family friend suggested to a captain that he establish a settlement in Minnesota for his company. Both he and his men thought it was an idea worth pursuing, and the troops "seemed gratified that any person had taken such an interest in their future welfare," yet he and they needed ample information before committing themselves. He wanted to know if the land was prairie or timber; what its access to water and market was; what was the quality of the soil; if it would be held for the men free from taxes until they left the service; and if the land went to their heirs in the event a soldier died. Although the officer was very cautious, fearing a shady deal that would rob his men of their hard-earned money and in which he would be implicated, he was hopeful. Apparently the project failed to come to fruition, and none of the troops lost money. Another plan came from the commander of the 58th U.S. Colored Infantry, who suggested that the government use the back pay it owed his men to acquire land in Mississippi. Families of soldiers could cultivate the soil while the men completed their service, and future pay and any profits from the harvest could pay off the remainder of the debt on the land. The project fell through when military authorities refused to violate a Mississippi law that forbade black ownership of land. Still another suggestion came from a black sergeant. He recommended a colony of black veterans in the Rio Grande Valley, where they could purchase land for a reasonable price. He also proposed the formation of the First United States Colored Pioneer Association to accumulate resources and acquire huge tracts for settlement. Evidently, nothing came of his suggestions.[41]

Particularly helpful in obtaining lands for enlisted men was the passage of a bounty law in 1865. This provided black soldiers with anywhere from one hundred to three hundred dollars, a sum that was unequal to bounties granted to whites but it did enable some soldiers to purchase land. Again in 1873 the United States Government altered its law and retroactively equalized bounties for black soldiers with those of whites, so that many men in the USCT received one large back payment. When Higginson returned to South Carolina and Florida in the late 1870s, his former soldiers nearly all owned land. "I rarely met an ex-soldier who did not own his house and ground, the inclosures varying from five to two hundred acres," asserted Higginson. Most had recently purchased their homes, he noted, and in all likelihood the equalization of bounties aided them.[42]

Over the next few decades the American economy was turbulent, and former officers and men had their ups and downs like the rest of society. The economy was expanding, yet in different ways than it had previously, and there were marked fluctuations as a result of erratic business practices, overproduction, and treasure seeking. Officers who left the service with a few thousand dollars and enlisted men with a couple of hundred dollars separated from their savings rapidly. The Panic of 1873 "swamped" many of them, while others did not hold out that long. So inconsistent, in fact, was the economy that by the late 1870s, sixteen of thirty-two former officers in the 59th U.S. Colored Infantry had been penniless at least once since leaving the service. Since all of them had received back pay of at least one thousand dollars when the government mustered them out of the army, which was enough to buy a nice farm, it indicates just how volatile the economy was after the war. In the end, many of the officers and men died in virtual squalor, their only source of income a piddling army pension.[43]

Among Northern whites—commonly called carpetbaggers—who went south to seek fortunes and power in reconstruction states, some of the most prominent had been officers in the USCT. Probably the most notorious was Milton Littlefield, a former commander of the 21st U.S. Colored Infantry who attempted to use his contacts illegally to become a railroad magnate. Yet most ex-officers in the USCT who played prominent roles in Southern politics after the war were not quite so self-serving. They tended to be men of mixed talents who saw nothing wrong with fulfilling personal ambitions in advocacy of black rights. As attorney general and governor of South Carolina, Daniel H. Chamberlain, former commander of the 5th Massachusetts (Colored) Cavalry, tried to be scrupulously fair, and Marshall Harvey Twitchell, who created his own fiefdom along the Red River in Louisiana after military service, included family and blacks as beneficiaries of his empire.

In the end, both Chamberlain and Twitchell fled the South, like virtually all carpetbaggers. Chamberlain was the sacrificial lamb in a disputed election for governor when President Rutherford P. Hayes sided with the opposition candidate, Wade Hampton, in hopes of burying the hatchet with Southern Democrats. Twitchell's fate was much more desperate. He had long been the target of violence, and in 1876 an assassin killed his brother-in-law and shot him six times. Although Twitchell survived he had both arms amputated and lost the use of a leg. Not long after recovering, he accepted a consular position in Canada that Hayes tendered him and left Louisiana permanently.[44]

Military service had long served as a springboard into politics, and this was no different among the black officers and men during reconstruction. The army had offered black soldiers an opportunity to display and develop leadership skills that was not readily available in peacetime and one that proved invaluable in the political arena. They had demonstrated the capacity to supervise men in crises and to formulate sensible decisions with lives hanging in the balance, which fostered a keen sense of responsibility and instilled confidence in themselves and their decision-making ability. They had also learned to work with others to achieve long-term goals and to exact the most work from soldiers without being abusive. Moreover, through their joint actions, such as the campaign for equal pay or work in the Freedmen's Bureau, these black soldiers had learned some valuable lessons in the art of politics.

Much to their disadvantage, however, the government had checked their level of promotion and therefore inhibited the growth of leadership skills among many outstanding individuals. Nevertheless, at least forty black delegates to Southern state constitutional conventions had served in the USCT, and a substantially larger number held elective and appointed government positions during reconstruction. Former enlisted man Josiah T. Walls served several years in the U.S. House of Representatives, and ex-Captain P. B. S. Pinchback was lieutenant governor and acting governor of Louisiana. One prominent black politician in Georgia, Edwin Belcher, actually served as an officer in a white regiment. He was born in South Carolina and, because he was very light in color, educated at an all-white school in Pennsylvania. When whites in Georgia learned of his ancestry in 1867, he responded, "My blood has died the soil of the Sunny South as deep as any other Soldier's." He then concluded with a touch of sarcasm, "My services during the war was just as acceptable as any other man's and they was appreciated." Belcher, no doubt, told the truth. He had been a prisoner of war twice and suffered two serious wounds, one of which was in the skull and caused epileptic-like seizures that plagued him for the rest of his life.[45]

Against their comrades-in-arms in the Southern states, few blacks in the North held comparable positions. Part of the reason was that many of the most talented black officers and enlisted men remained in the South after the war, where there were opportunities throughout reconstruction. Still, at least one black, George Washington Williams, served in the Ohio House of Representatives, and a number of others held various federal and state positions, such as ex-Lieutenant James M. Trotter, who was the recorder of deeds in Washington, D.C., a very lucrative post.[46]

Although other black veterans never held political offices, they demonstrated unusual organizational and lobbying ability. The men of the 60th U.S. Colored Infantry, for example, assembled at Davenport, Iowa, to generate support for the cause of equal rights for blacks. With a prominent black citizen as the convention's president and nine enlisted men as vice presidents, the body through its committees prepared some resolutions, an address to the people of Iowa, and a petition to the Iowa legislature seeking the vote. The resolutions declared that they had discharged their duties faithfully for the defense of "our" country and "respectfully urge that it is the duty of Iowa to allow us the use of our votes at the polls; believing, as we do and must, that he who is worthy to be trusted with the musket can and ought to be trusted with the ballot." They began the address to the people of Iowa with the words, "FELLOW COUNTRYMEN: We wish we could truthfully address you as 'fellow citizens' " and explained their need for equal rights, including the franchise. Although the scales of justice balanced slowly, by 1868 the people of Iowa passed a constitutional amendment to grant blacks the vote.[47]

Like the men of the 60th U.S. Colored Infantry, other black soldiers and citizens lobbied for equal rights, and especially the vote, based on the labors of the USCT. Eighteen months after the war some black veterans began calling for a Convention of Colored Soldiers and Sailors to meet in Philadelphia in 1867. The purpose of the organization, according to its founders, was to gather "all colored soldiers and sailors who served in the late war for the Union, and who believe they have not received a due recognition . . . in sustaining the Union with a musket, [and] have won their rights to the ballot." Others argued that black soldiers played a critical role in the Civil War and might have been the deciding factor in the Union victory. Frederick Douglass and several other prominent blacks hinted that the Union would not have won without black troops, and one black periodical asserted that "except for two hundred thousand muskets which the negro added to the army of the Union, the Federal Congress might not have been able to sit to-day." Maj. Martin Delaney, the ranking black officer, was even more blunt. Several months after the war, he told a black audience: "I want to tell you one thing. Do you know that if it was not for the black men this war never would have been brought to a close with success to the Union, and the liberty of your race if it had not been for the Negro? I want you to understand that."[48]

In response to such assertions, Northern whites challenged the wartime contributions of the USCT. The *New York Times* denounced such utterings as "preposterous claims." Its editors pointed out that Federals won at Gettysburg "before a single negro soldier was seen east of the Alleghenies," and that battle was the "turning point of the war." *Brownlow's Whig* concurred, insisting that black soldiers "came into the fight at the eleventh hour." In Florida, Governor William Marvin declared it was a white man's war and blacks "fought in no battles; or if engaged at all in such, they were trifling affairs." When the black newspaper in Jacksonville squawked over his comments, another periodical, the *Jacksonville Florida Union*, defended the governor and stated that white soldiers had carried the burden in the war.[49]

Despite such charges, black soldiers felt justifiably proud of their wartime contributions to Union victory. Approximately 180,000 had served as soldiers in the Union Army, and of those nearly 37,000 gave their lives for their country. They fought on 449 different fields, and in more than forty significant battles they played a prominent role. On many occasions black troops made the difference between victory and defeat or draw, while at other times the USCT saved Federal forces from catastrophes. During that critical summer of 1864, after the two principal Federal commands had suffered heavy casualties and the government was seeking replacements, more than one hundred thousand black soldiers were in uniform, one-ninth of the entire United States Army, and the number continued to increase into 1865. Their mere presence instilled terror in the minds of Southern whites and joy in the hearts of blacks. This psychological and emotional factor contributed substantially to the collapse of the Confederacy. Moreover, it spurred recruitment among Southern blacks and thus deprived the Confederacy of a huge labor force that helped to provide essentials to its soldiers in the field. All this they did with unequal pay, unfair work duties, severely limited opportunities for advancement, inadequate equipment, and inferior medical care.[50]

Probably the single greatest contribution of the USCT, though, was its efforts in logistics. Civil War armies consumed huge quantities of food and supplies, and black soldiers and laborers devoted much of their time to the transportation of war matériel. Black troops guarded key railroad bridges and vital passes, loaded boxes and barrels onto wagons, and drove and guarded supply trains. Although this work lacked the glamour and excitement of combat and rarely caught the attention of military and civilian observers, it was absolutely essential to Union success on the battlefield.

Nearly one year after the fighting had ended, a *New York Times* editorial concluded that, although it had not won the war, the USCT had proved that black soldiers were a valuable wartime resource.

It is evident from our experience that we can raise a large black army in this country; that the negroes are capable of being transformed into soldiers; that they can fight, and can do efficient work in all arms of service; that they have the sentiment of loyalty, and are capable of devotion to the flag. We have tried the experiment of African soldiers, in a civilized army, upon a scale of magnitude never before attempted or approached in the history of the world. The experience we have acquired may possibly be of service to our country in the future.

In short, the newspaper that had cautiously advised experimenting with a handful of black troops now declared the use of black soldiers to be a resounding success.[51]

Yet, amid this apparent victory and the great strides blacks were making in the early years of reconstruction, there were countercurrents in both the South and the North bent on demeaning black achievements in the war and nullifying their postwar civil rights gains. Former Captain-turned-politician P. B. S. Pinchback realized, "There is a false sense of security displayed by our people that is really alarming. They seem to think that . . . the Great Battle has been fought and the victory won." Clearly the war had laid to rest the debate over secession, but it had done little to eliminate race prejudice in American society. Strangely enough, for many black veterans and their families, the fight had just begun after the Confederate surrender.[52]

A majority of Southern whites intended to undercut the advances of blacks, and one of their most effective techniques was to punish those who had turned against them and fought for the Union Army. During duty in the army of occupation, black troops were subject to harassment and violence, but the Union blue uniform shielded them somewhat. Once they left the service, former black soldiers were victims of all sorts of retaliatory brutality and abuse. "The immediate future of our Colored soldier is not flattering," reported a chaplain in early 1866. "Defeat has brought with it bitterness and especially toward those who have assisted to bring about that result." The chaplain insisted that as soon as authorities mustered him out of service, local whites marked him as a target. "His life is insecure. He is looked upon as a runaway 'nigger' who has been fighting against his old master and now returns full of imputent notions of a freeman." Violence was so common against former soldiers that Elijah Marrs slept with a loaded pistol under his head and a rifle at his side. In Maryland a crowd of whites assaulted a former soldier, one man "striking me first with a large stone, in the head—& then hit my nose." Several others then pinned him to the ground while one man kicked him repeatedly. Eventually the black man escaped, but whites pursued him on foot and horseback for one mile. Even worse was an attack the wife of an ex-soldier endured in Georgia. One evening a party of whites came to the door in search of her husband, whom she said was out at the watermelon patch. The white men then seized her and took her some distance from the house, where they tied her over a log, pulled her dress over her head, and beat her about the buttocks, with two men securing both legs and another with his foot on her neck to hold her down. They then shifted her on the log and flailed her hip and thigh. Bored with this, they next threw her on the ground, one man standing on her breast and the other two pulling apart her legs, and beat her about the groin. Finally, an ex-Confederate amputee raped her. When they held her down, one man pulled a pistol on her and swore "they ought to Shoot me, as my husband had been in the 'God damned Yankee Army,' and Swore they meant to kill every black Son-of-a-bitch they could find that had ever fought against them." After they finished with the woman, they returned to the house, beat her two daughters, and plundered their home.[53]

Probably the most famous case of violence directed toward black veterans in the South was the assassination of Benjamin Randolph in South Carolina in 1868. Randolph, who had graduated from Oberlin College, was a Methodist minister and served in the Freedmen's Bureau in South Carolina after his work as chaplain in the 26th U.S. Colored Infantry. After the war, Randolph became a prominent black in the Republican party in South Carolina, where he served as state senator and was elected chairman of the Republican state central committee. While stumping the up-country region for equality among the races, he was catching a train at Cokesbury, South Carolina, when three armed white men approached and one fired three shots, all of which hit the mark. The men then climbed back on their horses and rode away while Randolph lay dead. Authorities never apprehended anyone for the murder.[54]

In conjunction with intimidation tactics, several other factors enabled Southern whites to regain control of the South. President Andrew Johnson, a vigorous proponent of rapid reconstruction, used the power of the pardon liberally to restore full rights to Southern whites. Then, drawing upon their vast political experience, these Southerners took advantage of some divisions among the more liberal forces in the South and regained control of state governments and expelled many of the black and liberal white elected officials. Finally, they preyed on Northern racial prejudice to secure acquiescence to their resumption of control in the South. Southern whites claimed that the corruption during early years of reconstruction was evidence that blacks were incapable of running their own affairs. For centuries Southern whites had always assumed the responsibility of caring for blacks, and Northerners again had to let those with experience shape race relations in the South. With most Northerners tired of the battles and more interested in the reconstruction of their own lives, rather than the black population, this appeared to be a simple solution to Southern racial problems. They provided blacks with the same legal rights as other citizens and let them fend for themselves, under the guidance of Southern whites. Gradually, Southern whites whittled away at those rights until the status of blacks bore little resemblance to citizenship.[55]

In the North, too, any momentum that the war produced for equality among the races seemed to dissipate rapidly. Part of the reason for this was that the war had done little to dispel prejudice, despite sentiments within the Union Army during the latter stages of the fighting that blacks made good soldiers. More importantly, the

United States Sanitary Commission, a semiofficial organization designed to study and improve the physical and moral condition of Union soldiers, and the Provost Marshal General's Office each used the war as an opportunity to compile a huge array of data on the anatomy of Federal troops. The results of their investigations, widely published and broadly accepted by scientific and nonscientific communities, provided "statistical" justification for white attitudes of the inferiority of the black race.[56]

The Sanitary Commission published its data in 1869 under the title *Investigations in the Military and Anthropological Statistics of American Soldiers.* Underwritten in part by life insurance companies and under the overall supervision of a prominent scientist named Benjamin Gould, the Sanitary Commission had begun studies of white troops, but once the War Department began enlisting blacks it revised its examinations and measuring devices and expanded its program. The examiners, who had no training and admitted that they carried out their work under unfavorable conditions, measured nearly 16,000 soldiers and sailors, of whom more than 2,000 were "full-blooded" Africans and 863 were mulattoes. The results vindicated nearly all the stereotyped features of the groups. Full blacks had elongated heels and arms that were disproportionately long for their body size, thus resembling those of apes. Mulattoes' arms were shorter than blacks' but longer than those of whites. In addition, statistics vindicated arguments that mixture with whites was no cure for the inferiority of the black race. Physical dimensions of mulattoes were below those of blacks and well below those of whites.[57]

Six years after the publication of the Sanitary Commission's investigations, with the scientific community still buzzing over its findings, the Provost Marshal General's Office released its compilations in *Statistics, Medical and Anthropological, of the Provost Marshal-General's Bureau.* This massive study generally corroborated the statistics of the Sanitary Commission study, and accompanying testimony from physicians again endorsed the argument that interracial breeding resulted in an inferior being. Mulattoes, physicians claimed, did not withstand the hardships of military service as well as full-blooded blacks.[58]

The most damaging Civil War study of all, though, came from a physician's report to the Sanitary Commission, which the author published in two different journals shortly after the war. In "The Negro As a Soldier," Dr. Sanford B. Hunt drew on personal observation and more than four hundred autopsies, nearly all of them of black soldiers. Hunt argued that blacks' imitative qualities and fondness for rhythmical movements made them exceptional in drill. Their "large, flat, inelastic foot, . . . almost splay-footed" enabled them to march well, as did their "large joints." The physician concluded that blacks endured hunger better than whites but not prolonged fatigue duty. Slavery, while inculcating discipline, also crushed their wills, even to live, and many black troops succumbed to illnesses suddenly because they had lost hope. Moreover, they had difficulty describing symptoms properly and were prone to blame illness on supernatural causes. Fortunately, wrote Hunt, several of these qualities "are not intrinsic to [the black] race, but are to a great extent educational and may be expected to disappear under the energising influences of freedom & the teacher." [59]

What made the Hunt study so important were his data on brains. "As a rule," wrote Hunt, "the size of the brain has much to do with mental power," and he found the brains of white Americans to be 10 percent larger than those of American blacks. Brains of blacks averaged five ounces less than whites', and those of mulattoes three ounces less, which supported racial views of the times that whites were the most gifted, with mulattoes intellectually superior to full-blooded blacks but physically inferior.[60]

With this vast amount of "scientific" data that verified societal attitudes of the racial inferiority of blacks, as well as recent studies in evolution and sociology, Southern physicians and scientists joined in the debate, drawing upon inaccurate census data to argue that Southern blacks were a declining species. Since emancipation, disease and moral degradation had been on the rise. In the Union Army, blacks had suffered almost three times the fatalities per one thousand men due to disease than white soldiers did—a clear signal that freedom had negative effects on the health and well-being of blacks. Beyond the structure and discipline of slavery, blacks were reverting to their previous state of savagery, particularly an inability to control their sexual impulses. These whites, ignoring Civil War medical records that reported venereal disease nearly twice as likely to occur among white as black soldiers, began to view blacks as a syphilitic race that might become extinct as a result of the disease and its effects on the rate of infant mortality.[61]

By emphasizing heredity over environment, both Northern and Southern scientists declared blacks an inferior species with limited ability to progress. They chided Northern philanthropists who argued that through education and religion blacks could compete on the same level as whites, when only evolution over thousands and thousands of years could equalize the races. Reversing roles, the scientific community attacked racially liberal elements in society for refusing to admit the inferiority of blacks in the face of irrefutable evidence and charged them with racial prejudice in favor of blacks.[62]

As arguments of racial inferiority spread from the scientific community to the population at large, Union veterans began to dismiss the wartime contributions of the USCT. If blacks were inferior as the best minds now claimed, pondered whites, how could they have aided the war effort significantly? Slowly yet steadily white veterans and non-veterans questioned the performance of the USCT and in their own minds reduced the contributions of black soldiers to a negligible level. The Grand Army of the Republic, the Union veterans' organization, tolerated more and more discrimination against black ex-soldiers, acquiescing in public opinion on the USCT in the war. It permitted black soldiers to join but had separate posts for blacks and whites in the South and throughout much of the North. In a debate over segregated chapters at a national encampment, one white veteran in 1885 insisted that blacks who had served in the war were not soldiers "in the same sense" as white volunteers. While whites enlisted for altruistic and patriotic motives, blacks sought personal gain in the war. In histories of the war, authors downplayed the efforts of black soldiers. One black man, who never served in the army because of a childhood injury he had received that went untreated and left him crippled for life, complained, "It is a fact to be lamented that the historians of our country speak so little about the heroic deeds of the colored troops; in fact by some no mention is made of them at all." James Ford Rhodes, in his monumental seven-volume *History of the United States from the Compromise of 1850 to 1877*, devoted a scant few pages to the USCT, other than a section on Confederate atrocities against it. Some years earlier, William F. Fox prepared his *Regimental Losses in the American Civil War, 1861–1865*. Near the back of the book, Fox included the tremendous number of fatalities that the 9th Louisiana (Colored) Infantry, later the 5th U.S. Colored Heavy Artillery, suffered at Milliken's Bend, as well as the strength of the regiment in the battle, but he conveniently omitted it from the list and narrative of regiments with the greatest number of fatalities in a single battle in the war. Evidently, he thought it would be impolitic to argue that black soldiers had endured the single greatest battlefield catastrophe in the war, yet he was too conscientious to alter or exclude data from his book.[63]

Even more revealing was the experience of ex-Lieut. Col. Cyrus Sears of the 49th U.S. Colored Infantry, a Medal of Honor winner who decided to read a paper on the Battle of Milliken's Bend, in which he had fought, before the Ohio Commandery of the Loyal Legion of the United States. Sears, who candidly believed that blacks were an "inferior race," described the engagement and criticized Fox for excluding the 9th Louisiana (Colored) Infantry from the list of highest percentage of battlefield fatalities. On motion without dissent, the body agreed to publish the paper, as was customary. Several days later, however, he received word that the organization had reversed itself and decided not to publish the paper, ostensibly because Sears argued that the 23rd Iowa Infantry had fled the battlefield, which supposedly contradicted reports in the War Department, although the Confederate commander in the battle had also confirmed Sears's recollection of the events. In truth, Sears charged, "without spectacles, it seemed easy to read between the lines of the discussion that the kick was largely, if not mainly, on account of lingering prejudice against giving the negro a 'square deal.'" Sears promptly resigned from the organization and financed the publication of the paper himself.[64]

In defense of the USCT stepped forward George Washington Williams, the former black legislator whose book entitled *A History of the Negro Troops in the War of the Rebellion, 1861–1865*, was written out of personal interest and because "he was anxious to emphasize the patriotic role of the blacks," according to his biographer. In the book Williams complained that

> The deathless deeds of the white soldier's valor are not only embalmed in song and story, but are carved in marble and bronze. But nowhere in all this free land is there a monument to brave Negro soldiers, 36,847 of whom gave up their lives in the struggle for national existence. Even the appearance of the Negro soldier in the hundreds of histories of the war has always been incidental. These brave men have had no champion, no one to chronicle their record, teeming with interest and instinct with patriotism.[65]

Not surprisingly, some of the greatest defenders of black soldiers were their former commanders. One ex-officer wrote, "The colored soldier of the Union takes his stand by divine right side by side with all those troops who, in any age, have bravely fought and died for liberty." Samuel Duncan, who had been a regimental and brigade commander of black troops and had suffered a severe wound fighting alongside blacks, announced

> It is my verdict, and I believe that you will all coincide with me, that the colored troops deserved well of the Republic; and when the artist-historian of the coming age shall seek to represent in enduring marble or bronze the magnificent events of the period of the Great Rebellion, high among the crowning figures of the structure will he uprear a full-armed statue of a negro soldier, and the Muse of History, with truthful pen, shall inscribe at the front of that statue of legend: "The colored troops fought nobly."

In complete concurrence, another former officer explained that to understand how well the USCT contributed to the Union victory, one merely has to look at the Regular Army: "the fact that ever since the Rebellion there have been four regiments of negroes, two of cavalry and two of infantry, constantly in the service of our Government, forming part of the regular army, is perhaps the best answer that can be given to any one who doubts their capacity as soldiers." [66]

Moreover, many of the white officers continued their battle for equal justice among the races. Throughout his life Penrose Hallowell fought for the black race at every opportunity. He reminded the editors of the *Boston Herald* that "there was no segregation at Fort Wagner," and to his aunt he wrote of Southerners: "I believe that a compassionate Father will let them into Heaven, and I pray that he will let me too inside at least long enough to enjoy their surprise when they find out that the Kingdom is not run on the Jim Crow system." He also took issue with the Republican party for using race and prejudice as factors for appointments. Again to the *Boston Herald* he criticized President William Howard Taft because "He proclaims that negro office-holders shall not be forced upon unwilling white communities. It never occurs to him to proclaim that white postmasters and other officials shall not be forced on unwilling negro communities." He insisted that the government had no need to know the color of a citizen's skin and called the policy "vicious and subversive to the last degree." Charles Trowbridge joined the chorus of protest over the deprivation of the vote for Southern blacks. It made him furious that Sgt. Fred Brown, who had saved the lives of his entire regiment, and all Brown's comrades who remained in the South after the war had lost their right to vote and many other rights of citizenship while those whites who murdered Lieutenant Furman and nearly killed the entire regiment enjoyed full privileges as U.S. citizens. [67]

Others continued to labor with blacks to uplift the race, too. Former Col. Samuel Armstrong, despite some strong views on black inferiority, established Hampton Institute to inculcate discipline, general knowledge, and a cooperationist attitude toward Southern whites. The school turned out thousands of black teachers, who in turn labored on behalf of fellow blacks. Much more supportive of the black race and its quest for equality was ex-Maj. Horace Bumstead. Long an opponent of prejudice, Bumstead became the president of Atlanta University and a leading white spokesman for black rights. He argued that the range of individual ability within each race overlapped, and if the average white outperformed the average black, it was only the result of generations of slavery and discrimination. No one had a right to expect blacks to overcome more than 150 years of abuse in four decades. On retiring as university president in 1907, Bumstead became an active force in the National Association for the Advancement of Colored People.[68]

Probably the most important advocate of black equality among former officers was Dr. Burt G. Wilder, previously an assistant surgeon in the USCT. After the war, Wilder became one of the most distinguished scientists in the United States, professor of neurology and zoology at Cornell Medical College, and his area of expertise was the study of the brain. Thus he was admirably suited to challenge racists on the basis of personal and scientific knowledge. Wilder continually battled racism by emphasizing the physical similarities between blacks and whites. In moments of frustration he admitted being sorely tempted to exclaim, "Yes, a white man is as worthy as a colored man—provided he behaves himself as well." World renowned for his work on animal and human brains, Wilder challenged various studies of the dimensions of human brains, including Hunt's, by insisting that he had seen a considerable number of brains of blacks larger than those of whites, and adding, "As yet there has been found no constant feature by which the Negro brain may be certainly distinguished from that of a Caucasian."[69]

Of course, some white officers never had an interest in the black race, and they were unlikely to take a stand against racism at the height of its popularity. Yet at one time most of the white men who commanded black soldiers had cared deeply about blacks, and now their voices were silent. For quite a number of them, the war had been a disillusioning experience that had sapped their reformist spirit. Many of the white officers, motivated by evangelicalism, had hopes that the elimination of the evil of slavery would pave the way for the coming of the millennium, or the one thousand years of calm before the arrival of Christ. But after six hundred thousand deaths, and hundreds of thousands more who suffered terribly, evil and sin were no less powerful than before the war. In fact, with the huge urban expansion in the postwar world, immorality seemed to be on the rise. Still others viewed slavery as the great impediment in the United States' rise to greatness among the nations of the world. With slavery removed, and a free labor system in place in the South, they had assumed that endless years of prosperity and political calm would set in. Somehow, though, the postwar decades appeared even more turbulent than those prior to the war, and although politicians no longer grappled with slavery, they had equally complex social and political problems to deal with. No single one was likely to replace slavery or generate such hostility as to lead to secession, but together they appeared just as troublesome as before the war. And still there was a handful of others who continued their reformist work but had abandoned the black cause. Some became clergymen who tended to their flocks, and others channeled their efforts toward the benefit of other needy segments of society.[70]

In the face of such powerful racism, a large number yielded all or in part to public sentiment. Palemon Smalley, for example—a young Minnesotan who served in the 4th Wisconsin Infantry, 99th U.S. Colored Infantry, and the Freedmen's Bureau and after the war became a lawyer, newspaper editor, and prominent Democrat— attributed his about-face on the race issue to maturity. "I was an ardent young Republican, because I was an abolitionist, the cause appealing strongly to my sense of right," he explained. "In common with all of my class I knew nothing of the negro but idealized him, endowing him with the same love of freedom and aspirations that moved us. Had I known him as I afterwards came to I should not have been so eager to bestow upon him the burden and, often, the curse, of freedom before a long process in gradual emancipation had prepared him for it, so far as that race can be prepared." In part Smalley's views may have been the result of decades of marriage to a Southern woman, but he also found reconstruction duty extremely disagreeable. He despised the "unmanly, cowardly oppression of the South for so many years" and the carpetbagger regimes that "exploited the negro" and bound "the intelligence of the state"— the wealthy white population. He considered the enfranchisement of blacks ludicrous:

> No greater cruelty was ever perpetrated in the name of humanity than was the enfranchisement of the negroes, persons with the matured bodies of men and the immature brains of children. Ignorant, utterly unused to self-help, with no conception of what freedom meant for them, the emancipation act cast them out upon the world and the enfranchisement act put into their hands for their self-defense the ballot which they could not use and which, by making them tools of designing men, only made for them enemies of the only persons who really cared for them, their old masters.[71]

Many others paid homage to the racist views of their day while at the same time arguing that the USCT had performed valuable service in the war. Because so many of them genuinely believed that blacks were not their equals, they had little difficulty discussing the peculiar experiences they had with black soldiers in the war and showed no reluctance to analyze the character and habits of black troops negatively. But at the same time, few of them could endure the psychological and emotional trauma of admitting that the USCT had been worthless in the war, that they and their comrades had suffered death, injury, hardship, and illness uselessly. The simple solution was to claim that blacks were bad raw material, but by dint of hard work and unusual ability, their white officers had made soldiers and men out of them. In speech and print, former officers in the USCT hammered home the argument that these black commands had performed well in the war and that much of the responsibility for their success belonged to the officer corps. "That the colored troops acquitted themselves with credit," a former major asserted, "has been fully demonstrated, and that the success they achieved was due to the patriotism and unflinching bravery of their white officers, must also be admitted. It is needless to say that without efficient white officers the experiment would have been a total failure. The officers of negro troops have not received the credit to which they are so deservedly entitled, and for which the great service they rendered their country in its darkest hour of peril demands." [72]

Fortunately for these white ex-officers, service in the USCT was never a hindrance or impediment to postwar life. Because so many of them served more than three years in both white and black units, few Northerners could criticize the extent of their sacrifices and commitment to reunion. A number of them, for example, entered politics and suffered no penalty for commanding black soldiers. Samuel Crawford was governor and U.S. senator from Kansas, and Alonzo J. Edgerton held numerous political positions throughout his career, including U.S. senator and president of South Dakota's constitutional convention. Other white officers also had success, gaining seats in the nation's capital as well as state and local posts. Nevertheless, ex-officers were usually cautious about service with the USCT. When Samuel P. Snider sought a seat in Congress, the Republican newspaper continually referred to him as Captain Snider and freely discussed his extensive military service and wounds in battle, but it never mentioned his unit. Nor did his opponent attack him for commanding a company of black soldiers. Apparently, neither side considered it an issue, but his party newspaper preferred not to take any unnecessary risks. [73]

Because their military service had been such an important part of their lives, numerous units held occasional reunions over the years. Frequently they were for officers only, but in a few commands officers encouraged black soldiers to attend also. In most cases, though, officers and enlisted men had little contact. Personally, professionally, intellectually, and culturally, they seldom had much in common, and it was not surprising that few kept in touch. And because black regiments had officers assigned to the troops, they seldom lived in the same vicinity or visited one another. Charles Trowbridge, an exception, had the pleasure of seeing numerous soldiers on two business trips to South Carolina. On the first excursion, in 1884, he found his trusted ex-Sergeant Fred Brown working on the docks. Six years later, when he returned, he visited Brown, who was dying of dropsy. During that trip all his former soldiers who lived nearby held a "campfire" for Trowbridge, and they had an excellent time. There he made his old comrades promise to see that Brown, the regimental hero, received a military funeral and asked them to forward the funeral bill to him.[74]

Other times white and black veterans came together over pension fights. Dr. Anderson Patton, formerly of the 60th U.S. Colored Infantry, had a surprise visit once from Oscar Blue. Blue was seeking a pension for an accidental wound, and there was no record of treatment and Patton was unable to recall the affair. Blue traveled from Missouri to Nevada, Iowa, Patton's hometown, and once the doctor saw Blue, the entire episode came back to him and he signed the affidavit verifying the injury. Another officer, Stuart Hall, aided one of his enlisted men years after their service together. An imposter was collecting the soldier's pension, and when the War Department rejected his application, the man sought help from his old commander. Working with the soldier, Hall had a federal official arrest the phony soldier for fraud and got the pension awarded to the real veteran.[75]

In 1887 black veterans held their own convention in Boston. About three hundred ex-soldiers, some from as far away as Ohio, converged to honor those who had worked so hard for the creation of black units and to celebrate the accomplishments of the USCT. James Monroe Trotter, one of the few black officers and at the time a prominent government official, presided, and several white ex-officers, Alfred S. Hartwell and Penrose Hallowell among them, and former sergeant and Medal of Honor winner William Carney of Fort Wagner fame, addressed the crowd. On the second and final day, they passed resolutions reminding the public of their contributions to the war effort, complaining that these veterans were now suffering political and physical abuse and asserting that "it is the plain duty of the Government of this great nation by every proper means and influence it may possess to see to it that the colored defenders of its life in its day of peril, and their kindred or race, have the full and equal protection of the laws." [76]

The years tended to be hard on old soldiers in the USCT. Prolonged and difficult service, with its accompanying illnesses and injuries, took a heavy toll on officers and men, as nearly all suffered from rheumatism or arthritis and many other ailments. Few of them were able to save much money for retirement, and they depended almost exclusively on their military pensions for support. Too enfeebled to care for themselves, quite a number lived their final days in old soldiers' homes that popped up in most Northern states, but those who resided in the South had no such luxury. These veterans simply coped as best they could on their own or under the care of their families.

As decades passed, the United States government and the white public had a very selective memory of the performance of black soldiers in the Civil War and after. Beyond any doubt, they had demonstrated that blacks made fine soldiers, and in the postwar army the regular black regiments served ably, even if authorities also stationed them in isolated areas that made them nearly invisible to the general public. During the Spanish-American War and fighting in the Philippines, black troops again conducted themselves skillfully in combat, yet some whites, including Theodore Roosevelt, resurrected old charges of black cowardice, which were untrue. In addition Congress displayed its attachment to racial half-truths when it raised ten black regiments, nicknamed the "immunes" because it presumed the troops possessed "immunity from diseases incident to tropical climates." While many blacks did possess a biological shield from malaria and possibly yellow fever, others did not, and they exhibited no special resistance to some other illnesses prevalent in tropical climates. Moreover, prolonged service in these unhealthy regions enhanced the likelihood that black troops would contract a serious tropical disease, as they had in the Civil War, when black soldiers suffered a vastly higher proportional death rate from malaria and typhoid fever than did whites.[77]

In the years before World War I, assumptions of black inferiority by the white population in and out of military service strengthened, and on two separate occasions racial violence involving black regulars cast doubts on the trustworthiness of black soldiers. Thus, by World War I, the two races were fighting old battles all over again—whites questioning the ability of blacks to handle the rigors of combat and blacks resenting such charges and being forced to prove their valor.[78]

Despite their excellent performance, the military legacy of the USCT was mostly negative. The U.S. Army continued the practice of having segregated units through World War II, and its reluctance to commission blacks as officers extended well beyond that. Nevertheless, blacks put aside their grievances over discrimination both inside and outside the military to offer their services in huge numbers in times of national crises. Military authorities continued to employ black soldiers disproportionately for fatigue duty and to restrict their presence in combat units. When they received an opportunity, blacks fought well, often under white officers, but prejudice deprived them

of their due, as it had in the decades after the Civil War. In fact,
through World War II blacks made very little headway in the army.
Racial attitudes in society advanced at a snail's pace, and without
the watchful eye of a president like Abraham Lincoln, the federal
government retained many of the worst aspects of service in the
USCT.

Every Fourth of July, it was customary for Civil War veterans to
parade through the streets as part of the day's festivities. With bands
blaring, a column usually proceeded down the main thoroughfare
amid the cheers of onlookers and the crack and boom of fireworks.
Led by a dignitary or high-ranking officer, next came the white ex-
soldiers, and at the tail end of the column marched black veterans.
To James F. Mitchell and his friends, it was embarrassing to bring
up the rear guard each year, yet they did it as long as they were
able physically, which was nearly sixty years. In their opinion it
was much more important to endure the insult and participate in
the parade, to remind the local citizenry that blacks sacrificed for
the country and to show everyone how proud they were to have
taken part in the war for reunion and freedom, than to snub the
community and help them forget the role of the United States Colored
Troops in the Civil War.[79]

1

Statistics Samples

In support of this study, I created two samples, one of the white officers and another of black enlisted men in the USCT. For the officers, I obtained 400 numbers randomly from 1 to 7,683 and began counting from the *Official Army Register of the Volunteer Forces of the United States Army, 1861–1865.* After eliminating black officers, repeated individuals, and those who had their commissions revoked, my sample was 386. At the National Archives I then requested their pension files (approximately 90 percent of the officers or their families filed for a pension), examined many of their compiled military service records, particularly from white volunteer units, and looked at carded medical files. I also checked county histories, obituaries in local newspapers, and census data for those whose military records lacked specific data. The results are provided below

Date of Birth. Before 1825: 30; 1825–29: 20; 1830–34: 64; 1835–39: 109; 1840–44: 133; after 1844: 14; not available: 16.

1. Place of birth; 2. Prewar Residence; 3. Postwar Residence a (residence of longest duration); 4. Postwar Residence b (residence of second longest duration); 5. Postwar Residence c (residence of third longest duration).

Appendix 1

Location	1	2	3	4	5
AL	1	0	2	0	1
AR	1	0	0	3	0
AZ	0	0	0	0	1
CA	0	2	10	10	9
Canada	6	1	1	0	0
CO	0	1	4	5	0
CT	7	12	5	4	0
DE	0	1	0	1	0
DC	0	0	11	3	1
FL	0	1	2	3	1
France	1	0	0	0	0
GA	0	1	2	1	2
Germany	10	0	0	0	0
Great Britain	15	0	0	0	0
IL	11	57	44	14	6
IN	11	19	10	5	1
IA	0	34	19	12	5
Ireland	6	0	0	0	0
Japan	0	0	0	1	0
KS	0	4	16	8	6
KY	7	1	1	0	0
LA	0	2	8	2	1
ME	19	13	5	3	1
MD	0	2	1	0	0
MA	31	37	27	8	3
Mexico	0	0	0	1	1
MI	5	15	10	8	4
MN	0	8	7	5	2
MS	1	0	1	2	3
MO	2	13	10	8	4
NE	0	0	5	1	1
Netherlands	1	0	0	0	0
NH	10	7	5	3	2
NJ	3	4	10	8	1
NY	75	68	37	18	7
NC	1	0	1	0	0
ND	0	0	0	1	0
OH	48	31	24	8	6
OR	0	0	0	0	1
PA	28	14	7	6	3
Prussia	3	0	0	0	0
RI	3	1	2	1	0
SC	0	0	1	0	0
SD	0	0	1	2	2
TN	0	0	1	6	0
TX	0	0	2	2	1
UT	0	0	0	1	1
VT	17	8	2	2	1
VA	0	0	0	3	3
WA	0	0	0	2	2
WI	0	15	7	4	3
WV	1	1	1	1	0
not available	51	14	47	—	—

Of those white officers born in NY, only ten were born in New York City, Long Island, Westchester County, or Rockland County. In Iowa before the war, twenty-three of thirty-four future officers in the USCT lived within 80 miles of the Missouri border and twenty-nine of thirty-four lived within 120 miles of the border. Likewise, nearly 30 percent of Illinois whites who commanded black soldiers lived within 80 miles of Missouri.

Number of Times an Ex-Officer Moved from One State to Another After the War. One move—85; two moves—73; three moves—56; four moves—31; five moves and more—94.

1. Prewar Occupation; 2. Postwar Occupation a (primary occupation); 3. Postwar Occupation b (secondary occupation).

Occupation	1	2	3
artist	3	1	0
blacksmith	6	3	0
bricklayer	2	0	0
carpenter	15	15	4
clerk	35	15	6
cooper	2	0	0
customs official	0	2	0
engineer	5	10	0
farmer	76	35	18
journalist/author	0	3	0
laborer	7	9	4
lawyer	10	20	2
lumberman	3	1	0
machinist	5	1	0
manager	0	7	0
merchant	3	6	5
minister	8	15	0
painter	4	2	0
physician	15	25	3
politician	0	0	4
postmaster	0	0	3
printer	5	0	0
publisher	0	2	0
salesman	0	13	2
shoe cutter	1	3	0
shoemaker	5	0	0
soldier	6	6	0
student	27	0	0
teacher	26	3	0
not available	62	69	—

Occupations in which only one officer served have been omitted.

Year of Death. Before 1866: 27; 1866–69: 6; 1870–74: 7; 1875–79: 9; 1880–84: 12; 1885–89: 13; 1890–99: 48; 1900–09: 69; 1910–19: 77; after 1919: 56; not available: 62.

Cause of Death. Accident: 11; alcoholism: 2; apoplexy: 5; cerebral hemorrhage: 6; chronic diarrhea;* 6: heart problem: 31; Kidney Problem: 19; killed in action: 8; liver problem: 7; lung problem: 8; malaria or typhoid fever: 9; pneumonia: 14; suicide: 4; not available: 200.

* Chronic diarrhea is not fatal. This was the diagnosis of the attending physician. More likely, the causes of death were dysentery or something similar.

Total Wealth at or Near Time of Death. I have added all assets and subtracted any mortgages or money owed.

Poor (\$1,000 or Less)	Moderate (\$1,001–\$5,000)	Wealthy (Over \$5,000)
47	22	13

Not available: 304.

Number Who Served in white volunteer units prior to USCT. 347. (I accumulated the names of the regiments or batteries, although that is of little interest to the reader. Sixty-seven of them served in two white volunteer units before entering the USCT. Some sixty-six officers served in two or more USCT units.).

Year of Original Enlistment. Before 1861: 5; 1861: 191; 1862: 130; 1863: 10; 1864: 10; 1865: 1.

Year discharged from white volunteer unit. 1861: 3; 1862: 17; 1863: 160: 1864: 126; 1865: 40; 1866: 1.

Length of White Volunteer Service in Months

1–9	10–9	20–9	30–9	40–9	50 and over
28	110	140	48	11	5

Length of Detached Service From White Volunteer Unit in Months (includes assignments away from unit, illness, pow, etc.).

Y*	0	1–4	5–9	10–9	20–9	30–9
46	172	29	31	39	9	6

* Y indicates there was a compelling reason other than detachment from the Volunteer Unit why the soldier left a volunteer unit to enter the USCT, such as reduction in rank, being passed over for promotion, dissolution of original command, or consolidation of original command with another unit.

Prisoner of War in White Volunteer Service, POW once: 20.

Number of Occasions When Wounds Were Sustained in White Volunteer Units. Once: 61; twice: 4; three times: 5; four or more times: 3.

Number of Battles in Which These Whites Fought Prior to Entering the USCT (list does not include skirmishes).

0	1	2	3	4–6	7–9	10 and over	*Not Appropriate or Available*
38	57	58	52	75	29	24	53

Year Appointed to USCT. 1862: 5; 1863: 187; 1864: 151; 1865: 40. 1866: 2.

Length of Service in Months, USCT.

1–9	10–9	20–9	30–9	40 and over
84	130	102	58	6

Year Officers Left USCT. 1863: 12; 1864: 91; 1865: 143; 1866: 122; 1867: 16.

Low and High Rank, White Volunteer and USCT.
1. Low rank, volunteer unit. 2. high rank, volunteer unit. 3. low rank, USCT. 4. high rank, USCT.

Rank	1	2	3	4
private	255	14	0	0
teamster	1	1	0	0
hospital steward	1	4	5	0
corporal	14	46	0	0
sergeant	38	145	17	0
second lieutenant	12	20	133	92
first lieutenant	8	10	100	116
captain	9	17	86	120
major	0	0	8	17
lt. colonel	0	3	4	7
colonel	0	0	8	9
medical cadet	2	1	0	0
contract surgeon	1	1	0	0
assistant surgeon	4	6	14	13
surgeon	0	1	3	4
chaplain	1	1	8	8

Cause for Leaving the Service, Other Than Death. Resigned for personal reasons: 106; resigned for incompetency: 9; resigned for disability: 53; discharged for disability: 2; dishonorably dismissed or cashiered: 15; mustered out: 211.

Selected Major Illnesses Recorded in Medical Records. This is a list of the number of soldiers who had this problem at least once. (These are incomplete and underestimate the number of illnesses and injuries incurred in military service. For example, there are only sixty-four recorded soldiers with gunshot or shell wounds, when in fact seventy-three men officially sustained these injuries in white volunteer units alone.)

Alcoholism: 8; diarrhea: 24; dysentery: 7; gunshot or shell wound: 64; hernia: 6; injury: 12; malaria; 40; pneumonia: 1; rheumatism: 8; typhoid fever: 7; Venereal Disease: 4; No Records Available: 9.

Number of Marriages.

0	1	2	3	4	Not Available
21	205	65	14	1	80

Date of First Marriage.

1861 or Before	1862–65	1866–69	1870–80	After 1880	Not Available
85	46	68	59	7	132

Number of Divorces. 0: 251; 1: 24; 2: 4; not available or appropriate: 107.

Number of Desertions or Abandonments. 0: 288; 1: 10; 2: 2; not available or appropriate: 107.

Number of Children. 0: 32; 1–3: 99; 4–7: 48; 8 or more: 13; Not available or appropriate: 194.

Selected Religions. Baptist: 9; Catholic: 12; Congregationalist: 5; Episcopalian: 9; Methodist: 15. Presbyterian: 15.

In the case of black troops, a valid sample would require a minimum of 1,000 soldiers, far too large to accomplish in any reasonable length of time. Therefore, I selected black regiments whose recruits came from specific regions, randomly selected a company within those units, and examined every eighth pension record, approximately 140 in all, and some compiled military service records. The purpose was mainly to get a feel for the pension records of black soldiers and draw upon more traditional information in affidavits and depositions. I also went to the Regimental Descriptive Books and compiled data on all the men in those companies. These units were: Battery A, 3rd USCHA in TN; Battery M, 11th USCHA in RI; Co. G. 5th USCC in KY; Co. C, 10th USCI in VA; Co. K, 21st USCI in SC; Co. C, 23rd USCI in VA; Co. I, 26th USCI in NY; Co. B, 28th USCI in IN; Co. A, 36th USCI in NC; Co. G, 39th USCI in MD; Co. F, 46th USCI in AR; Co. I, 50th USCI in LA; Co. H, 57th USCI in AR; Co. D, 65th USCI in MO; Co. D, 74th USCI in LA; Co. C, 83rd USCI (New) in KS; Co. D, 107th USCI in KY; Co. B, 138th USCI in GA; and Co. A, 55th Mass. (Colored) Inf. in MA.

Battery A, 2nd USCLA in TN

Place of birth: AL—20; GA—18; KY—77; LA—1; MD—1; MS—2; MO—2; NC—4; PA—1; SC—5; TN—49; TX—1; VA—30.

Occupations by place of birth: Blacksmith—AL, GA, TN, TN; boatman—TN; carpenter—VA, VA; clergyman—SC; cook—AL, KY; hostler—MO; ironworker—KY, KY; mason—KY, LA, SC; servant—AL, KY, NC, TN, TN, VA, VA; shoemaker—KY; teamster—GA; tobacconist—VA; wagoner—KY; waiter—KY; all others field hands or laborers.

Battery A, 3rd USCHA in TN

Place of birth: AL—5; GA—3; IL—1; KY—7; MD—3; MS—6; MO—3; NY—1; NC—9; SC—3; TN—36; TX—1; VA—11; unknown—45.

Occupations by Place of Birth: Blacksmith—TN; cook—TN; cooper–NC; farmer—KY, TN, TN, TN, VA; mason—NY; shoemaker—TN; student of medicine—IL; waiter—TN; all others laborers.

Battery M, 11th USCHA in RI

Place of birth: AL—6; GA—4; KY—2; LA—2; MD—2; MS—34; MO—1; NC—5; SC—5; TN—29; VA—11; Unknown—1.

Occupations by place of birth: Brickmaker—GA; carpenter—KY; hostler—GA, MS; mason—MD, TN; shoemaker—MS; waiter—MS, SC, TN, TN, TN, TN; all others laborers or field hands.

Company G, 5th USCC in KY

Place of birth: AL—3; GA—2; KY—95; MS—1; VA—2.
Occupation by place of birth: All field hands.

Company C, 10th USCI in VA

Place of birth: DC—1; MD—1; VA—99.
Occupation by place of birth: All field hands except one laborer.

Company K, 21st USCI in SC

Place of birth: AL—1; FL—4; GA—6; MD—1; Nassau—1; NY—1; NC—1; SC—59; VA—4; Unknown—9.

Occupation by place of birth: Blacksmith—SC—3 (all slaves); boatman—SC (slave); butler—SC—2 (both slaves); carpenter—SC—5 (four slaves); cartman—SC—2 (both slaves); coachman—FL (slave); cooper—SC (slave); driver—SC, VA (both slaves); engineer—SC (slave); fireman—SC—2 (both slaves); hostler—SC (slave); mail carrier—SC (slave); stockman—FL, SC (both slaves); teamster—NC, SC—5 (all slaves); wagoner—SC (slave); waiter—AL, NY, SC—3 (all slaves); all others laborers or field hands.

Company C, 23rd USCI in VA

Place of birth: AL—6; DE—2; DC—2; GA—1; Jamaica—1; KY—11; LA—1; MD—52; MA—1; MS—3; MO—2; OH—3; PA—4; TN—9; VA—48.

Occupation by place of birth: Blacksmith—VA; brickmaker—MD; carder—TN; farmer—AL—2; KY—7; MD—2; MA; MS—2; MO—2;

TN—8; VA; mariner—VA; servant—PA; waterman—MD; all others laborers.

Company I, 26th USCI in NY

Place of birth: AL—1; AR—1; Canada—5; Chile—2; CT—1; DE—4; DC—1; KY—1; MD—10; Mexico—1; MS—1; NJ—5; NY—63; NC—4; OH—2; PA—10; RI—1; VA—10; West Indies—1; Unknown—2.

Occupation by place of birth: Barber—CT, MD, NY—5; NC, PA; blacksmith—MD, NC, VA; boatman—NY, OH, PA, VA; butcher—NY—2; carpenter—MD; cartman—NY; coachman—Can., NY; cook—NJ, NY, VA; hatter—AR; hostler—NY—2; lumberman—NY; porter—NY; sailor—DE, MD, NY, West Indies; servant—MD; spoke maker—NY; steward—KY, NY; tailor—Can., Chile, Chile, NY; teamster—PA—2; waiter—NY—3; all others farmers and laborers.

Company B, 28th USCI in IN

Place of birth: AL—4; DE—4; IL—9; IN—29; KY—12; MD—21; MS—1; NC—10; OH—2; TN—6; VA—11; unknown—46.

Occupations by place of birth: Barber—IN; cook—IN; driver—MD; sawyer—NC; teamster—TN; waiter—MD; all others farmers or laborers.

Company A, 36th USCI in NC

Place of birth: NC—87; VA—13.

Occupation by place of birth: Barber—NC; caulker—NC; cobbler—NC; cooper—NC—2; fisherman—NC; lumberman—VA; porter—NC; servant—NC—2, VA; shingler—NC; teamster—NC; all others field hands.

Company G, 39th USCI in MD

Place of birth: Africa—1; CT—2; DC—1; FL—1; GA—1; KY—1; MD—95; MS—1; NY—4; NC—3; OH—1; PA—4; VA—11.

Occupation by place of birth: Barber—NY; blacksmith—MD; cook—CT, GA, VA; hostler—MS; musician—MD; quarryman—OH; sailor—MD; waiter—MD; all others laborers or field hands.

Company F, 46th USCI in AR

Place of birth: AL—11; AR—6; GA—4; KY—11; LA—2; MS—24; MO—9; NC—9; OH—1; PA—1; SC—7; TN—13; VA—17; unknown—2.

Occupation by place of birth: Barber—PA; blacksmith—SC; carpenter—TN, VA; cook—MO; engineer—NC; mason—MS; riverman—MS; servant—MS; waiter—KY, VA; all others farm hands or laborers.

Company I, 50th USCI in LA

Place of birth: AL—14; DC—1; GA—2; IN—1; LA—23; MD—1; MS—41; MO—7; NC—6; SC—4; TN—4; TX—1; VA—13; unknown—68.

Occupation by place of birth: Blacksmith—IN, VA; boatman—TX; cabin boy—LA; gunsmith—SC; sailor—MO; servant—MS—2; all others laborers or field hands.

Company H, 57th USCI in AR

Place of birth: AL—4; AR—15; DE—1; GA—2; IL—1; KY—3; MD—1; MS—9; MO—3; NC—15; SC—2; TN—33; VA—6; unknown—3.

Occupation by place of birth: Carpenter—VA; farmer—IL, TN; sawyer—DE; servant—KY; all others laborers or field hands.

Company D, 65th USCI in MO

Place of birth: AL—3; IN—1; KY—19; LA—4; MS—12; MO—101; NC—3; SC—2; TN—14; VA—25; unknown—1.

Occupation by place of birth: Barber—TN; blacksmith—VA; boatman—MS—2; TN; carpenter—SC; cook—unknown; all others laborers or field hands.

Company D, 74th USCI in LA

Place of birth: AL—1; DE—1; GA—2; KY—2; LA—80; MD—1; MS—11; MO—1; TN—1; VA—4.

Occupation by place of birth: Blacksmith—LA, LA; bricklayer—18 from LA; brickmaker—DE; carpenter—11 from LA; cigar maker—6 from LA; clerk—LA; cook—LA; MS; VA; cooper—5 from LA; fisherman—LA; gardener—LA; mechanic—LA; painter—LA; plasterer—6 from LA; servant—LA; shoemaker—13 from LA; MS; steamboat hand—LA—2; tailor—LA; teamster—TN; tinsmith—LA—2; MS; Wagoner—VA.

Company C, 83rd USCI in KS

Place of birth: AR—1; Cherokee Nation—2; DC—1; IN—1; KY—18; MO—42; NC—1; TN—5; VA—6; unknown—4

Occupation by place of birth: Barber—IN; all others field hands.

Company D, 107th USCI in KY

Place of birth: AR—1; KY—100; VA—2.

Occupation by place of birth: Blacksmith—KY; carriage driver—AR; miller—KY; servant—KY; all others laborers or farm hands.

Company B, 138th USCI in GA

Place of birth: AL—29; GA—54; MS—5; NC—1; SC—6; TN—1; VA—7.

Occupation by place of birth: Blacksmith—GA—2, TN; coachman—GA; coal burner—GA; cook—GA; mason—AL; miller—GA; printer—SC; railroader—GA; servant—AL, GA; shoemaker—AL—2, GA—2, VA; waiter—AL, GA, SC, VA; all others farm hands.

Company A, 55th Mass. (Colored) Inf. in MA

Place of birth: Can.—4; Chile—1; CT—3; DC—2; Great Britain—1; GA—1; Haiti—1; IL—12; IN—23; KY—6; ME—1; MD—2; MA—7; MI—2; MO—16; NY—3; NC—3; OH—23; PA—5; VT—1; VA—3; unknown—3.

Occupation by place of birth: Barber—5 from IN, MA, OH, PA; blacksmith—IN—2, MA, PA; bricklayer—OH; butcher—MA; carpenter—MD; cigar maker—MD; cook—IN, MA, NY; cooper—OH; coppersmith—CT; groom—OH; ironworker—PA; mechanic—IN; painter—IN, OH—2; ropemaker—NY; seaman—Can., Chile, DC, Great Britain, Haiti, IL, VA; shoemaker—ME; steward—Can., GA; teamster—MO; wagoner—KY; waiter—Can., IL, IN, KY, MA, NC, OH—4.

2

Congressional Medal of Honor Winners in the USCT

The following list of Congressional Medal of Honor winners was taken from *American Decorations: A List of Awards of the Congressional Medal of Honor, the Distinguished-Service Cross, and the Distinguished-Service Medal, 1862–1926.* Compiled by the Office of the Adjutant General of the Army. Washington, DC: Government Printing Office, 1927.

First Lt. William Appleton, Co. H, 4th USCI, at Petersburg, VA, 15 June 1864 and New Market Heights, VA, 29 Sep. 1864. The first man of the Eighteenth Corps to enter the enemy's works and valiant service in a desperate assault, inspiring the Union troops by his example of steady courage.

Pvt. William H. Barnes, Co. C, 38th USCI, at Chapin's Farm, VA, 29 Sep. 1864. Among the first to enter the enemy's works, although wounded.

First Lt. Charles L. Barrell, Co. C, 102nd USCI, near Camden, SC, Apr. 1865. Hazardous service in marching through the enemy's country to bring relief to his command.

Col. Delavan Bates, 30th USCI, at Cemetery Hill, VA, 30 July 1864. Gallantry in action where he fell, shot through the face, at the head of his regiment.

First Sgt. Powhatan Beaty, Co. G, 5th USCI, at Chapin's Farm, VA, 29 Sep. 1864. Took command of his company, all officers having been killed or wounded, and gallantly led it.

First Lt. Orson W. Bennett, Co. A, 102nd USCI, at Honey Hill, SC, 30 Nov. 1864. After several unsuccessful efforts to recover three pieces of abandoned artillery, this officer gallantly led a small force fully one hundred yards in advance of the Union lines and brought in the guns, preventing their capture.

First Sgt. James H. Bronson, Co. D, 5th USCI, at Chapin's Farm, VA, 29 Sep. 1864. Took command of his company, all the officers having been killed or wounded, and led it gallantly.

Lt. George W. Brush, Co. B, 34th USCI, at Ashepoo River, SC, 24 May 1864. Voluntarily commanded a boat crew, which went to the rescue of a large number of Union soldiers on board the stranded steamer *Boston*, and with great gallantry succeeded in conveying them to shore, being exposed during the entire time to heavy fire from a Confederate battery.

Sgt. William H. Carney, Co. C, 54th Mass. Col. Inf., at Fort Wagner, SC, 18 July 1863. When the color sergeant was shot down, this soldier grasped the flag, led the way to the parapet, and planted the colors thereon. When the troops fell back he brought off the flag, under a fierce fire in which he was twice severely wounded.

First Lt. Andrew Davidson, Co. H, 30th USCI, at the mine, Petersburg, VA, 30 July 1864. One of the first to enter the enemy's works, where, after his colonel, major, and one-third of the company officers had fallen, he gallantly assisted in rallying and saving the remnant of the command.

Sgt. Decatur Dorsey, Co. B, 39th USCI, at Petersburg, VA, 30 July 1864. Planted his colors on the Confederate works in advance of his regiment, and when the regiment was driven back to the Union works he carried the colors there and bravely rallied the men.

First Lt. Nathan H. Edgerton, 6th USCI, at Chapin's Farm, VA, 29 Sep. 1864. Took up the flag after three color bearers had been shot down and bore it forward, though himself wounded.

Capt. Thomas F. Ellsworth, Co. B, 55th Mass. Col. Inf., at Honey Hill, SC, 30 Nov. 1864. Under a heavy fire carried his wounded commanding officer from the field.

Capt. Ira H. Evans, Co. B, 116th USCI, at Hatcher's Run, VA, 2 Apr. 1865. Voluntarily passed . . . between the lines, under a heavy fire from the enemy, and obtained important information.

Sgt. Maj. Christian A. Fleetwood, 4th USCI, at Chapin's Farm, VA, 29 Sep. 1864. Seized the colors, after two color bearers had been shot down, and bore them nobly through the fight.

Pvt. James Gardiner, Co. I, 36th USCI, at Chapin's Farm, VA, 29 Sep. 1864. Rushed in advance of his brigade, shot a rebel officer who was on the parapet rallying his men, and then ran him through with his bayonet.

Sgt. James H. Harris, Co. B, 38th USCI, at New Market Heights, VA, 29 Sep. 1864. Gallantry in the assault.

Sgt. Maj. Thomas Hawkins, 6th USCI, at Deep Bottom, VA, 21 July 1864. Rescue of regimental colors.

Sgt. Alfred B. Hilton, Co. H, 4th USCI, at Chapin's Farm, VA, 29 Sep. 1864. When the regimental color bearer fell, this soldier seized the color and carried it forward, together with the national standard, until disabled at the enemy's inner line.

Sgt. Maj. Milton M. Holland, 5th USCI, at Chapin's Farm, VA, 29 Sep. 1864. Took command of Company C, after all the officers had been killed or wounded, and gallantly led it.

Cpl. Miles James, Co. B, 36th USCI, at Chapin's Farm, VA, 29 Sep. 1864. Having had his arm mutilated, making immediate amputation necessary, he loaded and discharged his piece with one hand and urged his men forward; this within 30 yards of the enemy's work.

First Sgt. Alexander Kelly, Co. F, 6th USCI, at Chapin's Farm, VA, 29 Sep. 1864. Gallantly seized the colors, which had fallen near the enemy's lines of abatis, raised them and rallied the men at a time of confusion and in a place of the greatest danger.

Lt. Col. Henry C. Merriam, 73rd USCI, at Fort Blakely, AL, 9 Apr. 1865. Volunteered to attack the enemy's works in advance of orders and, upon permission being given, made a most gallant assault.

Capt. Henry C. Nichols, Co. E, 73rd USCI, at Fort Blakely, AL, 9 Apr. 1865. Voluntarily made a reconnaissance in advance of the line held by his regiment and, under a heavy fire, obtained information of great value.

First Sgt. Robert Pinn, Co. I, 5th USCI, At Chapin's Farm, VA, 29 Sep. 1864. Took command of his company after all officers had been killed or wounded and gallantly led it in battle.

First Sgt. Edward Ratcliff, Co. C, 38th USCI, at Chapin's Farm, VA, 29 Sep. 1864. Commanded and gallantly led his company after commanding officer had been killed; was the first enlisted man to enter the enemy's works.

Second Lt. Walter Thorn, Co. G, 116th USCI, at Dutch Gap Canal, VA, 1 Jan. 1865. After the fuse of the mined bulkhead had been lit this officer, learning that the picket guard had not been withdrawn, mounted the bulkhead and at great personal peril warned the guard of its danger.

Pvt. Charles Veal, Co. D, 4th USCI, at Chapin's Farm, VA, 29 Sep. 1864. Seized the national colors, after two color bearers had been shot down, close to the enemy's works, and bore them through the remainder of the battle.

Capt. Albert D. Wright, Co. G, 43rd USCI, at Petersburg, VA, 30 July 1864. Advanced beyond the enemy's lines, capturing a stand of colors and its color guard; was severely wounded.

APPENDIX

3

Black Officers in the Union Army *

73rd USCI (1st Louisiana Native Guards)

Captains: Alfred Bourgeau, André Cailloux, Edward Carter, Edgard C. Davis, John DePass, Joseph Follin, James H. Ingraham, Alcide Lewis, James Lewis, Henry L. Rey.

Lieutenants: John Crowder, Emile Detiege, William Harding, Louis D. Larrien, Victor Lavigne, Jules Mallet, Joseph L. Montieu, Morris W. Morris, Ehurd Moss, Oscar Orillion, Paul Poree, Eugene Rapp, Henry Louis Rey, Charles Sentmanat, Hyppolite St. Louis, Louis A. Thibaut, Charles Warfield.

74th USCI (2nd Louisiana Native Guards)

Majors: Francis E. Dumas.

Captains: William B. Barrett, William Belley, Arnold Bertonneau, Hannibal Carter, Edward P. Chase, Robert H. Isabelle, P. B. S. Pinchback, Samuel W. Ringgold, Joseph Villeverde, Samuel J. Wilkinson.

Lieutenants: Alfred Annis, Jr., Louis De Gray, Peter O. Depremond, Alphonso Fleury, Jr., Calvin B. Glover, Solomon Hayes, Ernest Hubeau, Joseph Jones, John W. Latting, Jules P. Lewis, Theodore A. Martin, Ernest Morphy, Octave Rey, Jasper Thompson, Frank L. Trask, George F. Watson, Joseph Wellington.

* This list may not be complete, because of the records at the National Archives, and it does not include blacks who posed as whites and commanded in white volunteer units. The list is based predominantly on Berlin et al., *Freedom*, II, pp. 310–11. Several black officers, originally in the 73rd USCI, served briefly in the 91st USCI.

75th USCI (3rd Louisiana Native Guards)

Captains: Leon G. Forstall, Peter A. Gardener, Charles W. Gibbons, Jacques A. Gla, John C. Holland, Samuel Lawrence, Joseph B. Oliver.

Lieutenants: Charles Butler, Chester W. Converse, Octave Foy, William Hardin, Valdes Lessassier, Ernest Longpré, Jr., G. B. Miller, James E. Moore, E. T. Nash, Joseph G. Parker, Louis Petit, Hypolite Ray, Charles Schermerhorn, G. W. Talmon, A. F. Tervalon.

104th USCI

Majors: Martin R. Delany.

Captains: O. S. B. Wall.

Independent Battery, USCLA

Captains: H. Ford Douglas.

Lieutenants: William D. Matthews, Patrick H. Minor.

54th Mass. (Col.) Inf.

Lieutenants: Stephen A. Swails, Peter Vogelsang, Frank M. Welch.

55th Mass. (Col.) Inf.

Lieutenants: William H. Dupree, John F. Shorter, James M. Trotter.

Chaplains: John R. Bowles, Francis A. Boyd, Samuel Harrison, William H. Hunter, William Jackson, Chauncey B. Leonard, George W. LeVere, Benjamin F. Randolph, David Stevens, Henry M. Turner, James Underdue, William Waring, Garland H. White.

Surgeons: Anderson R. Abbott, Alexander T. Augusta, John V. De Grasse, William B. Ellis, William Powell, Charles B. Purvis, John Rapier, Alpheus Tucker.

Notes

ABBREVIATIONS

Repositories

American Antiquarian Society	AAS	Minnesota Historical Society	MNHS
Arkansas History Commission	ARHC	National Archives	NA
		Record Group	RG
Bentley Library, U. of Michigan	BL, UMI	New Hampshire Historical Society	NHHS
Boston Public Library	BPL	Ohio Historical Society	OHS
Clements Library, U. of Michigan	CL, UMI	Rhode Island Historical Society	RIHS
Schoff Collection	SC	Sophia Smith Collection, Smith College	SSC, Smith College
Emory University	EU		
Illinois State Historical Library	ILSHL	State Historical Society of Wisconsin	SHSW
Indiana Historical Society	INHS	U.S. Army Military History Institute	USAMHI
Iowa State Historical Society	IASHS	Civil War Miscellaneous Collection	CWMC
Kansas State Historical Society	KASHS	Civil War Times Illustrated Collection	CWTIC
Library of Congress	LC	University of Arkansas	UAR
Civil War Miscellany	CWM	University of Iowa	UIA
Massachusetts Historical Society	MAHS	Vermont Historical Society	VTHS
Michigan State University	MISTU		

281

Western Historical Collection—State Historical Society of Missouri	WHC-SHSMO	Western Reserve Historical Society Sterling Library, Yale University	WRHS YU

Other Abbreviations

Adjutant General's Office	AGO	Military Order of the Loyal Legion of the United States	MOLLUS
After Action Report	AAR		
Compiled Military Service Records	CMSR	Special Field Order	SFO
General Orders	GO	Special Order	SO
Headquarters	HQ	War Department	WD
Inspector General's Office	IGO		

Preface

1. S. A. Harrison to Vane, 6 Nov. 1863, 18 Nov. 1863. Harrison Family Papers, SHSW.

2. G. H. White to Mr. Editor, 28 Sep. 1865 in *Christian Recorder*, 4 Nov. 1865.

CHAPTER 1
Breaking Down the Resistance

1. Catton, *America Goes to War*, p. 14. Also see Durden, *The Gray and the Black* on Confederate consideration of using blacks in the army. I am, of course, referring to John Brown here.

2. Deposition of Sarah Reed, 26 May 1924 in Pension File of Charles Cull. RG 15, NA. Also see Litwack, *Been in the Storm So Long*, pp. 4–5. For excellent overviews of the coming of the war, see Sewell, *A House Divided: Sectionalism and Civil War, 1848–1865*, and McPherson, *Battle Cry of Freedom*.

3. See Litwack, *Been in the Storm So Long*, p. 46, for ex-slaves who regretted not trying to revolt. Boles, *Black Southerners*, pp. 183–86, gives an excellent summary of the issues that confronted slaves.

4. Quoted in McPherson, *The Negro's Civil War*, p. 24; Deposition of Jackson Carter and Carry Ann Carter, 8 Apr. 1869. Pension File of Hamilton Robison. RG 15, NA; James Parton, *General Butler of New Orleans*, p. 130. Hamilton Robison died of disease in 1865.

5. Morris, et al., "Sentiments of the Colored People of Boston Upon the War," *Boston Journal*, 24 Apr. 1861. "The Negro in the Military Service of the United States," pp. 804–8. RG 94, NA; W. T. Boyd and J. T. Alston to Simon Cameron, 15 Nov. 1861. Berlin et al., *Freedom*, II, p. 80. Also see Wm. A. Jones to Cameron, 27 Nov. 1861. Berlin et al., *Freedom*, II, pp. 80–81, as well as sundry letters in "The Negro," pp. 813–42. RG 94, NA.

6. I. L. Stevens to Hon. Mr. Cameron, 10 Aug. 1861. Edward Vernon to Cameron, 17 Sep. 1861. "The Negro," pp. 818, 822. RG 94, NA.

7. Extract of Message of George W. Johnson, Provisional Governor of Kentucky, 26 Nov. 1861. "The Negro," p. 721. RG 94, NA.

8. See Quarles, *The Negro in the Civil War*, pp. 58–61, for an excellent description of the event.

9. "An Act to Confiscate Property used for Insurrectionary Purposes," 6 August 1861. J. H. Lane to General S. D. Sturgis, 3 Oct. 1861. "The Negro," pp. 419, 431. RG 94, NA. Also see Cameron to Maj. Gen. Butler, 30 May 1861. "The Negro," pp. 408–10. RG 94, NA; Thos. W. Higginson to ?, 13 Aug. [1861]. Mary Thatcher Higginson, *Letters and Journals of Thomas Wentworth Higginson, 1846–1906*, p. 156.

10. See Sam Evans to father and mother, 21 Sep. 1862. Evans Family, OHS; Henry W. Halleck to Col. B. G. Farrar, 18 Dec. 1861. D. C. Buell to J. R. Underwood, 6 Mar. 1862. GO No. 27. AGO. 21 Mar. 1862. GO No. 26. HQ, Mitchell's Brigade, Central Army of Mississippi. 18 June 1862. GO No. 27. HQ, Dept. of the South. 19 Aug. 1862. "The Negro," pp. 451–52, 476, 486, 542, 593. RG 94, NA.

11. Stuart to friends at home, 20 Mar. 1863. M. S. Hall Papers, BL, UMI. Also see William to Zetty, 15 Nov. 1862. William Parkinson Papers, EU.

12. Halleck to Grant, 31 Mar. 1863. Berlin, *Freedom*, II, p. 143. Also see Samuel J. Kirkwood to General [Halleck], 5 Aug. 1862. Berlin et al., *Freedom*, II, pp. 85–86; Grant to Colonel Richard Oglesby, 15 Mar. 1862. Q. A. Gillmore to Maj. Gen. Gordon Granger, 11 Dec. 1862, with endorsements; GO No. 9. HQ, 2d Division, Army of Kentucky, 22 Oct. 1862; Q. A. Gillmore to M. R. Keith, 8 Dec. 1862. "The Negro," pp. 482, 692–98. RG 94, NA.

13. Thomas to Stanton, 1 Apr. 1863. "The Negro," p. 1156. RG 94, NA. Also see John A. Andrews to Maj. John A. Bolles, 16 Oct. 1862. "The Negro," pp. 980–82. RG 94, NA.

14. Oliver W. Norton to Sister L, 17 Jan. 1862. Norton, *Army Letters*, pp. 41–42. Also see Norton, *Army Letters*, p. 102; Edw. W. Bacon to Bro, 28 Sep. 1862. Edward W. Bacon Papers, AAS; Jos. J. Scroggs diary, 23 July 1862. CWTIC, MHI; Edward Stanley to Stanton, 12 June 1862. N. H. Swayne to Stanton, 21 July 1862. "The Negro," pp. 517–22, 559. RG 94, NA.

15. Thomas A. Scott to Brig. Gen. Thomas W. Sherman, 14 Oct. 1861. *The War of the Rebellion: A Compilation of the Official Records of the Union and Confederate Armies.* I. vol. 6, p. 176 (hereafter *OR*). Also see Cornish, *The Sable Arm*, pp. 18–21 for an excellent discussion of the entire affair.

16. See Cornish, *The Sable Arm*, pp. 31–55, for a full discussion of the Hunter affair.

17. Militia Act of 17 July 1862. "The Negro," pp. 915–16. RG 94, NA; George Tate to friend Cranston, 29 May 1862. Rudolph Haerle Collection, MHI. Also see Surg. Morris W. Townsend to Maj. Cha. G. Halpine, 14 May 1862. "The Negro," p. 854. RG 94, NA.

18. [Hunter] to Stanton, 23 June 1862. Berlin et al., *Freedom*, II, pp. 50–53.

19. See Cornish, *The Sable Arm*, pp. 69–78, for an excellent discussion of the entire Lane affair. Also see C. P. Buckingham to Hon. Jas. H. Lane, 22 July 1862. "The Negro," pp. 909, 937–39. RG 94, NA; Stanton to Lane, 23 Sep. 1862. *OR*, III, 2, p. 582.

20. Butler to Stanton, 25 May 1862. "The Negro," pp. 859–65. RG 94, NA.

21. See J. W. Phelps to Capt. R. S. Davis, 30 July 1862. Phelps to Butler, 2 Aug. 1862. Berlin et al., *Freedom*, II, pp. 62–65; Butler to Stanton, 18 June 1862. Stanton to Butler, 29 June 1862. Davis to Phelps, 31 July 1862. Phelps to Davis, 31 July 1862. Butler to Phelps, 2 Aug. 1862. "The Negro," pp. 526–28, 547, 920–28. RG 94, NA; Cornish, *The Sable Arm*, pp. 65–68.

22. See Descriptive Books for the 73rd and 74th USCI. RG 94, NA; Joshi and Reidy, " 'To Come Forward,' " pp. 326–27.

23. See Sandburg, *Lincoln: The War Years*, 1, pp. 582–85, and 2, p. 17–18 for a discussion of Lincoln's thoughts and actions surrounding the Emancipation Proclamation. Also see Cox, *Lincoln and Black Freedom*, pp. 11–15.

24. See Sandburg, *Lincoln: The War Years*, 1, pp. 582–85; Stanton to Saxton, 25 Aug. 1862. *OR* I, 14, pp. 377–78.

25. Robt. Kirkshaw to Gov. Yates, 28 Jan. 1863. Maj. A. E. Berey to Lincoln, 18 Feb. 1863. "The Negro," pp. 1103–4 and 1910–11. RG 94, NA. Also see Address of Governors to President Lincoln, 24 Sep. 1862. "The Negro," pp. 614–17 and 1105–6. RG 94, NA; Joseph J. Scroggs diary, 1 Oct. 1862. CWTIC, MHI. Hicken, "The Record of Illinois' Negro Soldiers" discusses the negative reaction to the Emancipation Proclamation in Illinois units.

26. I am, of course, talking about the armies they supervised in person in the campaigns of Northern Virginia and Atlanta. Technically speaking, Grant was commanding general in the U.S. Army and had charge of more than one million servicemen, and Sherman, commander of the Military Division of the Mississippi, headed hundreds of thousands of men. See Cornish, *The Sable Arm*, pp. 205–6; GO No. 143. 22 May 1863. GO No. 144. 22 May 1863. WD. *OR* III, 3, pp. 215–16; "The Negro," p. 1370. RG 94, NA; *OR* III, 5, p. 138.

CHAPTER 2
The White Man's War

1. George R. Sherman, "The Negro As a Soldier," pp. 7–8.

2. Jeff to Tillie, 28 Sep. 1860. Wise-Clark Family, UIA; Charles F. Adams to H. L. Higginson, [Nov. 1864?]. Perry, *Life and Letters of Henry Lee Higginson*, pp. 235–36. Also see Robert G. Shaw to Minni, 20 Feb. 1863. Robert Gould Shaw Papers, MAHS.

3. Lewis Ledyard Weld to Mother, 24 Sep. [1850]. Lewis Weld Family, YU.

4. Edelstein, *Strange Enthusiasm*, pp. 40–52.

5. Hallowell, *Selected Letters and Papers*, p. 67. Also see Henry C. Corbin, "Reminiscences," p. 13. Henry C. Corbin Papers, LC; Greely, *Reminiscences of Adventure and Service*, p. 11.

6. Benjamin W. Thompson, "Reminiscences," p. 10. CWTIC, MHI; Warren Olney, "Nagging the South," a paper read before the California Commandery of the Military Order of the Loyal Legion of the United States, November 20, 1896, p. 4.

7. See CSR for Lark S. Livermore, 16th Wisconsin Infantry and 5th USCHA; James B. Rogers, 14th Wisconsin Infantry and 64th USCI;

James M. Alexander, 66th Illinois Infantry and 55th USCI; Edwin M. Wheelock, 15th New Hampshire Infantry and 76th USCI; and John Eaton, Jr., 27th Ohio Infantry and 63rd USCI. RG 94, NA; T. Montgomery to Parents and Brothers, 7 July 1864. Montgomery Papers, MNHS; Rugoff, *The Beechers: An American Family*, pp. 451–57. Rank, but not pay, was equivalent to a captain.

8. See Appendix 1; Stewart, *Holy Warriors: The Abolitionists and American Slavery*; Sorin, *The New York Abolitionists*; Kraut, "The Forgotten Reformers"; Kraditor, *Means and Ends in American Abolitionism*; Donald, *Lincoln Reconsidered*; Barnes, *The Antislavery Impulse*; Perry, *Radical Abolitionism*; Duberman, *The Antislavery Vanguard*.

9. Tom Hoge to Tillie, 7 Nov. 1860. Wise-Clark Family Papers, UIA. Compared to American society in 1860, there were proportionally more than six times as many teachers in the sample of white officers in the USCT. While it was impossible to determine with accuracy the number of men in the sample who graduated from college, alumni records from a number of schools indicate strong support for the USCT. Among those who attended college, eighty-six matriculated at Harvard, followed by forty-five who went to Yale and thirty-eight to Dartmouth. Smaller numbers came from such liberal arts colleges as Amherst, Union, Brown, Oberlin, Wabash, Princeton, and Ohio Wesleyan, to name just a few.

10. See Appendix 1; Joseph C. G. Kennedy, *Population of the United States in 1860; Compiled From the Original Returns of the Eighth Census*, pp. 656–80.

11. See Appendix 1. Of course, in most cases the military experience forged bonds within the units that were very powerful, even for units recruited in frontier areas. Yet in most cases, too, these bonds were not as tight as they were in commands raised on the local level, where the young men had grown up together.

12. Dela to Mother & Katy, 11 Feb. 1855. R. D. Mussey Papers, Dartmouth College. Also see Lewis L. Weld To Brother, 6 April 1855. Lewis Weld Family, YU; F. Minot Weld to Miss Adie, 23 Sep. 1860. Blake, *Diaries and Letters of Francis Minot Weld*, p. 82; James Brisbin, U.S. Army Generals' Reports of Civil War Service, 1864–1887. RG 94, NA; David Cornwell memoir, "Dan Caverno," p. 6, CWMC, MHI.

13. *Memorial of Colonel John A. Bross, Twenty-Ninth U.S. Colored Troops*, p. 9; Jeff to Tillie, 28 Sep. 1860 and 25 Nov. 1860. Wise-Clark Family Papers, UIA. Also see Samuel D. Barnes diary, 3 Jun. 1860. CWM, LC; McMurray, *Recollections of a Colored Troop*, p. 8.

14. John A. Wilder, "Will the American Experiment Fail?" a commencement speech at Union College, 23 July 1856. Loomis-Wilder Family, YU; Joseph J. Scroggs diary, 1 Jan. 1861. CWTIC, MHI.

15. Charles Francis Adams, Jr., to Father, 10 June 1861. Ford, *A Cycle of Adams Letters, 1861–1865*, 1, p. 10; S. M. Q. to Mother, 31 Jul. 1861. Quincy, Wendell, Holmes and Upham Families Papers, MAHS. Also see Minos Miller to Mother, 20 Aug. 1864. Minos Miller Papers, UAR; W. H. E. to Samuel, 19 Feb. 1862. Andrew Evans to Sam, 9 Mar. 1862. Evans Family Papers, OHS; [Sol Starbird to Sis], 13 July 1862. SC, CL, UMI.

16. James Horrocks to Parents, 20 Oct. 1863, 5 Sep. 1863. Lewis, *My Dear Parents*, pp. 11–22, 23, 37, 39.

17. William Spurgin to the President of the Confederate States of America,

   2 Apr. 1861. Confederate Papers Relating to Citizens or Business Firms.
   Citizen File: Spurgin, William F. RG 109, NA. Thanks to my friends
   at the Jefferson Davis Papers for pointing it out to me.

18. John to Brother & Sister, 17 Nov. 1861. John L. Mathews Papers,
    IASHS. Also see Jn. L. Mathews to Friend, 22 Dec. 1861. John L.
    Mathews Papers, IASHS.

19. Frank to Father, 22 Feb. 1862. Frank Harding Papers, SHSW; N. T.
    Kirk to Robert Crouse, 24 Oct. 1862. Robert Crouse Papers, BL, UMI.
    Also see John to Sister, 23 Oct. [1861]. John L. Mathews Papers, IASHS;
    C. Riggs to Brother, 8 Sep. [1861]. Charles R. Riggs, IASHS.

20. T. W. Hopes to Father & Mother, 12 Oct. 1863. Thomas W. Hopes
    Pension File, RG 15, NA. Also see Charles R. Riggs to Brother, 17
    Nov. 1861. Charles R. Riggs Papers, IASHS.

21. C. P. Lyman to ones at Home, 13 Feb. 1862. Lyman Papers, WRHS;
    Jeff to Aunt Tillie, 4 Jan. 1863. Wise-Clark Family Papers, UIA. Also
    see Samuel Miller Quincy to Sir, 9 May 1862. Quincy, Wendell, Holmes
    and Upham Families, MAHS; Sam to Father & Mother, 16 Mar. 1862.
    Evans Family Papers, OHS; Henry to Parents & all, 22 Dec. [1863].
    Henry M. Crydenwise Papers, EU.

22. Walter Chapman to Parents, 3 June [1863]. Walter A. Chapman Papers,
    YU; Frank D. Harding to Father, 14 June 1863. Frank Harding Papers,
    SHSW; Sam Evans to father and mother, 24 May 1862. Evans Family
    Papers, OHS; George Tate to Cranston, 16 Jul. [1862]. Rudolph Haerle
    Collection, MHI.

23. S. M. Quincy to Mary Jane, 1 June 1862. Quincy, Wendell, Holmes
    and Upham Family Papers, MAHS; James [Horrocks] to Parents, 17
    May 1864. Lewis, *My Dear Parents*, p. 79; David Torrance, "Two Trips
    to Richmond," in Frederick Chesson Folder, CWTIC, MHI.

24. Sam E. to father, [10 Apr. 1862]. Evans Family Papers, OHS. Also see
    Appendix 1.

25. Greely, *Adventures*, p. 88. Also see James to Parents, 9 Jan. 1864[5].
    Lewis, *My Dear Parents*, p. 115; [W. Goodale] to Children, 7 May 1865.
    Warren Goodale Papers, MAHS; Sam Evans to father, 1 May 1862.
    Evans Family Papers, OHS; Thomas Hopes to Sister, 23 Sep. 1862.
    Thomas Hopes Papers, OHS.

26. David Torrance, "Two Trips to Richmond," in Frederick Chesson Folder,
    CWTIC, MHI; T. J. Hoge to Aunt Tillie, 12 Nov. 1862. Wise-Clark Family
    Papers, UIA; Thomas Hopes to Sister, 23 Sep. 1862. Thomas W. Hopes
    Papers, OHS.

27. William to [Sarah?], 15 Apr. 1862. William H. Parkinson Papers, EU.

28. Norton, *Army Life*, p. 95. Also see J. B. Evans to Father, 10 Apr. [1862].
    Evans Family Papers, OHS.

29. Frank Holsinger, "How Does One Feel Under Fire?," *MOLLUS-Kansas*,
    p. 294.

30. T. J. Hoge to Aunt Tillie, 6 Nov. 1862. Wise-Clark Family Papers, UIA.
    Also see Appendix 1; "Military Record of George R. Sherman, Corporal,
    82 New York Infantry." George R. Sherman Papers, RIHS; T. J. Hoge
    to Parents, 16 Oct. [1862]. Wise-Clark Family Papers, UIA.

31. Richard C. Phillips to Friend Rhoda, 15 Aug. 1863. Phillips and Par-
    segian, *Richard and Rhoda*, p. 33; Rogers, *War Pictures*, pp. 46—49.

Medical school diplomas were not mandatory for posts as army doctors during the war.

32. H. H. Hood to Wife, 9 Jan. 1863. Humphrey H. Hood Papers, ILSHL.

33. George [Gaskill] to Sister, 10 May 1862. Spanish-American War Survey, Civil War File, MHI; [J. H. Meteer] to Prof, 14 Oct. 1863. Caleb Mills Papers, INHS; Stuart Hall to Sister Emma, 30 Jan. 1864. M. S. Hall Papers, BL, UMI.

34. Lawrence Van Alstyne diary, 11 Aug. 1863. Van Alstyne, *Diary of an Enlisted Man*, p. 165. Also see Lawrence Van Alstyne diary, 22 Aug. 1863. Van Alstyne, *Diary of an Enlisted Man*, p. 169.

35. Sam to father, 7 Jun. 1863. Evans Family Papers, OHS.

36. Walter Chapman to Brother, 19 Aug. 1863. Walter Chapman Papers, YU.

37. J. Pierson to Wife, [10 Jun. 1862]. SC, CL, UMI; Danl. to Brother Ben, 13 Dec. 1863. Densmore Family Papers, MNHS; George Tate to friend & School-mate, 20 Dec. 1861. Rudolph Haerle Collection, MHI.

38. Frank to Father, 13 Jul. 1863. Frank Harding Papers, SHSW.

39. Sol [Starbird] to Sister, 23 Jan. 1863. SC, CL, UMI; Minos Miller to Mother, 24 Jan. 1863. Minos Miller Papers, UAR; Hen [Marshall] to Hattie, 13 Dec. [1863]. SC, CL, UMI. Also see Gus to Wife, 4 Jan. 1863. Charles Augustus Hill Papers, Richard S. Tracy Collection; George Tate to Cranston, 12 Feb. 1864. Rudolph Haerle Collection, MHI; C. P. Lyman to Brother Howard, 25 Dec. 1863. Carlos P. Lyman Papers, WRHS; John Pierson to Wife, 8 July and 13 Sep. 1862. SC, CL, UMI; S. E. to father, 21 Feb. 1863. Evans Family Papers, OHS; George W. Grubbs Memorandum, 4 Mar. 1864. George W. Grubbs Papers, INHS; Walter Chapman to Parents, 28 Dec. 1863. Walter Chapman Papers, YU; Frank to Father, 13 July 1863. Frank Harding Papers, SHSW; Jeff to Tillie, 22 Feb. 1863. Wise-Clark Family, UIA.

40. John Pierson to Wife, 11 Aug. 1862. SC, CL, UMI. Also see John Pierson to Wife, 8 Aug. 1862. SC, CL, UMI; H. H. Hood to Wife, 27 Apr. 1863. Humphrey H. Hood Papers, ILSHL.

41. Minos Miller to Mother, 30 June 1862. Minos Miller Papers, UAR. Also see Walter Chapman to Brother, 18 Aug. 1863. Walter Chapman Papers, YU; George W. Grubbs Memorandum, 2 Mar. 1864 and diary, 24 May 1864. George W. Grubbs Papers, INHS; John Pierson to Daughter, 21 May 1864. SC, CL, UMI; Sam to father, 6 Dec. 1862. Evans Family Papers, OHS; E. C. D. Robbins to Father & Mother, 11 Nov. 1862 and 22 Feb. 1863. Edward C. D. Robbins Pension File, RG 15, NA. Initially, the destruction disgusted many of the future officers in the USCT. It is interesting to see the gradual shift over the war years. See Glatthaar, *The March to the Sea*, for a discussion of destruction on a massive scale.

42. William Reed to [Thomas McCleary], 20 Feb. 1863. William Reed Papers, Iowa State Historical Department; William to ?, 24 Feb. 1863. William Parkinson Papers, EU.

43. C. P. Lyman to Father, 2 Jan. 1863. Carlos P. Lyman Papers, WRHS; Madison [Bowler] to Wife, 9 Oct. 1863. Bowler Papers, MNHS. Also see Palemon Smalley, "Dad's Memoirs," p. 47. Smalley Papers, MNHS; Hen [Marshall] to Hattie, 1 Mar. 1863. SC, CL, UMI; George E. Suther-

land, *MOLLUS-Wisconsin*, I, p. 173; Rufus Kinsley diary, 3 Oct. 1862, 1 Jan. 1863. Rufus Kinsley Papers, VTHS.

44. See Sutherland, "The Negro in the Late War," p. 169.

45. John Pierson to Wife & Daughter, 16 Aug. 1862 and John Pierson to Daughter, 15 Mar. 1863. SC, CL, UMI. Also see GO, No. 7. HQ, Ullmann. 10 June 1863. "The Negro," p. 1316. RG 94, NA.

46. Halleck to Grant, 31 Mar. 1863. Berlin et al., *Freedom*, II, p. 144; Sam to father, 8 Feb. 1863. Evans Family Papers, OHS; Robert Cowden, *59th USCI*, p. 177. Also see Maj. Gen. Samuel Curtis to Brig. Gen. E. A. Carr, 21 Oct. 1862. "The Negro," p. 985. RG 94, NA; Sol [Starbird] to Sister, 28 Sep. 1862. SC, CL, UMI; H. H. Hood to Wife, [6 Jan. 1863]. Humphrey H. Hood Papers, ILSHL; Edwin M. Main, *3rd USCC*, p. 5.

47. Oliver W. Norton to Cousin L, 28 Jan. 1862. Norton, *Army Letters*, p. 43; Henry to Parents and all, 19 Aug. 1862. Henry Crydenwise Papers, EU; J. H. Meteer to Prof., 20 Oct. 1862. Caleb Mills Papers, INHS. Also see Edward W. Bacon to Father, 30 Apr. 1862. Edward W. Bacon Papers, AAS; John Pierson to Wife, 8 Aug. 1862. SC, CL, UMI.

48. Henry to Parents and all, 5 Feb. 1862. Henry M. Crydenwise Papers, EU; H. H. Hood to Wife, 10 Jan. 1863. Humphrey H. Hood Papers, ILSHL. Also see H. H. Hood to Wife, 19 Nov. 1862, 16 Dec. 1862. Humphrey H. Hood Papers, ILSHL; John Pierson to Wife, 11 Aug. 1862. SC, CL, UMI; Sam Evans to Grand Mother, 25 Jul. 1862. Evans Family Papers, OHS; Frank Harding to Father, 17 Sep. 1862. Frank Harding Papers, SHSW; Henry to Parents and all, 19 Aug. 1862. Henry Crydenwise Papers, EU; Danl. to Father, 28 Jan. 1864. Densmore Family, MNHS.

49. Jeff to Tillie, 25 Mar. 1864. Wise-Clark Family Papers, UIA; John Pierson to Wife, 19 Jan. 1864. SC, CL, UMI. Also see H. H. Hood to Wife, 16 Apr. 1863. Humphrey H. Hood Papers, ILSHL.

50. Sam to father, 17 May 1863. Evans Family Papers, OHS; L. C. Drake, "Reminiscence," p. 6. L. C. Drake Papers, BL, UMI; Jeff to Tillie, 6 Feb. 1863. Wise-Clark Family Papers, UIA. Also see Wm. Winthrop to F. W. Seward, Esq., 25 Aug. 1863. "The Negro," pp. 1528–30. RG 94, NA; Wm. A. Jones to Cameron, 27 Nov. 1861. Berlin et al., *Freedom*, II, pp. 80–81.

51. Hen [Marshall] to Hattie, 12 June 1863. SC, CL, UMI; Lawrence Van Alstyne diary, 4 Apr. 1863. Van Alstyne, *Diary of an Enlisted Man*, p. 96; Henry to Bro, 17 June 1863 (this was his first mention of blacks). Henry Burrell Papers, MHI. Also see Papa to Children, 10 Nov. 1864 and 27 Nov. 1864. Warren Goodale Papers, MAHS; John Pierson to Wife & Daughter, 13 Sep. 1863. SC, CL, UMI.

52. Andrew J. McGarrah to Parents, 8 Mar. 1863. Andrew J. McGarrah Papers, INHS; George L. Stearns to Gov. Andrew, 3 Apr. 1863. "The Negro," p. 1163. RG 94, NA. Also see Walter Chapman to Brother, 24 Dec. [1862]. Walter Chapman Papers, YU; Chas. F. Stinson to Mother, 3 Mar. 1863. Michael P. Musick Collection, MHI; H. H. Hood to Wife, 4 July 1863. Humphrey H. Hood Papers, ILSHL; Cous. Adam to Cousin Sam, 22 Feb. 1864. Sam Bloomer Papers, MNHS; Henry to Parents & all, 22 Dec. [1863]. Henry Crydenwise Papers, EU; Glatthaar, *The March to the Sea*, p. 52.

53. J. H. Meteer to Proff, 10 Feb. [18]64. Caleb Mills Papers, INHS.

CHAPTER 3
Recruiting the Officers

1. See Banks to Thomas, 12 Feb. 1863. *OR* III, 3, p. 46; Banks to Lincoln, 17 Aug. 1863. *OR* I, 26, Pt. 1, p. 688–89.

2. Hunter to Gen. I. I. Stevens, 8 Mar. 1862. "The Negro," pp. 844–45, RG 94, NA. The Fessenden Papers are at Bowdoin College and cover his experiences with this black unit. Also see GO No. 99. Dept. of the South. 6 Mar. 1863. "The Negro," pp. 1120–21. RG 94, NA.

3. Testimony of Col. Thomas Wentworth Higginson before the American Freedmen's Inquiry Commission (AFIC). "The Negro," p. 2553. RG 94, NA. For the establishment and purpose of the commission, see Stanton to Robert Dale Owen, James McKaye and Samuel G. Howe, 16 Mar. 1863. *OR* III, 3, pp. 73–74. Their report is in *OR* III, 3, pp. 430–54. Field officers are colonels, lieutenant colonels, and majors.

4. For a roster of officers in the 33rd U.S. Colored Infantry, see Higginson, *Army Life in a Black Regiment*, pp. 269–72. Also see Ullmann to Maj. Thomas A. Vincent, 27 Jan. 1863. "The Negro," pp. 1079–80. RG 94, NA.

5. [Gov. Andrew] to Francis G. Shaw, 30 Jan. 1863. Emilio, *A Brave Black Regiment*, pp. 3–5.

6. Cornish, *The Sable Arm*, pp. 112–15, provides a good description of the dealings of Stanton and Thomas. Also see Thomas to Stanton, 5 Oct. 1865. *OR* III, 5, pp. 118–24 and Stanton to Thomas, 25 Mar. 1863. *OR* III, 3, pp. 100–101.

7. See David Cornwell's memoir, "Dan Caverno," p. 117. CWMC, MHI; William to Sarah, 13 Apr. 1863. William H. Parkinson Papers, EU; Thomas to Stanton, 9 Apr. 1863 and 12 Apr. 1863. *OR* III, 3, p. 121. According to Thomas, Logan spoke eloquently for the policy too.

8. See Thomas to Maj. Gen. Fred. Steele, 15 Apr. 1863. "The Negro," p. 1187. RG 94, NA; Cornish, *The Sable Arm*, pp. 205–6; GO No. 143. 22 May 1863. GO No. 144. 22 May 1863. WD. *OR* III, 3, pp. 215–16; "The Negro," p. 1370. RG 94, NA; Chetlain, *Recollections After Seventy Years*, p. 101.

9. Thomas to Rosecrans, 15 June 1863. Circular. HQ, Com'r Org'n U.S. Colored Troops, 15 Feb. 1864. "The Negro," pp. 1324, 2383. RG 94, NA; GO, No. 24. 12 Dec. 1864. Brig. Gen. A. L. Chetlain in Williams, *A History of the Negro Troops*, p. 126. Also see Thomas to J. M. Schofield, 5 Aug. 1863. C. W. Foster to Brig. Gen. E. R. S. Canby, 29 Apr. 1864. "The Negro," pp. 1468, 2501. RG 94, NA.

10. Alfred to Caroline, 11 Aug. 1863. Alfred M. Brigham Papers, EU; L. Grim to Aunt Tillie, 27 June 1864. Wise-Clark Family Papers, UIA; Henry to Parents & all, 31 Jan. 1864. Henry M. Crydenwise Papers, EU. Also see John P. Hawkins to Caleb Mills, 12 Nov. 1863. Caleb Mills Papers, INHS.

11. Henry to Parents & all, 28 Nov. 1863. Henry Crydenwise Papers, EU. Also see James to Father, 27 Apr. 1863. James to Father, [July 1863]. Tarbox, *Memoirs of James H. Schneider*, pp. 102–4, 117, 121; CMSR of Lark S. Livermore, 16th Wisconsin Infantry and Chaplain John Eaton, 27th Ohio Infantry. RG 94, NA; W. Goodale to Bro. David, 21 Feb. 1865. Warren Goodale Papers, MAHS.

12. Blake, *Diaries and Letters of Francis Minot Weld*, p. 150; Jas. Rogers to ?, 11 Jan. 1863. Jas. Rogers to ?, 24 May 1863. SSC, Smith College.

13. Joseph J. Scroggs diary, 19 Oct. 1863. CWTIC, MHI; Sam to Brother, 9 Jun. 1863. Evans Family Papers, OHS. Also see Dew. W. Bacon to Dr. Father, 17 Aug. 1862. Edward W. Bacon Papers, AAS; Col. Edward McCook to Stanton, 3 June 1863. "The Negro," pp. 1285–87. RG 94, NA; Saml. Duncan to ?, 30 July 1863. Duncan-Jones Papers, NHHS.

14. See William Baird, "Reminiscences," p. 9. William Baird Papers, BL, UMI; W. Goodale to Mrs. Chamberlain, 27 Sep. 1864 and Warren to Bro. David, 5 Nov. 1864. Warren Goodale Papers, MAHS. Survey the diary of Albert Rogall, Albert Rogall Papers, OHS, for someone who sought a commission in the USCT purely for promotion and it turned out to be a terrible experience.

15. Walter Chapman to Parents, 10 Mar. [1863]. Walter Chapman Papers, YU; Oliver W. Norton to Sister L, 15 Oct. 1863. Norton, *Army Letters*, p. 183. Also see Solomon [Starbird] to Sister, 12 Aug. 1862. SC, CL, UMI; Stuart to Sister Emma, 9 Mar. 1864. M. S. Hall Papers, BL, UMI; C. F. Stinson to Mother, 16 June 1863. Michael P. Musick Collection, MHI; Henry to Brother Louis, 30 Jan. 1862. Henry Burrell Papers, MHI. One soldier, George Gaskill, turned down two offers of commissions. George to Mary, 24 Sep. [1862] and Geo. Lee to Sister, 10 Nov. 1863. Spanish-American War Survey, Civil War Folder, MHI.

16. David Cornwell memoir, "Dan Caverno," p. 120. CWMC, MHI. Also see Bowley, *A Boy Lieutenant*, pp. 14–15; Jamie to Father and Mother, 17 Jan. and 19 Nov. 1864 and 24 Feb. [1865]. Lewis, *My Dear Parents*, pp. 61–62, 107, 125; Palemon Smalley, "Dad's Memoirs," p. 94. Smalley Papers, MNHS.

17. See Wm. R. Stuckey to Wife, 4 July 1864. William R. Stuckey Papers, INHS; Duren Kelley to Emma, 15 Feb. 1864. Offenberg and Parsonage, *Letters of Duren F. Kelley*, pp. 91–92.

18. Henry to Parents & all, 22 Dec. [1863]. Henry M. Crydenwise Papers, EU. Also see Jocelyn, *Mostly Alkili*, p. 12; Benjamin Thompson, "Reminiscences," p. 55. CWTIC, MHI.

19. According to the sample of nearly four hundred white officers in the USCT, one-half of them had just such experience. Hen [Marshall] to Ones at Home, 4 Nov. [1863]. SC, CL, UMI. Also see Appendix 1; M. H. Twitchell, "Reminiscence," pp. 57, 62, 69. Marshall H. Twitchell Papers, VTHS; George Tate to Cranston, 27 June 1864. Rudolph Haerle Collection, MHI; Frank to Father, 24 Aug. 1862 and 18 Dec. 1862. Frank Harding Papers, SHSW; Sol to Bro. Geo., 9 Dec. 1862. SC, CL, UMI; Walter Chapman to Brother, 27 Jan. [1864]. Walter Chapman Papers, YU.

20. Lieut. Chas. A. Ball to Adjutant General, 15 July 1863. Lieut. Glenn Lowe to General, 25 July 1863. M. K. Taylor, Surgeon to General, 31 July 1863. Deane Papers, AHC; Petition to Brig. Gen. W. S. Smith, 17 May 1863. Charles R. Riggs Papers, IASHS. Also see Applications for Commissions in the Colored Units, AGO. RG 94, NA; Letter of Recommendation for Commanding a Colored Unit, June 1863. Densmore Papers, MNHS; GO No. 26. HQ, Dept. of the Missouri. 18 Feb. 1864.

"The Negro," pp. 2383–84. RG 94, NA; [Col. Montgomery] to Maj. Foster, 27 Feb. 1864. Montgomery Papers, KASHS.

21. George N. Albee to Stanton, 6 Mar. 1863. Walter H. Angell to Stanton, 26 May 1863. Applications for Commission in Colored Units, AGO. RG 94, NA. Also see Capt. Richard Ballinger to General, 25 Apr. 1863. CMSR of Richard H. Ballinger, 3rd Illinois Cavalry. RG 94, NA.

22. Hen [Marshall] to Folks at Home, 29 Nov. 1863. SC, CL, UMI; GO No. 26. HQ, Dept. of the Missouri. 18 Feb. 1864. "The Negro," pp. 2383–84. RG 94, NA; George W. Allen to Gen. Casey, 27 May 1863, plus endorsements. Applications for Commissions in the Colored Units, AGO. RG 94, NA.

23. Application of Baron Engelbert de Brackel. Applications for Commissions in the Colored Units, AGO. RG 94, NA. Also see Application of Frank J. Dobie. Applications for Commissions in the Colored Units, AGO. CMSR of Edelmiro Mayer, 4th USCI, 7th USCI, 45th USCI. RG 94, NA.

24. W. R. Porter to [Adjutant General], 1 June 1863. Application for Commissions in Colored Units, AGO. RG 94, NA; Col. William Birney to President of the Board of Examiners, 11 Sep. 1863, with enclosure, Theodore D. Weld to Birney and L. Miller McKay, 6 Sep. 1863. Lewis Weld Family, YU. Also see letter of endorsement for Benjamin Densmore, June 1863. Densmore Family Papers, MNHS.

25. 1st Lt. Anselem Hobbs to Lt. N. J. Gilson, 11 June 1864. CMSR of James A. Johnston, Co. B, 11th Indiana Infantry. RG 94, NA. Also see Appendix 1 for USCT officers with drinking problems.

26. See Appendix 1 for venereal disease in USCT. See Coffman, *The Old Army*, for a discussion of venereal disease in the U.S. Army. Also, Dennis Wrynn, formerly of the New York Civil War Round Table, provided me with the CMSR of his ancestor, Sgt. Orville Tuck of the 19th Maine Infantry, who was discharged from the 8th USCI for physical disability, "from a loathsome disease, contracted through his own imprudence," as stated in SO, No. 182. AGO. 20 May 1864.

27. See Benjamin to Brother, 18 Feb. 1864. Densmore Family, MNHS; Lewis to Mason, 25 Sep. 1863. Lewis Weld Family, YU; Sol [Starbird] to Brother George, 29 Jan. 1864. SC, CL, UMI.

28. Danl to Brother, 26 Feb. 1864. Densmore Family, MNHS. Also see Foster to Brig. Gen. J. C. Rice, 24 Nov. 1863. "The Negro," p. 1763. RG 94, NA.

29. See Thomas Webster to Stanton, 22 Apr. 1864 and Stanton to Webster, 21 Mar. 1864. "The Negro," pp. 2495–99, 2450. RG 94, NA; Taggart, *Free Military School; Cornish, The Sable Arm*, pp. 218–21; Wilson, "Thomas Webster."

30. Silas Adams, "My Observations and Service With the Colored Troops," delivered 3 Dec. 1913, p. 3. MOLLUS Collection, MHI. Also see Taggart, *Free Military School*, pp. 18–19; William Baird, "Reminiscences," p. 9. William Baird Papers, BL, UMI; C. P. Lyman diary, 31 Mar.–16 May 1864. Carlos P. Lyman Papers, WRHS; Broadside. Free Military School for Applicants for Command of Colored Troops, CPL.

31. See Samuel Campbell diary, 19 Mar.–11 Apr. 1864. Rudolph Haerle Collection, MHI.

32. William Baird, "Reminiscences," p. 8. William Baird Papers, BL, UMI.

33. See Samuel W. Campbell diary, 12–13 Apr. 1864. Rudolph Haerle Collection, MHI; Broadside. Free Military School for Applicants for Command of Colored Troops, CPL; Wilson, "Thomas Webster," p. 110.

34. See C. P. Lyman to Father, 26 Feb. 1864. Carlos P. Lyman Papers, WRHS; GO No. 125. AGO. 29 Mar. 1864. *OR* III, 4, p. 207.

35. See William Baird, "Reminiscences," pp. 8–9, 37–38, and 41. William Baird Papers, BL, UMI.

36. Cornish, *The Sable Arm*, p. 221. The prospectus lists some information on past graduates, which indicates its Eastern orientation. Western troops do not even mention the existence of the school. There was an examination process to rid the army of incompetent officers but very few appeared before it. See Shannon, *The Organization and Administration of the Union Army*, 1, pp. 186–87.

37. GO No. 144, AGO. 22 May 1863. *OR* III, 3, p. 216.

38. Foster to Maj. Thomas Duncan, 15 Mar. 1864. "The Negro," pp. 2432–33. RG 94, NA.

39. Mussey to Col. R. W. Barnard, Maj. Wm. Inness, & Maj. E. Grosskopff, 3 Nov. 1864. Letters Sent by the Commissioner, Department of the Cumberland, Mar. 1864–Feb. 1865. RG 393, NA.

40. Hen [Marshall] to Ones at Home, 22 Jan. [1864]. SC, CL, UMI. Also see Danl to Benj, 26 Mar. 1864. Densmore Family, MNHS; Samuel W. Campbell diary, 16 Apr. 1864. Rudolph Haerle Collection, MHI.

41. Bowley, *A Boy Lieutenant*, pp. 23–27.

42. Stuart Hall, "Reminiscences," p. 9. M. S. Hall Papers, BL, UMI. Also see Examination of Maj. J. Smith Brown, 126th New York Infantry. Proceedings of the Examining Board, St. Louis, Missouri. RG 94, NA; Silas Adams, "My Observations," p. 4. MOLLUS Collection, MHI; C. P. Lyman to Brother, 4 May 1864. Carlos P. Lyman Papers, WRHS; Joseph J. Scroggs diary, 31 Oct. 1863. CWTIC, MHI; William Baird, "Reminiscences," p. 55. William Baird Papers, BL, UMI.

43. See Examination of James T. Moss, Sergeant, Co. I, Eighty-fifth Infantry. Nashville, 22 Mar. 1864. Proceedings of the Boards of Examination for Commissions in the U.S. Colored Troops, 1863–1864. Departments of Cumberland and Tennessee. RG 393, NA; W. A. Nichols to Brig. Gen. J. C. Caldwell, 8 Apr. 1865. Letters Regarding Recruiting, Division of Colored Troops. RG 94, NA; Report of the Board of Examiners for Officers in U.S. Colored Troops, St. Louis, Missouri. RG 393, NA.

44. Examination of a member of the Mass. Rifle Club before Gen. Casey's Board at Washington. Papers of the 43d USCT, probably Horace Bumstead, BPL. Also see McMurray, *Recollections*, pp. 1–2; J. W. Patterson to Duncan, 7 Aug. 1863. Samuel A. Duncan Papers, Dartmouth College.

45. Examination of George Tinker. Proceedings of the Examining Board, St. Louis, Missouri, 1863–1865, RG 94, NA.

46. Examinations of 1st Lieut. Isaac Gannett and George P. Tinker. Proceedings of the Examining Board, St. Louis, Missouri, 1863–1865. RG 94, NA.

47. Danl to Brother, 26 Feb. 1864. Densmore Family, MNHS.

48. D. O. Van Trump to Editors, *Missouri Democrat*, 6 Mar. 1864. Proceed-

ings of the Examining Board, St. Louis, Missouri, 1863–1865. RG 94, NA. Also see James to [Friend, 1863]. Tarbox, *Memoirs of James H. Schneider*, p. 126.

49. Proceedings of GCM. Trial of Maj. W. S. Long, LL 2999. RG 153, NA.

50. Mussey to Maj. Foster, 16 May 1864. Mussey to Thomas, 18 May 1864. Letters Sent by the Commissioner, Dept. of the Cumberland, Mar. 1864–Feb. 1865. RG 393, NA. Also see Foster to Gov. Yates, 20 June 1864. Letters Regarding Recruiting, Division of Colored Troops. RG 94, NA; Col. Geo. B. Drake to Col. Sypher, President, Board of Examiners, 2 Oct. 1864. "The Negro," pp. 2796–97. RG 94, NA.

51. See Jocelyn, *Mostly Alkili*, p. 26; SO, No. 289. HQ, Dept. of the Missouri. 18 Oct. 1864. Proceedings on the Fitness of Officers of the Volunteer Service, St. Louis, Missouri. RG 393, NA; Silas Adams, "My Observations," p. 4. MOLLUS Collection, MHI.

52. See Report of Maj. Foster, 20 Oct. 1865. *OR* III, 5, pp. 137–40; Military Examining Board at Nashville, Tenn. 4–9 Jan. 1864. Col. C. M. Lum to Capt. Wm. Russell, 5 Sep. 1863. Proceedings of the Board of Examination for Commissions in the Colored Troops for the Departments of the Cumberland and Tennessee. RG 393, NA; Record of the Examining Board at Cincinnati, Ohio, 1–31 Mar. 1864. Proceedings of the Examining Board in Cincinnati, Ohio, 1863–1864. RG 94, NA; Foster to Stanton, 31 Oct. 1863 and Foster to Canby, 29 Apr. 1864. "The Negro," pp. 1719, 2500–501. RG 94, NA.

53. Testimony of Surgeon James Thompson. Proceedings of GCM. Trial of James Thompson. MM 2636. RG 153, NA; Mussey to Brig. Gen. Davis Tillson, 17 May 1864. Letters Sent by the Commissioner, Dept. of Cumberland, Mar. 1864–Feb. 1865. RG 393, NA.

54. Edw. W. Bacon to Kate, 21 June 1864. Edward Woolsey Bacon Papers, AAS; Also see Hen [Marshall] to Hattie, 27 June 1864. Hen to Folks at Home, 5 Mar. 1864. SC, CL, UMI; Examination of W. R. Shafter, lieut. col., 19th Michigan Infantry. Examination of 1st Lieut. Thomas J. Morgan, 70th Indiana Infantry. Proceedings of the Board of Examination for Commissions in the Colored Troops for the Departments of the Cumberland and Tennessee. RG 393, NA.

55. McMurray, *Recollections*, p. 2. Also see Henry Romeyn, "With Colored Troops in the Army of the Cumberland," *MOLLUS-DC*, pp. 5–6. Read at Meeting of 6 Jan. 1904; Benjamin to Brother Daniel, 20 Mar. 1864. Densmore Family Papers, MNHS.

56. See Foster to Banks, 22 June 1864. Foster to Hon. J. Donnelly, 28 June 1864. Letters Regarding Recruiting, Division of Colored Troops, RG 94, NA.

57. Maj. E. F. Dutton to Captain, 7 May 1864. Proceedings of the Board of Examinations for Commissions in the Colored Troops for the Departments of the Cumberland and Tennessee. RG 393, NA.

58. Col. Frank R. Cahill et al. to Maj. C. T. Christensen, 16 Aug. 1864. CMSR. Edward Martindale, 38th USCI. RG 94, NA. Article 12 of SO, No. 17 and 19, Dept. of the Gulf, gave them the authority. Also see Brisbin to L. Thomas, 5 Feb. 1865. Discreet Letters Sent, Feb.–Mar. 1865. USCT. Dept. of Kentucky. RG 393, NA; C. H. Howard to Lizzie, 5 Feb. 1865. O. O. Howard Papers, Bowdoin College; Foster to Maj.

Gen. J. G. Foster, 20 May 1864. GO No. 6. Dept of the South. 14
Jan. 1864. "The Negro," pp. 2593, 3555. RG 94, NA; Mussey to Lt.
O'Neill, 6 Apr. 1864. Mussey to Thomas, 17 May 1864. Mussey to Foster,
15 Feb. 1865. Letters Sent by the Commissioner, Dept. of the Cumber-
land, Mar. 1864–Feb. 1865. RG 393, NA; Sam to Father, 29 May 1864,
31 July 1864. Evans Family Papers, OHS; Jeff to Tillie, 14 Aug. 1864.
Wise-Clark Family Papers, UIA; John Beatty journal, 31 Aug. [1863].
Beatty, *Memoirs of a Volunteer*, pp. 240–41.

59. Mussey to Maj. Foster, 16 May 1864. Letters Sent by the Commissioner,
Dept. of the Cumberland, Mar. 1864–Feb. 1865. RG 393, NA. Also
see Lincoln to Andrew Johnson, 26 Mar. 1863. Stanton to Johnson,
28 Mar. 1863. Foster to Stearns, 13 Aug. 1863. Stanton to Stearns,
16 Sep. 1863. Johnson to Stanton, 17 Sep. 1863. Johnson to Rosecrans,
17 Sep. 1863. Stanton to Johnson, 18 Sep. 1863. Stanton to Stearns,
18 Sep. 1863, Stanton to Johnson and Stearns, 21 Oct. 1863. *OR* III,
3, pp. 103, 105–6, 676, 816–17, 819–20, 823, and 908; SO No. 15.
9 Feb. 1864. Mussey to Foster, 10 Oct. 1864. *OR* III, 4, pp. 90, 762–
64.

60. Edwin Ph to son, 22 Jan. 1864. Rhoda to Richard, 15 Jan. 1864.
Phillips and Parsegian, *Richard and Rhoda*, p. 38; O. Densmore to
Son, 1 Jan. 1865. Densmore Family Papers, MNHS; Henry to Parents
& All, 28 Nov. 1863. Henry M. Crydenwise Papers, EU. Also see Henry
to Parents & All, 22 Dec. [1863] and 31 Jan. 1864. Henry M. Crydenwise
Papers, EU; W. A. Coffut to Friend Marshall, 3 May 1863. Mary A.
Marshall to brother, 29 Apr. 1863. SC, CL, UMI; Wm. Parkinson to
Sarah, 6 May 1863. William Parkinson Papers, EU; Thomas Montgomery
to Parents and Brothers, 23 Jan. 1864. Montgomery Papers, MNHS.

61. Sam Evans to Sister, 13 Oct. 1863. Peet Family Papers, MNHS.

62. Andrew Evans to Son, 18 May 1863. Sam to father, 1 June 1863.
Evans Family Papers, OHS. Also see Amos to Sam, 14 May 1863. Andrew
Evans to Saml. Evans, 7 June 1863. Sam Evans to father, 14 June
1863. Evans Family Papers, OHS.

63. L. Grim to Aunt, 20 July 1864. Wise-Clark Family Papers, UIA. Also
see L. Grim to Aunt, 21 Aug. 1864. Wise-Clark Family Papers, UIA.

64. Alonzo C. Rembaugh to Capt, 28 Feb. 1864. Loomis-Wilder Family Papers, YU. Also see David Cornwell memoir, "Dan Caverno," p. 121.
CWMC, MHI; Hobart, *Semi-History of a Boy Veteran*, pp. 21–2; Sam
to father, 10 May 1863. Evans Family Papers, OHS; Thomas Montgomery
to Parents and Brothers, 23 Jan. 1864. Montgomery Papers, MNHS.

65. See Thompson, *Thirteenth Regiment of New Hampshire*, p. 626. Chester L. Sommers pointed this out to me; Van Alstyne, *Diary of an Enlisted
Man*, p. 173; F. W. Browne, "My Service in the U.S. Colored Cavalry,"
p. 3, CWM, LC; Main, *3rd USCC*, pp. 148–55; SO No. 3. AGO. 7 Apr.
1863. "The Negro," pp. 1177–79. RG 94, NA.

66. Hobart, *Semi-History of a Boy Veteran*, pp. 22–23; Hen [Marshall] to
Folks at Home, 26 Apr. 1863. SC, CL, UMI. Also see Saml. A. Duncan
to [Julia], 6 Sep. 1863. Saml. to Mother, 21 Sep. 1863. Duncan-Jones
Papers, NHHS; Lawrence Van Alstyne diary, 1 Sep. 1863. Van Alstyne,
Diary of an Enlisted Man, p. 174; Henry to Parents & All, 2 Nov.
[1863]. Henry to Charles, 8 Dec. 1863. Henry M. Crydenwise Papers,
EU; M. Miller to Mother, 3 Aug. 1863. Minos Miller Papers, UAR.

67. Testimony of Maj. George Stearns before AFIC. "The Negro," p. 2570. RG 94, NA; Silas Casey to ?, 30 Nov. 1875. Califf, *Record of the Services*, pp. 5–6. Also see R. B. Irwin to Col. Townsend, 10 Mar. 1864. "The Negro," p. 2413. RG 94, NA.

CHAPTER 4
Filling the Ranks

1. Marrs, *Life and History*, pp. 17–20. No information regarding the fate of the minor exists.
2. Botkin, *Lay My Burden Down*, pp. 198–99. Depositions of Richard Patterson and Mrs. Kate Patterson, 18 Sep. 1924. Pension File of Charles Reed, aka Charles Cull. RG 15, NA.
3. Affidavit of Edward Caufy, undated. Pension File of George Ellis. Affidavit of William J. Haynes, 3 Sep. 1907. Pension File of William J. Haynes, RG 15, NA.
4. Discussion in Senate over an Amendment to the Enrollment Act, 12 Jan. 1864. Resolution of the House of Representatives, 1 Feb. 1864. "The Negro," pp. 2322, 2344. RG 94, NA. Also see Thomas Webster to Lincoln, 30 July 1863. Gov. Andrew to Col. Robert G. Shaw, 11 July 1863. Amos A. Lawrence et al. to Stanton, 10 Dec. 1863. Speech of Sen. James W. Grimes of Iowa, 12 Jan. 1864. "The Negro," pp. 1395, 1448, 1804–6, 2321. RG 94, NA.
5. Circular, HQ, U.S. Colored Cavalry. 8 Aug. 1864. Instructions and Reports Sent, Organization of U.S. Colored Cavalry, Department of Kentucky. RG 393, NA. Also see Proceedings of GCM. Trial of James Thompson. MM 2636. RG 153, NA; Thomas to Stanton, 9 Apr. 1863 and 12 Apr. 1863. *OR* III, 3, p. 121.
6. See Stearns to Stanton, 17 Aug. 1863. Berlin et al., *Freedom*, II, p. 100; Public—No. 196. 4 July 1864. Message of the Governor of Massachusetts, John A. Andrew, to the State Legislature, 8 Jan. 1864. "The Negro," pp. 2664, 2311; Lincoln to Sherman, 18 July 1864. *OR* 1, 38, pt. 5, p. 169.
7. See Report of the Provost Marshal General, 15 Nov. 1864. "The Negro," p. 2823. RG 94, NA; *OR* III, 5, p. 138; Thomas to Stanton, 15 June 1864. SFO, No. 16. Mil. Div. of the Mississippi. 3 Jun. 1864. Sherman to Thomas, 26 June 1864. *OR* III, 4, pp. 433–34, 454–55; Sherman to Halleck, 14 July 1864. Lincoln to Sherman, 18 Jul. 1864. *OR* I, 38, pt. 5, pp. 136, 137, 169.
8. Mussey to Major, 6 Aug. 1864. [Mussey] to Mr. McKine, 14 Aug. 1864. Letters Sent by the Commissioner, Department of the Cumberland. RG 393, NA.
9. See Mussey to Lt. George Mason, 11 Apr. 1864. Act of the General Assembly of Maryland, 6 Feb. 1864. "The Negro," pp. 2368–69, 2478–79. RG 94, NA; Maj. Foster to Lt. Col. H. A. Oakman, 18 Apr. 1864. Unbound Letters Received, 45th USCI. RG 94, NA; Saxton to Stanton, 29 Oct. 1862. Col. S. M. Bowman to Maj. Foster, 22 June 1864. Gov. Tod to Stanton, 21 June 1863. Stanton to Tod, 27 June 1863. Tod to Stanton, 14 July 1863. Webster to Stanton, 30 July 1863. Berlin et al., *Freedom*, II, pp. 53–4, 223–26, 370–73. See Table 14, Report of the Provost Marshal General, 17 Mar. 1866, *OR* III, 5, pp. 740–49, for bounties paid by districts and states throughout the war. See Report

of the Provost Marshal General, 17 Mar. 1866, *OR* III, 5, pp. 654–62, for a discussion of various laws that pertained to recruitment and bounties of blacks by the federal government. After the war, an "Act to Place Colored Persons Who Enlisted in the Army on the Same Footing As Other Soldiers As to Bounty and Pension, 3 Mar. 1873," redressed the discrimination. "The Negro," pp. 3825–26. RG 94, NA.

10. See Sherman to Halleck, 14 July 1864. Lincoln to Sherman, 18 July 1864. *OR* I, 38, pt. 5, pp. 136, 137, 169; Thomas to Stanton, 15 June 1864. SFO, No. 16, HDQRS. Mil. Div. of the Mississippi. 3 June 1863. Sherman to Thomas, 26 June 1864. *OR* III, 4, pp. 433–34, 454–55; Capt. Alfred Sears to Lt. Col. Chas. G. Halpine, 3 Apr. 1863. Affidavit of Jacob Forrester. Endorsement by Banks to E. R. S. Canby to letter of S. B. Bevans to Canby, 2 Aug. 1864. Geo. B. Drake to Brig. Gen. T. W. Sherman, 15 Aug. 1864. Berlin et al., *Freedom*, II, pp. 55–57, 57–58, 163, 164; Col. Jos. G. Totten to Thomas, 27 Feb. 1863. GO No. 106. HQ, Dept. of the Gulf. 2 Aug. 1864. "The Negro," pp. 1112–14, 2735. RG 94, NA.

11. Col. T. J. Cram et al. to Maj. Gen. John E. Wool, 20 Mar. 1862. Orders, No. 29. AGO. 15 Dec. 1864. "The Negro," pp. 789 and 2844. RG 94, NA. Also see GO No. 34. 1 Nov. 1861. SO No. 72. 14 Oct. 1861. GO No. 5. 30 Jan. 1862. HQ. Dept. of Virginia. John A. Dix to Stanton, 22 Nov. 1862. Dix to Brig. Gen. Corcoran, 26 Nov. 1862. Stearns to Stanton, 19 Sep. 1863. "The Negro," p. 489, 645–46, 648, 1592. RG 94, NA; Affidavit of Joseph Miller, 26 Nov. 1864. Affidavit of Abisha Scofield, 16 Dec. 1864. T. E. Hall to Major Genl. Howard, 22 Jan. 1865. Berlin et al., *Freedom*, II, pp. 269–71, 715–18.

12. See Chetlain, *Recollections*, pp. 103–4; Stearns to Stanton, 17 Aug. 1863. Berlin et al., *Freedom*, II, p. 100; Jas. Rogers to ?, 24 Apr. 1863. SSC, Smith College; Saxton to Stanton, 29 Oct. 1862. "The Negro," pp. 986–87. RG 94, NA; Mussey to Capt. Geo. B. Halstead, 30 May 1864. Letters Sent by the Commissioner, Dept. of the Cumberland. RG 393, NA; Statement of Armstead Lewis, [Sep. 1863]. Berlin et al., *Freedom*, II, p. 177.

13. See GO No. 60. HQ, District of North Carolina. 1 Sep. 1864. "The Negro," pp. 2760–61. RG 94, NA; Mussey to Lt. C. P. Brown, 28 Sep. 1864. Mussey to Brig. Gen. W. D. Whipple, 1 Nov. 1864. Letters Sent by the Commissioner, Dept. of the Cumberland. RG 393, NA; Proceedings of GCM. Trial of Col. Thomas J. Downey. LL 3193. Trial of Lieut. Col. Cyrus F. Jackson. OO 281. RG 153, NA.

14. Butler to Stanton, 10 Aug. 1864. "The Negro," p. 2742. RG 94, NA. Also see Thomas to Stanton, 5 Sep. 1864. GO No. 90. Dept. of Virginia and North Carolina. 4 Aug. 1864. "The Negro," pp. 2769–70, 2737. RG 94, NA.

15. Duren to Emma, 4 Feb. 1865. Offenberg, *Letters of Duren F. Kelley*, p. 146. Also see Monthly Report of Chap. Geo. W. Carruthers, 51st USCI, 31 Dec. 1864. CWM, LC.

16. See Hugh L. Bond to Stanton, 15 Aug. 1863. Capt. John Frazier, Jr., to Stanton, 21 Sep. 1863. Andrew Johnson to Lincoln, 23 Sep. 1863. Comments by Lincoln, in response to Stanton to Lincoln, 1 Oct. 1863. GO No. 329. AGO. 3 Oct. 1863. Maj. W. Slidell to Brig. Gen. Burbridge, 4 Apr. 1864. Act of 24 Feb. 1864. "The Negro," pp. 1484–90, 1593–94, 1597, 1642–44, 1654–56, 2436–39, 2393. RG 94, NA.

17. James A. Carr to Major L. Wolfey, 18 Mar. 1865. CMSR of Capt. Thomas Bunch, 5th USCC. RG 94, NA.

18. See Col. J. P. Creager to Col. Wm. Birnie, 19 Aug. 1863. Birney to Adjutant General, 20 Aug. 1863. Birney to Foster, 26 Aug. 1863. Foster to Birney, 9 Sep. 1863. In Berlin, *Freedom*, II, pp. 203–5 and "The Negro," pp. 1508–13. RG 94, NA.

19. See Califf, *Record of the Services*, pp. 11–12; Maj. W. H. Slidell to Colonel James B. Fry, 14 Mar. 1864. "The Negro," pp. 2424–27. RG 94, NA. J. Thomas Scharf, who wrote his version in the late nineteenth century, explained it differently in *History of Maryland from Earliest Period to the Present Day*, vol. 3, pp. 571–72.

20. John to Eben, 10 Aug. 1863. Loomis-Wilder Papers, YU. Also see Report on the Death of Lt. Anson L. Sanborn, 11 Jul. 1863. Col. Birney to Adjutant General, 16 July 1863. C. A. Dana to Gideon Wells, 29 Oct. 1864. "The Negro," pp. 1409, 1414, 2812. RG 94, NA; Hen [Marshall] to Mother & Mary, 23 Oct. 1863. SC, CL, UMI.

21. Col. S. M. Bowman to Lt. Col. Lawrence, 11 May 1864. Testimony of Col. Pile before the AFIC. "The Negro," pp. 2530–31, 2577. RG 94, NA.

22. See Capt. James M. Fidler to Brig. Gen. J. B. Fry, 31 May 1864. "The Negro," p. 2600. RG 94, NA; Fidler Historical Report, 15 June 1865. Capt. John L. Bullis to Maj. Gen. Burbridge, 17 Sep. 1864. Berlin, *Freedom*, II, pp. 257–59, 267; Testimony of R. A. Watt, [30 Nov. 1863]. Affidavit of Aaron Mitchell, 4 Jan. 1864. Jeff A. Mayhall to Col. C. W. Marsh, 9 Jan. 1864. Berlin et al., *Freedom*, II, pp. 235–38; Foster to Stanton, 7 June 1864. "The Negro," p. 2604. RG 94, NA.

23. Brig. Gen. Thomas Ewing to Lt. Col. C. W. Marsh, 3 Aug. 1863. Berlin et al., *Freedom*, II, pp. 228–30. Also see Berlin et al., *Freedom*, II, p. 189; Johnson to Lincoln, 17 Sep. 1863. Johnson to Stanton, 17 Sep. 1863. Johnson to Rosecrans, 17 Sep. 1863. Stanton to Johnson, 18 Sep. 1863. *OR* III, 3, pp. 819–20, 823.

24. Wm. A Pile to Rosecrans, 23 Feb. 1864. Martha to My Dear Husband, 30 Dec. 1863. Berlin et al., *Freedom*, II, pp. 244–46. Also see Affidavit of Patsey Leach, 25 Mar. 1865. Capt. A. J. Hubbard to Pile, 6 Feb. 1864. H. G. Moses to Stanton, 1 Apr. 1865. Berlin et al., *Freedom*, II, pp. 268–69, 687–88, 696.

25. Capt. Louis F. Green to Alexander Calhoun, 14 Feb. 1864. Odon Guitar Papers, WHMC-SHSMO. Also see GO No. 35. HQ, Dept. of the Missouri. 1 Mar. 1864. Capt. John Gould to Sec. of War, 21 Jan. 1864. S. S. Burdett to Rosecrans, 9 Feb. 1864. "The Negro," pp. 2398, 2332–35. RG 94, NA; Pile to Maj. O. D. Greene, 11 Feb. 1864. Lt. William P. Deming to Pile, 1 Feb. 1864. Berlin et al., *Freedom*, II, pp. 242–43.

26. Jeff to Tillie, 24 May [1864]. Wise-Clark Family Papers, UIA. Also see Statement of Joseph L. Coppoc, 18 July 1863. Berlin et al., *Freedom*, II, p. 149; Christian A. Fleetwood to Dr. James Hall, 8 June 1865. Carter G. Woodson Papers, LC.

27. B. F. Randolph to E. D. Townsend, 1 Nov. 1864. 972 R 1864. Letters Received, AGO. RG 94, NA; Post, *Soldiers' Letters*, p. 421. Calculations were made from Report of Maj. Foster, 20 Oct. 1865, in *OR* III, 5, p. 138, and *Eighth U.S. Census for 1860*, p. xiii.

28. Supervisory Committee on Colored Enlistments, 27 June 1863. OHS.

Later, the War Department ruled that because of unequal pay, blacks could not serve as substitutes for whites, and this provided impetus for the equalization of pay.

29. Foster to Lt. Col. Louis Wagner, 7 Oct. 1864. "The Negro," p. 2798. RG 94, NA; Higginson to [William Brown?], 26 Dec. 1862. Thomas W. Higginson Papers, AAS. Also see Ullmann to Gov. Andrew, 28 Feb. 1863. Stanton to Stearns, 16 Sep. 1863. Stearns to Foster, 26 Sep. 1863. Geo. Bliss, Jr., to Stanton, 4 Jan. 1864. L. Noble, Adjutant General of Indiana to Brig. Gen. Fry, 4 Sep. 1864. "The Negro," pp. 1115–16, 1581–82, 1611, 2307, 2768. RG 94, NA.

30. See Califf, *Record of the Services*, pp. 9–11; SO, No. 22. HQ, 115th USCI. 2 Sep. 1864. Myron E. Billings Papers, University of Kentucky; Madison to Lizzie, 17 June 1864. J. M. Bowler Papers, MNHS.

31. Henry Whitney journal, 22 May 1864. Whitney Family Papers, Rutgers U. Also see William D. Matthews to Hon. James H. Lane, 12 Jan. 1863. Berlin et al., *Freedom*, II, pp. 69–70. James Rogers performed a daring rescue of two runaways in a dugout canoe as some twenty Confederate cavalrymen fired at them. This must have won him tremendous respect within the unit. Jas. Rogers to ?, 10 May 1863. SSC, Smith College.

32. See Thomas to Col. S. M. Bowman, 27 July 1864. J. Holt to Stanton, 28 July 1864. "The Negro," pp. 2719–20. RG 94, NA; Lt. Robt. M. Campbell to Col. H. Scofield, 18 July 1863. C. T. Buddeck to Banks, [5] Aug. [1863]. Berlin et al., *Freedom*, II, pp. 148–50; Higginson, *Army Life*, p. 173.

33. *The Colored Citizen*, 7 Nov. 1863. U. of Cincinnati, and McPherson, *The Negro's Civil War*, pp. 205–6.

34. James Rogers to ?, 6 Jan. 1865. James Rogers to ?, 24 Apr. 1863. SSC, Smith College; Dr. Seth Rogers to ?, 27 May 1863. MOLLUS Collection, MHI. Also see Capt. Geo. G. Davis to Brig. Gen. James Bowen, 21 Aug. 1863. Berlin et al., *Freedom*, II, p. 157.

35. Sherman to Thomas, 26 June 1864. *OR* III, 4, pp. 454–55. Also see Sgt. Joseph J. Harris to Gen. Ullman, 27 Dec. 1864. Pvt. Aaron Oats to Stanton, 26 Jan. 1865 with enclosures. Brig. Gen. A. Schimmelfennig to Capt. W. L. M. Burger, 2 June 1864. GO No. 46. Commander of the Dept. of Virginia and North Carolina. 5 Dec. 1863. Berlin et al., *Freedom*, II, pp. 691–94, 397–98, 135–36; Col. S. M. Bowman to Lieut. Col. Lawrence, 6 June 1864. "The Negro," p. 2542. RG 94, NA.

36. J. O. Halsey to E. B. Paine, Esq., 10 Dec. 1864. Wm. S. Studley, *Final Memorials of Major Joseph Warren Paine*, p. 15. Also see Butler to John T. Dent, 22 Mar. 1864. Col. James Montgomery to Brig. Gen. J. B. Hatch, 2 May 1864. "The Negro," pp. 2451–53, 2525–28. RG 94, NA; Montgomery to Sen. Wilson, 22 Jan. 1864. Montgomery Papers, KASHS; Higginson, *Army Life*, p. 184; "Obituary of Maj. Joseph W. Paine" by Col. J. G. Wilson in Studley, *Final Memorials*, p. 18; Jas. to Wife, 14 Feb. 1864, and Jas. to H., 24 Feb. 1864. Peet Family Papers, MNHS.

37. David Cornwell memoir, "Dan Caverno," pp. 123–24. CWMC, MHI; Madison Bowler, "Reminiscences," p. 19. James M. Bowler Papers, MNHS; [William] to Wife, 17 May 1863. William Parkinson Papers, EU. Also see Stanton to Stearns, 10 Nov. 1863. GO No. 6. HQ, Dept. of the Ohio. 6 Jan. 1864. "The Negro," pp. 1732, 2306. RG 94, NA; Jane

Wallis to Prof. Woodburry, [10 Dec. 1863]. H. S. Beals to Butler, 10 Dec. 1863. Statement of John Banks, 2 Jan. 1864. P. F. Mancosas to Banks, 7 Aug. 1863. Berlin et al., *Freedom*, II, pp. 138–39, 140, 152. Maj. Davidson to Lt. Col. W. A. Gage, 31 Oct. 1864. Letters Sent. Sep. 1864 to Mar. 1865. USCT. Dept. of Kentucky. RG 393, NA; GO No. 106. HQ, Dept. of the Gulf. 2 Aug. 1864, CPL.

38. Inspection Report of Milliken's Bend, Vidalia, and Bullet's Bayou, Aug. 1865, by First Lt. Charles Robinett. Letters Received, IGO, RG 159, NA. Also see P. W. Bruce to General, 23 Feb. 1865. Ben Warfield to General Brisbin, 21 Feb. 1865. Letters Received, 119th USCI. RG 94, NA; Sam to father, 22 Nov. 1863. Evans Family Papers, OHS; Duren to Emma, 4 Feb. 1865. Offenberg, *Letters of Duren F. Kelley*, p. 146. Letters Received Regarding Recruiting, Bureau of Colored Troops. RG 94, NA, are filled with examples. Col. James Brisbin adopted the Regular Army practice of holding the recruiting officer and original examining physician financially responsible for government expenses in these types of cases. See Circular. HQ, U.S. Colored Cavalry. 8 Aug. 1864. Instructions and Reports Sent. Organization of USCC, Dept. of Kentucky. RG 393, NA.

39. George Johnson of Mississippi. Substitute Book of Drafted Men, Illinois, Sep. 1864. Charles Smith of Mississippi and Joseph Haskel of South Carolina. Medical Exams of Recruits and Substitutes, 13th District, Illinois. RG 110, NA. Also see Medical Exams of Substitutes, 12th District, Illinois. Medical Exams of Recruits and Substitutes, 12th District, Illinois. RG 110, NA.

40. Lawrence Van Alstyne diary, 6 Nov. 1863. Van Alstyne, *Diary of an Enlisted Man*, pp. 213–14; H. H. Hood to Wife, 4 May, 1 July, 16 July 1863. Humphrey H. Hood Papers, ILSHL.

41. H. H. Hood to Wife, 1 July 1863. Humphrey H. Hood Papers, ILSHL; Henry to Parents & all, 28 Sep. 1864. EU. Also see Hallowell, "The Negro as a Soldier," in *Selected Letters*, p. 27; CMSR of David Briggs, Company G, 39th USCI. RG 94, NA.

42. Jeff to Tillie, 31 July 1864. Wise-Clark Family Papers, UIA. Also see Thomas Montgomery to Parents and Brothers, 23 Jan. 1864. Montgomery Papers, MNHS.

43. The quotation is the author's. See [Capt. Benjamin Densmore] to Capt. Chas. E. Howe, 25 Dec. 1865. Densmore Family Papers, MNHS; John Habberton diary, 12 Feb. 1864. John Habberton Papers, MHI; H. H. Hood to Wife, 30 Apr. 1863. Humphrey H. Hood Papers, ILSHL; James Rogers to ?, 24 Apr. 1863. SSC, Smith College.

44. Cowden, *59th USCI*, p. 45; Quoted in Litwack, *Been in the Storm So Long*, p. 101.

45. Quoted in Cimprich, *Slavery's End*, p. 90; Marrs, *Life and History*, p. 22; Silas Adams, "My Observations and Service with the Colored Troops," del. 3 Dec. 1913. MOLLUS Collection, MHI.

46. John W. Pratt to Sir, 30 Nov. 1864. *Christian Recorder*, 24 Dec. 1864; Quoted from a letter from Alexander Atwood to his partner, n.d., in Obituary of Sgt. Alexander Atwood. *Christian Recorder*, 4 Nov. 1865; Jas. C. Beecher to [Frankie, July-Aug. 1863?]. Beecher Family Papers, Stowe-Day Library.

47. John Habberton diary, 12 Feb. 1864. John Habberton Papers, MHI.

CHAPTER 5
Coping with Racism

1. [Gus] to Sister Bine, 15 Oct. 1864. Charles Augustus Hill Papers, Richard S. Tracy Collection; C. P. Lyman to Sister Celia, 12 Feb. 1865. Carlos P. Lyman Papers, WRHS; J. O. Moore to Lizzie, 25 Sept. 1864. James O. Moore Papers, Duke U. Also see SAD to Julia, 22 Jan. 1865. Duncan-Jones Papers, NHHS; C. H. Howard to brother, 3 Mar. 1865. O. O. Howard Papers, Bowdoin College.

2. Silas Adams, "My Observations and Service with the Colored Troops," pp. 11–12. delivered 3 Dec. 1913. MOLLUS Collection, MHI. Also see Higginson, *Army Life*, p. 244; T. W. Higginson journal, 22 Aug. 1863. Higginson Papers, Harvard U.; Henry Whitney journal, 26 Apr. 1864. Whitney Family Papers, Rutgers U.

3. John Habberton diary, 14 Apr. 1864. John Habberton Papers, MHI; D. Densmore to Brother, 3 Mar. 1864. Densmore Family Papers, MNHS. For a discussion of white attitudes toward blacks, see Jordan, *White Over Black; Davis, The Problem of Slavery;* Frederickson, *The Black Image in the White Mind.*

4. George Sutherland, *MOLLUS-WI,* 1, p. 180; An Officer of the 9th Army Corps, *Notes on Colored Troops,* p. 5; John Habberton diary, 10 Feb. 1864. John Habberton Papers, MHI. Also see John Habberton diary, 14 Apr. 1864. John Habberton Papers, MHI. For additional testimony that blacks did not function well in cold weather, see reports of Dr. J. W. Compton, 20 May 1865, and Dr. E. P. Buckner, 15 Jun. 1865. *Statistics, Medical and Anthropological, of the Provost Marshal General's Bureau.* 1, pp. 368, 379.

5. B. Marshall Mills to Father, 4 Mar. 1864. Caleb Mills Papers, INHS; T. W. Higginson diary, 27 Nov. 1862. Higginson, *Army Life*, p. 10; Officer, *Notes on Colored Troops,* p. 6; Thomas Montgomery to Brother, 26 Oct. 1864. Montgomery Papers, MNHS; T. W. Higginson diary, 27 Nov. 1862. Higginson, *Army Life*, p. 10. Also see Mary J. McKitrick on William Shafter, undated. William Shafter Papers, BL, UMI; Rogers, *War Pictures,* p. 217.

6. Officer, *Notes on Colored Troops,* pp. 5–6; William to Wife, 17 May 1863. William Parkinson Papers, EU.

7. Testimony of Benjamin Butler before AFIC. "The Negro," p. 2257. Also see Thomas to Hon. H. Wilson, 30 May 1864. Berlin, et al., *Freedom,* II, pp. 530–31.

8. Col. R. B. Marcy to Thomas, 30 Nov. 1864. Testimony of John Eaton, Jr. before AFIC. Col. M. S. Littlefield to Henry Wilson, 25 Jan. 1864. "The Negro," pp. 2831, 2565, and 2352. RG 94, NA; James D. Fessenden to Father, 10 May 1862. Fessenden Papers, Bowdoin College. Also see GO, No. 99. HQ, Dept. of the South. 6 Mar. 1863. Col. R. B. Marcy to Thomas, 30 Nov. 1864. "The Negro," pp. 1120, 2831–32. RG 94, NA.

9. W. Goodale to Mother, 7 May 1865. Warren Goodale Papers, MAHS; Col. R. B. Marcy to Thomas, 30 Nov. 1864. Testimony of John Eaton, Jr., before the AFIC. "The Negro," pp. 2831–32, 2564. RG 94, NA. Also see Butler to Elizabeth T. Upshur, 10 Jan. 1864. "The Negro," p. 2314. RG 94, NA; Cowden, *59th USCI,* p. 46.

10. Capt. Joseph Walker to Maj. T. B. Brooks, 11 Sep. 1863. Col. M. S.

Littlefield to Henry Wilson, 25 Jan. 1864. "The Negro," pp. 1617–19, 2353; Silas Adams, "My Observations and Service with the Colored Troops," p. 6, del. 3 Dec. 1913. MOLLUS Collection, MHI. Also see Circular. Colored Troops for Work. Engineer's Office, Morris Island, S.C., 10 Sep. 1863. "The Negro," pp. 1615–17; Hallowell, *Selected Letters and Papers*, p. 33.

11. Simon Prisby to Honerable E. M. Staunton, 20 July 1865. Garland H. White to Stanton and Wm. H. Seward, 14 June 1864. Berlin et al., *Freedom*, II, pp. 424–25, 141. Note the characterization as animals.

12. S. M. Quincy to Mother, 7 Jan. 1864. Quincy, Wendell, Holmes and Upham Families, MAHS; Dr. Seth Rogers to ?, 26 Jan. 1863. MOLLUS Collection, MHI; Testimony of Capt R. J. Hinton, 79th USCI, before the AFIC. "The Negro," pp. 2582–83. RG 94, NA.

13. William to Sarah, 13 Apr. 1863. William Parkinson Papers, EU; John Pierson to Daughter, 23 Nov. 1864. SC, CL, UMI; J. O. Moore to Lizzie, 8 Jun. 1864. James O. Moore Papers, Duke U. Also see Hen [Marshall] to Hattie, 19 Nov. 1862. SC, CL, UMI.

14. H. H. Hood to Wife, 11 Jul. 1865. Humphrey H. Hood Papers, ILSHL; Testimony of Capt. R. J. Hinton, 79th USCI, before AFIC. "The Negro," p. 2582. RG 94, NA; Coln. N. P. Chipman to General, 16 Oct. [1862]. Berlin et al., *Freedom*, II, p. 71; Benjamin to Brother, 25 Oct. 1863. Densmore Family, MNHS; Testimony of Maj. George Stearns before AFIC. "The Negro," pp. 2569–70. RG 94, NA; H. H. Hood to Wife, 1 July 1863. Humphrey H. Hood Papers, ILSHL; S. M. Quincy, *A Manual of Camp and Garrison Duty*, p. 43. Also see Brig. Gen. Alonzo Draper to Gov. Andrew, 15 Dec. 1864. "The Negro," p. 2845. RG 94, NA.

15. Higginson, *Army Life*, p. 249. Also see Proceedings of GCM. Trial of Richard Mills. MM 3069. RG 153, NA.

16. For comments on the temptation of army life, see Henry to Parents & all, 28 Sep. 1864. Henry M. Crydenwise Papers, EU.

17. See Proceedings of GCM. Trial of Capt. Orin H. Granville. MM 3067. RG 153, NA; Col. Benj. R. Townsend to Thomas, 6 Nov. 1865. Endorsements, 2nd USCI. RG 94, NA; SO, No. 264. HQ, District of Memphis. 30 Oct. 1864. Miscellaneous Papers and Letters, 2nd USCLA. RG 94, NA; GO, No. 20. HQ, 50th USCI. 23 Oct. 1864. Orders, 50th USCI. RG 94, NA; G. A. Rockwood to Sir, 31 Oct. 1864. 890 R 1864. Letters Received, AGO. RG 94, NA; H. H. Hood to Wife, 9 Aug. 1864, 4 and 5 July 1865. Humphrey H. Hood Papers, ILSHL; John Habberton diary, 24 Jan. 1865. John Habberton Papers, MHI; Proceedings of GCM. Trial of Lt. Col. Dexter Clapp. MM 1937. Trial of Capt. John F. Devereaux. MM 3167. Trial of Lt. H. R. Gardner. OO 1774. Trial of Capt. Samuel Aikins. MM 3553. RG 153, NA.

18. See Foster to Maj. Gen. Dodge, 9 July 1865. Miscellaneous Papers and Letters Received, 2nd USCLA. RG 94, NA; GO, No. 19. HQ, 119 USCI. 15 Nov. 1865. Order Book, 119th USCI. RG 94, NA.

19. See CMSR of Lt. Henry W. Keaster, B, 12th USCHA. CMSR of Capt. Aaron Hanger, G, 54th USCI. RG 94, NA.

20. Proceedings of GCM. Trial of Capt. C. H. Cole. LL 2051. RG 153, NA. Also see GO No. 147. HQ, Dept. of Virginia and North Carolina. 20 Nov. 1864. Miscellaneous Papers and Letters Received, 2nd USCLA. RG 94, NA.

21. Rufus Kinsley diary, 20 Dec. 1863, 2 Apr. 1864. Rufus Kinsley Papers, VTHS; Newton, *Out of the Briars*, p. 82.

22. Palemon Smalley, "Dad's Memoirs," p. 104. Also see O. Densmore to Son, 21 Aug. 1864. Densmore Family Papers, MNHS; Edwin Phillips to son, 28 May 1865. Phillips and Parsegian, *Richard and Rhoda*, p. 72; John Pierson to Wife, 1 Sep. 1862. SC, CL, UMI; T. Montgomery to Mother, [?] August 1864. Montgomery Papers, MNHS.

23. H. H. Hood to Wife, 3 Jul. 1864. Humphrey H. Hood Papers, ILSHL; GO, No. 31. HQ, Camp William Penn. 16 Jun. 1864. Regimental Order Book, 45th USCI. RG 94, NA. Also see Brother George to Sister Mary, 28 Aug. 1864. George Gaskill File, Civil War Folder, Spanish-American War Survey, MHI; Orrin to Brother, 7 Nov. 1864. Densmore Family, MNHS. Although the order at Camp William Penn did not specify blacks, other evidence, including this order, indicates that it was directed at black women. GO, No. 1. HQ, 45th USCI. 20 July 1864. Regimental Orders, 45th USCI. RG 94, NA.

24. Proceedings of GCM. Trial of Lt. H. E. Blakeslee. LL 2744. Trial of Capt. Charles Goff. LL 2744. RG 153, NA.

25. Proceedings of GCM. Trial of Capt. John Gossman. LL 2717. RG 153, NA.

26. R. H. B. to Sir, 30 Jun. 1864. *Christian Recorder*, 6 Aug. 1864.

27. See H. H. Hood to Wife, 24 Aug. 1864. Humphrey H. Hood Papers, ILSHL; T. W. Higginson diary, 16 Dec. [1862]. Higginson, *Army Life*, pp. 28–29; Trial of Pvt. Dock Wilson, in Unbound Issuances, 107th USCI. RG 94, NA; Frank [Moulton] to Father, 20 Feb. 1865. Palmer Collection, WRHS; Trial of James Gripen. Trial of Danbridge Brooks. Trial of John Sheppard. Trial of William Jackson. Trial of John Wesley Cork. Trial of John Smith. Trial of Lloyd Spencer. GCM of United States Soldiers Executed by United States Authorities During the Civil War. RG 153, NA.

28. Higginson, *Army Life*, pp. 221, 52–53. Also see Ullmann to Hon. Henry Wilson, 4 Dec. 1863. Testimony of Col. T. W. Higginson before AFIC. "The Negro," pp. 1785, 2552; Testimony of Col. T. W. Higginson before AFIC. Berlin et al., *Freedom*, II, pp. 59–60; Proceedings of GCM. Trial of Richard Mills. MM 3069. RG 153, NA.

29. Monthly Report of Chaplain George N. Carruthers, 51st USCI., 30 Nov. 1864. CWM, LC. Also see [W. Goodale] to Children, 20 Apr. 1865 and 12 July 1865. Warren Goodale Papers, MAHS; Lt. Fred Smith to Rev. Dr. Brown, 3 Apr. 1864. Letters Sent, 1st USCC. RG 94, NA; Brig. Gen. Jas. S. Brisbin to ?, Mar. 1865. Press Copies of Letters Sent, Mar.–Sep. 1865. USCC. Dept. of Kentucky. RG 393, NA; Thomas Conway to Thomas, 13 June 1864 and 11 July 1864. 779 C 1864, 944 C 1864. Letters Received, AGO. RG 94, NA; Lists of Enlisted Men's Families, 18 June 1865. Unbound Miscellaneous Papers, 119th USCI. RG 94, NA; Marrs, *Life and History*, pp. 55–57.

30. See Andrew Jordan to Mrs. Esther H. Hawks, 14 Feb. 1864. J. M. and Esther Hawks Papers, LC; Willis Gardner to father, 14 Nov. 186[4]. Pension File of Willis Gardner. RG 15, NA.

31. See Jas. Rogers to ?, 10 May 1863. James S. Rogers Papers, SSC, Smith College; Thos. Montgomery to Bro, 18 Mar. 1864. Montgomery Papers, MNHS; Stephen P. Jocelyn diary, 13 Feb. 1865. Jocelyn, *Mostly Alkili*, pp. 45–46.

32. Sgt. George W. Generals to Major H. Bumstead, 19 Jan. 1865. Papers
    of the 43rd U.S. Colored Infantry, BPL; Pa to Mary Peet, 5 Mar. 1864.
    Peet Family Papers, MNHS; Bowley, *Boy Lieutenant,* p. 44.

33. Adolphus W. Greely to Brother, 21 Nov. 1864. A. W. Greely Papers,
    Duke U. Also see B. G. Kinsley to Cousin, 29 Sep. 1863. E. W. Kinsley
    Papers, MAHS; Stuart to Mother, 17 Jan. 1865. Morris Stuart Hall
    Papers, BL, UMI; John [Wilder] to Eben, 4 Dec. 1863. Loomis-Wilder
    Family, YU; Capt. L. F. Dewey in account with Co. C, 2nd USC Inf.
    1865. Capt. E. R. Moore in account with Company Fund, Co. K, 2
    USCI for Jan.–Apr. 1865. Miscellaneous Papers, 2nd USCI. RG 94,
    NA; Proceedings of the Council of Administration of the 43d Regt. USCT.
    12 Nov. 1864. Papers of the 43rd U.S. Colored Infantry, BPL; Battery
    Order, No. 14. Battery D, 2 USCLA. 21 Jun. 1865. Orders, Battery D,
    2nd USCLA. RG 94, NA.

34. B. Marshall Mills to Father, 16 Jun. 1865. Caleb Mills Papers, INHS;
    Affidavit of B. F. Frick, undated. Pension File of Stephen Planter. RG
    15, NA.

35. Resignation of Capt. Oliver S. Daugherty, K, 46th USCI. Pension File
    of Oliver S. Daugherty. RG 15, NA; Resignation of Asst. Surg. Elias
    W. Gray. CMSR of Elias W. Gray, 58th USCI. RG 94, NA; Endorsement
    of Lt. Col. Edelmiro Mayer on letter of resignation of 1st Lt. James
    Souder. CMSR of James Souder, K, 45th USCI. RG 94, NA. Also see
    endorsement by Brig. Gen. Geo. L. Andrews to letter of resignation of
    Charles B. Fullington. CMSR of Charles B. Fullington, 75th USCI. RG
    94, NA; Albert Rogall diary, 19, 21 Sep. 1864. Albert Rogall Papers,
    OHS.

36. Gus to Wife, 13 Oct. 1863, 15 Nov. 1863. Charles Augustus Hill Papers,
    Richard S. Tracy Collection; Dr. Seth Rogers to ?, 6 Jan. 1863. MOLLUS
    Collection, MHI; Hen [Marshall] to Hattie, 17 Apr. 1864. SC, CL, UMI.
    Also see Dr. Seth Rogers to ?, 16 Jan. 1863. MOLLUS Collection, MHI;
    Silas Adams, "My Observations and Service with the Colored Troops,
    p. 1, del. 3 Dec. 1913. MOLLUS Collection, MHI; Mussey to Joseph
    Parish, MD, 27 Mar. 1864. Letters Sent by the Commissioner, Dept.
    of the Cumberland. RG 393, NA; James S. Rogers to ?, 26 Dec. 1862.
    James S. Rogers Papers, SSC, Smith College; Wm. Parkinson to Sarah,
    6 May 1863. William Parkinson Papers, EU; Testimony of Brig. Gen.
    R. Saxton before AFIC. Ullmann to Thomas, 19 May 1863. Saxton to
    Stanton, 25 Jan. 1863. "The Negro," pp. 2548, 1249–51, 1073–74.
    RG 94, NA.

37. Lewis to Mother, 6 Aug. 1864. Lewis Weld Family Papers, YU; Joseph
    Mitchell to Sir, 7 Nov. 1864. Edward W. Kinsley papers, MAHS; Willis
    A. Bogart to Mrs. Colonel Bross, [July? 1864]. *Memorial to Lt. Col.
    Bross,* pp. 32–33. Also see James M. Trotter to Friend, 1 July 1865.
    Edward W. Kinsley Papers, Duke U.

38. Higginson, *Army Life,* p. 253.

39. O. Densmore to Son, 1 July 1863. Densmore Family Papers, MNHS.

CHAPTER 6
Training and Discipline

1. Hobart, *Semi-History of a Boy Veteran,* p. 23; Greely, *Reminiscences,*
   p. 91; Stuart to Sister Emma, 28 Sept. 1864. M. S. Hall Papers, BL,
   UMI; Danl to Brother, 11 Mar. 1865. Densmore Family Papers, MNHS.

Also see Edward W. Bacon to Kate, 31 Mar. 1865. Edward W. Bacon Papers, AAS; [Marshall] to Mother & Father, 7 June 1864. Caleb Mills Papers, INHS.

2. Crawford, *Kansas in the Sixties*, p. 107.

3. See *Memorial to Lt. Col. Bross*, p. 10; Thos. Montgomery to Father and Mother, 10 May 1864 and to Father, 4 Apr. 1866. Montgomery Papers, MNHS; Testimony of Col. T. W. Higginson before AFIC. "The Negro," p. 2555. RG 94, NA; GO, No. 1. HQ, USCT. 21 Jan. 1865. Order Book, 50th USCI. RG 94, NA; Jas H. Mead to Ellen, 19 Nov. 1865. Mead Family Papers, UIA.

4. See B. Marshall Mills to Father, 2 May 1865. Caleb Mills Papers, INHS; Capt. Josiah V. Meigs to Brig. Gen. Chetlain, 10 June 1864. Letter Book, Battery A, 2nd USCLA. RG 94, NA; Stuart to Sister Emma, 4 June 1864. M. S. Hall Papers, BL, UMI; Walter Chapman to Bro, 16 Apr. 1865. Walter A. Chapman Papers, YU; Ullmann to Maj. Vincent, 27 Jan. 1863. Joseph Parker to Stanton, 30 May 1863. S. M. Bowman to Thomas, 5 Feb. 1864. "The Negro," pp. 1079–80, 1275, 2362–64. RG 94, NA; Hen [Marshall] to Folks at Home, 26 Apr. [1864]. SC, CL, UMI.

5. Thomas Montgomery to Parents and Brothers, 8 Mar. 1864. Montgomery Papers, MNHS. Also see GO, No. 13. HQ Camp William Penn. 8 Nov. 1863. Regimental Order Book, 45th USCI. RG 94, NA; Cowden, *59th USCI*, pp. 134–35.

6. Wilbur Nelson diary, 23 June 1864. Nelson Family Papers, MISTU; David Cornwell's memoir, "Dan Caverno," p. 129. CWMC, MHI; B. Marshall Mills to Father, 11 Apr. 1864. Caleb Mills Papers, INHS. Also see William to James, 11 May 1863. William Parkinson Papers, EU.

7. Private, 43d U.S.C.T. to Editor, 23 Dec. 1864. *Christian Recorder*, 28 Jan. 1865; Lt. Edwin Harrington to Capt. W. Van Bechtold, 13 Jan. 1865. Letters Sent, 45th USCI. RG 94, NA. Also see GO, No. 7. HQ 45th USCT. 27 Sept. 1864. GO, No. 10. 2 Nov. 1864. GO, No. 12. 18 Nov. 1864. GO, No. 18. 22 Mar. 1865. Regimental Orders, 45th USCI; SO, No. 19. 25 Jan. 1864. SO, No. 21. 28 Jan. 1864. SO, No. 25. 1 Feb. 1864. SO, No. 30. 14 Feb. 1864. 1st USCC. SO, 1st USCC; Co. Orders, No. 7. HQ Battery E, 2nd USCLA. Orders, Battery E, 2nd USCLA; Capt. F. C. Choate to Maj. R. S. Davis, 2 Sep. 1864. Rosters, Reports and Lists, B, 2nd USCLA. RG 94, NA; Paul E. Steiner, *Medical History of a Civil War Regiment*, p. 10.

8. Gen. Silas Casey to ?, [Feb. or Mar. 1863]. "The Negro," pp. 1107–10. RG 94, NA. Also see Casey, *Infantry Tactics*; Coffman, *The Old Army*, pp. 141, 175.

9. Col. H. Leib to Thomas, 14 Aug. 1863. "The Negro," p. 1483. RG 94, NA; T. J. Hoge to "Sam" and "Tillie," 14 May 1865. Wise-Clark Family Papers, UIA. Also see George Sutherland, *MOLLUS-WI*, I, p. 180.

10. Benjamin to Mother, 5 Nov. 1863. Densmore Family Papers, MNHS; Lt. L. L. Billings to E. W. Kinsley, Esq., 10 Apr. 1864. Edward A. Kinsley Papers, Duke U. Also see Lawrence Van Alstyne diary, 8 Nov. 1863. Van Alstyne, *Diary of an Enlisted Man*, p. 216; Jas. Rogers to ?, 9 Jan. 1863, 27 May 1863. James S. Rogers Papers, SSC, Smith College; John Habberton diary, 5 Apr. 1864. John Habberton Papers, MHI; Higginson, *Army Life*, p. 49; Dr. Seth Rogers to ?, 10 Feb. 1863. Rogers

Papers, MHI; B. Densmore to Capt. Geo. Russell, 9 July 1864. Densmore Letterbook, Densmore Family Papers, MNHS; Capt. Wm. Lee Apthorp to Lt. R. H. S. Jewett, 9 Sep. 1863. Montgomery Papers, KASHS; Testimony of Col. T. W. Higginson before AFIC. Berlin et al., *Freedom*, II, p. 59.

11. See Silas Adams, "My Observations and Service with the Colored Troops," pp. 6–7, del. 3 Dec. 1913. MOLLUS-MA Collection, MHI.

12. See Col. Jeptha Garrard to Maj. Davis, 26 Jan. 1864. Letters Sent, 1st USCC; GO, No. 11. HQ 1st USCC. 18 Jan. 1864. GO, 1st USCC; GO, No. 2. HQ, and Brig., 2nd Div., 25 A.C. 12 Dec. 1864. GO, No. 3. 15 Dec. 1864. Regimental Order Book, 45th USCI; SO, No. 19. HQ, 45th USCI. 26 Dec. 1864. Regimental Orders, 45th USCI; Circular. US Forces at Deep Bottom, Virginia. 23 Oct. 1864. Unbound Letters Received, 107th USCI. RG 94, NA; Sam Evans to Father, 16 Sep. 1864. Evans Family Papers, OHS; Christian Fleetwood diary, 18 Dec. 1863. Christian Fleetwood Papers, LC.

13. David Cornwell memoir, "Dan Caverno," pp. 128–29. CWMC, MHI.

14. Danl to Brother, 15 Dec. 1864. Densmore Family Papers, MNHS; Thomas J. Morgan to General, 22 Aug. 1864. CMSR of Col. Thomas J. Morgan, 14th USCI. Also see Capt. Geo. E. Gourand to Capt. W. S. M. Burger, 22 Aug. 1864. Rosters, Reports and Lists, 2nd USCLA. Joe. V. Meigs to Col. Donaldson, 10 May 1864. Letter Book, Battery A, 2nd USCLA. RG 94, NA; GO, No. 4. HQ 2nd USCI. 22 Jan. 1864. Order Book, Co. A, 2nd USCI. RG 94, NA; GO, No. 1. HQ 50th USCI. 14 Oct. 1863. Order Book, 50th USCI. RG 94, NA; Harry Wadsworth to Aunt, 5 May 1864. Frederick and Sarah Cutler Papers, Duke U.

15. Banks to AG, 27 Mar. 1864. *OR* III, 4, p. 205. Also see Foster to Banks, 14 Apr. 1864. *OR* III, 4, p. 231; Banks to Lincoln, 17 Aug. 1863. *OR* I, 26, Pt. 1, p. 688; Brig. Gen. Hawkins to Thomas, 19 Aug. 1864. "The Negro," p. 2752. RG 94, NA; Col. E. Martindale to Capt. Wheeler, 31 Oct. 1864. Letters Received, USCT. Dept. of Virginia and North Carolina, 1864–65. RG 393, NA; Lt. Col. Townsend to Brig. Gen. Woodbury, 2 Jul. 1864. Letters Received, 2nd USCI. RG 94, NA; Higginson, *Army Life*, p. 223.

16. Inspection Report of 15 Aug. 1864 by Maj. Gen. N. J. T. Dana. Inspection Reports, 1865. RG 159, NA; Inspection Report of Milliken's Bend, Vidalia, and Bullet's Bayou, Aug. 1865 by Lt. Chas. Robinett. Letters Received, IGO. RG 159, NA. Also see Inspection Report of 57th USCI on 30 June 1864 by Col. Marcy. Inspection Report of Colored Troops in the Depts. of Miss. and the Gulf by Col. R. B. Marcy, 16 May 1865. Letters Received, IGO. RG 159, NA; Benjamin to Mother, 3, 5 Nov. 1863. Densmore Family Papers, MNHS.

17. Jas. Rogers to ?, 18 Apr. 1863. James S. Rogers Papers, SSC, Smith College. Also see Jas. Rogers to ?, 11 June [1863]. James S. Rogers Papers, SSC, Smith College; Proceedings of Board of Examiners of Field Officers of Colored Troops, 15 Aug. 1864. CMSR of Edward Martindale, 83rd USCI. RG 94, NA.

18. See Jas. Rogers to ?, 11 June [1863]. James S. Rogers Papers, SSC, Smith College; GO, No. 11. HQ 1st USCC. 18 Jan. 1864. GO, 1st USCC. RG 94, NA; GO, No. 13. HQ, 119th USCI. 11 Jun. 1865. Order Book, Co. I, 119th USCI. RG 94, NA; GO, No. 10. HQ, 3rd Div., 10 A.C. 14

Oct. 1864. Regimental Order Book, 45th USCI. RG 94, NA; GO, No. 4. HQ. 30 July 1863. Order Book, Co. B, 2nd USCI. RG 94, NA; Saml. to Mother, 21 Sep. 1863. Duncan-Jones Papers, NHHS; A. W. Greely diary, 15, 16 July 1864 and throughout diary. A. W. Greely Papers, LC; B. Marshall Mills diary, 6 Mar. 1865. Caleb Mills Papers, INHS; Minos Miller to Mother, 14 Apr. 1864. Minos Miller Papers, UAR; Mussey to Capt. C. P. Brown, 24 Oct. 1864. Letters Sent by the Commissioner, Dept. of the Cumberland. RG 393, NA.

19. William to Sarah Ann, 19 Apr. 1863. William H. Parkinson Papers, EU; L. C. Drake, "Reminiscence," p. 8. L. C. Drake Papers, BL, UMI. Also see Saml. Gardner to Sir, 3 Dec. 1864. 890 G 1864. Letters Received, AGO. RG 94, NA; Sam Evans to father, 14 June 1863. Evans Family Papers, OHS; T. W. Higginson diary, 3 Dec. 1862. Higginson, *Army Life*, p. 19; Duren to Emma, 4 Feb. 1865. Offenberg, *Letters of Duren F. Kelley*, p. 145.

20. Quotation is the author's. See Col. R. B. Marcy to Thomas, 30 Nov. 1864. "The Negro," p. 2833. RG 94, NA.

21. David Cornwell memoir, "Dan Caverno," p. 159. CWMC, MHI. Also see Morgan, "Reminiscences of Service," p. 12.

22. Walter Chapman to Parents, 17 Jul. 1864. Walter Chapman Papers, YU; B. Marshall Mills to Father, 12 Sep. 1864. Caleb Mills Papers, INHS; Charles Francis Adams to John Quincy Adams, 2 May 1865. Ford, ed., *A Cycle of Adams Letters*, p. 269. Also see John Habberton diary, 18 Feb. 1864, 1 May 1864, 11 Feb. 1865. John Habberton Papers, MHI; Thomas Scott Johnson to Folks, 17 Dec. 1864. Johnson, "Letters from a Civil War Chaplain," p. 229.

23. John Habberton diary, 13 June 1864. John Habberton Papers, MHI; Duren to [Emma], 31 Mar. 1865. Offenberg, *Letters of Duren F. Kelley*, pp. 162–63. Also see *War Record of Col. W. M. Grosvenor*. Rare Book Room, New York Public Library; Sam Evans to Father, 25 Dec. 1864. Evans Family Papers, OHS; CGGM to Father, 22 July 1865. Charles G. Merrill Papers, YU; Testimony of Surg. James Thompson. Proceedings of GCM. Trial of James Thompson. MM 2636. RG 153, NA; Edw. W. Bacon to Kate, 30 Aug. 1864. Edward W. Bacon Papers, AAS; Danl. to Brother, 22 June 1864. Densmore Family Papers, MNHS.

24. Maj. J. J. Comstock, Jr., to Col. Charles E. Bailey, 16 Apr. 1864. "The Negro," p. 2485. RG 94, NA. Also see S. M. Quincy to Grandfather, 8 Dec. 1863. Quincy, Wendell, Holmes, and Upham Families, MAHS; R. G. Shaw to Charley, 3 Jul. 1863. Robert G. Shaw Papers, MAHS; GO, No. 93. HQ U.S. Forces, Morris Island, SC. 16 Dec. 1863. Montgomery Papers, KASHS; John Habberton diary, 25 Nov. 1864. John Habberton Papers, MHI.

25. Higginson, *Army Life*, p. 259. Also see GO, No. 7. HQ, Brig. Gen. Ullmann's Brigade. 10 June 1863. Col. Marcy to Thomas, 30 Nov. 1864. "The Negro," pp. 1281–83, 1314, 2832. RG 94, NA.

26. Thos. Montgomery to Mother, 19 Apr. 1864. Montgomery Papers, MNHS; Henry C. Harmon to Friend, 23 Oct. 1863. *Christian Recorder*, 7 Nov. 1863; Jas. Rogers to ?, 9 Jan. 1863. James S. Rogers Papers, SSC, Smith College. Also see Higginson, *Army Life*, pp. 44, 260; Jas. Rogers to ?, 11 Jan. 1863. James S. Rogers Papers, SSC, Smith College; Lt. Col. Ed. W. Smith to Col. Higginson, 1 Jun. 1863. "The Negro," pp. 1281–82. RG 94, NA.

27. Quoted in Cimprich, *Slavery's End*, pp. 88–99. The Articles of War are in the back of tactics manuals. See Regimental Order, No. 37. 1st USCI. 31 July 1863 in Proceedings of GCM. NN 813. RG 153, NA; GO, No. 2. HQ, 83rd USCI. (New). 5 Dec. 1863. Order Book, 83rd USCI (New). RG 94, NA; Proceedings of GCM. Trial of William Walker. MM 1320. RG 153, NA.

28. See M. H. Twitchell, "Reminiscences," p. 71. M. H. Twitchell Papers, VTHS; Maj. Geo. L. Paddock to Lt. Chas. P. Brown, 19 July 1864. Rosters, Reports and Lists, 2nd USCLA. GO, No. 5. A, 2nd USCLA. 15 July 1864. Orders, Battery A, 2nd USCLA. RG 94, NA.

29. See Proceedings of GCM. Trial of Lt. Col. Dexter Clapp, Lt. S. B. Bancroft, and Lt. John E. White. MM 1937. RG 153, NA; Mussey to Foster, [late Jun. 1864]. Mussey to Maj. Gen. Geo. H. Thomas, 14 Aug. 1864. Letters Sent by the Commissioner, Dept. of the Cumberland. RG 393, NA.

30. See Willis Gardner diary, 21 Mar. 1864. Pension File of Willis Gardner. RG 15, NA; Wm. Parkinson to Sarah, 6 May 1863. William Parkinson Papers, EU. Many officers in the USCT were prosecuted for offenses.

31. Quincy, *A Camp and Garrison Manual*, p. 22. Also see GO, No. 26. HQ, 2nd USCI. 14 June 1864. Order Book, Co. A, 2nd USCI. RG 94, NA; Capt. Densmore to Capt. F. H. Chapman, 7 Jan. 1865. Letterbook, Densmore Family Papers, MNHS; Testimony of Capt. R. J. Hinton before AFIC. "The Negro," p. 2583. RG 94, NA.

32. GO, No. 3. HQ, 100th USCI. 30 Jan. 1865. Berlin et al., *Freedom*, II, pp. 457–58. Also see Quincy, *A Camp and Garrison Manual*, p. 43.

33. Proceedings of GCM. Trial of Pvt. Henry Brown. MM 3226. RG 153, NA; GO, No. 13. HQ, District of Key West and Tortugas. 1 Aug. 1864. Issuances, 2nd USCI. RG 94, NA; GCM Orders, No. 12. 11 Nov. 1865. Trial of Pvt. John Higgins. Berlin et al., *Freedom*, II, pp. 475–76.

34. See Banks to Halleck, 11 Dec. 1863. Brig. Gen. William Dwight to Brig. Gen. Charles Stone, 15 Dec. 1863. Banks to Halleck, 17 Dec. 1863. Testimony of Col. Charles W. Drew before Court of Inquiry for Fort Jackson Mutiny. "The Negro," pp. 1807–09, 1827–28, 1834–52. For a description of the mutiny and punishments, see "The Negro," pp. 1843–44 and 1846–51. RG 94, NA; Proceedings of GCM. Trial of Lt. Col. Augustus W. Benedict. NN 1301 (Transcript missing). Trial of Lt. John A. David. NN 813. Trial of Lt. Cornelius Cain. MM 2036. RG 153, NA; Testimony of Capt. James Miller before Court of Inquiry for Fort Jackson Mutiny. OR I, 26, pt. 1, pp. 467–68.

35. Close Observer to Mr. Editor, 9 Aug. 1864. *Christian Recorder*, 27 Aug. 1864. Also see GO, No. 36. HQ, 62nd USCI. 9 Nov. 1864. Chaplain Saml. L. Gardner to Ullmann, 19 Dec. 1864. Berlin et al., *Freedom*, II, pp. 454, 417–18; James Peet diary, 8 Feb. 1865. Peet Family Papers, MNHS; Ben to Brother, 7 Mar. 1864. Densmore Family Papers, MNHS.

36. Proceedings of GCM. Trial of George Douglass. MM 3067. RG 153, NA. Also see GO, No. 36. HQ, 1st Div. USCT. 28 Aug. 1864. GO, No. 7. HQ 52nd USCI. 17 Feb. 1865. Simon Prisby to Honerable E. M. Staunton, 20 July 1865. Berlin et al., *Freedom*, II, pp. 452, 485, 424–25; Duren to little darling, 16 July 1865. Offenberg, *Letters of Duren F. Kelley*, pp. 164–65; H. H. Hood to Wife, 8 Oct. 1864. Humphrey H. Hood Papers, ILSHL; Lt. Col. John Wilder to Capt. H. D. Brown, 4 Oct. 1864. CMSR of John Wilder, 2nd USCI. RG 94, NA; Lorenzo Gould diary, 2 May 1865. CWMC, MHI; Proceedings of GCM. Trials of George

L. Young and Henry Standbeck. LL 2676. Trial of Henry Bird. MM 3226. Trial of Robert Cuffey. MM 3067. RG 153, NA.

37. See *List of U.S. Soldiers Executed by United States Military Authorities During the Late War*, 1 Aug. 1885. AGO. RG 94, NA. One is included in the GCM of *United States Soldiers Executed by United States Authorities During the Late War*, RG 153, NA. A perusal of transcripts demonstrates the frequency of mutiny charges in the USCT.

38. See Proceedings of GCM. Trial of Sgt. A. Tolliver. MM 2179. RG 153, NA; Maj. J. J. Comstock, Jr., to Col. Chas. E. Bailey, 16 Apr. 1864. "The Negro," pp. 2484–85. RG 94, NA; Capt. Thomas W. Fry to ?, 21 Sep. 1864 in Chenery, *The 14th RIHA (Col.)*, p. 66.

39. Col. M. D. Littlefield to Col. P. P. Brown, Jr., 3 June 1864. Berlin et al., *Freedom*, II, pp. 394–95; Proceedings of GCM. Trial of William Walker. MM 1320. RG 153, NA; Price Warefield et al. to Stanton, 20 Feb. 1865. Berlin et al., *Freedom*, II, pp. 459–60; B. Marshall Mills to Father, 12 Sep. 1864. Caleb Mills Papers, INHS. Also see B. M. Mills to Father, 28 June 1864. Caleb Mills Papers, INHS; Fox *Record of the Service*, p. 33.

40. Proceedings of GCM. Trial of William Walker. MM 1320. RG 153, NA.

41. Cain, *Autobiography*, pp. 38–39. Also see Lawrence Van Alstyne diary, 1 Oct. 1862. Van Alstyne, *Diary of an Enlisted Man*, pp. 42–43; Oliver to Father, 15 June. 1861. Norton, *Army Letters*, p. 15; H. H. Hood to Wife, 27 Mar. 1863. Humphrey H. Hood Papers, ILSHL; SO, No. 6. AGO. 10 Apr. 1863. *Report of the Adjutant General of the State of Illinois*, 2, p. 477.

42. See Article 67, Articles of War. Also, see Regimental Order Book, 45th USCI. RG 94, NA.

43. See Articles 64–90, Articles of War.

44. Proceedings of GCM. Trial of William Jackson. OO 786. RG 153, NA; GO, No. 10. HQ, Dept. of the South. 20 Jan. 1864. "The Negro," p. 2330. RG 94, NA. Also see Trial of Thomas Four (Fore) et al. MM 2079. *United States Soldiers Executed by United States Authorities During the Late War*, RG 153, NA; B. Marshall Mills to Father, 26 May 1864. Caleb Mills Papers, INHS.

45. Trial of Fortune Wright. OO 1494. *Trials of United States Soldiers Executed by United States Authorities During the Late War*. RG 153, NA. Also see *List of U.S. Soldiers Executed by United States Authorities During the Late War*, 1 Aug. 1885; Trial of Aaron Collins. MM 2571. For all other trials of black soldiers, see *Trials of United States Soldiers Executed by United States Authorities During the Late War*. RG 153, NA.

46. See Proceedings of GCM. Trials of Cage Heath and James Johnson. MM 3226. RG 153, NA. Although Heath stole considerably more money, the sentence was harsh, especially when Johnson was also drunk in camp and received a sentence that was only one-half as severe. Generally speaking, two years was a lengthy jail term for thievery in the Army.

47. Proceedings of a Regimental Courts Martial. Trials of George Spencer and Reddich Watson. Miscellaneous Letters, 1st USCC. RG 94, NA. Also see GO, No. 18. HQ 1st USCC. 3 Mar. 1864. GO, 1st USCC; Guard Report Book and Unbound Issuances, 119th USCI; GO, No. 15. 1st

USCC. 29 Jan. 1864. GO, 1st USCC; GO, No. 14. HQ 2nd USCI. 4 Apr. 1864. GO, No. 15. HQ 2nd USCI. 9 Apr. 1864. Order Book, Co. A, 2nd USCI. RG 94, NA. RCM punishments were standard for white volunteer units too.

48. J. H. Meteer to Prof, 10 Feb. [18] 64. Caleb Mills Papers, INHS; Edw. W. Bacon to Kate, 26 Sep. 1864. Edward W. Bacon Papers, AAS; Jas. C. Beecher to friend Kinsley, 27 July 1863. Beecher Family Papers, Stowe-Day Library. Also see Col. S. Fellows to Capt. H. W. Bowers, 19 Apr. 1864. Letters Received, 2nd USCI. RG 94, NA; T. W. H. to James, 24 Nov. 1862. T. W. Higginson Papers, AAS; Danl to friends at home, 19 Feb. 1865. Densmore Family Papers, MNHS; Col. C. H. Adams to Brig. Gen. Hawkins, 28 Sep. 1863. Regimental Orders, No. 69. HQ, 1st USCI. 3 Jan. 1864. GO No. 25. HQ, Tenth Army Corps. 19 Aug. 1864. Quarterly Return of 50th USCI for 3rd Quarter of 1864. "The Negro," pp. 1630, 2300, 2750, 2814. RG 94, NA.

49. John Habberton diary, 28 Mar. 1864. John Habberton Papers, MHI. Also see James S. Rogers to ?, 28 Dec. [1862]. James S. Rogers Papers, SSC, Smith College.

CHAPTER 7
Proving Their Valor

1. *New York Times*, 16 Feb. 1863. Also see *New York Times*, 6 June 1863 for a summary of prejudicial doubts about black troops.

2. Cornish, *The Sable Arm*, p. 77. Also see *Chicago Tribune*, 10 Nov. 1862.

3. Dr. Seth Rogers to ?, 5 Feb. 1863. MOLLUS Collection, MHI; *OR* I, 14, p. 198; James Rogers to ?, 1 Feb. 1863. James S. Rogers Papers in SSC, Smith College. Also see Higginson, *Army Life*, pp. 62–96; *OR* I, 14, pp. 195–98.

4. Brown, *The Negro in the American Rebellion*, p. 165–66. Also see AAR of Col. N. W. Daniels in Brown, *The Negro in the American Rebellion*, pp. 159–66; Daniels to Brig. Gen. T. W. Sherman, 10 Apr. 1863. *OR* I, 52, pt. 1, p. 61.

5. For a detailed examination of the battle of Port Hudson, see Hewitt, *Port Hudson*; Edmonds, *The Guns of Port Hudson*.

6. Edmonds, *The Guns of Port Hudson*, vol. 2, p. 49.

7. See *New York Times*, 13 June, 8 Aug. 1863; George W. Williams, *A History of the Negro Troops*, pp. 218–19; Brown, *The Negro in the American Rebellion*, pp. 168–69.

8. Affidavit of Mrs. Maria Wilson, 18 Oct. 1873; Deposition of Rev. John M. Brown, 29 Apr. 1875; Affidavit of Mrs. Maria Wilson, 24 Aug. 1874. Pension File of John H. Crowder. RG 15, NA. Also see Deposition of Rev. John M. Brown, 29 Apr. 1875; Deposition of Martha Ann Stars, 28 Oct. 1872. Affidavit of Jane Ellison, 24 Aug. 1874. Pension File of John H. Crowder. RG 15, NA.

9. See Affidavit of Martha Ann Stars, 23 Mar. 1877; Affidavit of Edward A. Tyler, 16 Oct. 1873; Deposition of Martha Ann Stars, 28 Oct. 1872. Pension File of John H. Crowder. RG 15, NA.

10. See Deposition of Rev. John M. Brown, 29 Apr. 1875; Deposition of Martha Ann Stars, 28 Oct. 1872; Affidavit of Edward A. Tyler, 28 Oct. 1872. Pension File of John H. Crowder. RG 15, NA.

11. Affidavit of Mrs. Maria Wilson, 18 Oct. 1873; John H. Crowder to Mother, 23 Apr. [1863]. Pension File of John H. Crowder. RG 15, NA.

12. John H. Crowder to Mother, 26 Nov. 1862 and 3 Jan. 1863. Pension File of John H. Crowder. RG 15, NA.

13. John H. Crowder to Mother, 27 Apr. 1863. Pension File of John H. Crowder. RG 15, NA. Also see John H. Crowder to [foster sister], 18 Apr. 1863. Pension File of John H. Crowder. RG 15, NA.

14. John H. Crowder to [foster sister], 18 Apr. 1863. John H. Crowder to Mother, 23 Apr. [1863]. Pension File of John H. Crowder. RG 15, NA.

15. See Williams, *A History of Negro Troops*, pp. 214–15; Hewitt, *Port Hudson*, p. 147.

16. See Hewitt, *Port Hudson*, pp. 133, 148; Edmonds, *The Guns of Port Hudson*, vol. 2, pp. 53–54.

17. See Hewitt, *Port Hudson*, pp. 148–49; Edmonds, *The Guns of Port Hudson*, pp. 52–55.

18. See *New York Times*, 13 June 1863; Hewitt, *Port Hudson*, pp. 148–49.

19. See *New York Times*, 13 June 1863; Hewitt, *Port Hudson*, p. 150; Banks to Halleck, 30 May 1863. *OR* I, 26, pt. 1, p. 45.

20. Quoted in Quarles, *The Negro in the Civil War*, p. 214; *New York Times*, 13 June 1863; George R. Sanders to Mr. Burnham, 15 July 1863. Burnham File, Civil War Miscellaneous, YU. Also see *New York Times*, 13 June 1863; Hewitt, *Port Hudson*, pp. 148–49.

21. It was certainly to their advantage that Northerners did not know that the Confederates had not suffered any casualties. See *New York Times*, 8 Aug. 1863, for a revised casualty figure of 197; Edmonds, *The Guns of Port Hudson*, p. 58. The *Official Army Register of the Volunteer Officers*, pp. 247, 251, lists the casualties much lower, but it appears to be wrong.

22. *New York Times*, 8 Aug. 1863. Also see *New York Times*, 13 June 1863; Williams, *The Negro Troops*, pp. 218–19.

23. Capt. Elias D. Strunke to Ullmann, 29 May 1863. Berlin et al., *Freedom*, II, p. 529; letter from an officer in Banks's Army, 28 May 1863. *New York Times*, 11 June 1863; Banks to Halleck, 30 May 1863. *OR* I, 26, pt. 1, p. 45; Ullmann to Stanton, 6 June 1863. "The Negro," p. 1298. RG 94, NA; *New York Times*, 11 June 1863. Clearly the unidentified officer exaggerated when he claimed they "carried all before them."

24. Roy, "Our Indebtedness to the Negroes," p. 359.

25. See AAR of Maj. Gen. Richard Taylor, *OR* I, 24, pt. 2, pp. 457–62.

26. See AAR of Col. H. Lieb, 8 Jun. 1863. David Cornwell memoir, "Dan Caverno," p. 136. CWMC, MHI; AAR of Brig. Gen. Elias Dennis, 12 Jun. 1863. *OR* I, 24, pt. 2, p. 447.

27. AAR of Col. H. Lieb, 8 Jun. 1863, in David Cornwell memoir, "Dan Caverno," p. 136. CWMC, MHI.

28. David Cornwell memoir, "Dan Caverno," p. 130. CWMC, MHI. Also see Main, *3rd USCC*, pp. 65–70; Banks to Halleck, 30 May 1863. "The Negro," pp. 2124–25. RG 94, NA.

29. AAR of Col. Herman Lieb, 8 Jun. 1863, in Cornwell, "Dan Caverno," pp. 136–38. CWMC, MHI. Also see AAR of Brig. Gen. Elias Dennis, 12 June 1863. *OR* I, 24, pt. 2, p. 447.

30. See *OR* I, 24, pt. 2, p. 463; David Cornwell memoir, "Dan Caverno," pp. 131–32. CWMC, MHI; Cyrus Sears, *Paper of Cyrus Sears. Read Before the Ohio Commandery of the Loyal Legion*, October 7th, 1908, pp. 12–14.

31. AAR of Col. Herman Lieb, 8 June 1863, in David Cornwell memoir, "Dan Caverno," p. 136. CWMC, MHI.

32. AAR of Col. Herman Lieb, in David Cornwell memoir, "Dan Caverno," pp. 136–37. CWMC, MHI. Also see AAR of Brig. Gen. H. E. McCulloch, 8 June 1863. *OR* I, 24, pt. 2, p. 469; [Marshall Mills] to Mother & Father, 7 June 1864. Caleb Mills Papers, INHS. The official rosters indicate the executions.

33. M. M. Miller to Aunt, 10 June 1863. *OR.* III, 3, pp. 452–53. Also see AAR of Col. Herman Lieb, 8 June 1863, in Cornwell memoir, "Dan Caverno," p. 136–37. CWMC, MHI.

34. See David Cornwell memoir, "Dan Caverno," p. 133. CWMC, MHI.

35. AAR of Brig. Gen. H. E. McCullough, 8 June 1863. *OR* I, 24, pt. 2, p. 467. Also see M. M. Miller to Aunt, 10 June 1863. *OR* III, 3, p. 453; AAR of Col. Herman Lieb, 8 June 1863 in Cornwell, "Dan Caverno," p. 138. CWMC, MHI.

36. David Cornwell memoir, "Dan Caverno," p. 134. CWMC, MHI.

37. See Cornwell, "Dan Caverno," p. 134, and AAR of Col. Herman Lieb, 8 June 1863 there in, p. 137. CWMC, MHI.

38. See AAR of Maj. Gen. J. G. Walker, 10 June 1863. *OR* I, 24, pt. 2, pp. 462–65.

39. David D. Porter to Grant, 7 Jun. 1863. *OR* I, 24, pt. 2, p. 454. Also see AAR of Brig. Gen. H. E. McCulloch, 8 June 1863. *OR* I, 24, pt. 2, pp. 469–70; AAR of Col. Herman Lieb, 8 June 1863, in Cornwell, "Dan Caverno," pp. 136–38. CWMC, MHI; Cyrus Sears, *Paper*, pp. 11–12. These statistics come from Fox, *Regimental Losses*, pp. 26–27, 521. If we rely on the information in the *Register of Officers in the Volunteer Service of the United States*, pt. 8, p. 153, it would still be 37 percent killed.

40. Annual Report (Extract) of 1st Mississippi AD, for 7 June 1863. "The Negro," p. 2143. RG 94, NA. Also see Cornwell, "Dan Caverno," p. 140. CWMC, MHI.

41. M. M. Miller to Aunt, 10 June 1863. *OR* III, 3, p. 452; AAR of Capt. Abraham E. Strickle, 9 June 1863. *OR* I, 24, pt. 2, p. 456; C. A. Dana to Stanton, 22 June 1863. *OR* I, 24, pt. 1, p. 106.

42. See John A. Andrew to Francis G. Shaw, 30 Jan. 1863. Emilio, *Brave Black Regiment*, pp. 3–5, 12, 30.

43. Speech of Gov. Andrew, 18 May 1863. Emilio, *Brave Black Regiment*, pp. 23, 27, 31–33.

44. Quote in *To Colored Men. Freedom, Protection, Pay, and a Call to Military Duty. Circular.* "The Negro," p. 1822. RG 94, NA. Also see Burchard, *One Gallant Rush*, pp. 107–8.

45. Testimony of Nathaniel Paige, Special Correspondent of the *New York Tribune*, before the AFIC. "The Negro," pp. 2586–87. RG 94, NA. Also see Shaw to Strong, 6 July 1863. Emilio, *Brave Black Regiment*, p. 49.

46. At the time, Gillmore had no plans for an attack on Charleston. See AAR of Maj. Gen. Q. A. Gillmore, 28 Feb. 1864. *OR* I, 28, pt. 1, pp. 6–7, 13.

47. See Emilio, *Brave Black Regiment,* pp. 68–70.

48. See AAR Addendum to AAR of General P. G. T. Beauregard, 18 Sep. 1864. AAR of Brig. Gen. Wm. B. Taliaferro, 21 July 1863. *OR* I, 28, pt. 1, pp. 76–77, 417.

49. See Emilio, *Brave Black Regiment,* pp. 72–73.

50. See Emilio, *Brave Black Regiment,* pp. 73–76.

51. Emilio, *Brave Black Regiment,* p. 77.

52. Emilio, *Brave Black Regiment,* p. 78.

53. See Emilio, *Brave Black Regiment,* pp. 79–80.

54. Lewis [Douglass] to Amelia, 20 July [1863]. Carter Woodson Papers, LC. Also see Emilio, *Brave Black Regiment,* pp. 80–81.

55. See Emilio, *Brave Black Regiment,* pp. 81–82; Burchard, *One Gallant Rush,* pp. 137–38.

56. See Emilio, *Brave Black Regiment,* p. 81; AAR of General P. G. T. Beauregard inclosed with AAR of Beauregard, 18 Sep. 1864. *OR* I, 28, pt. 1, pp. 76–77.

57. See Emilio, *Brave Black Regiment,* p. 84.

58. See Emilio, *Brave Black Regiment,* pp. 84–85, 93; E. N. Hallowell to William Schouler, 18 Dec. 1865. Brown, *The Negro in the American Rebellion,* pp. 210–11; Burchard, *One Gallant Rush,* pp. 131, 139.

59. Brown, *The Negro in the American Rebellion,* p. 203; Francis George Shaw to Gillmore, 24 Aug. 1863. Emilio, *Brave Black Regiment,* pp. 102–3. Also see AAR of Col. E. N. Hallowell, 7 Nov. 1863. *OR* I, 28, pt. 1, pp. 210, 362–63.

60. A. S. Fisher to dear afflicted Captin and Most Obedient kind Sir, 31 July 1863. A. S. Fisher Papers, Gettysburg College.

61. *New York Times,* 7 Mar. 1864.

CHAPTER 8
Leaving Their Mark on the Battlefield

1. Furness, "The Negro As a Soldier," pp. 457–58.

2. William Baird, "Reminiscences," pp. 64–65. William Baird Papers, BL, UMI; Danl to friends at home, 2 June 1864. Densmore Family Papers, MNHS; Oliver Norton to Father, 1 May 1864. Norton, *Army Letters,* p. 202. Also see Danl to Friends, 17 June 1864. Densmore Family Papers, MNHS.

3. John C. Brook to Recorder, 30 Oct. 1864. *Christian Recorder,* 12 Nov. 1864. Luther Bingham to Father, no date. Bingham, *Young Quartermaster,* pp. 97–98. Also see Lewis to Mason, 16 Feb. 1864. Lewis Weld Family Papers, YU.

4. Higginson, *Army Life,* p. 246; Newton, *Out of the Briars,* p. 39. Also see Jas. Rogers to ?, 1 Feb. 1863. James S. Rogers Papers, SSC, Smith College; Seth Rogers to ?, 5 Feb. 1863. MOLLUS Collection, MHI; Ullmann to Stanton, 6 June 1863. "The Negro," p. 1298. RG 94, NA.

5. Oliver Norton to Sister L, 29 Feb. 1864. Norton, *Army Life,* pp. 198–

99; L. Grim to Aunt, 1 Feb. 1865. Wise-Clark Family Papers, UIA. Also see Maj. Quincy McNeil to Brig. Gen. Jno. A. Rawlins, 13 Aug. 1864. Berlin et al., *Freedom*, II, pp. 602–3; Oliver Norton to Father, 1 Mar. 1864. Norton, *Army Letters*, p. 202; C. G. G. M. to Father, 28 Feb. 1864. Charles G. Merrill Papers, YU.

6. Higginson, *Army Life*, p. 25.

7. Bowley, *Boy Lieutenant*, pp. 47–48, 69–70. Also see Emilio, *Brave Black Regiment*, pp. 77–78; M. H. Twitchell, "Reminiscences," p. 76. M. H. Twitchell Papers, VTHS.

8. Gus to Wife, 24 [25] May 1864. Charles Augustus Hill Papers, Richard S. Tracy Collection; Walter Chapman to Bro, 16 Apr. 1865. Walter A. Chapman Papers, YU. Also see Col. T. W.˙Higginson testimony before AFIC. "The Negro," pp. 2551–52. RG 94, NA; Hallowell, "The Negro as a Soldier," in Hallowell, *Selected Letters and Papers*, pp. 46–47; AAR of Col. Frank A. Kendrick, 7 Dec. 1863. *OR* 1, 31, pt. 1, 585.

9. Holsinger, *MOLLUS-Kansas*, 1, pp. 300–301. Also see Stuart to Sister Emma, 16 May 1865. Morris Stuart Hall Papers, BL, UMI; A. S. Fisher to dear afflicted Captin, 31 July 1863. A. S. Fisher Papers, Gettysburg College.

10. John Habberton diary, 7 Apr. 1864. John Habberton Papers, MHI. Also see Jos. J. Scroggs diary, 29 Sep. 1864. CWTIC, MHI; HQ. Dept. of Virginia & North Carolina. 11 Oct. 1864. George R. Sherman Papers, RIHS.

11. Newton, *Out of the Briars*, p. 47. Also see A. S. Fisher to dear afflicted Captin, 31 July 1863. A. S. Fisher Papers, Gettysburg College.

12. Henry to Parents & all, 24 July 1864. Henry M. Crydenwise Papers, EU. Also see Rickard, "Service with Colored Troops," pp. 40–41.

13. Edward W. Bacon to Kate, 31 Oct. 1864. Edward W. Bacon Papers, AAS.

14. McMurray, *Recollections*, p. 36; Joseph J. Scroggs diary, 29 Sep. 1864. CWTIC, MHI; Lewis to Mother, 17 Aug. 1864. Lewis Weld Family, YU. Also see Lewis to Amelia, 20 Jul. [1863]. Carter Woodson Papers, LC; Stuart Hall, "Reminiscence," p. 40. Morris Stuart Hall Papers, BL, UMI.

15. *New York Times*, 8 Jan. 1865.

16. August V. Kautz to Mrs. Savage, 29 Mar. 1865. August V. Kautz Papers, ILSHL. Also see Testimony of Nathaniel Paige, Special Correspondent of the *New York Tribune*, before AFIC. "The Negro," pp. 2586–87. RG 94, NA.

17. Sutherland, "The Negro in the Late War," p. 180; [Gus] to Wife, 21 Jun. 1864. Charles Augustus Hill Papers, Richard S. Tracy Collection.

18. Albert Rogall diary, 30 July 1864. Albert Rogall Papers, OHS; D. E. Proctor to Harvey, 1 Aug. 1864. David E. Proctor Papers in possession of Chester L. Somers. Also see William Baird, "Reminiscence," p. 20. William Baird Papers, BL, UMI; *OR* I, 40, pt. 1, pp. 46, 137, 246–49; *Memorial to Lt. Col. Bross*, p. 17.

19. Saml. A. Duncan to Julia, 22 Oct. 1864. Duncan-Jones Papers, NHHS. Also see James Henry to Father, 4 Oct. 1864. James Henry Wickes Papers, BPL; McMurray, *Recollections*, pp. 52–58; Solon A. Carter, "Fourteen Months' Service," pp. 170–71; George R. Sherman, "Reminiscence," pp. 10–11. George R. Sherman Papers, RIHS; *OR* I, 42, pt. 1, pp. 133–36.

20. Main, *3rd USCC,* pp. 200–203; GO No. 81. Hdqrs. Military Division of the West Mississippi. 9 Dec. 1864. *OR* I, 45, pt. 1, p. 778. Also see AAR of Col. E. D. Osband, 4 Dec. 1864. *OR* I, 45, Pt. 1, pp. 781–82.

21. Joseph J. Scroggs diary, 29 Sep. 1864. CWTIC, MHI. Also see Quarles, *The Negro in the Civil War,* pp. 15, 214, 219; Joseph B. Mitchell, *The Badge of Gallantry,* p. 139; AAR of Lt. Col. Jno. C. Chadwick, 13 June 1864. *OR* I, 34, pt. 1, p. 444; Dr. Seth Rogers to ?, 27 Jan. 1863. MOLLUS Collection, MHI; George R. Sanders to Mr. Burnham, 15 July 1863. Burnham File, Civil War Miscellaneous Papers, YU.

22. G. A. Rockwood to Sir, 31 Oct. 1864. 890 R 1864. Letters Received, AGO. RG 94, NA; T. W. H. to James, 24 Nov. 1862. T. W. Higginson Papers, AAS. Also see AAR of Col. S. J. Crawford, 20 May 1864. Stanton to ?, 16 June 1864. Lt. Col. I. C. Terry to Lt. Proudfit, ND. "The Negro," pp. 3107–9, 3164, 3420. RG 94, NA; Extract of Annual Report of 51st U.S. Colored Infantry for 1863. "The Negro," p. 2143. RG 94, NA.

23. C. P. Lyman to ones at home, 19 June 1864. Carlos P. Lyman Papers, WRHS. Also see List of Camp and Garrison Equipage Lost in George W. Strong Papers, UIA; Maj. S. W. Pickens et al. Statement, 17 Oct. 1864. Berlin, ed., *Freedom,* II, pp. 553–56.

24. Danl to Brother, 24 July 1864. Densmore Family Papers, MNHS; Gus to Wife, 3 Aug. 1864. Charles Augustus Hill Papers, Richard S. Tracy Collection. Also see Reports of Surg. Daniel D. Hanson and Lt. Col. W. W. Marple. Pension File of B. Ryder Corwin. RG 15, NA; Danl to Brother, 11, 30 Aug. 1864. Danl to Friends at home, 5 Oct. 1864. Densmore Family Papers, MNHS; Proceedings of GCM. Trial of J. H. Clendening. LL 3110. RG 153, NA; Rickard, "Service with Colored Troops," pp. 22–23; Lewis to Mason, 7 Oct. 1864. Lewis Weld Family, YU; McMurray, *Recollections,* p. 35; Albert Rogall diary, 19 Aug. 1864. Albert Rogall Papers, OHS; Foster to Bvt. Brig. Gen. Brice, 12 Dec. 1864. Letters Regarding Recruiting, Division of Colored Troops. RG 94, NA; Henry Whitney journal, no date. Whitney Family Papers, Rutgers U; CMSR of Chap. Alvah R. Jones, 10th USCI. RG 94, NA. These were white men.

25. See GO, No. 9. HQ 3 Div., 25 A.C. 9 Mar. 1865. Unbound Issuances, 107th USCI. RG 94, NA; McMurray, *Recollections,* p. 36.

26. Bowley, *Boy Lieutenant,* p. 12; Testimony of Col. T. W. Higginson before AFIC. "The Negro," pp. 2551–52. RG 94, NA; AAR of Lt. Col. Hubert A. McCaleb, 9 Feb. 1864. *OR* I, 34, pt. 1, p. 130. Also see Sutherland, "The Negro in the Late War," p. 182; Higginson, *Army Life,* p. 112; AAR of Col. T. W. Higginson, 1 Feb. 1863. Berlin et al., *Freedom,* II, p. 524.

27. Ben F. Stevens to Mother, 12 Aug. 1863. Ellis, "The Civil War Letters of an Iowa Family," p. 582. Also see Jas. Rogers to ?, 18 Mar. 1863. James S. Rogers Papers, SSC, Smith College; Saxton to Stanton, 4 Apr. 1863. "The Negro," pp. 1168–69. RG 94, NA.

28. Lt. Col. Theo. Trauernicht to Mussey, 23 Oct. 1863. Letters Received, 2nd USCI. RG 94, NA; E. O. C. Ord to Grant, 20 Aug. 1864. "The Negro," p. 2754. RG 94, NA; Samuel D. Barnes diary, 24 Apr., 1 May 1864. CWM, LC.

29. See AAR of Brig. Gen. Geo. B. Andrews, 6 Aug. 1863. *OR* I, 26, pt. 1, p. 240; Jas. to Wife, 5 Mar. 1864. Peet Family Papers, MNHS; Lt. Com-

mander E. K. Ewen to Act'g Rear Admiral David D. Porter, 16 June
1863. Affidavit of Sgt. Samuel Johnson, 11 July 1864. Col. Jno. Logan
to Col. E. B. Ewell, 3 Sep. 1863 and Col. Frank Powers to Col. Jno.
Logan, 2 Sep. 1863. Col. Williams to Maj. T. R. Livingston, 21 May
1863. Berlin et al., *Freedom*, II, 574–75, pp. 581, 584–85, 588–89.

30. AAR of Col. J. M. Williams, 24 Apr. 1864. *OR* I, 34, pt. 1, p. 746.
Also see Bowley, *Petersburg Mine Run*, pp. 14–15; AAR of Col. James
Brisbin, 20 Oct. 1864. Report of Surg. William H. Gardner, 13th Ken-
tucky Infantry, of the shooting of Union prisoners, 26 Oct. 1864. *OR*
I, 39, pt. 1, pp. 554–55, 557.

31. For the most recent and probably the best account of Fort Pillow, see
John Cimprich and Robert C. Mainforth, Jr., "Fort Pillow Revisited,"
pp. 293–306 (percentage losses are on page 295). For testimony about
the massacre, see *OR* I, 32, pt. 1, pp. 519–40. For Forrest's side of
the story, see *OR* I, 32, pt. 1, pp. 586–619.

32. See Notes of George N. Carruthers. CWM, LC; Return of the 51st USCI
for Feb. 1864. "The Negro," p. 3018. RG 94, NA; Stuart to Sister Emma,
14 Feb. 1865. Morris Stuart Hall Papers, BL, UMI; Maj. Cochrane[?]
to Foster, 9 Jan. 1865. Letters Sent by the Commissioner, RG 393,
NA; Walter Chapman to Parents, 17 July 1864. Walter A. Chapman
Papers, YU; Extract from the Annual Return of the 108th USCI, 1864.
Capt. Ben S. Nicklin to Maj. B. H. Polk, 10 Oct. 1864. "The Negro,"
p. 3302. RG 94, NA; W. C. Ream to Cousin Tillie, 11 Feb. 1864. Wise-
Clark Family Papers, UIA.

33. Maj. Gen. N. B. Forrest to Col., 15 Apr. 1864. *OR* I, 32, Pt. 1, p. 610;
AAR of Brig. Gen. August Chetlain, 14 Apr. 1864. "The Negro," p.
3072. RG 94, NA; Gus to Wife, 6 May 1864. Charles Augustus Hill
Papers, Richard S. Tracy Collection; Lieut. Anson S. Hemingway to ?,
17 May 1864. Post, *Soldiers' Letters*, p. 366; E. R. Manson to Friend
John, 19 Oct. 1864. E. R. Manson Papers, Duke U.; Walter Chapman
to Parents, 11 Apr. 1865. Walter A. Chapman Papers, YU. Also see
Alonzo Rembaugh to Capt., 28 Feb. 1864. Loomis-Wilder Papers, YU;
Brig. Gen. B. H. Robertson to Maj., 14 July 1864. "The Negro," p.
3200. RG 94, NA; H. M. Turner to Mr. Editor, 30 June 1864. *Christian
Recorder*, 9 July 1864.

34. Edward W. Bacon to Kate, 26 Sep., 31 Oct. 1864. Edward W. Bacon
Papers, AAS. Also see Hen [Marshall] to Hattie, 25 Nov. 1864. SC, CL,
UMI; AAR of Col. A. G. Draper, 15 May 1864. "The Negro," pp. 3114–
16. RG 94, NA; George R. Sherman, "Reminiscences," p. 9. George R.
Sherman Papers, RIHS.

35. Rickard, "Service with Colored Troops," p. 29; Joseph K. Nelson, "Reminiscences," p. 47. CWMC, MHI. Also see Stuart Hall, "Reminiscences,"
pp. 41–2. Morris Stuart Hall Papers, BL, UMI; William Baird, "Reminiscences," pp. 20, 79–81. William Baird Papers, BL, UMI; Hall, "Mine
Run to Petersburg," p. 24; George R. Sherman, "Reminiscences." George
R. Sherman Papers, RIHS.

36. Higginson, *Army Life*, pp. 255–56; M. Miller to Mother, 27 Jul. 1863.
Minos Miller Papers, UAR; J. H. Welch to Brother in Christ, 15 Oct.
1863. *Christian Recorder*, 24 Oct. 1863; Thomas J. Morgan, *PNRISSHS*,
Ser. 3, No. 13, p. 29. Also see Sam to Father, 13 Sep. 1863. Evans
Family Papers, OHS.

37. GO, No. 5. HQ, 100th USCI. 2 Feb. 1865. "The Negro," pp. 3512–513. RG 94, NA; Thomas B. Webster to Editor, Dec. 1864. *Christian Recorder*, 7 Jan. 1865. Also see *The Medical and Surgical History of the War of the Rebellion.* Pt. First, Medical Volume and Appendix, pp. xl–xli; McMurray, *Recollections*, p. 59; Hallowell, "The Negro as a Soldier," in Hallowell, *Selected Letters and Papers*, p. 37.

38. See Holsinger, "How Does One Feel Under Fire?" pp. 303–4.

39. Surg. Henry O. Marcy to Mrs. Reed, 16 Mar. 1864. Pension File of William N. Reed. RG 15, NA; Sam to father, 2 Nov. 1863. Evans Family Papers, OHS; Morgan, "Reminiscences of Service," pp. 32–33; Bowley, *Boy Lieutenant*, p. 111; Deposition of Capt. Jacob M. Wells, 23 Apr. 1900. Pension File of Gooding T. Newsom. RG 15, NA. Also see A. S. Hartwell to K, 4 Dec. 1864. E. W. Kinsley Papers, MAHS.

40. See Weist, "The Medical Department in the War," p. 84; Ch. G. G. Merrill to Father, 2 Aug. 1864. Charles Merrill Papers, YU.

41. Rufus S. Jones to Christian Recorder, 20 Mar. 1864. *Christian Recorder*, 16 Apr. 1864; J. O. Moore to Lizzie, 23 Feb. 1864. James O. Moore Papers, Duke U.; Charles to Mother, 8 Sep. 1864 and Charles to Father, 23 June 1864. Charles Merrill Papers, YU. Also see Adams, *Doctors in Blue*, pp. 66–67; Ch. G. G. Merrill to Father, 2 Aug. 1864. Charles Merrill Papers, YU; Lewis to wife, 2 May 1864. Jonathan Lewis Whitaker Papers, SHC, UNC.

42. Ch. G. G. Merrill to Father, 2 Aug. 1864 Charles Merrill Papers, YU. Also see Adams, *Doctors in Blue*, pp. 66–69.

43. [Francis] to Aunt Margie, 1 Aug. 1864. Blake, ed., *Diaries and Letters of Francis Minot Weld*, p. 166; Charles to Annie, 16 June 1864. Ch. G. G. Merrill to Father, 1 Aug. 1864. Charles Merrill Papers, YU. Also see Charles to Mother, 8 Sep. 1864. Charles Merrill Papers, YU.

44. Charles to Father, 3 July 1864. Charles Merrill Papers, YU; Jas. C. Beecher to Kinsley, 8 Dec. [1864]. Edward W. Kinsley Papers, MAHS; Hattie to Tillie, 13 June 1865. Wise-Clark Family Papers, UIA. Also see Ch. G. G. Merrill to Father, 18 Jan. 1864[5]. Charles Merrill Papers, YU.

45. McMurray, *Recollections*, pp. 61–2; Surgeon's Certificate for Maj. J. W. M. Appleton, by Surg. Charles E. Briggs. CMSR for J. W. M. Appleton. RG 94, NA; Albert Rogall diary, 14 June 1864. Albert Rogall Papers, OHS. Also see Carded Medical Records of John McMurray. RG 94, NA; Albert Rogall diary, 8, 10, 11 June, 1 July 1864. Albert Rogall Papers, OHS. Rogall had no Carded Medical Records at NA. For comments on the sense of isolation, see J. H. Mead to Ellen, 31 Mar. 1865. Mead Family Papers, UIA; Sam to Father, 8 Jun. 1864. Evans Family Papers, OHS.

46. See *OR* III, 5, pp. 668–70. Also see Ella Lonn, *Desertion During the Civil War*, 1966. Some sixty-seven black troops deserted per one thousand, whereas sixty-three white troops per one thousand deserted. Authorities recruited the bulk of the white units on the local level, while that was not really the case with black soldiers, and that alone could easily account for the difference.

47. Jeff [Hoge] to Tillie, 4 Nov. 1864. Wise-Clark Family Papers, UIA; AAR of Col. James S. Brisbin, 20 Oct. 1864. *OR* I, 39, pt. 1, p. 557. Also

see Col. John Shaw, Jr. to Bvt. Lt. Col. George Lee, 15 Aug. 1866. "The Negro," p. 3199. RG 94, NA; AAR of Col. Ed. Bouton, 17 Jun. 1864. Testimony of Col. Edward Bouton in the Sturgis hearings. *OR* I, 39, Pt. 1, pp. 125–27 and 213–14; Bowley, *The Petersburg Mine*, p. 14; Affidavit of Sgt. Samuel Walker, undated. Pension File of George Turner, Co. G, 5th USCC. RG 15, NA.

48. Morgan, "Reminiscences of Service," p. 32; Edward W. Bacon to Kate, 31 Oct. 1864. Edward W. Bacon Papers, AAS. Also see G. A. Rockwood to Sir, 31 Oct. 1864. 890 R 1864. Letters Received, AGO. RG 94, NA.

49. Testimony of Col. T. W. Higginson before AFIC. AAR of Lt. Col. John Foley, 11 Oct. 1864. "The Negro," pp. 2552, 3374–75. RG 94, NA; HQ Dept. of Virginia and North Carolina. 11 Oct. 1864. George R. Sherman Papers, RIHS. Also see Gus to Wife, 15 June 1864. Charles Augustus Hill Papers, Richard S. Tracy Collection; G. A. Rockwood to Sir, 31 Oct. 1864. 890 R 1864. Letters Received, AGO. RG 94, NA; AAR of Col. A. G. Draper, 15 May 1864. "The Negro," pp. 3114–16. RG 94, NA; Medals of Honor Awarded in the Virginia Campaign, *OR* I, 42, pt. 1, pp. 849–50.

50. AAR of Col. S. G. Hicks, 6 Apr. 1864. *OR* I, 32, pt. 1, p. 549; Gus to Wife, 15 June 1864. Charles Augustus Hill Papers, Richard S. Tracy Collection. Also see Higginson, *Army Life*, p. 123; GO No. 50. HQ, 14th USCT. 23 Nov. 1864. Berlin et al., *Freedom*, II, p. 559.

51. Stuart Hall, "Reminiscence," p. 40. Morris Stuart Hall Papers, BL, UMI. Also see *OR* I, 46, pt. 1, p. 61; Glatthaar, "Hood's Tennessee Campaign," pp. 191–93, 199–201; *OR* I, 45, pt. 1, pp. 59, 103.

52. Walter Chapman to Parents, 11 Apr. 1865. Walter A. Chapman Papers, YU. Also see Henry to parents & all, 10 Apr. 1865. Henry M. Crydenwise Papers, EU; AAR of Brig. Gen. John P. Hawkins, 16 Apr. 1865. *OR* I, 49, pt. 1, p. 287.

53. John Pierson to Daughter, 3 Oct. 1864. SC, CL, UMI; Lewis to Mother, 17 Aug. 1864. Lewis Weld Family Papers, YU. Also see Hunter to Gov. Andrew, 4 May 1863. Ullmann to Stanton, 6 June 1863. Dana to Stanton, 22 June 1863. Thomas to Stanton, 7 Nov. 1864. "The Negro," pp. 1219–20, 1298, 1343, 2819. RG 94, NA.

54. L. Grim to Aunt Tillie, 27 June 1864. Wise-Clark Family Papers, UIA; Ullmann to William C. Bryant, 7 Mar. 1864. "The Negro," p. 2412. RG 94, NA; Sam S. Gardner to Sir, 13 Apr. 1865. 339 G 1865. Letters Received, AGO. RG 94, NA; C. P. Lyman to ones at Home, 21 June 1864. Carlos P. Lyman Papers, WRHS.

CHAPTER 9
Prejudice in the Service

1. Stanton to Saxton, 25 Aug. 1862. *OR* I, 14, p. 377; James Rogers to ?, 3 Mar. [1863]. SSC, Smith College. Also see N. P. Hallowell Folder, Loomis-Wild Family Papers, YU, for a recruiting leaflet.

2. See Cornish *The Sable Arm*, p. 187; GO, No. 163. AGO. 4 Jun. 1863. *OR* III, 3, p. 252.

3. Edward W. Kinsley to Col., 30 Jun. 1864. CWM, LC; Col. E. N. Hallowell to Governor Andrew, 23 Nov. 1863. Berlin et al., *Freedom*, II, p. 387. Also see N. P. Hallowell, "The Meaning of Memorial Day," an address

delivered 30 May 1896, in Hallowell, *Selected Letters and Papers*, p. 61; John Habberton diary, 14 May 1864. John Habberton Papers, MHI; Gov. Andrew to George J. Downing, Esq., 23 Mar. 1863 and to John Wilder, Esq., 23 May 1863. "The Negro," pp. 1132–33, 1264–65. RG 94, NA.

4. Hiram A. Peterson to Mr. Babcock, 24 Oct. [1863]. Berlin et al., *Freedom*, II, pp. 374–75; A. S. Fisher to Dear friend And Strange acquaintance, 14 Mar. 1864. A. S. Fisher Papers, Gettysburg College; Thomas D. Freeman to Martha, 25 Apr. 1864. Brown Family Papers, AAS; E. D. W. to Editor, 13 Mar. 1864. *Christian Recorder*, 2 Apr. 1864; Corp. James Henry Gooding to Lincoln, 28 Sep. 1863. "The Negro," pp. 1622–24. RG 94, NA.

5. Samuel Roosa to Abraham Lincoln, 24 Jan. 1864[5]. Berlin et al., *Freedom*, II, pp. 477–79; A. S. Fisher to Dear friend And Strange acquaintance, 14 Mar. 1864. A. S. Fisher Papers, Gettysburg College; A. S. Hartwell to Kinsley, 7 Apr. 1864. Edward A. Kinsley Papers, Duke U.; T. D. Freeman to William, 24 Mar. 1864. Brown Family Papers, AAS. Also see George Rodgers et al. to Mr. President, [Aug.] 1864. Berlin et al. *Freedom*, II, pp. 680–81; T. D. Freeman to William, 26 Mar. 1864. Brown Family Papers, AAS; Wilbur Nelson diary, 27 Apr. 1864. Nelson Family Papers, MISTU. Even after equal pay the problem continued. See Lt. Col. E. Mayer to Lt. Wm. M. Barrows, 4 Feb. 1865. Letters Sent, 45th USCI. RG 94, NA.

6. Comment by John A. Andrew on letter from A. S. Hartwell to Kinsley, 7 Apr. 1864. Edward A. Kinsley Papers, Duke U.

7. GO No. 46. Dept. of Virginia and North Carolina. 5 Dec. 1863. *OR* III, 3, p. 1140; Col. Montgomery to Sen. Wilson, 22 Jan. 1864. Montgomery Papers, KAHS; Joseph J. Scroggs diary, 30 Mar. 1864. CWTIC, MHI. Also see Chetlain to Thomas, 5 Apr. 1864. Lt. Col. A. G. Bennett to Thomas, 21 Nov. 1863. Wm. Birney to Foster, 12 Apr. 1864. "The Negro," pp. 2472, 1758–59, 2480. RG 94, NA; Col. Wm. A. Pile testimony before AFIC. Warren D. Hamilton to Stanton, May 1865. Bennett to Capt. Wm. L. M. Burger, 30 Nov. 1863. Berlin et al., *Freedom*, II, pp. 375–76, 384–85, 388–90.

8. Quoted in N. P. Hallowell, *Selected Letters and Papers*, p. 42. Also see Lt. Col. J. M. Williams to Capt. Loring, 21 Apr. 1863. Berlin et al., *Freedom*, II, pp. 72–73; Maj. J. J. Comstock to Col. E. Bailey, 16 Apr. 1864. "The Negro," pp. 2484–85. RG 94, NA; Capt. Thomas W. Fry to ?, 21 Sep. 1864. Chenery, *14th RIHA*, p. 66; Proceedings of GCM. Trial of Sgt. William Walker. MM 1320. RG 153, NA; Col. M. S. Littlefield to Col. P. P. Brown, Jr., 3 June 1864. Berlin et al., *Freedom*, II, pp. 394–95.

9. Circular, HQ, 55th Mass. Vols., 11 Jun. 1864 of Lt. Col. Chas. B. Fox to Col. A. S. Hartwell, 14 June 1864. "The Negro," pp. 2623–24. RG 94, NA. Also see Col. Hartwell to Governor, 12 June 1864 and Col. Hartwell to Sec. of War, 13 June 1864. "The Negro," pp. 2609–10, 2614. RG 94, NA.

10. See Edward Bates to President, 23 Apr. 1864. *OR* III, 4, pp. 271–74; Circular, No. 54. Provost Marshal General's Office, 20 July 1863. *OR* III, 3, p. 548; Thomas Webster to Lincoln, 30 July 1863. "The Negro," p. 1445. RG 94, NA.

11. Emilio, *Brave Black Regiment*, pp. 220–21. Also see *OR* III, 5, pp. 657–59; Higginson, *Army Life*, pp. 281–91.

12. Hill, *A Sketch of the 29th*, pp. 9–10. Also see Fox. *Record of the Service*, pp. 35–36.

13. G. H. White to Sir, 8 Sep. 1864. *Christian Recorder*, 17 Sep. 1864; Ferdinand H. Hughes to Mr. Editor, 28 Nov. 1864. *Christian Recorder*, 14 Jan. 1865; Wm. Paul Green to Mr. Editor, 2 Jan. 1865. *Christian Recorder*, 4 Feb. 1865. A perusal of the *Christian Recorder* for the final nine months of 1864 provides a good survey of the battle among black soldiers. Unfortunately, one of the most controversial articles, in the 15 Oct. edition, is missing, although one can readily infer the contents from the letters in response.

14. Testimony of Maj. Gen. Benjamin Butler before the AFIC. "The Negro," pp. 2560–61. RG 94, NA.

15. Capt. J. M. Williams et al. to Gen. James H. Lane, 9 Jan. 1863. Berlin et al., *Freedom*, II, pp. 334–35; Banks to Thomas, 12 Feb. 1863. *OR* III, 3, p. 46. Also see Gov. Andrew to Stanton, 3 Feb. 1863 and Stanton to Andrew, 13 Feb. 1863. *OR* III, 3, pp. 36, 47; Andrew to Charles Sumner, 7 Feb. 1863. "The Negro," pp. 1086–87. RG 94, NA; Richard J. Hinton to General, 12 Jan. 1863. Berlin et al., *Freedom*, II, pp. 335–36; Joshi and Reidy, "To Come Forward," pp. 331–32.

16. George W. Grubbs Memorandum, 28 Feb. 1864. George W. Grubbs Papers, INHS; J. B. McPherson et al. to Abraham Lincoln, February 1864. "The Negro," pp. 2377–78. RG 94, NA. Also see Banks to Lincoln, 17 Aug. 1863. *OR* I, 26, pt. 1, p. 688; Endorsement by Brig. Gen. Geo. L. Andrews, 28 Nov. [18]64 to letter of Privit Solomon Moses to Asst. Adjt. Gen. Geo. B. Drake, 19 Nov. 1864. Berlin et al., *Freedom*, II, p. 331; Maj. H. B. Scott to Maj. Gen. G. Wentzel, 21 Mar. 1865. "The Negro," pp. 3603–4. RG 94, NA. I failed to determine who that black officer in the 15th USCI was, but the source appears reliable.

17. Testimony of Chap. John Eaton, Jr., and Brig. Gen. Rufus Saxton before the AFIC. "The Negro," pp. 2565, 2548. RG 94, NA.

18. See Christian Fleetwood Papers, LC, and Louis Douglass letters in Carter G. Woodson Papers, LC; Thomas to Stanton, 7 Nov. 1864. *OR* III, 4, p. 922; Thomas To Stanton, 5 Oct. 1865. *OR* III, 5, p. 120; CMSRs of Sgt. William H. Combs, Sgt. Vanness V. Cook, and Sgt. Elijah Hair, 59th U.S. Colored Infantry. RG 94, NA; Foster to Maj. Gen. Canby, 30 Jan. 1865. "The Negro," p. 3546. RG 94, NA.

19. Late 2d Lieut. R. H. Isabelle to Ullman[n], 12 June 1863. Berlin et al., *Freedom*, II, p. 330; Joseph G. Parker to Stanton, 30 May 1863. "The Negro," pp. 1273–74. RG 94, NA; John H. W. N. Collins to Editor, 15 June 1864. *Christian Recorder*, 25 June 1864; Louis Douglass, et al. to Stanton, [Jan? 1865]. Berlin et al., *Freedom*, II, pp. 340–41; Rufus to Mr. Editor, 17 May 1864. *Christian Recorder*, 28 May 1864. Also see A Colored Man, Statements of, [Sep. 1863?]. J. H. W. N. Collins and John Shaffer to Honble Edwin M. Stanton, 11 Sep. 1864. Berlin et al., *Freedom*, II, pp. 153–56 and 339–40; Higginson, *Army Life*, p. 261; Testimony of Col. T. W. Higginson before the AFIC. "The Negro," p. 2552. RG 94, NA.

20. See Sgt. Swails to Capt. W. L. M. Burger, 15 Oct. 1864 with endorsements. J. G. Foster to Gov. Andrew, 18 Nov. 1864, with endorsements.

Memorandum of War Department, undated. Berlin et al., *Freedom*, II, pp. 342–46.

21. Gabriel Grays et al. to Capt. H. Ford Douglas, 19 Jun. 1865. Endorsement of Lt. Col. Gust. Heinricks to letter from Capt. H. Ford Douglas to Lieut. Jno. Barber, 20 Jun. 1865. Berlin et al., *Freedom*, II, pp. 421–22.

22. Chap. Francis A. Boyd to Butler, 5 Jan. 1865. Berlin et al., *Freedom*, II, p. 351. Also see Sgt. Francis A. Boyd to General, 4 Nov. 1864. Pvt. Francis A. Boyd to Your Excellency, 12 May 1865, with enclosures. Berlin et al., *Freedom*, II, pp. 350–54.

23. A Tribute of Regard To Chaplain White by Officers of 28th U.S.C.T., 11 Oct. 1865 in *Christian Recorder*, 25 Nov. 1865; ? to Stanton, 2 Oct. 1865. Berlin et al., *Freedom*, II, p. 655; Lewis to wife, 28 May 1864, 13 Mar. 1865. Jonathan Lewis Whitaker Papers, SHC, UNC. Also see James M. Trotter et al., Tribute to Rev. John R. Bowles, 7 May 1865 in *Christian Recorder*, 7 Jun. 1865; Geo. Washington Le Vere to Mr. Editor, 1 Dec. 1864 in *Christian Recorder*, 31 Dec. 1864.

24. H. M. Turner journal, 18 Dec. 1864 in *Christian Recorder*, 7 Jan. 1865; Louis Whitaker to wife, 13 Mar. 1865. Jonathan Lewis Whitaker Papers, SHC, UNC. Also see Chap. B. F. Randolph to Thomas, 31 May 1865. Berlin et al., *Freedom*, II, pp. 420–21.

25. See Maj. Gen. Curtis to Stanton, 29 Jun. 1864. Stanton to Curtis, 30 June 1864. John Shorter to Governor of Massachusetts, 9 June 1864. Andrew to Shorter, 12 June 1864. C. W. Foster to Hatch, 21 June 1864. J. T. Foster to Andrew, 18 Nov. 1864 and endorsements with comments by Andrew, 2 Dec. 1864; Col. Jas. A. Hardie, 10 Dec. 1864; C. W. Foster, 13 Dec. 1864. Col. A. S. Hartwell to Capt. W. L. M. Burger, 2 Feb. 1865. "The Negro," pp. 2650–51, 2608, 2824–27, and 3565–66; Hartwell to Kinsley, 28 Aug. 1864. E. W. Kinsley Papers, MAHS.

26. Quotation marks around the word *save* are the author's. Coln. N. P. Chipman to General, 16 Oct. [1862]. Berlin et al., *Freedom*, II, p. 71; Ullmann to Sen. Henry Wilson, 4 Dec. 1863. "The Negro," pp. 1784–85. RG 94, NA.

27. Capt. R. T. Auchmutz to Col. E. D. Townsend, 20 Dec. 1863. Berlin et al., *Freedom*, II, pp. 494–96; Capt. Joseph Walker to Maj. T. B. Brooks, 11 Sep. 1863. Butler to Stanton, 25 May 1862. "The Negro," pp. 1618–19, 864. RG 94, NA. Also see Stanton to Andrew, 11 July 1863. Grant to Halleck, 24 July 1863. "The Negro," p. 1383, 1429. RG 94, NA.

28. J. G. Foster to General, 7 July 1864. "The Negro," p. 2667. RG 94, NA; Inspection Report of U.S. Forces at Lafourche Dist., Louisiana, 26 Apr. 1864 by Lt. V. B. M. Bergen. Inspection Reports, Louisiana. RG 159, NA. Also see Mussey to Lieutenant, 11 Apr. 1864. Berlin et al., *Freedom*, II, p. 181; Testimony of Nathaniel Paige, Special Correspondent of the *New York Tribune*, before the AFIC. "The Negro," p. 2585. RG 94, NA.

29. [Nimrod Rowley] to My Dear Friend and X Pre., [Aug.] 1864. Berlin et al., *Freedom*, II, p. 501; A. S. Fisher to dear afflicted Captin, 31 July 1863. A. S. Fisher Papers, Gettysburg College; T. D. Freeman to William, 26 Mar. 1864. Brown Family Papers, AAS. Proceedings of GCM. Trial of Pvt. William G. Barcroft. LL 2675. RG 153, NA.

30. George J. Alden to Brig. Gen. Wilde, 9 Jan. 1864. Edward A. Wild Papers, MHI; Danl to Brother, 15 Dec. 1864. Densmore Family Papers, MNHS; Col. H. N. Frisbie to Lt. O. A. Rice, 24 Sep. 1864. Lt. Col. Morgan to Mussey, 6 Dec. 1863. Berlin et al., *Freedom*, II, pp. 511–12, 499. Also see James D. Fessenden to Father, 22 Feb. 1864. Fessenden Papers, Bowdoin College; Capt. O. J. Wright to Thomas, 3 Nov. 1864. Berlin et al., *Freedom*, II, p. 504; M. H. Twitchell, "Reminiscences," p. 73. M. H. Twitchell Papers, VTHS; Lt. H. Farrand to Maj. Brooks, 16 Sep. 1863. Capt. R. T. Auchmutz to Col. E. D. Townsend, 20 Dec. 1863. "The Negro," pp. 1619–21, 1854–55. RG 94, NA; Col. S. Fellows to Capt. H. W. Bowers, 19 Apr. 1864. Letters Received, 2nd USCI. RG 94, NA; Capt. Geo. Gourand to Capt. W. S. M. Burger, 22 Aug. 1864. Rosters, Reports and Lists, 2nd USCLA. RG 94, NA.

31. Col. H. N. Frisbie to Lt. O. A. Rice, 24 Sep. 1864. Col. J. C. Beecher to Brig. Gen. Wild, 13 Sep. 1863. Berlin et al., *Freedom*, II, pp. 511, 493–94. Also see McMurray, *Recollections*, 40–41, 46; Capt. W. von Bechtold to Lt. Col. H. J. Hall, 26 Nov. 1864. Letters Received (Unbound), 45th USCI. RG 94, NA; Report of Lt. Talcott, 12 Aug. 1863. "The Negro," pp. 1612–13. RG 94, NA; T. D. Freeman to William, 26 Mar. 1864. Brown Family, AAS; GO No. 47. HQ, Dept. of the South. 17 Sep. 1863. *OR* I, 28, pt. 2, p. 95; Col. S. Fellows to Capt. H. W. Bowers, 19 Apr. 1864. Letters Received, 2nd USCI. RG 94, NA; Capt. Geo. Gourand to Capt. W. S. M. Burger, 22 Aug. 1864. Rosters, Reports & Lists, 2nd USCLA. RG 94, NA.

32. Inspection Report of Provisional Brigade Attached to the 1st Division, USCT by Lt. George C. Haggerty, 20 July 1864. Inspection Reports, Arranged by States. MS. RG 159, NA; Meade to Grant, 26 Aug. 1864. *OR* I, 42, pt. 2, p. 519. Also see Mussey to Capt. Geo. B. Halstead, 6 June 1864; Brig. Gen. E. A. Wild to Col. Birney, 20 Oct. 1863; GO No. 105. HQ, Dept. of the South. 25 Nov. 1863; Ullmann to Thomas, 16 Apr. 1864. "The Negro," pp. 2603, 1684–85, 1766, 2486–87. RG 94, NA; Orders, No. 21. AGO. 14 June 1864; Thomas to Stanton, 7 Nov. 1864. *OR* III, 4, pp. 431, 922; Inspection of part of the 54th USCI. at Duvall's Bluff, Arkansas, 4 July 1864. Letters Received, IGO, RG 159, NA; Ullmann to Hon. Henry Wilson, 4 Dec. 1863. Berlin et al., *Freedom*, II, pp. 496–98; John Habberton diary, 28 June 1864. John Habberton Papers, MHI.

33. See Col. J. Garrard to Maj. Davis, 9 Apr. 1864. Letters Sent, 1st USCC. RG 94, NA; Inspection Report of Milliken's Bend, Vidalia, and Bullet's Bayou by Lt. Charles Robinett, Aug. 1865. Letters Received, IG. RG 159, NA; Orders. HQ, 107th USCI. 18 Jan. 1865. Unbound Issuances, 107th USCI. RG 94, NA. The government did not shortchange black units any more than white ones when it came to rations. The major debate over food within the USCT referred to the contrast between government rations and the food that slaves were accustomed to eating, specifically beef and wheat flour versus pork and corn meal.

34. Geo. Bliss, Jr., to Stanton, 4 Jan. 1864. "The Negro," p. 2308. RG 94, NA.

35. Capt. T. E. Ellsworth to Thomas, 25 Feb. 1864. Rosters, Reports and Lists, 2nd USCLA. RG 94, NA; Inspection Report of 82nd USCI by 1st Lt. W. Benham, July 1864. Inspection Reports, Louisiana. RG 159, NA. Also see Edw. W. Bacon to Kate, 6 Apr. 1864. E. W. Bacon Papers, AAS; C. A. Dana to Brig. Gen. John P. Hawkins, 2 Mar. 1864. "The

Negro," pp. 2401–2. RG 94, NA; Request of Officers of 4th USCHA that Artillery Pieces Be Repaired. Densmore Family Papers, MNHS; Col. Benj. R. Townsend to Thomas, 22 Aug. 1864. Lt. Col. John Wilder to Capt. E. B. Tracy, 18 Jan. 1865. Col. Townsend to Brig. Gen. Dyer, 22 Mar. 1865. Letters Sent, 2nd USCI. RG 94, NA; Brig. Gen. [Hinks] to Butler, 29 Apr. 1864. Ullmann to Henry Wilson, 4 Dec. 1863. Berlin et al., *Freedom*, II, pp. 548–49, 497.

36. See Inspection Report of Col. Marcy, 21 Jul. 1864. Letters Received, IG. RG 159, NA; Statement of Number, Kind, and Calibre of Arms Belonging to 2d Kans. Col'd Vols. (Infty) [83rd USCI]. Unbound Miscellaneous Papers, 83rd USCI (New). RG 94, NA; Inspection Report of U.S. Infantry (Colored) Serving with 2d Div. 13th Army Corps at Brownsville, Texas, 23 June 1864. Inspection Reports, Texas. RG 159, NA.

37. Inspection Report of Col. Randolph B. Marcy of 1st Kansas (Col) Inf. [79th USCI (New)]. Letters Received, IG. RG 159, NA; Report of Inspection of 3rd USCC by Maj. General N. J. T. Dana, 7 Aug. 1864. Letters Received, IG. RG 159, NA. Also see Inspection Report of 107th USCI in the field at Chapin's Farm, Virginia by Capt. Lewis Barnes, 20 Dec. 1864. Letters Received, USCT. Department of Virginia and North Carolina. RG 94, NA; Inspection Report of Col. Marcy of 54th USCI, 21 July 1864. Letters Received, IG. RG 159, NA; *OR* I, 34, pt. 1, p. 444.

38. See Final Report of the Provost Marshal General, 17 Mar. 1866. *OR* III, 5, pp. 667–69. Casualties by disease in the USCT were 141.39/1,000, and in general volunteers it was 59.22/1,000. Battlefield mortality was 16.11/1,000 in the USCT and 35.10/1,000 in the white volunteers.

39. General Summary of the Sickness and Mortality of Colored Troops During the War. *Medical and Surgical History*, Medical Volume, 1, pp. 710–12. The reason statistics were inaccurate was that doctors were so busy at times that they had no spare moments for paperwork. Even statistics on the number of white officers in the USCT who died was wrong. See Steiner, *Medical History*, p. 46, for a persuasive argument.

40. Annual Report of Joseph K, Barnes, Surgeon General, 20 Oct. 1864. *OR* III, 4, p. 792; C. H. Crane to Surg. Adam N. McLaren, 16 Oct. 1863. Personal Papers, Medical Officers and Physicians. Prior to 1912. Edgar L. Draper File. RG 94, NA.

41. C. W. Foster to Maj. Gen. J. G. Foster, 20 Dec. 1864. Letters Regarding Recruiting, Division of Colored Troops. RG 94, NA. Also see Mussey to C. W. Foster, 13 Mar. 1864. Letters Sent by the Commissioner, Dept. of the Cumberland. RG 393, NA.

42. See Berlin et al., *Freedom*, II, pp. 354–58 for excellent coverage of the Augusta affair. Also see Fort Green to Recorder, 24 Aug. 1864. *Christian Recorder*, 24 Sep. 1864.

43. See CMSR of Dr. John De Grasse. File of Dr. William C. Powell. Medical Officers & Physicians. Prior to 1910. RG 94, NA; Logan and Winston, *Dictionary of American Negro Biography*, pp. 169, 507–8.

44. Banks to Maj. C. T. Christenden, 18 July 1864. "The Negro," pp. 2694–95. RG 94, NA. Also see Pension File of Herman W. Dickinson. RG 15, NA; H. H. Hood to Wife, 20 Jan. 1863. Humphrey H. Hood Papers, ILSHL; [Col. Risdon] to Thomas, 11 May 1864. Risdon Papers, WRHS.

45. Mussey to Mr. Edwin H. Cooper, 20 Jan. 1865. Letters Sent by the

Commissioner, Dept. of the Cumberland. RG 393, NA. Also see Thomas to Stanton, 19 Sep., 7 Nov. 1864. *OR* III, 4, pp. 733, 922; Rufis Ollogin to Friend Moulton, 1 Mar. 1865. Palmer Collection, WRHS; J. K. Bandery to Stearns, 9 Dec. 1863. Proceedings of Boards of Examination for Commissions in the USCT, Dept. of the Cumberland, 1863–1864. RG 393, NA; Memo dated 19 May 1863 in Personal Papers, Medical Officers and Physicians. Prior to 1912. William Bidlack File. RG 94, NA; J. O. Moore to Lizzie, 10 July [1864]. James O. Moore Papers, Duke U.; C. G. G. Merrill Papers, YU, especially C. G. G. M. to Father, 22 Jan. 1864; George W. Adams, *Doctors in Blue*, p. 175.

46. Dover's Powder is a combination of ipecac and opium. James to Lizzie, 23 July 1865. James O. Moore Papers, Duke U.; H. H. Hood to Wife, 26 June 1865. Humphrey H. Hood Papers, ILSHL; [Francis Minot Weld] to Aunt, 3 May 1864. Blake, *Diaries and Letters of Francis Minot Weld*, pp. 152–53.

47. Inspection Report for the Dept. of Arkansas by Col. Marcy, 15 Aug. 1864. Inspection Reports, 1865. RG 159, NA; ? to Sir, 20 Aug. 1864. Berlin et al., *Freedom*, II, pp. 640–41. Also see Proceedings of GCM. Trial of George M. Potts. MM 3067. RG 153, NA; Charges and Specifications against Dr. S. F. Selby, A. A. Surgeon, undated. Letters Sent by the Commissioner, Dept. of the Cumberland. RG 393, NA; H. H. Hood to Wife, 2 Sep. 1864. Humphrey H. Hood Papers, ILSHL; Dr. E. P. Gray to Surg. R. H. Alexander, 20 Nov. 1863. Personal Papers, Medical Officers and Physicians. File of Elias W. Gray. RG 94, NA; John H. Wilkison to Honored Sir, 28 Nov. 1864. ? to unidentified official, 18 Oct. 1864. Berlin et al., *Freedom*, II, pp. 642–44.

48. Dr. Seth Rogers to ?, 4 Apr. 1863. MOLLUS Collection, MHI; W. W. McDowell, Dr. at Small Pox Hospital at Natchez, to Surg. George S. Kemble, 3 May 1864. File of Elias W. Gray. Personal Papers, Medical Officers and Physicians. Prior to 1912. RG 94, NA; Newton, *Out of the Briars*, p. 82; T. D. Freeman to William, 26 Mar. 1864. Brown Family Papers, AAS. Also see W. W. McDowell to Thomas, 7 May 1864. Court of Inquiry, 24 May 1864. E. W. Gray to Thomas, 7 May 1864. File of Elias W. Gray. Personal Papers, Medical Officers and Physicians. Prior to 1912. RG 94, NA.

49. ? to Sir, 20 Aug. 1864. Berlin et al., *Freedom*, II, pp. 640–41.

50. Proceedings of GCM. Trial of Surg. Lyman Allen, with endorsement by Brig. Gen. C. J. Paine. LL 3199. RG 153, NA. Also see Proceedings of GCM. Trial of Surg. E. Jackson. MM 1664. RG 153, NA.

51. Proceedings of GCM. George J. Potts to Thomas, 22 Mar. 1865. Lt. Col. M. L. Dempcy to E. W. Smith, 22 Mar. 1865. Report of Wm. A. Conover, Medical Director, 25th AC, 25 Mar. 1865. Trial of Dr. George J. Potts. MM 3067. RG 153, NA. Also see Edward W. Bacon to Kate, 24 Sep. 1865. Edward W. Bacon Papers, AAS.

52. See Danl to friends at home, 10 Dec. 1864. Densmore Family Papers, MNHS; G. C. C. M. to Father, 28 Feb. 1864. Charles Merrill Papers, YU; Dr. Seth Rogers to ?, 31 Dec. 1862. MOLLUS Collection, MHI; John M. Hawks diary, 20 Aug. 1864. John M. Hawks Papers, BPL; Steiner, *Medical History*, p. 120; Inspection Report of Dept. of Arkansas, 13 Jan. 1865 by Col. R. B. Sackett. Letters Received, IGO. RG 159, NA; H. H. Hood to Wife, 3 Oct. 1863. Humphrey H. Hood Papers, ILSHL.

An inspection in the West uncovered only one regimental hospital in poor condition in which medical officials were to blame.

53. Inspection of Medical Dept. for Dept. of Arkansas by Col. Marcy, 15 Aug. 1864. Inspection Report of Medical Dept., Dept. of the Mississippi by Col. Marcy, March 1865. Inspection Report of the Medical Dept. of the Mississippi by Col. Marcy, 7 June 1865. Inspection Reports, 1865. Inspection Report of Dept. of Arkansas, 13 Jan. 1865 by Col. R. B. Sackett. Letters Received, IGO. RG 159, NA. Also see Wm. M. Chambers et al., Report on the Conditions of U.S. (Small Pox) Hospital No. 11. 1 Oct. 1864. Letters Received Relating to Recruiting, RG 94, NA; Inspection Report of Troops at District of Vicksburg, 20 Aug. 1864 by Capt. S. Bostwick. Inspection Reports, Mississippi. RG 159, NA.

54. Albert Rogall diary, 24 Aug. 1864. Albert Rogall Papers, OHS; Col. Jeptha Garrard to Maj. Davis, 1 Mar. 1864. Letters Sent, 1st USCC. RG 94, NA.

55. Capt. Josiah V. Meigs to Thomas, 25 July 1864. Letter Book, Battery A, 2nd USCLA. RG 94, NA; Mussey to Capt. C. P. Brown, 21 Dec. 1864. Letters Sent by the Commissioner, Dept. of the Cumberland. RG 393, NA; Thomas to Colonel R. C. Wood, 16 Jan. 1865. Berlin et al., *Freedom*, II, p. 645. Also see Ch. G. G. Merrill to Sister, 11 Apr. 1863. Charles Merrill Papers, YU; Mussey to Capt. Rusling, 7 Feb. 1865. Letters Sent by the Commissioner, Dept. of the Cumberland. RG 393, NA.

56. [Duren Kelley] to Emma, 24 July 1864. Offenberg, *Letters of Duren F. Kelley*, p. 111. Also see Steiner, *Medical History*, pp. xvii, 45; [Ullmann] to Lt. Col. C. T. Christensen, 29 Oct. 1864. Berlin et al., *Freedom*, II, pp. 513–14; T. Montgomery to Father, 16 Sep. 1864. Montgomery Papers, MNHS; Chenery, *14th RIHA*, p. 105.

57. Col. Stark Fellows to Parents, [Nov. 1863]. Tarbox, *Memoirs of James H. Schneider*, p. 139; Chap. J. H. Schneider to AAG Samuel T. Brick, 29 Feb. 1864. Letters Received, 2nd USCI. RG 94, NA; Fellows to Parents, [Feb. 1864]. Tarbox, *Memoirs of James H. Schneider*, p. 163; Lt. Col. B. R. Townsend to Capt. H. W. Bowers, 5 July 1864. Letters Sent, 2nd USCI. RG 94, NA.

58. Albert Rogall diary, 26 Apr. 1864. Albert Rogall Papers, OHS; Lt. Col. S. Fellows to Maj. C. H. Raymond, 19 Nov. 1863. "The Negro," p. 1749. RG 94, NA. Also see Albert Rogall diary, 27 Apr. 1864. Albert Rogall Papers, OHS; Brig. Gen. B. F. Kelley to Lt. Col. Wm. Cheseborough, 3 Apr. 1863. "The Negro," p. 1165. RG 94, NA.

59. A. T. Augusta to the Editor of the *Republican*, 15 May 1863. *Christian Recorder*, 30 May 1863.

60. James C. Beecher to friend, 29 Apr. 1864. J. M. and Esther Hawks Papers, LC; Thomas to Stanton, 14 Jun. 1864. "The Negro," p. 2618. RG 94, NA; 1st Regt. Infty. Corps to A. A. A. Genl. G. Norman Lieber, 28 Mar. 1864. Berlin et al., *Freedom*, II, p. 416. Also see Thomas to Stanton, 20 Sep. 1864. *OR* III, 4, p. 734; Endorsement of Maj. Gen. Banks. "The Negro," pp. 1831–32. RG 94, NA; Mussey to Stearns, 17 Aug. 1864. Letters Sent by the Commissioner, Dept. of the Cumberland. RG 393, NA; A.A.G. J. H. Hammond to Br. Gen. Jno. A. Rawlins, 10 Mar. 1864. Orders No. 17. AGO. "The Negro," pp. 2414, 2420–22. RG 94, NA; Col. Chas. A. Gilchrist to Lt. T. Sumner Greene, 31 July

1864. Letter Book, 50th USCI. RG 94, NA; First Lt. J. R. McGinnis to Capt. James W. Grace, 3 Aug. 1864. Col. Hallowell to Capt. W. L. M. Burger, 24 Aug. 1864. Berlin et al., *Freedom*, II, pp. 502–3.

61. H. H. Hood to Wife, 10 Sep. 1863. Humphrey H. Hood Papers, ILSHL.

62. Capt. Josiah V. Meigs to Brig. Gen. Granger, 26 May 1864. Letter Book, 2nd USCLA. RG 94, NA.

63. Lt. Col. E. Mayer to Lt. Wm. M. Barrows, 14 Feb. 1865. Letters Sent, 45th USCI. RG 94, NA. Also see [Lewis] to Wife, 23 July, 4 Dec. 1864. Jonathan Lewis Whitaker Papers, SHC, UNC.

64. Thos. Montgomery to Father and Mother, 10 May 1864. Montgomery Papers, MNHS; J. Owen, Jr., to Fannie, 17 July 1864. John Owen, Jr., Papers, MAHS. Also see GO No. 64. HQ, Dept. of the Gulf. 29 Aug. 1863. *OR* I, 26, pt. 1, p. 704; Capt. B. H. Polk to Maj. T. E. Tupper, 26 Feb. 1864. Tupper to Mussey, 29 Feb. 1864. Col. J. M. Alexander to Lt. Col. Wilson, 10 Sep. 1863. Col. J. M. Alexander to Thomas, 17 Oct. 1863. GO No. 3. HQ, 2nd Div. 16th Army Corps. 13 Sep. 1863. "The Negro," pp. 2408, 1567, 1680, and 1579.

65. Stearns to Henry Wilson, 4 Mar. 1864. "The Negro," pp. 2404–6. RG 94, NA; GO No. 12. HQ U.S. Forces, Port Hudson, Louisiana. 30 July 1863. *OR* I, 26, pt. 1, pp. 663–64; GO No. 46. Commander, Dept. of Virginia and North Carolina. 5 Dec. 1863. *OR* III, 3, p. 1142. Also see Brig. Gen. E. A. Wild, U.S. Army General's Reports of Civil War Service, 1864–1887. RG 94, NA; A.A.G. J. H. Hammond to Col. W. H. Revere and Lt. Col. John S. Bishop, 1 Aug. 1864. Unbound Letters Received, 107th USCI. RG 94, NA; GO No. 29. HQ, Dept. of Virginia. 18 Mar. 1865. "The Negro," p. 3601. RG 94, NA.

66. H. H. Hood to Wife, 23 Jul. 1864. Humphrey H. Hood Papers, ILSHL; H. G. Crickmore to John G. Wellstood, 21 July 1865. 4th U.S.C.C. Folder, Regimental Papers, Palmer Collection, WRHS.

67. Dr. Seth Rogers to ?, 3 Jan. 1863. MOLLUS Collection, MHI; C. A. Dana to Gideon Wells, 29 Oct. 1864. "The Negro," p. 2811. RG 94, NA. Also see Mussey to Capt. C. P. Brown, 24 Nov. 1864 and to Lt. Geo. Mason, 14 Mar. 1864. Letters Sent by the Commissioner, Dept. of the Cumberland. RG 393, NA.

68. Dr. Seth Rogers to ?, 1 Feb. 1863. MOLLUS Collection, MHI; G. W. H. to Editor, 10 May 1864. *Christian Recorder*, 28 May 1864. Also see Thomas to Stanton, 5 Oct. 1863. Berlin et al., *Freedom*, II, pp. 414–15; Foster to Thomas, 13 July 1864, endorsed by Maj. Gen. J. B. McPherson. "The Negro," pp. 2674–75. RG 94, NA. Wild permitted freedmen to flog a cruel master. J. O. Moore to Lizzie, 12 May 1864. James O. Moore Papers, Duke U. Cook was later the hero of the battle at Big Black River Bridge.

69. See Proclamation of Jefferson Davis, 23 Dec. 1862. *OR* II, 5, p. 797; Joint Resolutions adopted by the Confederate Congress on the subject of retaliation, 30 Apr., 1 May 1863. *OR* II, 4, pp. 940–41; Col. Jno. R. F. Tattnall to Capt. S. Croom, 8 Nov. 1862. Berlin et al., *Freedom*, II, pp. 570–71; Matson, "The Colored Man in the Civil War," pp. 242–43; Lt. Gen. E. Kirby Smith to Maj. Gen. R. Taylor, 13 Jun. 1863. Berlin et al., *Freedom*, II, p. 578; Maj. Gen. G. E. P[ickett] to General, 15 Dec. 1863. "The Negro," pp. 2294–95; F. H. Pierpont to Sec. of War, 27 Jan. 1864. "The Negro," pp. 2341–42. RG 94, NA.

70. [Charles] to Father, 13 Mar. 1864. Charles G. Merrill Papers, YU. Also see [John Owen] to Mother, ND. John Owen, Jr. Papers, MAHS; [James] to Wife, 26 Apr. 1864. Peet Papers, MNHS; H. H. Hood to Wife, 31 Aug. 1864. Humphrey H. Hood Papers, ILSHL; Proceedings of GCM. Trial of Thomas Fore et al. Testimony of Pvt. Henry Johnson. MM 2079. RG 153, NA; Higginson, *Army Life*, p. 249.

71. See Thomas S. Johnson to People, 17 Dec. 1864. Thomas S. Johnson Papers, SHSW; Dr. Seth Rogers to ?, 14 May 1863. MOLLUS Collection, MHI.

72. Sutherland, "The Negro in the Late War," 1, p. 175; Hen [Marshall] to Folks at Home, 3 May 1863. SC, CL, UMI; William to Sarah Ann, 19 Apr. 1863. William H. Parkinson Papers, EU; J. Owen, Jr. to Aunt, 6 May [1864]. John Owen, Jr. Papers, MAHS. Also see John Pierson to Daughter, 25 Apr. 1864. SC, CL, UMI; Rufus Kinsley diary, 27 Sep. 1863. Rufus Kinsley Papers, VTHS; Jeff to Tillie, 14 Aug. 1864. Wise-Clark Family Papers, UIA.

73. Instructions for the Government of Armies of the United States in the Field, 24 Apr. 1863. *OR* III, 3, pp. 155. Also see Proclamation of the President, 30 July 1863, in GO No. 252. AGO. 31 July 1863. *OR* II, 6, p. 163.

74. Brig. Gen. Wild to Capt. George Johnson, 28 Dec. 1863. "The Negro," p. 2281. RG 94, NA. Also see R. Saxton to Stanton, 28 Nov. 1862. Letterpress Copybook, 1862 Jun. 8–1864 Oct. 15. R. and W. Saxton Papers, YU; Historical Sketch of the 79th U.S.C.I., by J. M. Williams. J. M. Williams Papers, KASHS; Col. J. M. Williams to Maj. T. R. Livingston, 21 May 1863. Berlin et al., *Freedom*, II, pp. 574–75; Butler to Stanton, 31 Dec. 1863. *OR* I, 29, pt. 2, pp. 595–96; SO No. 282. HQ, Dist. of Tennessee. 28 Nov. 1864. CMSR of Asst. Surg. Eli Hewitt, 15th USCI. RG 94, NA; Hunter to Col. James Montgomery, 9 June 1863. *OR* I, 14, p. 467; Milton M. Holland to Messenger, 19 Jan. 1864. Levstik, "From Slavery to Freedom," p. 12.

75. Crawford, *Kansas in the Sixties*, p. 108; Higginson, *Army Life*, pp. 150–51; GO, No. 16. HQ, 10th Regt. Corps d'Afrique [82nd USCI]. 7 Aug. 1863. Berlin et al., *Freedom*, II, p. 600. Also see Higginson, *Army Life*, p. 251; Walter Chapman to Brother, 3 Dec. 1862. Walter A. Chapman Papers, YU.

76. Charles W. Singer to Mr. Editor, 18 Sep. 1864. *Christian Recorder*, 8 Oct. 1864; Chenery, *14 RIHA*, p. 49; S. M. Quincy to Mother, 29 Dec. 1863. Quincy, Wendell, Holmes and Upham Families Papers, MAHS; Henry to Parents & all, 31 Jan. 1864. Henry Crydenwise Papers, EU. Also see H. H. Hood to Wife, 16 July 1863. Humphrey H. Hood Papers, ILSHL; Oliver Van Valin to Uncle, 25 Sep. 1864. Oliver Van Valin Papers, BL, UMI; J. O. Moore to Lizzie, 25 Sep. 1864. James O. Moore Papers, Duke U. For a discussion of Copperheads' views on blacks, see Abrams, "The Copperhead Newspapers and the Negro," pp. 131–52.

77. Lincoln to Hon. James C. Conkling, 26 Aug. 1863. Basler, *Abraham Lincoln: His Speeches and Writings*, p. 722; Lincoln to Albert G. Hodges, 4 Apr. 1864. Basler, *The Collected Works of Abraham Lincoln*, 7, p. 282.

78. L. Grim to Aunt Tillie, 27 June 1864. Wise-Clark Family Papers, UIA; H. H. Hood to Wife, 20 Sep. 1864. Humphrey H. Hood Papers, ILSHL.

79. See John Habberton diary, 5 Mar. 1864. John Habberton Papers, MHI; Lewis to Mother, 22 Nov. 1864. Lewis Weld Family, YU.

80. Matson, "The Colored Man in the Civil War," pp. 242–43. Also see Norton, *Army Letters*, pp. 285, 295.

81. Gus to Wife, 12 Dec. 1863. Charles Augustus Hill Papers, in Richard S. Tracy Collection. Also see John Pierson to Daughter, 4 Nov. 1864. SC, CL, UMI.

CHAPTER 10
Army of Occupation

1. Madison to Lizzie, 11 Sep. 1864. James M. Bowler Papers, MNHS; Chas. R. Riggs to Brother, 30 Sep. 1864. Charles R. Riggs Papers, IASHS; L. Grim to Aunt Tillie, 8 Sep. 1864. Wise-Clark Family Papers, UIA; James Henry to Father, 18 Oct. 1864. James Henry Wickes Papers, BPL. Also see Jeff to Tillie, 22 Nov. 1864. Wise-Clark Family Papers, UIA; Sam to Father, 16 Sep., 16 Oct. 1864. Evans Family Papers, OHS.

2. [Sam] to Dear friend, 15 Mar. 1865. Duncan-Jones Papers, NHHS. Also see Monthly Report of Chap. Geo. N. Carruthers, 31 Mar. 1865. CWM, LC; Thomas to Brother Barnabas, 2 Apr. 1865. Thomas S. Johnson Papers, SHSW; G. H. White to Mr. Editor, 12 Apr. 1865. *Christian Recorder*, 22 Apr. 1865; Sutherland, "The Negro in the Late War," p. 181.

3. Gus to Wife, 12 Dec. 1863. Charles Augustus Hill Papers, Richard S. Tracy Collection; J. H. Mead to Ellen, 4 May 1864[5]. Mead Family, UIA.

4. [George] to Sister, 23 Apr. 1865. George Gaskill Folder, SP-AM War Survey, Civil War, MHI; Papa to Children, 15 Apr. 1865. Warren Goodale Papers, MAHS. Also see Madison to Lizzie, Apr. 1865. James M. Bowler Papers, MNHS.

5. Chauncy Leonard to Thomas, 30 Apr. 1865. 287 L 1865. Letters Received, AGO. RG 94, NA; W. B. Johnson to Mr. Editor, 28 Apr. 1865. *Christian Recorder*, 20 May 1865; John C. Brock, "Death of the President," in *Christian Recorder* 6 May 1865.

6. For a letter calling for an increase in the enlistment of blacks after the war, see C. H. Howard to Brother, 24 May 1865. O. O. Howard Papers, Bowdoin. On all phases of Reconstruction, see Foner, *Reconstruction*.

7. See Coffman, *The Old Army*, pp. 215–20, 234–37; Sefton, *The United States Army and Reconstruction*.

8. See Foner, *Reconstruction*, pp. 77–175; McFeely, *Yankee Stepfather*.

9. His brother Charles and Lt. Col. William Beebe were in the 128th USCI and Lt. Joseph A. Sladen of 14th USCI remained on his staff.

10. Henry to Parents, 25 June 1865. Henry M. Crydenwise Papers, EU. Also see Henry to Parents & All, 14 May 1865. Henry M. Crydenwise Papers, EU.

11. Henry to Parents, 25 June 1865. Henry M. Crydenwise Papers, EU; Samuel D. Barnes diary, 3 Dec. 1965, with summary of his address in *Southern Sentinel*. CWM, LC.

12. See Joseph K. Nelson, "Reminiscences," p. 56. CWMC, MHI.

13. Madison to Lizzie, 26 July 1865. James M. Bowler Papers, MNHS; Henry to Parents, 25 June 1865. Henry M. Crydenwise Papers, EU; Saml Evans to Father, 17 Aug. 1865. Evans Family Papers, OHS.

14. C. P. Lyman to Ones at Home, 31 Aug. 1865. Carlos P. Lyman Papers, WRHS; [Gus] to Wife, 13 Aug. 1865. Charles Augustus Hill Papers, Richard S. Tracy Collection. Also see Addeman, "Reminiscences of Two Years," p. 35.

15. Col. Chas. G. Bartlett to Capt. W. T. Y. Schenck, 15 Jan. 1866. Press Copies, 119th USCT. RG 94, NA. Also see Saml Evans to Father, 17 Aug. 1865. Evans Family Papers, OHS; Frank to Father, 13 Sep.[Oct.] 1865. Palmer Collection, WRHS; ? to AAG, 25 Sep. 1865. Charles R. Riggs Papers, IASHS.

16. [Gus] to Wife, 13 Aug. 1865. Charles Augustus Hill Papers, Richard S. Tracy Collection; H. M. Turner to Stanton, 14 Feb. 1866. Berlin et al., *Freedom*, II, p. 757. Also see Frank to Father, 23 Apr. 1865. Palmer Collection, WRHS; B to Friends, 28 Jun. 1865. Densmore Family Papers, MNHS.

17. Henry to Mother, 29 Oct. 1865. Henry M. Crydenwise Papers, EU; Quotes in Foner, *Reconstruction*, p. 120. Also see Papa to Children, 15 Apr. and 20 Apr. 1865. Warren Goodale Papers, MAHS; Thos. Montgomery to Bro James Charles, 21 Jul. 1866. Montgomery Papers, MNHS; Sam Evans to Father, 9 Jul. and 8 Oct. 1865 and 7 Jan. 1866. Evans Family Papers, OHS.

18. See Lt. Thos. C. Bennett to Lt., 26 Aug. 1865. Berlin et al., *Freedom*, II, p. 743.

19. Stuart to Sister Fannie, 24 Feb. 1866. M. S. Hall, BL, UMI; Louis E. Granger to General, 19 Jan. 1866. Daniel Ullmann Papers, NYHS. Also see Capt. Edwin Latimer to Lt. Col. Chamberlain, 27 June 1865. Maj. Gen. Harstuff to Maj. Gen. Weitzel, 13 May 1865. Berlin et al., *Freedom*, II, 737–39; N. S. Andrews to Enlisted Men of 2nd Battalion, 12th USCHA, 23 May 1865. Resolution Requesting the President to Withdraw Negro Troops from Kentucky, 3 June 1865. "The Negro," pp. 3653–54, 3661. RG 94, NA; Proceedings of GCM. Trial of Lt. Frank Baird. MM 3864. RG 153, NA.

20. Statement of Sgt. Joe Brown, [11 Sep.] 1865. Berlin et al., *Freedom*, II, pp. 743–44. Also see Thomas To Brother James, 4 June 1866. Montgomery Papers, MNHS; Lovett, "Memphis Riots."

21. H. M. Turner to Stanton, 14 Feb. 1866. Berlin et al., *Freedom*, II, pp. 756–57. Also see Marrs, *Life and History*, pp. 73–74; N. B. Sterritt to Mr. Editor, 22 June 1865. *Christian Recorder*, 8 July 1865; Lt. Col. M. H. Tuttle to Lt. Will H. Williams, 21 Dec. 1865. Letters Received, 50th USCI. Capt. F. B. Clark to Lt. Lamberton, 26 June 1866. Unbound Letters Received, 107th USCI. RG 94, NA.

22. Thos. Montgomery to Brother Alexander, 22 Apr. 1866. Montgomery Papers, MNHS. Also see Sam Evans to Father, 18 Dec. 1865. Evans Family Papers, OHS; C. H. Howard to Brother, 27 Sep. 1865. O. O. Howard Papers, Bowdoin College; Charles T. Trowbridge, "Experiences in the Freedmen's Bureau," pp. 7–8. Trowbridge Papers, MNHS. Howard mentions the murder of two officers in South Carolina, but it seems

apparent from the time and Trowbridge's account that he was referring to the murder of Furman.

23. See Charles T. Trowbridge, "Experiences in the Freedmen's Bureau," pp. 1, 15–17. Trowbridge Papers, MNHS.

24. See E. S. Robinson to Maj. Gen. Q. A. Gillmore, 7 Aug. 1865. Berlin et al., *Freedom*, II, p. 742.

25. Capt. Will R. Story to Mr. John J. King, 15 Aug. 1865. Letter of Will Story, University of Tennessee Library. Also see Col. H. N. Frisbie to Thomas Conway, 2 Oct. 1865 and Conway to Frisbie, 5 Oct. 1865. Norman Riley to Dear wife, 12, 26 Aug., 22 Sep. 1865. Catherine Riley to Norman Riley, 28 Aug. 1865, with endorsement from Capt. F. P. Meigs. Capt. F. B. Clark to Lt. E. T. Manberton, 15 Nov. 1865 with endorsements from Lt. Col. Sells and Maj. Gen. Palmer. Berlin et al., *Freedom*, II, pp. 701–5, 750–51; Madison to Lizzie, 26 Jul. 1865. J. M. Bowler Papers, MNHS.

26. Col. Chas. B. Bartlett to Maj. I. H. Frazee, 14 Nov. 1865. Letter Book, 119th USCI. RG 94, NA; Wilbur Nelson diary, 2 Sep. 1865. Nelson Family, MISTU. Also see Capt. Densmore to Capt. Moss, 23 June 1865. Densmore Letterbook, Densmore Family Papers, MNHS; GO No. 21. HQ, First Div. USC Troops. 3 May 1865. Charles R. Riggs Papers, IASHS; GO, No. 17. HQ, Post of Nashville. 22 Sep. 1865. "The Negro," p. 3695. RG 94, NA; Proceedings of GCM. Trial of Polk Martin. MM 3614. RG 153, NA.

27. Report of Inspector for Dept. of Louisiana of 20th USCI for July 1865, stationed at Post Donaldsonville, in IG Hardie to Foster, 25 Aug. 1865. Berlin et al., *Freedom*, II, pp. 741–42; Wm. B. Johnson to Mr. Editor, 22 June 1865. *Christian Recorder*, 8 July 1865; Thomas to Brother James, 4 June 1866. Montgomery Papers, MNHS. Also see William P. Green to Rev. Sir, 8 Aug. 1865. *Christian Recorder*, 9 Sep. 1865, and Charles R. Riggs Papers, IASHS, which discusses altercations and punishments.

28. Special Inspection in Dept. of the Ohio relative to Military Instruction of the 125th Regiment USCI, 5 Mar. 1866, by Bvt. Brig. Gen. Hart. Letters Received, IGO. RG 159, NA. Also see J. C. B. to Col. William Gurney, 15 May [1866]. James C. Beecher Papers, Radcliffe College; B. Marshall Mills to Mother, 18 May 1865. Caleb Mills Papers, INHS; Lovett, *Tennessee Historical Quarterly*, 38, pp. 9–33.

29. See Inspection Report of Dept. of Kentucky by Maj. Chas. E. Behle, 5 Mar. 1866. Letters Received, IGO. Inspection Report of Milliken's Bend, Vidalia, & Bullet's Bayou, Aug. 1865 by Lt. Chas. Robinett. Inspection Reports, Louisiana. Inspection Report of Forts Pickens, Barrancas and McRae and Barrancas Redoubt, 4 Dec. 1865 by Lt. Col. J. Schuyler Crosby. Letters Received, IGO. RG 159, NA.

30. Halleck to Stanton, 28 Apr. 1865. *OR* I, 46, pt. 3, p. 990. Also see GO, No. 50. HQ Dept. of Virginia. 1 May 1865. *OR* I, 46, pt. 3, p. 1062.

31. See Ord to Brig. Gen. Gordon, 12 May 1865. Brig. Gen. Gordon to Capt. O. Brown, 6 Jun. 1865; Bvt. Brig. Gen. Cole to [25 AC HQ], [Jun. 1865]; Unsigned to sir, Dec. 1865. Berlin et al., *Freedom*, II, pp. 721–27; Maj. R. Dollard to Lt. Walter Munson, 15 Jun. 1865. "The Negro," pp. 3679–80. RG 94, NA.

32. Newton, *Out of the Briars*, p. 70; Hill, *A Sketch of the 29th*, p. 27; J. H. Mead to Ellen, 11 Jul. 1865. Mead Family Papers, UIA.

33. Lorenzo Gould diary, 30 June 1865. CWMC, MHI; Edward W. Bacon to Kate, 10 July 1865. Edward W. Bacon Papers, AAS. Also see Jocelyn, *Mostly Alkili*, p. 55; Lorenzo Gould diary, 23, 25 June 1865. CWMC, MHI.

34. Edward W. Bacon to Kate, 5 Jul. 1865. Edward W. Bacon Papers, AAS; J. H. M. to Ellen, 16 Aug. 1865. Mead Family Papers, UIA. Also see GO, No. 27. HQ, 45th USCT. 22 June 1865. Regimental Orders, 45th USCI. RG 94, NA; Clapp, *Sketches of Army Life*, pp. 35–36; Jamie to Mother, 29 July 1865. Lewis, *My Dear Parents*, p. 145; Lorenzo Gould diary, 20, 29 Sep. 1865. CWMC, MHI; Papa to Children, 6 Aug. 1865. Warren Goodale Papers, MAHS; Edw W. Bacon to Kate, 13 Aug. 1865. Edward W. Bacon Papers, AAS.

35. Report of William A. Hammond, Surg. Gen., 10 Nov. 1862. *OR* III, 2, p. 750. Also see Adams, *Doctors in Blue*, pp. 212–13; *Medical and Surgical History*, Medical Volume, First Part, pp. 710–12, 636–41; Third Part, p. 694.

36. Francis Minot Weld diary, 24 May 1865. Blake, *Diaries and Letters of Francis Minot Weld*, p. 203; Proceedings of GCM. Surg. Potts to Surgeon E. P. Mooney, 5 Aug. 1865. Monthly Report of July 1865 of Surg. George Potts. MM 3069. Trial of Surg. George Potts. RG 153, NA; Charles to Father, 13 Aug. 1865. Charles Merrill Papers, YU. Also see Hemenway, "Observations on Scurvy," pp. 582–85; Lorenzo Gould diary, 9 Sep. 1865. CWMC, MHI; Monthly Report for June 1865 and Monthly Report for July 1865 by Dr. Henry Grange. 7th USCI Regimental Hospital Records. RG 94, NA; Proceedings of GCM. Trial of Surg. George Potts. Surg. Potts to Thomas, 12 July 1865 and Potts to Major Genl. Jas. K. Barnes, 20 July 1865. MM 3069. RG 153, NA; Charles to Father, 29 Aug. 1865. Charles Merrill Papers, YU; *Medical and Surgical History*, Medical Volume, Third Part, pp. 694–96.

37. Main, *3rd USCC*, p. 162; Col. Sells to Capt., 30 June 1866. Unbound Letters Received, 107th USCI. RG 94, NA. Also see Lorenzo Gould diary, 4 July 1865. CWMC, MHI; Chas. Rumph to Comd'g Officer, 10 Oct. 1865. Charles R. Riggs Papers, IASHS; Post Order, No. 4. HQ Post Pass Christian, MS. 17 Aug. 1865. Carpenter Family Papers, ILSHL; ? to Stanton, 2 Oct. 1865. Berlin et al., *Freedom*, II, pp. 425–26; Thos. Montgomery to Father, 23 Feb. 1866. Montgomery Papers, MNHS.

38. See Thomas S. Johnson to People, 11 May 1865. Thomas S. Johnson Papers, SHSW; Proceedings of GCM. Trial of Capt. Willard Dagget. MM 3067. Trial of Capt. Edwin Cooper. MM 3614. Trial of Capt. Oren Granville. MM 3067. Trial of Lt. Lewis Brown. MM 3603. RG 153, NA; ? to Mr. Stanton, 22 Oct. 1865. Capt. Edward Pease to Thomas, 14 Nov. 1865. John Bowie to AG, 25 Aug. 1871. Late QM Sgt. Chas. Davis to Capt. Kennedy, 21 Feb. 1866. Berlin et al., *Freedom*, II, pp. 425–27, 429–32.

39. See Inspection Report of Dept. of Alabama by Maj. G. Grosskopff, 1 Nov. 1865. Letters Received, IGO. RG 159, NA; Post Orders, No. 2. HQ Pass Christian, MS. 1 Aug. 1865. Carpenter Family, ILSHL; Col. Risdon to Lt. Gleason, 3 June 1865. Risdon Papers, WRHS; [Capt. Densmore] to Lt. Sanders, 28 June 1865. Densmore Letterbook, Densmore Family Papers, MNHS.

40. H. S. Harmon to Mr. Editor, [Sep. or Oct. 1865]. *Christian Recorder*, 21 Oct. 1865; William P. Green to Rev. Sir, 8 Aug. 1865. *Christian Recorder*, 9 Sep. 1865; ? to Mr. E. M. Stanton, 22 Aug. 1865. Berlin et al., *Freedom*, II, p. 774. *Freedom* has sundry examples.

41. See Proceedings of GCM. Trial of Pvt. Alexander Benjamin. MM 3707. Trial of Pvt. Dudley Simes. MM 3067. Trial of Pvt. Benjamin McCloud. MM 3243. RG 153, NA; Lt James Barnett to Lt. Lamberton, 22 Jan. 1866. Unbound Letters Received, 107th USCI. RG 94, NA; Sefton, *The United States Army and Reconstruction*, p. 51.

42. Proceedings of GCM. Trial of Pvt. James Mudd. Trial of Pvt. Sandy Feuqua. Trial of Pvt. James O'Banan. Trial of Corp. Jake Matlinger. Also see Trial of Sheldon Penock. MM 3244. RG 153, NA.

43. Edw. W. Bacon to Kate, 16 May 1865. Edward W. Bacon Papers, AAS. Also see Edward W. Bacon to Kate, 18 July 1865. Edward W. Bacon Papers, AAS.

44. Proceedings of GCM. Trial of Pvt. Jacob Plowder. OO 1477. Also see Trials of James Allen, Joseph Grien, Thomas Howard, and Joseph Nathaniel. OO 1477. RG 153, NA.

45. Marrs, *Life and History*, p. 25.

46. Recommendation of Chap. Asa B. Randall. Michael P. Musick Collection, MHI. Also see B. Densmore to Father, 17 May 1865. Densmore Family Papers, MNHS. Jones, *Soldiers of Light and Love*, discusses Northern attitudes on religion and education and their impact on citizenship very effectively.

47. See Owen Riedy to Sir, 4 Jan. 1865. 55 R 1865. Letters Received, AGO. RG 94, NA.

48. Monthly Report of Chap. Geo. N. Carruthers, 31 Jan. 1866. CWM, LC. Also see G. A. Rockwood to Sir, 31 Aug. 1865. 902 R 1865. Letters Received, AGO. RG 94, NA; Proceedings of GCM. Trial of Pvt. Richard Frisly. Trial of Pvt. Jacob H. Brown. MM 3244. RG 153, NA; Stuart Hall, "Reminiscences," pp. 11–12. Morris Stuart Hall Papers, BL, UMI; T. Montgomery to Mother, 22 Aug. 1864. Montgomery Papers, MNHS.

49. C. P. Taylor to Sir, 30 Sep. 1864. 617 T 1864. Letters Received, AGO. RG 94, NA; J. C. B. to Frankie, 15 Jun. 1863. Beecher Family Papers, Stowe-Day Foundation. Also see James Schneider to ?, 25 Jan. 1865 and [ND, 1864]. Tarbox, *Memoirs*, pp. 151, 157; Jas. Rogers to ?, 15 Feb. [1863]. James S. Rogers Papers, SSC, Smith College; J. Rice Taylor to Thomas, 30 Apr. 1865. 285 T 1865. A. C. McDonald to Thomas, [30] Sep. 1865. 2171 M 1865. Letters Received, AGO. RG 94, NA; A. C. McDonald to Sir, 1 June 1865. Letters Received Relating to Recruiting. RG 94, NA; Luther Bingham to?, ND. Bingham, *The Young Quartermaster*, pp. 83–84.

50. Henry Carpenter Hoyle to Editor, 9 Feb. 1865. *Christian Recorder*, 18 Feb. 1865. Also see Report of Chap. Geo. N. Carruthers, 31 Aug., 30 Sep. 1864. CWM, LC; James Schneider to ?, 29 Jan. 1864. Tarbox, *Memoirs*, pp. 153–54; L. S. Livermore to Thomas, 31 Mar. 1865. CMSR of Lark Livermore, RG 94, NA; Owen Riedy to Sir, 1 Nov. 1864. 994 R 1864. Walter Yancy to Thomas, 1 Oct. 1864. 45 Y 1864. G. H. White to Thomas, 30 Aug. 1865. 1871 W 1865. B. F. Randolph to E. D. Townsend, 1 Nov. 1864. 972 R 1864. B. F. Randolph to Thomas, 31 May 1865. 462 R 1865. Letters Received, AGO. RG 94, NA; Cowden,

59th USCI, p. 63; Louis to wife, 16 Nov. 1864, 13 Mar. 1865. Jonathan
Lewis Whitaker Papers, SHC, UNC.

51. See Chap. Saml. Gardner to Gen. Ullman, 19 Dec. 1864. GO, No. 13.
HQ 49th USCI. 11 Apr. 1865. GO, No. 21. HQ 100th USCI. 2 Jun.
1865. Chap. J. R. Reasoner to Thomas, 30 Nov. 1865. Berlin et al.,
Freedom, II, pp. 417–18, 625–26, 631; GO, No. 39. HQ Second Div,
25 AC. Regimental Order Book, 45th USCI. C. P. Taylor to Thomas,
31 May 1865. 424 T 1865. Letters Received, AGO, RG 94, NA.

52. See Prucha, *Broadax and Bayonet*, pp. 209–10; GO, No. 169. HQ
Dept. of the Gulf. 30 Nov. 1864. "The Negro," p. 2839. RG 94, NA;
Marietta College, p. 51; Monthly Report of Chap. George Carruthers,
30 Apr. 1866. CWM, LC; GO, No. 9. 82nd USCI. 15 Mar. 1864. GO,
No. 35. 29 Oct. 1864 and GO, No. 4. 62nd USCI. 25 Jan. 1865. Berlin
et al., *Freedom*, II, pp. 616, 619–20; [James] to [Father], 16, 17 Dec.
1863, and James Schneider to ?, 2 Mar. 1864. Tarbox, *Memoirs*, pp.
145, 164–65; Recommendation of Chap. Asa B. Randall. Michael P.
Musick Collection, MHI; Chap. T. McRae to Thomas, 31 Aug. 1864.
Letters Received Regarding Recruiting. RG 94, NA.

53. Daniel Ullmann to General Richard C. Drum, 16 Apr. 1887. "The Negro,"
p. 3836. RG 94, NA; Lewis to Mason, 8 Feb. 1864. Lewis Weld Family
Papers, YU; J. M. Mickey to Sir, 31 Jan., 31 Aug. 1865. 296 M 1865
and 1999 M 1865. Letters Received, AGO. RG 94, NA. Also see Francis
A. Boyd to Thomas, 31 Dec. 1864. 1861 B 1864. G. A. Rockwood to
Sir, 31 Dec. 1864. 1128 R 1864. G. H. White to Genl., 1 Oct. 1865.
2015 W 1865. B. R. Randolph to E. D. Townsend, 1 Nov. 1864. 972
R 1864. B. F. Randolph to Thomas, 31 May 1865. 462 R 1865. Letters
Received, AGO. RG 94, NA; Stuart Hall, "Reminiscence," p. 10. Morris
Stuart Hall Papers, BL, UMI; D. Cornwell, "Dan Caverno," p. 166. CWMC,
MHI.

54. See Jones, *Soldiers of Light and Love*, pp. 198–200.

55. Quoted in Lovett, "Memphis Riots," p. 12.

56. W. A. Freeman to Mr. Editor, [May 1865]. *Christian Recorder*, 27 May
1865; Benj'n M. Boyd to [Editor, May or June 1865]. *Christian Recorder*,
17 June 1865; Garland H. White to Mr. Editor, 19 Sep. 1865. *Christian
Recorder*, 21 Oct. 1865; J. H. Payne to Mr. Editor, 12 Aug. 1865.
Christian Recorder, 19 Aug. 1865. Also see Andrew King to [Editor],
15 June [18]64. *Christian Recorder*, 18 July 1864; Wm. H. Davis to
Mr. Editor, 24 Sep. 1864. *Christian Recorder*, 15 Oct. 1864.

57. See Chap. Thomas Stevenson to Brig. Gen. Thomas, 11 Sep. 1864.
Chap. C. W. Buckley to Lt Austin Mills, 1 Feb. 1865. Berlin et al.,
Freedom, II, p. 624, 629; Undated Address to Troops by Col. John
Holman. Holman Papers, WHC-SHSMO; Duren to Emma, 14 May 1865.
Offenberg, *Letters to Duren F. Kelley*, p. 161.

58. Mickley, *43rd USCT*, pp. 87–88. Also see Ullmann, *Organization of
Negro Troops*, pp. 11–13. U.S. Army Generals' Reports of Civil War
Service, 1864–1887. Daniel Ullmann. RG 94, NA.

59. Thomas Montgomery to Father, 6 Oct. 1864. Montgomery Papers,
MNHS; Saml. Evans to father, 16 Oct. 1865. Evans Family Papers,
OHS; H. H. Hood to Wife, 30 May 1865. Humphrey H. Hood Papers,
ILSHL; Charles W. Smith to Parents, 22 Feb. 1865. Charles W. Smith
Papers, INHS; Palemon Smalley, "Dad's Memoirs," p. 122. Smalley Pa-

pers, MNHS. Also see George Tate to Cranston, 1 Sep. 1865. Rudolph Haerle Collection, MHI; Sam Evans to Brother, 21 July 1865. Evans Family Papers, OHS.

CHAPTER 11

Life After the USCT

1. H. H. Hood to Wife, 28 May 1865. Humphrey H. Hood Papers, ILSHL. Also see [W. Goodale] to Children, 8 Jun. 1865. Warren Goodale Papers, MAHS; Maj. Horace Bumstead to Asst. Adjt. Gen., 12 Jul. 1865. Papers of 43rd USCT, BPL.

2. Christian A. Fleetwood to Dr. James Hall, 8 June 1865. Carter G. Woodson Papers, LC.

3. Walter Chapman to Parents, 21 May 1865. Walter A. Chapman Papers, YU. Also see Louis to wife, 18 Nov. 1864. Jonathan Lewis Whitaker Papers, SHC, UNC; Samuel D. Barnes diary, 6 Sep. 1865, 28 Feb. 1867. CWM, LC; Edwin Phillips to Son, 16 Apr. 1865, 22 July 1866. Phillips and Parsegian, ed., *Richard and Rhoda,* pp. 66, 104; Thos. Montgomery to Mother, 11 June 1865. Montgomery Papers, MNHS. Chapman was killed in a warehouse explosion four days later.

4. Tilman F. Hardy to Sir Mr, 2 May 1866. Thomas S. Johnson Papers, SHSW; Jas. H. Mead to Mary, ? Mar. 1866. Mead Family Papers, UIA. Also see Roy, "Our Indebtedness to the Negro," p. 353.

5. Thomas to Parents and Brothers, 9 Jan. 1867. Montgomery Papers, MNHS. Also see John L to Sister, 11 Nov. 1865. John L. Mathews Papers, IASHS.

6. Jas. H. Mead to Ellen, 24 Feb. 1866. Mead Family Papers, UIA. Also see Mickley, *43rd USCT,* p. 83; Report of Horace Bumstead, Major, 43rd USCI, 17 Nov. 1865. Company Sergeants to Maj. Horace Bumstead, 17 Nov. 1865. Papers of 43rd USCT, BPL.

7. See Kiple and King, *Another Dimension,* pp. 147–48, for a description of its symptoms. Treatment often exacerbated the condition, because it further dehydrated the patient.

8. Report of Col. Charles Bentzoni, 18 Aug. 1866. Cholera Epidemic in 56th USCI. WHC-SHSMO. Also see *Missouri Democrat,* 17 Sep. 1866.

9. Undated speech of John Holman. Holman Papers, WHC-SHSMO; Col. T. H. Barrett to Officers & Men of the 62d U.S. Colored Infantry, 4 Jan. 1866. Orders, No. 43. HQ, 6th USCC. 16 Apr. 1866. Berlin et al., *Freedom,* II, pp. 784, 788. Also see Trowbridge, "Experiences in Freedmen's Bureau," p. 28. Charles Trowbridge Papers, MNHS; M. S. Hall, "Reminiscences," p. 13. M. S. Hall Papers, BL, UMI; Fox, *Record of the Service of the Fifty-fifth,* p. 84; Smith, *Autobiography,* pp. 121–22.

10. Mickley, *43rd USCT,* p. 48.

11. See Coffman, *The Old Army,* pp. 371–75; Fletcher, *The Black Soldier,* pp. 25–26.

12. Thos. Montgomery to Mother, 28 Nov. 1866. Montgomery Papers, MNHS. Also see Barton to Thomas, 8 Sep. 1866. Ira M. Barton Papers, ARHC. Several officers in the sample received commissions in the RA.

13. George H. Thomas, Recommendation for Promotion and Appointment in the Army of the United States, 18 Feb. 1866. Shafter Papers, BL, UMI.

14. Trial of Lt. Col. Henry Corbin. Henry Corbin Papers, LC. Also see Henry Corbin, "Autobiography," pp. 29–31. Henry C. Corbin Papers, LC; Court Martial was again published in Senate Document No. 214, Fifty-Sixth Congress, First Session.

15. L. Grim to Aunt, 5 Jan. 1864[5]. Wise-Clark Family Papers, UIA; Duren to Emma, 6 Oct. 1864. Offenberg, *Letters of Duren F. Kelley*, p. 120.

16. Thos. Montgomery to Mother, 19 Apr. 1864. Montgomery Papers, MNHS; Weber, *Autobiography*, p. 23.

17. Newton, *Out of the Briars*, p. 83; E. J. Woodward to Lt. Mead, 9 July 1865. Mead Family Papers, UIA.

18. Duren to Emma, 14 Mar. 1865. *Letters of Duren F. Kelley*, p. 151.

19. Pension File of Washington Young 74th USCI and others. RG 15, NA; Deposition of Sarah E. Randolph, 2 Feb. 1898. Pension File of Samuel P. Randolph. RG 15, NA. Also see Pension Files of ex-Capt. Samuel Ringgold of the 74th USCI; Levi Goens of 28th USCI; Esau Riley of 10th USCI; Seymour Wells of the 65th USCI. RG 15, NA. Of approximately 140 pension files of black soldiers that I sampled, only two divorced and four had drinking problems.

20. See Appendix 1; Robert L. Griswold, *Family and Divorce in California, 1850–1890*, p. 28; Elaine Tyler May, *Great Expectations*, p. 167; File of William Bidlack. Personal Papers, Medical Officers & Physicians. Prior to 1912. RG 94, NA. Pension File of George Cutler, D, 6th USCHA. Pension File of Alphonso Bullen. RG 15, NA; Carded Medical Records of Lt. Isaac A. Lewis. RG 94, NA. Family historian Steven Mintz of the University of Houston has told me the divorce statistics are extremely high. Interview with author, 29 May 1988.

21. Records of A. E. M. Lundy, 17 Aug. 1882 and Records of Bloomingdale Asylum. Pension File of William Charlsey. RG 15, NA.

22. *Washington Post*, 16 Jun. 1890. Also see Pension File of Clarence M. Clarke. RG 15, NA. I have discovered six suicides among officers in the USCT, four of whom were in my sample. If they were the only 6 out of 7,211 white officers, their suicide rate would still be more than five times higher than the highest suicide rate of a major city, New York. I have tried to be cautious with this because of the inaccuracy of suicide statistics. See Lane, *Violent Death in the City*, p. 15; Billings, *Vital Statistics of the District of Columbia and Baltimore*, p. 27; Billings, *Vital Statistics of New York City and Brooklyn*, p. 50; Billings, *Vital Statistics of Boston and Philadelphia*, p. 45; Futterman and Pumpian-Mindlin, "Traumatic War Neuroses Five Years Later," p. 402.

23. John A. Griffin to Sir, 4 Nov. 1864. E. C. D. Robbins to father & mother, 8 Oct. 1864. John A. Griffin to Sir, 4 Nov. 1864. Pension File of E. C. D. Robbins. RG 15, NA. Also see Thomas Smith to Sir, 17 Oct. 1864. B. S. Chase to Parents of the Late Captain Robbins, 16 Oct. 1864. Pension File of E. C. D. Robbins, GR 15, NA. A brain tumor may have also been the cause.

24. Dr. Thomas Cushing to Mrs. D. J. Stiles, 23 May 1864. Maj. A. P. Wells to Mrs. D. T. Stiles, 23 May 1864. Deposition of Dr. Thomas Cushing, undated. Pension File of Delos T. Stiles. RG 15, NA.

25. See Pension File and Carded Medical Records of Henry M. McCauley. RG 15, NA; *Atlanta Constitution*, 2 July 1879.

26. J. C. B. to Tom, undated, with Belle to Henry, 20 Apr. 1863. Beecher Family Papers, Stowe-Day Library; Undated Affidavit of George W. Taylor. Pension File of James C. Beecher, RG 15, NA.

27. J. C. B. to Tom, undated, with Belle to Henry, 20 Apr. 1863. Beecher Family Papers, Stowe-Day Library. Also see Physician's Affidavit of George W. Taylor, undated. Pension File of James C. Beecher, RG 15, NA; Belle to husband, [Mar. 1863]. Beecher Family Papers, Stowe-Day Library.

28. Physician's Affidavit of Henry O. Marcy, undated. Affidavit of William Birney, ? Feb. 1887. Pension File of James C. Beecher. RG 15, NA. Also see [J. C. Beecher] to beloved, 2 Aug. 1864. James C. Beecher Papers, Radcliffe College.

29. Physician's Affidavit of Ira Russell, undated. Pension File of James C. Beecher. RG 15, NA; [James] to beloved wife, Tuesday [1882]. [James] to beloved wife, 20 Aug. [1882]. [James] to wife, 18 [Oct. 1885?]. Mama to darling daughters, 29 Aug. [18]86. Beecher Family Papers, Stowe-Day Library; Wm. E. Conroy to Hon. John C. Black, 30 May 1887. Pension File of James C. Beecher, RG 15, NA. Also see [James] to beloved wife, [1884 after 9 Mar.]. Beecher Family Papers, Stowe-Day Library.

30. McMurray, *Recollections,* p. 62.

31. H. G. Crickmore to John G. Wellstood, 28 Sep. 1865. Regimental Papers, 4th USCC. Palmer Collection, WRHS; Affidavit of John Mixon, 3 Mar. 1899. Pension File of John Mixon. RG 15, NA. Also see Rev. J. M. Mickley to Lt. Phillips, 19 Mar. 1866. Phillips and Parsegian, *Richard and Rhoda,* p. 96. A considerable number of officers and men whose pension records I examined had physical ailments that inhibited their readjustment to civilian life.

32. See Pension File of William F. Blanchard. RG 15, NA; Clapp, *Sketches of Army Life,* p. 27.

33. Affidavit of Troy Isgrig, 3 Jun. 1907. Pension File of Troy Isgrig. RG 15, NA. Also see Pension File of Francis A. Bentley, including photograph. RG 15, NA.

34. Palemon Smalley, "Dad's Memoirs," p. 121. Smalley Papers, MNHS; T. Montgomery to Bro, 14 Jun. 1864 and to Mother, 16 May 1865. Montgomery Papers, MNHS. Also see T. J. Hoge to Aunt Tillie, 10 Jun [1867?]. Wise-Clark Family Papers, UIA.

35. Thos. Montgomery to Brother James Charles, 17 Aug. 1866. Montgomery Papers, MNHS; H. G. Crickmore to John G. Wellstood, 28 Sep. 1865. Regimental Papers, 4th USCC. Palmer Collection, WRHS. Also see Pension File of Ireneus C. Myers. Pension File of Nathan P. Pond. RG 15, NA. In the sample of white officers, sixty-five went from manual to nonmanual labor, three were so disabled that they never worked again, and five went from nonmanual to manual labor. See Appendix 1.

36. B. Marshall Mills to Father, 4 Mar. 1864. Caleb Mills Papers, INHS; William Baird, "Reminiscences," p. 9. William Baird Papers, BL, UMI; John Day to Friend Crickmore, 7 May 1865. Regimental Papers, 4th USCC. Palmer Collection, WRHS. Also see Pension Files of Jefferson Robinson, Elias F. Stall, and Buel A. Man. RG 15, NA; Steiner, *Medical History,* p. 25; J. O. Moore to Lizzie, 14 Feb. 1865. James O. Moore Papers, Duke U; Appendix 1.

37. John to Eben, 2 Nov. 1865. Loomis-Wilder Papers, YU. Also see [Sam] to Julia, 13 Oct. 1865. Duncan-Jones Papers, NHHS; A. W. Greely to Brother Augustus, 9 May, 14 Jun. and 5 Jul. 1866. A. W. Greely Papers, Duke U; Lewis to wife, 8 Feb. 1865. Jonathan Lewis Whitaker Papers, SHC, UNC; Lewis to Mason, 19 May 1864. Lewis Weld Family Papers, YU; Sam Evans to Father, 24 Oct. 1865. Evans Family Papers, OHS; L. F. Dewey to Col., 22 Apr. 1866. Loomis-Wilder Family Papers, YU; Chas. R. Riggs to Brother, 6 Sep. 1865. Charles R. Riggs Papers, IASHS; Main, *3rd USCC*, pp. 46–48, 55; Cowden, *59th USCT*, pp. 149–53, 259–60. The author recommends Powell's *New Masters*.

38. See J. B. Roberts to father, 19 Sep. 1865. CWM, LC; Romeyn, "With Colored Troops," pp. 9–10; Holt, *Black Over White*, p. 49; Higginson, "Some War Scenes Revisited," p. 3.

39. See Logan and Winston, *Dictionary of American Negro Biography*, pp. 18–19, 318–19, 507–8; Logan, *Howard University*, pp. 44–48; Dyson, *Howard University*, pp. 242–46.

40. Marrs, *Life and History*, pp. 77–78; Testimony of Henry H. Butler. Rawick, *The American Slave*, p. 559.

41. T. W. Higginson journal, 21 Nov. [1863]. Thomas W. Higginson Papers, Harvard U; Thomas Montgomery to Father, 22 Mar. 1865. Montgomery Papers, MNHS. Also see Oubre, *Forty Acres and a Mule*, pp. 29–30, 75.

42. Higginson, "Some War Scenes Revisited" p. 3. Also see OR III, 5, pp. 659–60; Act to Place Colored Persons Who Enlisted in the Army on the Same Footing As Other Soldiers As to Bounty and Pension, 3 Mar. 1873. "The Negro," pp. 3825–26. RG 94, NA.

43. Seth Wheaton to Comrades in the 59th, 1 Sep. 1879. Cowden, *59th USCT*, p. 272. Also see Cowden, *59th USCT*, pp. 272–73 and biographical sketches in circular letter; E. J. Woodward to Lt. Mead, 9 July 1865. Mead Family Papers, UIA; Edwin C. Latimer to Father, 19 Oct. 1869. Pension File of Edwin C. Latimer. RG 15, NA.

44. See Fenlon, "The Notorious Swepson-Littlefield Fraud"; Jonathan Daniels, *Prince of Carpetbaggers*, [1958]; McPherson, *The Abolitionist Legacy*, p. 43; "Autobiography of Marshall Harvey Twitchell," pp. 97, 100, 175–77. M. H. Twitchell Papers, VTHS; Ted Tunnell, *Crucible of Reconstruction*, pp. 173–209. Also see Foner, *Reconstruction*, and Current, *Those Terrible Carpetbaggers*.

45. Drago, *Black Politicians and Reconstruction*, pp. 69–70. Also see Drago, p. 39; Foner, *Reconstruction*, p. 318; Rabinowitz, *Southern Black Leaders*; Pension File of Edwin Belcher. RG 15, NA.

46. See Franklin, *George Washington Williams*, p. 110; *Boston Globe*, 7 Apr. 1890; Logan and Winston, *Dictionary of American Negro Biography*, pp. 602–3.

47. *Christian Recorder*, 18 Nov. 1865.

48. *Loyal Georgian*, 13 Oct. 1866; *New York Times*, 8 Feb. 1866; Ullman, *Martin R. Delaney*, p. 328.

49. *New York Times*, 8 Feb. 1866; *Jacksonville Florida Union*, 21 Oct. 1865, quoting from *Brownlow's Whig*, 27 Sep. 1865, and 7 Oct. 1865.

50. See Williams, *A History of Negro Troops*, p. 324; Wm. W. Belknap, Sec. of War, to Military Committee, House of Representatives, 15 Apr. 1872. "The Negro," p. 3819. RG 94, NA.

51. *New York Times*, 26 Mar. 1866.

52. Quoted in Foner, *Reconstruction*, p. 307.

53. Monthly Report of Chap. Geo. N. Carruthers, 31 Jan. 1866. CWM, LC; Statement of Essex Barbour, 7 Feb. 1866. Affidavit of Roda Ann Childs, 25 Sep. 1866. Berlin et al., *Freedom*, II, pp. 803–4, 807. Also see Marrs, *Life and History*, p. 90; CMSR of John W. Parrington, 4th USCI, RG 94, NA.

54. See *New York Times*, 28 Oct. 1868.

55. See Foner, *Reconstruction*, and Holt, *Black Over White.*

56. Quote is author's. See John S. Haller, Jr., *Outcasts from Evolution*, pp. 19–29.

57. Haller, *Outcasts from Evolution*, p. 26. Also see Haller, pp. 19–29.

58. See Haller, *Outcasts from Evolution*, pp. 29–32.

59. Hunt, "The Negro As a Soldier," pp. 166, 175, 172.

60. Hunt, "The Negro As a Soldier," p. 179. Also see Hunt, p. 180.

61. Haller, *Outcasts from Evolution*, p. 34. Also see *Medical and Surgical History*, Medical Volume, first part, pp. 710–12, 636–41, third part, p. 891; Jones, *Bad Blood*, ch. 2.

62. See Haller, *Outcasts from Evolution*, p. 85.

63. Dearing, *Veterans in Politics*, p. 414; Smith, *Autobiography*, p. 113. Also see Deposition of Henry Cooper, 27 May 1924 in Pension File of Charles Cull. RG 15, NA; Dearing, *Veterans in Politics*, pp. 120, 412–13; Fox, *Regimental Losses*, pp. 26–27, 521.

64. Sears, *Papers*, p. 3.

65. Franklin, *George Washington Williams*, p. 110; Williams, *A History of Negro Troops*, p. 328.

66. Freeman, "A Colored Brigade." Furness, "The Negro as a Soldier," pp. 421, 486–87. Also see Armstrong, "The Negro as a Soldier," pp. 316–17.

67. N. P. Hallowell to Editor of the *Herald*, 1 Dec. 1913. N. P. Hallowell to Aunt Lucia, Feb. 1910. N. P. Hallowell to Editors of the *Boston Herald*, 9 Mar. 1909. Hallowell, *Selected Letters and Papers*, pp. 78, 95–96, 73–74; Trowbridge, "Experiences in the Freedmen's Bureau," p. 17. Charles Trowbridge Papers, MNHS.

68. See Spivey, *Schooling for the New Slavery*, pp. 7–9, 16–38; "Popular Prejudice," by Horace Bumstead in Papers of the 43d USCT, BPL; McPherson, *Abolitionist Legacy*, pp. 345, 391; Savage, *The History of Lincoln University*, pp. 1–12.

69. Wilder, "The Negro Brain," p. 40.

70. George Hepworth continued to perform charitable work, such as running a relief fund during the Irish famine, and Frank McAulliff became a social worker in NYC.

71. Palemon Smalley, "Dad's Memoirs," pp. 47, 121, 127–28, 122. Smalley Papers, MNHS.

72. Address of Ed. Main, ex-Maj., Third USCC, 5 May 1893. Main, *3rd USCC*, pp. 3–4. Also see *Third USCC Organization*, p. 11, and virtually any book or article written by officers in the USCT after the war, from which I have quoted throughout the text.

73. Fleetwood, "The Negro as a Soldier," p. 15. Also see Pension File of Alonzo Edgerton. RG 94, NA; *Minneapolis Evening Journal,* 11 Oct. 1888 and through mid-Nov. 1888; Main, *3rd USCC,* p. 65. Charles Augustus Hill and John A. Weber were also U.S. congressmen, and numerous individuals held state positions.

74. See Trowbridge, "Experiences in the Freedmen's Bureau," pp. 30–32. A few of the units that had reunions were the 11th USCHA, 3rd USCC, 7th USCI, 59th USCI, 109th USCI, and 55th Mass. (Col.) Infantry.

75. See Pension File of Oscar Blue in Louis Benecke Papers, WHC-SHSMO; Stuart Hall, "Reminiscences," addition p. 15. Morris Stuart Hall Papers, BL, UMI.

76. *Boston Journal,* 3 Aug. 1887. George Thompson Garrison Papers, SSC, Smith College. Also see *Boston Journal,* 2 Aug. 1887 and *Boston Herald,* 3 Aug. 1887. George Thompson Garrison Papers, SSC, Smith College.

77. Foner, *Blacks and the Military,* p. 85. Also see Kiple and King, *Another Dimension,* p. 27; Foner, pp. 75, 87–88.

78. See Fletcher, *The Black Soldier and Officer,* pp. 153–60. For the black soldier in World War I, see Coffman, *The War to End All Wars,* Barbeau and Henri, *The Unknown Soldiers.*

79. See Deposition of James F. Mitchell, 27 May 1924. Pension File of Charles Cull. RG 15, NA.

Bibliography

MANUSCRIPTS

American Antiquarian Society

Edward Woolsey Bacon Papers
Brown Family Papers: Thomas D. Freeman, John J. Johnson, and R. Robin-
son
John Francis Gleason Papers
Thomas Wentworth Higginson Papers

Arkansas History Commission

Ira McLean Barton Papers
G. A. A. Deans Papers

Bentley Library, University of Michigan

William Baird Papers
Robert Crouse Collection: Newton J. Kirk
Abram E. Garrison Papers
Morris Stuart Hall Papers
MOLLUS-Michigan Commandery Papers: Ludlum C. Drake
Nina Ness Collection: Norman S. Andrews
William R. Shafter Papers
Oliver Van Valin Papers

Boston Public Library

William Lloyd Garrison Papers
John M. Hawks Papers
Thomas Wentworth Higginson Papers
Benjamin C. Lincoln Papers

Papers of the Forty-Third USCT, probably Horace Bumstead
James A. Reeder Papers
James Henry Wickes Papers

Bowdoin College

Fessenden Family Papers: James D. Fessenden
Oliver Otis Howard Papers: W. M. Beebe, Charles H. Howard, and Davis
   Tillson

Chicago Historical Society

Hiram Bixby Papers
John A. Hawkins Papers

Clements Library, University of Michigan

Schoff Collection: Henry G. Marshall, John Pierson, and Solomon Bates
   Starbird

Dartmouth College

Samuel A. Duncan Papers: Samuel A. Duncan and Stark Fellows
Reuben Delavan Mussey Papers

Duke University

I. H. Carrington Papers
John Snider Cooper Papers
Frederick and Sarah Cutler Papers: Harry Wadsworth
Charles A. R. Dimon Papers: Mr. Lowenstein
Adolphus W. Greely Papers
Edward W. Kinsley Papers: L. L. Billings, James Spencer Drayton, A. S.
   Hartwell, B. G. Kinsley, William Logan, W. C. Manning, James M. Trotter,
   and Edward A. Wild
Luther and James Lawrence Papers: D. M. Drie
Edwin R. Manson Papers
James Otis Moore Papers
Charles H. Remick Papers

Emory University

Alfred Milo Brigham Papers
Henry M. Crydenwise Papers
Papers of the 38th USCT
William M. Parkinson Papers: William M. Parkinson, H. H. McHenry, and
   Frederick Smith

Gettysburg College

A. S. Fisher Papers

Harvard University

Thomas Wentworth Higginson Papers

Illinois State Historical Library

Carpenter Family Papers: George D. Carpenter and Samuel L. Carpenter
John Gayle Davis Papers
John A. Griffin Papers
Humphrey Hughes Hood Papers
August V. Kautz Papers
C. E. Lanstrum Papers
McClernand Papers: James Grant Wilson
Theodore E. True Papers

Indiana Historical Society

John H. Ferree Papers
George W. Grubb Papers
Andrew J. Johnson Papers
Kinder Family Papers: John C. Hackhiser
Andrew J. McGarrah Papers
Caleb Mills Papers: John P. Hawkins, J. H. Meteer, Benjamin Marshall
    Mills, and Lycurgus Railsback
Charles W. Smith Papers
William R. Stuckey Papers
Wallace Papers: Robert G. Shaw

Iowa State Historical Department

William Reed Papers

Iowa State Historical Society

John A. Hart Papers
John L. Mathews Papers: John L. Mathews and Frank M. Pickett
Charles R. Riggs Papers

Kansas State Historical Society

R. J. Hinton Papers
James Montgomery Papers
B. F. Van Horn Papers
James M. Williams Papers

Library of Congress

Black History Miscellaneous Collection: F. W. Browne
Civil War Miscellaneous Collection: George N. Carruthers and Samuel D.
    Barnes
Henry C. Corbin Papers
Adolphus W. Greely Papers
J. M. and Esther H. Hawks Papers: John M. Hawks, James C. Beecher,
    Lemuel G. Benton, John A. Bouldon, Henry Clark, Thomas Cooper, Henry
    Cork, George Delevan, James C. Green, Thorndike Hodges, Lewis Jones,
    Andrew Jordan, Henry O. Marcy, V. Mayo, Edward Mils, J. R. Morgan,
    Edward William Moris, Joseph A. Palmer, Freeman Pugh, James William
    Ringgold, Burrill Smith, Benjamin Thompson, Edward Williams, and
    Isaiah Wilson

Edward W. Kinsley Papers: G. Williams Dewhurst, A. S. Hartwell, and Edward A. Wild
Edward McPherson Papers: William Nellis
Miscellaneous Manuscripts Collection: William R. Shafter
Quincy-Wendell-Upham-Holmes Family Papers: Samuel M. Quincy
Roberts Family Papers: Junius Roberts
Carter Woodson Papers; Horace Bumstead, Lewis Douglass, and Christian Fleetwood

Lincoln Shrine

George H. Gordon Papers
George L. Stearns Papers

Litchfield Historical Society

D. C. Kilbourn Papers: Richard Watson for Albert Wadhams

Massachusetts Historical Society

John M. Andrew: John M. Forbes
Atkinson Papers: Thomas Wentworth Higginson
Charles B. Fox Papers
Warren Goodale Papers
James Family Papers: Wilky James in letter of Horace James
Edward W. Kinsley Papers: James C. Beecher, A. S. Hartwell, B. G. Kinsley, and Joseph Mitchell
Amos A. Lawrence Papers: Robert Gould Shaw and George L. Stearns
H. H. Mitchell Papers
James A. Munroe Papers
John Owne, Jr., Papers
Robert Gould Shaw Papers

Michigan State University

Nelson Family Papers: Wilbur Nelson

Minnesota Historical Society

Sam Bloomer Papers: Adam
James M. Bowler Papers
George C. Clapp Papers
Densmore Family Papers: Benjamin Densmore and Daniel Densmore
Thomas Montgomery Papers
Peet Family Papers: James Peet
Palemon Smalley Papers
Charles C. Trowbridge Papers

National Archives

Record Group 15

Civil War Pension Files

Record Group 94

Address Books, 1860–1894
Adjutant General's Office (AGO) Miscellaneous File ("Colored Troops")
Applications for Commissions in the Colored Units

Circulars of the First Division of U.S. Colored Troops, Mar.–Dec. 1864
and Feb.–July 1865
Compiled Military Service Records
Daniel Ullmann Papers
Field Records of Hospitals
Index to Letters Received, Adjutant General's Office
Letters Received, Adjutant General's Office
Letters Received, Division of Colored Troops, 1863–68
Letters Received Relating to Recruiting, 1863–68
Letters Regarding Recruiting, Division of Colored Troops
Letters Sent, Division of Colored Troops. Dec. 1863–Mar. 1888
Letters Sent Relating to Examinations of Applicants for Commission of
Colored Troops
List of Applicants Before Board of Examination for Officers in U.S. Colored
Troops Convened in Washington, D.C. Aug. 19–Oct. 18, 1865
Lists of Persons Who Have Passed Examining Boards, 1863–65
The Negro in the Military Service of the United States, 1607–1889
Personal Papers, Medical Officers and Physicians. Prior to 1912
Proceedings of Examining Board, Cincinnati, OH, 1863–64
Proceedings of Examining Board, St. Louis, MO, 1863–65
Regimental Descriptive Books
Regimental Hospital Records, Seventh U.S.C. Infantry
Regimental Letterbooks
Regimental Order Books
Regimental Unbound Papers
Register of Officers of U.S. Colored Troops, 1863–65
Surgeon's Morning Reports, Hospital Records and Letters, Fourth U.S.C.C.
U.S. Army Generals' Reports of Civil War Service, 1864–87

Record Group 110

Circulars of the Provost Marshal General's Office, the Surgeon General's
Office, the Ordnance Department, and Headquarters of the Department
of Susquehanna, June 1863–Apr. 1865
Letters Sent, Camp William Penn, July 1863–June 1865

Record Group 112

Letters Sent, June 1863–Apr. 1865
Minutes of Meetings, June 1863–May 1865
Reports of Results of Examinations of Candidates Seeking Appointment
as Surgeons with U.S. Volunteers ("Merit Rolls"), 1861–65

Record Group 153

Index to Proceedings of General Courts Martial (GCM)
Proceedings of General Courts Martial
Proceedings of General Courts Martial of Soldiers Executed in the Civil
War
United States Soldiers Executed by United States Authorities During the
Late War

Record Group 159

Inspection Reports, 1865
Inspection Reports, Arranged by States
Letters Received, Inspector General's Office, 1864

Record Group 393

Applications for Commissions and Reports of Boards of Examiners for Officers in U.S. Colored Troops, Dept. of the Gulf, 1863–64

Daily Reports, Dept. of Missouri, 1864

Discrete Letters Sent, Dept. of Kentucky. Feb.–May 1865

Endorsements Received and Sent, Instructions and Reports Sent, Special Orders Sent, Telegrams Received, Telegrams Sent, Organization of U.S. Colored Troops, Dept. of Kentucky

General Orders and Special Orders, Dept. of the Gulf, Oct.–Dec. 1864

Letters and Endorsements Sent, Dept. of the Gulf. Nov. 1864–Feb. 1865

Letters Received by Boards of Examiners, Dept. of the Gulf, Oct. 1863–Feb. 1864

Letters Received, Dept. of Virginia and North Carolina. 1864–65

Letters Sent by the Commissioner, Dept. of the Cumberland. Mar. 1864–Feb. 1865

Letters Sent, Dept. of Missouri

Letters Sent, Dept. of Virginia and North Carolina, Oct. 1864–May 1865

Letters Sent and Letters and Orders Received (Board of Examination of Improper Enlistments), Dept. of the Gulf, May 1864–Mar. 1865

Letters Sent and Orders Issued by the Medical Director, Dept. of the South

Letters Sent, Organization of USCT, Dept. of Kentucky. Sep. 1864–Mar. 1865

Letters Sent, Special Orders Issued, Telegrams Sent, Organization of U.S. Colored Cavalry, Dept. of Kentucky

Press Copies of Letters Sent by the Commissioner, Dept. of the Cumberland. June 1864–Jan. 1865

Press Copies of Letters Sent, Organization of USCT, Dept. of Kentucky, Mar.–Sep. 1865

Proceedings of the Board for the Examination of Officers, Dept. of Missouri

Proceedings of the Board of Examiners for Officers in U.S. Colored Troops, Dept. of the Gulf, Sep.–Nov. 1864

Proceedings of the Boards of Examination for Commissions in U.S. Colored Troops, Dept. of the Cumberland and Tennessee, 1863–64

Proceedings, Dept. of the Gulf, May 1864–Mar. 1865

Proceedings, Dept. of Missouri, Aug. 1863–June 1864. June 1864–Jan. 1865. Sep. 1864.

Proceedings on the Fitness of Officers of the Volunteer Service, Dept. of Missouri, Oct. 1864–July 1865

Records of Capt. R. D. Mussey, 19th U.S. Infantry, Mustering Officer, Nashville, Relating to the Organization of Colored Troops, and of Maj. George L. Stearns, Committee on the Organization of Colored Troops, Dept. of the Cumberland, 1863–64

Register of Applicants for Commissions in the U.S. Colored Troops, Dept. of the Cumberland and Tennessee, 1864

Reports of Examinations of Officers, Dept. of Virginia and North Carolina, 1864

Special Orders Issued by the Commissioner, Dept. of the Cumberland, Mar. 1864–May 1865

New Hampshire Historical Society

Duncan-Jones Papers: Samuel A. Duncan

New-York Historical Society

Clifford Thomson Papers and Daniel Ullmann Papers

Ohio Historical Society

Adjutant General's Report of Examination of Candidates for Officers in
    Colored Troops, July 1863–Feb. 1864 for 5th USCI
Evans Family Papers: Samuel Evans
Gustave W. Fahrion Papers
Nicholas A. Gray Papers
Thomas W. Hopes Papers
Albert Rogall Papers
Supervisory Committee on Colored Enlistments Papers
Julius Birney Work Papers

Radcliffe College

James C. Beecher Papers
Browne Family Papers: Lewis Ledyard Weld

Rhode Island Historical Society

George R. Sherman Papers: George R. Sherman and James A. Gregg
Nelson Viall Papers

Rutgers University

Adelbert C. Sherman Papers
Whitney Family Papers: Henry Whitney

Smith College

Sophia Smith Collection: George Thompson Garrison and James M. Rogers

Society for the Preservation of New England Antiquities

Silas Casey Papers

Chester Somers Private Collection

David Edwin Proctor

Southern Historical Collection, University of North Carolina

J. Lewis Whitaker Papers

State Historical Society of Wisconsin

Frank D. Harding Papers
Harrison Family Papers: Samuel A. Harrison
Thomas S. Johnson Papers: Thomas S. Johnson, Tilman F. Hardy, (?)
    Meekins, and Merritt Pool

Stowe-Day Library

Beecher Family Papers: James C. Beecher

Richard S. Tracy Private Collection

Charles Augustus Hill Papers

United States Army Military History Institute

Hattie Burleigh Papers: Albert James
Henry Burrell Papers

Civil War Miscellaneous Collection: David Cornwell, Lorenzo Gould, Albert H. Hollister, Joseph K. Nelson, James Thompson in Marcus, A. Stults folder, and John B. Wilson

Civil War Times Illustrated Collection: John Q. Adams and William Seagrave in Seagrave folder, Joseph J. Scroggs, Benjamin W. Thompson, David Torrence in Frederick Chesson folder, and Union Army—Tenth Corps, unidentified letter, possibly 29th Connecticut Infantry.

John Habberton Papers

Rudolph Haerle Collection: Samuel William Campbell and George Tate in George W. Cranson folder

Harrisburg Civil War Round Table: Gregory Coco Collection: John W. Ames; and Steljes Collection: Harvey J. Covell

Hawkins-Canby-Speed Papers: John P. Hawkins

Earl M. Hess Collection: John C. Hackhiser

August V. Kautz Papers

Michael P. Musick Collection: Asa B. Randall and Charles F. Stinson

MOLLUS-Massachusetts Collection: Silas Adams and Seth Rogers

Levi Neville Papers

William Prince Collection: Papers of the 3rd USCHA

Sladen Family Papers: Joseph Sladen

Spanish American War Survey, Civil War folder: George L. Gaskill

Thomas R. Stone Collection: Daniel Butler and Oliver Cromwell

John W. Turner Papers

Edward A. Wild Papers

University of Arkansas

Minos Miller Papers

University of Iowa

Mead Family Papers: James H. Mead and E. J. Woodward

George W. Strong Papers

Wise-Clark Family Papers: Lycurgus Grim, Thomas J. Hoge, and William Ream

University of Kentucky

Myron E. Billings Papers

University of Tennessee

Will R. Story Letter

Vermont Historical Society

Rufus Kinsley Papers

Marshall Harvey Twitchell Papers

Washington and Lee University

Edwin J. Harkness Papers

Western Historical Collection—State Historical Society of Missouri

Alley-Brewer Papers

Louis Benecke Papers

Odon Guitar Papers
John Holman Papers

Western Reserve Historical Society

Carlos P. Lyman Papers
Palmer Collection: Moulton Papers—Charles Macklin and Frank Moulton;
   Regimental Papers, 4th USCC folder—J. S. Bangs, H. G. Crickmore, John
   M. Day, Nathaniel C. Mitchell, Samuel White, and James Grant Wilson
Orlando C. Risdon Papers

Yale University

Beecher Family Papers: James C. Beecher
Walter A. Chapman Papers
Civil War Miscellaneous Papers: George R. Sanders in Burnham file
Loomis-Wilder Family Papers: John Wilder, Benjamin Townsend, and Con-
   sider Willett
Josiah V. Meigs Papers
Charles G. G. Merrill Papers
Saxton Family Papers: Rufus Saxton and S. Willard Saxton
Lewis Ledyard Weld Family Papers: Lewis Ledyard Weld and Theodore Dwight
   Weld

PUBLISHED PRIMARY SOURCES

Addeman, J. M. "Reminiscences of Two Years With the Colored Troops,"
   *Personal Narratives, Rhode Island Soldiers and Sailors Historical Soci-
   ety,* series, 2, no. 7.
Allen, William P. "Three Frontier Battles." *Military Order of the Loyal Legion
   of the United States—Minnesota,* 4, 478–93.
Ames, John W. "The Victory at Fort Fisher." *Overland Monthly,* 9 (1872),
   323–32.
Armstrong, William H. "The Negro As a Soldier." *Military Order of the Loyal
   Legion of the United States—Indiana,* 316–33.
Balch, John A. *History of the 116th Regiment U.S.C. Infantry.* Philadelphia:
   King & Baird, Printers, 1866.
Bangs, I. S. "The Ullmann Brigade." *Military Order of the Loyal Legion of
   the United States—Maine,* 2, 290–310.
Beatty, John. *Memoirs of a Volunteer, 1861–1863.* New York: W. W. Norton
   & Company, 1946.
Berlin, Ira; Fields, Barbara J., Glymph, Thaviola, Reidy, Joseph P., and
   Rowland, Leslie S., eds. *Freedom: A Documentary History of Emancipa-
   tion, 1861–1867.* series I, vol. 1. New York: Cambridge University Press,
   1985.
Berlin, Ira; Reidy, Joseph P., and Rowland, Leslie S., eds. *Freedom: A
   Documentary History of Emancipation, 1861–1867,* series II, vol. 1. New
   York: Cambridge University Press, 1982.
Blake, Sarah Swan Weld, ed. *Diaries and Letters of Francis Minot Weld.*
   Boston: [Stetson Press], 1925.
Botkin, B. A., ed. *Lay My Burden Down: A Folk History of Slavery.* Chicago:
   University of Chicago Press, 1945.

Bowley, F. S. *A Boy Lieutenant.* Philadelphia: Henry Altemus Company, 1906.

———. "The Petersburg Mine." *Military Order of the Loyal Legion of the United States—California.* War papers, no. 3.

———. "Seven Months in Confederate Military Prison." *Military Order of the Loyal Legion of the United States—California.* War papers, no. 6.

Brown, William Wells. *The Negro in the American Rebellion: His Heroism and His Fidelity.* New York: Lee & Shepard, 1867. Reprint Johnson Reprint Corporation, 1968.

Burnell, G. W. "The Development of Our Armies—1861–1865." *Military Order of the Loyal Legion of the United States—Wisconsin,* 2, 70–80.

Cain, William S. *Autobiography of W. S. Cain.* Topeka: Printed by Crane & Co., 1908.

Califf, Joseph M. *Record of the Services of the Seventh Regiment, U.S. Colored Troops.* Providence: E. L. Freeman & Co., Printers, 1878.

Carter, Solon A. "Fourteen Months' Service With Colored Troops." *Military Order of the Loyal Legion of the United States—Massachusetts,* 1, 155–79.

Chenery, William H. *The Fourteenth Regiment Rhode Island Heavy Artillery (Colored).* Providence: Snow & Farnham, 1898.

Chetlain, Augustus L. *Recollections of Seventy Years.* Galena, IL: Gazette Publishing Company, 1899.

Clapp, Henry S. *Sketches of Army Life in the Sixties.* Newark, OH; n.p., 191(?).

Cleland, Jno. E. "The Second March to the Ohio." *Military Order of the Loyal Legion of the United States-Indiana,* 220–38.

Cowden, Robert. *A Brief Sketch of the Organization and Services of the Fifty-Ninth Regiment, United States Colored Infantry.* Dayton: United Brethren Publishing House, 1883.

Crawford, Samuel J. *Kansas in the Sixties.* Chicago: A. C. McClurg & Co., 1911.

Day, James Byron. *The Surviving Soldiers Step and Reward of 1861–1865,* 1911.

Eaton, John. *Grant, Lincoln, and the Freedmen.* New York: Negro Universities Press, 1966.

Ellis, Richard N., ed. "The Civil War Letters of an Iowa Family." *Annals of Iowa,* series 3, 39, no. 8 (Spring 1969), 561–85.

Emilio, Luis F. *A Brave Black Regiment: History of the Fifty-Fourth Regiment of Massachusetts Volunteer Infantry.* Boston: Boston Book Company, 1894.

Fleetwood, Christian A. *The Negro as a Soldier.* Washington, D.C.: Prof. George William Cook, 1895.

Ford, Washington Chauncey, ed. *A Cycle of Adams Letters, 1861–1865.* 2 vols. Boston: Houghton Mifflin Company, 1920.

Fox, Charles Bernard. *Record of the Service of the Fifty-Fifth Regiment of Massachusetts Volunteer Infantry.* Cambridge: Press of John Wilson and Son, 1868.

Freeman, Henry V. "A Colored Brigade in the Campaign and Battle of Nashville." *Military Order of the Loyal Legion of the United States—Illinois,* 2, 399–422.

Furness, William Eliot. "The Negro as a Soldier." *Military Order of the Loyal Legion of the United States—Illinois,* 2, 457–88.

Goulding, Joseph Hiram. "The Colored Troops in the War of the Rebellion." *Proceedings of the Reunion Society of Vermont Officers*, 2, 137–54.

———. "A Month on a Transport." *Military Order of the Loyal Legion of the United States—Vermont.* War paper no. 5.

Greely, A. W. *Reminiscences of Adventures and Service: A Record of Sixty-Five Years.* New York: Charles Scribner's Sons, 1927.

Green, Alfred M. *Letters and Discussions on the Formation of Colored Regiments.* Philadelphia: Ringwalt & Brown, 1862.

Hall, Henry Seymour. "Mine Run to Petersburg." *Military Order of the Loyal Legion of the United States—Kansas*, 206–49.

Hallowell, N. P. *Selected Letters and Papers of N. P. Hallowell.* Peterborough, NH: Richard R. Smith Co., Inc., 1963.

Hemenway, S. "Observations on Scurvy, and Its Causes Among U.S. Colored Troops of the 25th Army Corps, During the Spring and Summer of 1865." *Chicago Medical Examiner*, 7 (Oct. 1866), 582–86.

Hepworth, George Hughes. *The Whip, Hoe, and Sword; or Gulf Department in '63.* Boston: Walker, Wise, and Co., 1864.

Higginson, Mary Thatcher, ed. *Letters and Journals of Thomas Wentworth Higginson, 1846–1906.* Boston: Houghton Mifflin Company, 1921.

Higginson, Thomas Wentworth. *Army Life in a Black Regiment.* Boston: Beacon Press, 1962.

———. "The Reoccupation of Jacksonville in 1863." *Military Order of the Loyal Legion of the United States—Massachusetts*, 467–74.

———. "Some War Scenes Revisited." *Atlantic Monthly*, 42, no. 249 (July 1878), 1–9.

Hill, Isaac J. *A Sketch of the 29th Regiment of Connecticut Colored Troops.* Baltimore: Daugherty, Maguire & Co., 1867.

Hinton, Richard J. *Rebel Invasion of Missouri and Kansas.* Chicago: Church & Goodman, 1865.

Hobart, Edwin L. *Semi-History of a Boy Veteran.* Denver: n.p., 1909.

Holsinger, Frank. "How Does One Feel Under Fire?" *Military Order of the Loyal Legion of the United States—Kansas*, 290–304.

Hunt, Sanford B. "The Negro As a Soldier." *Journal of Psychological Medicine and Jurisprudence*, 1, 161–86.

Johnson, Mary E., ed. "Letters from a Civil War Chaplain." *Journal of Presbyterian History*, 46, no. 3 (September 1968), 219–35.

Jones, Howard J., ed. "Letters in Protest of Race Prejudice in the Army During the American Civil War." *Journal of Negro History*, 61, 97–98.

Levstik, Frank R., ed. "From Slavery to Freedom: Two Wartime Letters of One of the Conflict's Few Black Medal of Honor Winners." *Civil War Times Illustrated*, 11, 10–15.

Lewis, A. S., ed. *My Dear Parents: The Civil War Seen By an English Union Soldier.* New York: Harcourt Brace Jovanovich, 1982.

Mallory, William. *Old Plantation Days.* Hamilton (?), Ont.: n.p., 190ff.

Main, Edwin M. *The Story of the Marches, Battles and Incidents of the Third United States Colored Cavalry.* Louisville: Globe Print Co., 1908.

Marcy, Henry O. "Sherman's Campaign in the Carolinas." *Military Order of the Loyal Legion of the United States—Massachusetts*, 2, 331–48.

Marrs, Elijah P. *Life and History of the Rev. Elijah P. Marrs.* Louisville: The Bradley & Gilbert Company, 1885.

Matson, Daniel. "The Colored Man in the Civil War." *Military Order of the Loyal Legion of the United States—Iowa*, 2, 236–54.

Mattson, H. "Early Days of Reconstruction in Northeastern Arkansas." *Military Order of the Loyal Legion of the United States—Minnesota*, 2, 322–37.

McCord, William B. "Battle of Corinth, the Campaigns Preceding and Leading Up to This Battle, and Its Results." *Military Order of the Loyal Legion of the United States—Minnesota*, 4, 567–84.

McMurray, John. "A Union Officer's Recollections of the Negro as a Soldier." ed. Horace Montgomery. *Pennsylvania History*, 28, (April 1961), 156–86.

———. *Recollections of a Colored Troop*. Brookville, PA: n.p., 1916.

Mickley, Jeremiah Marion. *The Forty-Third Regiment United States Colored Troops*. Gettysburg: J. E. Wible, Printer, 1866.

Morgan, Thomas J. "Reminiscences of Service With Colored Troops in the Army of the Cumberland." *Personal Narratives, Rhode Island Soldiers and Sailors Historical Society*, series 3, no. 13.

Newton, Alexander H. *Out of the Briars: An Autobiography and Sketch of the Twenty-Ninth Regiment Connecticut Volunteers*. [Philadelphia: A.M.E. Book Concern, 1910].

Norton, Henry Allyn. "Colored Troops in the War of the Rebellion." *Military Order of the Loyal Legion of the United States—Minnesota*, 5, 59–73.

Norton, Oliver Willcox. *Army Letters, 1861–1865*. [Chicago: Printed by O. L. Deming, 1903].

Offenberg, Richard S., and Parsonage, Robert Rue, eds. *The War Letters of Duren F. Kelley*. New York: Pageant Press, 1967.

An Officer in the 9th Army Corps. *Notes on Colored Troops and Military Colonies on Southern Soil*. New York: n.p., 1863.

Olney, Warren. "Nagging the South." *Military Order of the Loyal Legion of the United States—California*. Read November 20, 1896.

Perry, Bliss, ed. *Life and Letters of Henry Lee Higginson*. Boston: Atlantic Monthly Press, 1921.

Phillips, Marion G., and Parsegian, Valerie Phillips, eds. *Richard and Rhoda: Letters from the Civil War*. Washington, DC: Legation Press, 1981.

Post, Lydia Minturn, ed. *Soldiers' Letters From Camp, Battle-Field and Prison*. New York: Bunce & Huntington, Publishers, 1865.

Powell, E. Henry. "The Colored Soldier in the War of the Rebellion." *Military Order of the Loyal Legion of the United States—Vermont*. War paper no. 3.

Quincy, S. M. *A Camp and Garrison Manual for Volunteers and Militia*. New Orleans: Peter O'Donnell, 1865.

Rawick, George P., ed. *The American Slave: A Composite Autobiography*. Texas Narratives, part 2. Westport, CT: Greenwood Press, 1979.

Richard, James H. "Service with Colored Troops in Burnside's Corps." *Personal Narratives, Rhode Island Soldiers and Sailors Historical Society*. series 5, no. 1.

Riddle, Francis A. "The Soldier's Place in Civilization." *Military Order of the Loyal Legion of the United States—Illinois*, 2, 515–38.

Rogers, James B. *War Pictures: Experiences and Observations of a Chaplain in the U.S. Army*. Chicago: Church & Goodman, 1863.

Romeyn, Henry. "With Colored Troops in the Army of the Cumberland." *Military Order of the Loyal Legion of the United States-District of Columbia*. War papers, no. 51.

Sears, Cyrus. *Papers of Cyrus Sears, Read Before the Ohio Commandery of the Loyal Legion, October 7th 1908.* Columbus, OH: F. J. Heer Printing Co., 1909.

Shaw, James. "Our Last Campaign and Subsequent Service in Texas." *Personal Narratives, Rhode Island Soldiers and Sailors Historical Society.* series 6, no. 9.

Sherman, George R. "The Negro As a Soldier." *Personal Narratives, Rhode Island Soldiers and Sailors Historical Society.* series 7, no. 7.

Simonton, Edward. "The Campaign Up the James River to Petersburg." *Military Order of the Loyal Legion of the United States—Minnesota,* 5, 481–95.

Smith, Charles W. "Lights and Shadows, a Sketch of Five Sundays." *Military Order of the Loyal Legion of the United States—Indiana,* 433–50.

Smith, James Lindsay. *Autobiography of James L. Smith.* Norwich, CT: Thames Printing Co., 1976 (Reprint of 1881 ed.)

Snider, Samuel P. "Reminiscences of the War." *Military Order of the Loyal Legion of the United States—Minnesota,* 2, 234–44.

Sutherland, George E. "The Negro in the Late War," *Military Order of the Loyal Legion of the United States—Wisconsin,* 1, 164–88.

———. "Abraham Lincoln and Jefferson Davis, As Commanders-in-Chief." *Military Order of the Loyal Legion of the United States—Wisconsin,* 2, 110–36.

Taggart, John H. *Free School for Applicants For Commands Of Colored Troops.* Philadelphia: King & Baird, 1863. 2nd ed., 1864.

Taylor, Susie King. *Reminiscences of My Life in Camp With the 33d United States Colored Troops.* Boston: Susie King Taylor, 1902.

Third United States Colored Cavalry Organization. Chicago: 1893.

Thomas, Henry Goddard. "The Colored Troops at Petersburg." *Battles and Leaders of the Civil War,* 4, 563–67.

———. "Twenty-Two Hours Prisoner in Dixie." *Military Order of the Loyal Legion of the United States—Maine,* 1, 29–48.

Thompson, S. Millett. *Thirteenth Regiment of New Hampshire Volunteer Infantry-In the War of the Rebellion, 1861–1865.* Boston: Houghton Mifflin and Co., 1888.

Ullmann, Daniel. *Address of the Organization of Colored Troops and the Regeneration of the South.* Washington: Great Republican Office, 1868.

Van Alstyne, Lawrence. *Diary of an Enlisted Man.* New Haven: Tuttle, Morehouse & Taylor Co., 1910.

Vanderslice, Catherine H., ed. *The Civil War Letters of George Washington Beidelman.* New York: Vantage Press, 1978.

War Record of Col. W. M. Grosvenor, Editor of the Missouri Democrat. N.p., 1864.

Weber, John B. *Autobiography of John B. Weber.* Buffalo: J. W. Clement Co., 1924.

Weist, J. R. "The Medical Department in the War." *Military Order of the Loyal Legion of the United States—Ohio,* II, 71–95.

Wilder, Burt G. "The Negro Brain," in *Proceedings of the National Negro Conference,* 1909.

Williams, George Washington. *A History of the Negro Troops in the War of the Rebellion, 1861–1865. Preceded by a Review of the Military Service of Negroes in Ancient and Modern Times.* New York: Negro Universities Press, 1969. Reprint, New York: Harper & Brothers, 1888.

Wilson, James Grant. "The Red River Dam, With Comments on the Red River Campaign." *Military Order of the Loyal Legion of the United States–New York*. I, 78–95.

GOVERNMENT PUBLICATIONS

Billings, John S. *Vital Statistics of Boston and Philadelphia Covering a Period of Six Years Ending May 31, 1890*. Washington, DC: Government Printing Office, 1895.

――――. *Vital Statistics of the District of Columbia and Baltimore Covering a Period of Six Years Ending May 31, 1890*. Washington, DC: Government Printing Office, 1893.

――――. *Vital Statistics of New York City and Brooklyn Covering a Period of Six Years Ending May 31, 1890*. Washington, DC: Government Printing Office, 1894.

Gould, Benjamin A. *Investigations in the Military and Anthropological Statistics of the American Soldier*. New York: Hurd and Houghton, 1869.

Heitman, Francis B. *Historical Register and Dictionary of the United States Army, 1789 to 1903*. Washington, DC: Government Printing Office, 1903.

The Medical and Surgical History of the War of the Rebellion. Washington, DC: Government Printing Office, 1870–88.

Official Army Register of the Volunteer Forces of the U.S. Army, 1861–1865. Washington, DC: Government Printing Office, 1865.

Report of the Adjutant General of the State of Illinois, 2. Springfield: Baker, Bailache & Co., 1867.

A Report of the Surgical Cases Treated in the Army of the United States from 1865 to 1861. Circular No. 3. War Department, Surgeon General's Office, 17 August 1871. Washington, DC: Government Printing Office, 1871.

Statistics, Medical and Anthropological, of the Provost-Marshal-General's Bureau. 2 vols. Washington, DC: Government Printing Office, 1875.

The War of the Rebellion: A Compilation of the Official Records of the Union and Confederate Armies. Washington, D.C.: Government Printing Office.

NEWSPAPERS AND PERIODICALS

Atlanta Constitution
Augusta Colored American
Augusta Loyal Georgian
Boston Herald
Boston Journal
Charleston South Carolina Leader
Chicago Times
Chicago Tribune
Cincinnati Colored American
Frank Leslie's Illustrated Weekly
Harper's Weekly
Newburgh Free Press
New Orleans Black Republican
New York Times
New York Tribune
Philadelphia Christian Recorder

SELECTED SECONDARY SOURCES

Abbott, Richard H. "Massachusetts and the Recruitment of Southern Negroes, 1863–1865." *Civil War History*, 14, 197–210.

Abrams, Ray H. "The Copperhead Newspapers and the Negro." *Journal of Negro History*, 20 no. 2 (Apr. 1935), 131–52.

Adams, George W. *Doctors in Blue: The Medical History of the Union Army in the Civil War.* New York: Henry Schuman, 1952.

Armstrong, Warren B. "Union Chaplains and the Education of the Freedmen." *Journal of Negro History*, 52, 104–15.

Barbeau, Arthur E., and Henri, Florette. *The Unknown Soldiers: Black American Troops in World War I.* Philadelphia: Temple University Press, 1974.

Barnes, Gilbert. *The Antislavery Impulse, 1830–1844.* New York: D. Appleton–Century Company, 1933.

Belz, Herman. "Law, Politics and Race in the Struggle for Equal Pay During the Civil War." *Civil War History*, 22, 197–213.

Berlin, Ira. *Slaves Without Masters: The Free Negro in the Antebellum South.* New York: Vantage Books, 1974.

Berry, Mary F. "Negro Troops in Blue and Gray: The Louisiana Native Guards, 1861–1863." *Louisiana History*, 8, no. 2 (Spring 1967), 165–90.

Bingham, Luther G. *The Young Quartermaster: The Life and Death of Lieut. L. M. Bingham.* New York: Board of Publications of the Reformed Protestant Dutch Church 1863.

Blassingame, John W. *Black New Orleans, 1860–1880.* Chicago: University of Chicago Press, 1973.

_____. "Negro Chaplains in the Civil War." *Negro History Bulletin*, 27, no. 1 (Oct. 1963), 23–24.

_____. "The Recruitment of Colored Troops in Kentucky, Maryland, and Missouri, 1863–1865." *Historian*, 24, no. 4 (Aug. 1967), 533–45.

_____. "The Recruitment of Negro Troops in Maryland." *Maryland Historical Magazine*, LVIII, No. 1 (Mar. 1963), 20–9.

_____. "The Recruitment of Negro Troops in Missouri During the Civil War," *Missouri Historical Review*, 58, no. 3 (Apr. 1964), 326–38.

_____. "The Selection of Officers and Non-Commissioned Officers of Negro Troops in the Union Army, 1863–1865." *Negro History Bulletin*, 30, no. 1 (Jan. 1967), 8–11.

_____. "The Union Army As an Educational Institution for Negroes, 1861–1865." *Journal of Negro Education*, 34, no. 2 (Spring 1965), 152–59.

Boles, John B. *Black Southerners, 1619–1869.* Lexington: University of Kentucky Press, 1984.

Brown, Francis H. *Harvard University in the War of 1861–1865.* Boston: Cupples, Upham, and Company, 1886.

Burchard, Peter. *One Gallant Rush: Robert Gould Shaw and His Brave Black Regiment.* New York: St. Martin's Press, 1965.

Burnham, W. Dean. *Presidential Ballots, 1836–1892.* Baltimore: Johns Hopkins Press, 1955.

Burrage, Henry S. *Civil War Record of Brown University.* Providence: Alumni Association, 1920.

Cahill, Carl. "Note on Two Va. Negro War Soldiers, One Union, One Confederate." *Negro History Bulletin*, 24, 39–40.

Carter, Dan T. *When the War Was Over: The Failure of Self-Reconstruction in the South, 1865–1867.* Baton Rouge: Louisiana State University Press, 1985.

Castel, Albert. "Civil War Kansas and the Negro." *Journal of Negro History*, 51, no. 2 (Apr. 1966), 125–38.

_____. "The Fort Pillow Massacre: A Fresh Examination of the Evidence." *Civil War History*, 4, no. 1 (Mar. 1958), 37–50.

Catton, Bruce. *America Goes to War*. Middletown, CT: Wesleyan University Press, 1958.

Cimprich, John. *Slavery's End in Tennessee*. University, AL: University of Alabama Press, 1985.

Cimprich, John, and Mainfort, Robert C., Jr. "Fort Pillow Revisited: New Evidence about an Old Controversy." *Civil War History*, 28, no. 4 (Dec. 1982), 293–306.

Clark, Peter. H. *The Black Brigade of Cincinnati*. New York: Arno Press/ *New York Times*, 1969.

Cochrane, John. *Arming the Slave in the War for the Union: A Prelude to the Destruction of African Slavery Throughout the World*. New York: Rogers & Sherwood, 1879.

Coffman, Edward M. *The Old Army: A Portrait of the American Army in Peacetime, 1784–1898*. New York: Oxford University Press, 1986.

———. *The War to End All Wars: The American Military Experience in World War I*. Madison: University of Wisconsin Press, 1986.

Conn, Granville P. *History of the New Hampshire Surgeon in the War of the Rebellion*. Concord: Ira C. Evans Co., 1906.

Cornish, Dudley T. *The Sable Arm: Negro Troops in the Union Army, 1861– 1865*. New York: Longmans Green & Co., 1956.

Cox, LaWanda. *Lincoln and Black Freedom: A Study in Presidential Leadership*. Columbia: University of South Carolina Press, 1981.

Cross, Whitney R. *The Burned-Over District: The Social and Intellectual History of Enthusiastic Religion in Western New York, 1800–1850*. Ithaca: Cornell University Press, 1950.

Current, Richard Nelson. *Those Terrible Carpetbaggers*. New York: Oxford University Press, 1988.

Daniels, Jonathan. *Prince of the Carpetbaggers*. Philadelphia: Lippincott, 1958.

Davis, David Brion. *The Problem of Slavery in Western Culture*. Ithaca: Cornell University Press, 1966.

Davis, J. Barnard. "On the Weight of the Brain in the Negro." *Anthropological Review*, 25 (Apr. 1869), 190–92.

Davis, William C. "Massacre at Saltville." *Civil War Times Illustrated*, 9, 4–11.

Dearing, Mary R. *Veterans in Politics: The Story of the G.A.R..* Baton Rouge: Louisiana State University Press, 1952.

Donald, David. *Lincoln Reconsidered: Essays on the Civil War Era*. New York: Alfred A. Knopf, Inc., 1947.

Drago, Edmund L. *Black Politicians and Reconstruction in Georgia: A Splendid Failure*. Baton Rouge: Louisiana State University Press, 1982.

Duberman, Martin B., ed. *The Antislavery Vanguard: New Essays on the Abolitionists*. Princeton: Princeton University Press, 1965.

Durden, Robert F. *The Gray and the Black: The Confederate Debate on Emancipation*. Baton Rouge: Louisiana State University Press, 1972.

Dyer, Brainerd. "The Treatment of Colored Union Troops by the Confederates, 1861–1865." *Journal of Negro History*, 20 (July 1935), 273– 86.

Dyer, Frederick H. *A Compendium of the War of the Rebellion*, 1. New York: Thomas Yoseloff, 1959.

Dyson, Walter. *Howard University: The Capstone of Negro Education, A History, 1867–1940*. Washington, DC: Graduate School, Howard University, 1941.

Edelstein, Tilden G. *Strange Enthusiasm: A Life of Thomas Wentworth Higginson*. New Haven: Yale University Press, 1968.

Edmonds, David C. *The Guns of Port Hudson: The Investment, Siege, And Reduction*. 2 vols. Lafayette, LA: Arcadiana Press, 1984.

Eliot, Ellsworth, Jr. *Yale in the Civil War*. New Haven: Yale University Press, 1932.

Engs, Robert Francis. *Freedom's First Generation: Black Hampton, Virginia, 1861–1890*. Philadelphia: University of Pennsylvania Press, 1979.

Fearey, Thomas H. *Union College Alumni in the Civil War, 1861–1865*. Schenectady, NY: n.p., 1915.

Fen, Sing-nan. "Notes on the Education of Negroes in North Carolina during the Civil War." *Journal of Negro History*, 36, no. 1 (Winter 1967), 24–31.

Fenlon, Paul E. "The Notorious Swepson-Littlefield Fraud: Railroad Financing in Florida (1868–1871)." *Florida Historical Quarterly*, 32, no. 4 (Apr. 1954), 231–61.

Fishel, Leslie H., Jr. "Repercussions of Reconstruction: The Northern Negro, 1870–1883." *Civil War History*, 14, no. 4 (Dec. 1968), 325–45.

Fletcher, Marvin. *The Black Soldier and Officer in the United States Army, 1891–1917*. Columbia: University of Missouri Press, 1974.

Foner, Eric. *Reconstruction: America's Unfinished Revolution, 1863–1877*. New York: Harper & Row, 1988.

Foner, Jack D. *Blacks and the Military in American History: A New Perspective*. New York: Praeger Publishers, 1974.

Fowler, Arlen L. *The Black Infantry in the West, 1869–1891*. Westport, CT: Greenwood Publishing Corp., 1971.

Fox, William F. *Regimental Losses in the American Civil War, 1861–1865*. Albany, NY: Albany Publishing Company, 1893.

Franklin, John Hope. *George Washington Williams: A Biography*. Chicago: University of Chicago Press, 1985.

Frederickson, George M. *The Black Image in the White Mind: The Debate on Afro-American Character and Destiny, 1817–1914*. New York: Harper & Row, 1971.

_____. *The Inner Civil War: Northern Intellectuals and the Crisis of the Union*. New York: Harper & Row, 1965.

French, Earl A., and Royce, Diana, eds. *Portraits of a Nineteenth Century Family: A Symposium on the Beecher Family*. Hartford: The Stowe-Day Foundation, 1976.

Gatewood, Willard B., Jr. *"Smoked Yankees" and the Struggle for Empire: Letters from Negro Soldiers, 1898–1902*. Urbana: University of Illinois Press, 1971.

Genovese, Eugene D. *From Rebellion to Revolution: Afro-American Slave Revolts in the Making of the Modern World*. Baton Rouge: Louisiana State University Press, 1979.

Glatthaar, Joseph T. *The March to the Sea and Beyond: Sherman's Troops in the Savannah and Carolinas Campaigns*. New York: New York University Press, 1985.

Gossett, Thomas F. *Race: The History of an Idea in America*. New York: Schocken Books, 1963.

Griswold, Robert L. *Family and Divorce In California, 1850–1890: Victorian Illusions and Everyday Realities*. Albany: State University of New York Press, 1982.

Guthrie, James M. *Camp-Fires of the Afro-American*. Philadelphia: Afro-

American Pub. Co., 1899 (reprinted in New York by Johnson Reprint Corporation, 1970).

Haller, John S., Jr. *Outcasts from Evolution: Scientific Attitudes of Racial Inferiority, 1859–1900.* Urbana: University of Illinois Press, 1971.

Hewitt, Lawrence Lee. *Port Hudson: Confederate Bastion on the Mississippi River.* Baton Rouge: Louisiana State University Press, 1987.

Hicken, Victor. "The Record of Illinois' Negro Soldiers in the Civil War." *Illinois State Historical Society Journal,* LVI, No. 3 (Autumn 1963), 529–51.

Holt, Thomas. *Black Over White: Negro Political Leadership in South Carolina during Reconstruction.* Urbana: University of Illinois Press, 1977.

Jocelyn, Stephen Perry. *Mostly Alkili.* Caldwell, Idaho: The Caxton Printers, Ltd., 1953.

Jones, Jacqueline. *Soldiers of Light and Love: Northern Teachers and Georgia Blacks, 1865–1873.* Chapel Hill: University of North Carolina Press, 1980.

Jones, James H. *Bad Blood: The Tuskegee Syphilis Experiment.* New York: Free Press, 1981.

Jordan, Winthrop. *White Over Black: American Attitudes Toward the Negro, 1550–1812.* New York: W. W. Norton & Company, 1977.

Joshi, Manoj K., and Reidy, Joseph P. " 'To Come Forward and Aid in Putting Down This Unholy Rebellion': The Officers of Louisiana's Free Black Native Guard During the Civil War Era." *Southern Studies,* 21, no. 3 (Fall 1982), 326–42.

Kiple, Kenneth F., and King, Virginia Himmelsteib. *Another Dimension to the Black Diaspora: Diet, Disease, and Racism.* Cambridge: Cambridge University Press, 1981.

Kolchin, Peter. *First Freedom: The Response of Alabama's Blacks to Emancipation and Reconstruction.* Westport, CT: Greenwood Press, 1972.

Kraut, Alan M. "The Forgotten Reformers: A Profile of Third Party Abolitionists in Antebellum New York." In *Antislavery Reconsidered: New Perspectives on the Abolitionists,* ed. Lewis Perry and Michael Fellman. Baton Rouge: Louisiana State University Press, 1979.

Lane, Roger. *Violent Death in the City: Suicide, Accident, and Murder in Nineteenth-Century Philadelphia.* Cambridge: Harvard University Press, 1979.

Litwack, Leon F. *Been in the Storm So Long: The Aftermath of Slavery.* New York: Alfred A. Knopf, 1979.

———. *North of Slavery: The Negro in the Free States, 1790–1860.* Chicago: University of Chicago Press, 1961.

Litwack, Leon, and Meier, August, eds. *Black Leaders of the Nineteenth Century.* Urbana: University of Illinois Press, 1988.

Logan, Rayford W. *Howard University: The First Hundred Years, 1867–1967.* New York: New York University Press, 1969.

Logan, Rayford W., and Winston, Michael R. *Dictionary of American Negro Biography.* New York: W. W. Norton & Company, 1982.

Lonn, Ella. *Desertion During the Civil War.* Gloucester, MA: Peter Smith, 1966.

Lovett, Bobby L. "Memphis Riots: White Reaction to Blacks in Memphis, May 1865–July 1866." *Tennessee Historical Quarterly,* 38, (Spring 1979), 9–33.

———. "The Negro's Civil War in Tennessee, 1861–1865." *Journal of Negro History,* LXI, 36–50.

Luck, Wilbert H. *Journey to Honey Hill*. Washington, DC: Wiluk Press, 1985.

Maher, Jane. *Biography of Broken Fortunes: Wilkie and Bob, Brothers of William, Henry and Alice James*. Hamden, CT: Archon Press, 1986.

Marietta College in the War of Secession, 1861–1865. Cincinnati: Peter G. Thompson, Publishers, 1878.

Marsden, George. "Kingdom and Nation: New School Presbyterian Millennialism in the Civil War Era." *Journal of Presbyterian History*, 46, no. 4 (Dec. 1968), 254–73.

May, Elaine Tyler. *Great Expectations: Marriage & Divorce in Post-Victorian America*. Chicago: University of Chicago Press, 1980.

Mays, Joe H. *Black Americans and Their Contributions Toward Union Victory in the American Civil War, 1861–1865*. Lanham, MD: University Press of America, 1984.

McFeely, William S. *Yankee Stepfather: General O. O. Howard and the Freedmen*. New Haven: Yale University Press, 1968.

McPherson, James M. *The Abolitionist Legacy: From Reconstruction to the NAACP*. Princeton: Princeton University Press, 1975.

_____. *Battle Cry of Freedom: The Civil War Era*. New York: Oxford University Press, 1988.

_____. *The Negro's Civil War: How American Negroes Felt and Acted During the War for the Union*. New York: Vintage Books, 1965.

McRae, Norman. *Negroes in Michigan During the Civil War*. Lansing: Michigan Civil War Centennial Observance Commission, 1966.

Memorial of Colonel John A. Bross, Twenty-Ninth U.S. Colored Troops. Chicago: Tribune Book and Job Office, 1865.

Mills, Gary B. "Patriotism Frustrated: The Native Guards of Confederate Nachitoches." *Louisiana History*, 18, no. 4 (Fall 1977), 437–51.

Mitchell, Lt. Col. Joseph B. *The Badge of Gallantry: Recollections of Civil War Medal of Honor Winners*. New York: The Macmillan Company, 1968.

Murray, Donald M. and Rodney, Robert M. "Colonel Julian E. Bryant: Champion of the Negro Soldier." *Illinois State Historical Society Journal*, 56, no. 2 (Summer 1963), 257–81.

Nalty, Bernard C. *Strength for the Fight: A History of Black Americans in the Military*. New York: Free Press, 1986.

Oubre, Claude F. *Forty Acres and a Mule: The Freedmen's Bureau and Black Land Ownership*. Baton Rouge: Louisiana State University Press, 1978.

Parton, James. *General Butler of New Orleans*. New York: Mason Brothers, 1864.

Perry, Lewis. *Radical Abolitionism: Anarchy and the Government of God in Antislavery Thought*. Ithaca: Cornell University Press, 1973.

Powell, Lawrence N. *New Masters: Northern Planters During the Civil War and Reconstruction*. New Haven: Yale University Press, 1980.

Prucha, Francis Paul. *Broadax and Bayonet: The Role of the United States Army in the Development of the Northwest, 1815–1860*. Madison: State Historical Society of Wisconsin, 1953.

Quarles, Benjamin. *The Negro in the Civil War*. Boston: Little, Brown and Company, 1953.

Rabinowitz, Howard N., ed. *Southern Black Leaders of the Reconstruction Era*. Urbana: University of Illinois Press, 1982.

Redkey, Edwin S. "Black Chaplains in the Union Army." *Civil War History*, 33, no. 4, (December 1987), 331–50.

Ritter, E. Joy. "Congressional Medal of Honor Winners." *Negro History Bulletin*, 26, 135–36.

Robbins, Gerald. "Recruiting and Arming of Negroes in the South Carolina Sea Islands." *Negro History Bulletin*, XXVIII, 150–51.

Robertson, James I., Jr. "Negro Soldiers in the Civil War." *Civil War Times Illustrated*, 7, 21–32.

Roll of the Alumni and Former Students of the College of New Jersey Who Served in the Army or Navy of the United States in the War for the Union. Philadelphia: McCalla & Stavely, 1867.

Roll of the Graduates and Undergraduates of Amherst College Who Served in the Army of Navy of the United States, During the War of the Rebellion. Amherst: Henry M. McCloud, 1871.

Roy, Joseph E. "Our Indebtedness to the Negro For Their Conduct During the War." *New Englander and Yale Review*, 51 (Nov. 1889), 353–64.

Rugoff, Milton. *The Beechers: An American Family in the Nineteenth Century.* New York: Harper & Row, 1981.

Sandburg, Carl. *Abraham Lincoln: The War Years.* 4 vols. New York: Harcourt, Brace & Company, 1939.

Savage, W. Sherman. *The History of Lincoln University.* Jefferson City, MO: Lincoln University, 1939.

Scharf, J. Thomas. *History of Maryland from Earliest Period to the Present Day*, 3. Hatboro, PA: Tradition Press, 1967.

Sefton, James E. *The United States Army and Reconstruction, 1865–1877.* Baton Rouge: Louisiana State University Press, 1967.

Seraile, William. "The Struggle to Raise Black Regiments in New York State, 1861–1864." *New York Historical Society Quarterly*, 58, 215–33.

Sewell, Richard H. *The House Divided: Sectionalism and the Civil War, 1848–1865.* Baltimore: Johns Hopkins University Press, 1988.

Shannon, Fred A. "The Federal Government and the Negro Soldier, 1861–1865." *Journal of Negro History*, 11, no. 4 (Oct. 1926), 563–83.

———. *The Organization and Administration of the Union Army, 1861–1865*, 2 vols. Gloucester, MA: Peter Smith, 1965.

Shattuck, Gardiner H., Jr. *A Shield and Hiding Place: The Religious Life of the Civil War Armies.* Macon: Mercer University Press, 1987.

Singletary, Otis A. *Negro Militia and Reconstruction.* New York: McGraw-Hill Book Company, Inc. 1963.

Smallwood, James M. *Time for Hope, Time for Despair: Black Texans During Reconstruction.* Port Washington, NY: Kennikat Press, 1981.

Smith, John David. "The Recruitment of Negro Soldiers in Kentucky, 1863–1865." *Register of the Kentucky Historical Society*, 72, 364–90.

Sommers, Richard J. "The Dutch Gap Affair: Military Atrocities and the Rights of Negro Soldiers." *Civil War History*, 21, 51–64.

———. *Richmond Redeemed: The Siege at Petersburg.* Foreword by Frank E. Vandiver. Garden City, NJ: Doubleday, 1981.

Sorin, Gerald. *The New York Abolitionists: A Case Study of Political Radicalism.* Westport, CT: Greenwood Press, 1971.

Spivey, Donald. *Schooling for the New Slavery: Black Industrial Education, 1865–1915.* Westport, CT: Greenwood Press, 1978.

Stanton, William. *The Leopard's Spots: Scientific Attitudes Toward Race in America, 1815–59.* Chicago: University of Chicago Press, 1960.

Steiner, Paul E. *Medical History of a Civil War Regiment: Disease in the Sixty-Fifth United States Colored Infantry.* Clayton, MO: Institute of Civil War Studies, 1977.

Stewart, James Brewer. *Holy Warriors: The Abolitionists and American Slavery.* New York: Hill & Wang, 1976.

Studley, W. S. *Final Memorials of Major Joseph Warren Paine.* Boston: John Wilson and Sons, 1865.

Tarbox, Increase N. *Memorials of James H. Schneider and Edward M. Schneider.* Boston: Massachusetts Sabbath School Society, 1867.

Tunnell, Ted. *Crucible of Reconstruction: War, Radicalism and Race in Louisiana, 1862–1877.* Baton Rouge: Louisiana State University, 1984.

Ullman, Victor. *Martin R. Delany: The Beginnings of Black Nationalism.* Boston: Beacon Press, 1971.

Vincent, Charles. Black Legislators in Louisiana During Reconstruction. Baton Rouge: Louisiana State University Press, 1976.

Voegeli, Jacques. *Free But Not Equal: The Midwest and the Negro During the Civil War.* Chicago: University of Chicago Press, 1967.

Webb, Nathan B. *East Maine Conference Seminary War Record.* Boston: Albert Wright, 1877.

Werstein, Irving. *The Storming of Fort Wagner: Black Valor in the Civil War.* New York: Scholastic Book Services, 1970.

Westwood, Howard C. "Benjamin Butler's Enlistment of Black Troops in New Orleans in 1862." *Louisiana History,* 26, no. 1 (Winter 1985), 5–22.

——. "Captive Black Union Soldiers in Charleston—What to Do?" *Civil War History,* 27, 28–44.

——. "The Cause and Consequence of a Union Black Soldier's Mutiny and Execution." *Civil War History,* 31, 222–36.

Wiley, Bell Irvin. *Southern Negroes, 1861–1865.* Baton Rouge: Louisiana State University Press, 1974.

Williamson, Joel. *After Slavery: The Negro in South Carolina During Reconstruction, 1861–1877.* Chapel Hill: University of North Carolina Press, 1965.

Wilson, Keith. "Thomas Webster and the 'Free Military School for Applicants for Commands of Colored Troops.'" *Civil War History,* 24, 101–22.

Wyatt-Brown, Bertram. *Yankee Saints and Southern Sinners.* Baton Rouge: Louisiana State University Press, 1985.

THESES AND DISSERTATIONS

Glatthaar, Joseph T. "Hood's Tennessee Campaign." Master's thesis, Rice University, Houston, TX, 1981.

Wilson, Keith Philip. "White Officers in Black Units in the Civil War." Ph.D. dissertation, La Trobe University, 1985.

Index